# Health Promotion and Aging
## Second Edition

**David Haber, PhD,** is a Professor in the School of Allied Health Sciences at the University of Texas Medical Branch in Galveston. Dr. Haber was the director of Creighton University's shopping mall-based Center for Healthy Aging. He received his PhD in sociology in 1976 from the University of Southern California.

Dr. Haber authored *Health Care for an Aging Society* and has been Project Director or Principal Investigator of 18 grant-funded research or demonstration projects for such agencies as the Administration on Aging, AARP Andrus Foundation, Bureau of Health Professions, Fund for the Improvement of Postsecondary Education, Health Future Foundation, and others.

Typically, these projects involve health profession students leading exercise and health education programs with older adults, and contributing to the evaluation of the impact of these programs. The model upon which these programs are based received a "Best Practices" award from the Health Promotion Institute of the National Council on the Aging in 1998, and will be included in its forthcoming book, *Best Practices in Health Promotion and Aging.*

*Second Edition*

# Health Promotion and Aging

*Implications for the Health Professions*

David Haber, PhD

*Springer Publishing Company*

Springer Publishing Company, Inc.
536 Broadway
New York, NY 10012-3955

*Cover design by Janet Joachim*
*Acquisitions Editor: Helvi Gold*
*Production Editor: Jeanne Libby*

99 00 01 02 03/5 4 3 2 1

---

**Library of Congress Cataloging-in-Publication Data**

Haber, David, 1944–
    Health promotion and aging : implications for the health
professions / by David Haber. — 2nd ed.
        p.   cm.
    Includes bibliographical references and index.
    ISBN 0-8261-8461-8
    1. Preventive health services for the aged—United States.
2. Health promotion—United States.   3. Health education—United
States.   I. Title.
    [DNLM: 1. Primary Prevention—in old age. 2. Health Promotion.
WA 108 H114h 1999]
RA564.8.H33   1999
362.1'9897—dc21
DNLM/DLC
for Library of Congress                                    98-42976
                                                              CIP

---

Printed in the United States of America

# Contents

# Foreword

Welcome to the new American millennium. It is a gray one. The sheer numbers of older adults who will be on the scene present us with incredible opportunities and untold challenges. The largest and most potent arena these challenges and opportunities will play out is healthcare.

As the eminent geriatrician, Robert Butler, MD, has noted, "We have created a health system in this country that is brilliant but irrelevant to the health needs of most older people." He is right. Our healthcare system makes heroic and powerful efforts to sustain people through the last year of life with high-tech, high-cost care, but does relatively little for them during the years when they are coping with and managing chronic illness.

Dr. David Haber, in this second edition of *Health Promotion and Aging*, helps health professionals construct a bridge between the biomedical realities of aging, and what can be done to help older adults reclaim health and vitality, and also manage chronic illness, through health promotion. For many people, health promotion is one pathway to feeling good now and preventing health problems in the future. For older adults, health promotion is much more.

> For older women at high risk for hip fractures, health promotion, in the form of exercise programs, nutrition counseling, and medication management, can make the difference between nursing home dependence and independent living.

> For retirees coping with arthritis, health promotion in the form of a chronic disease self-management program can make the difference between just "getting by" and living lives filled with purpose and meaning.

> For older people with life-threatening illnesses, health promotion, in the form of shared medical decision-making and medical consumerism, can make the difference between wasted medical care that adds no value to life and effective care that adds quality to both living and dying.

Years of innovative programming in a wide variety of settings have shown that older people have the interest and ability to better control their health and their health care through health promotion. Research shows that the payback is substantial: better health, reduced health care costs, and improved quality of life.

However, considering that health promotion can benefit all older adults, health promotion for this age group has had a history of being under-funded, under-researched, and unavailable to large segments of the population, especially minority elders and those living in inner cities and rural areas. How then, do we move the disease prevention and health promotion agenda forward, effectively and efficiently, with our aging population?

As health professionals, we value prevention. Most of us would like to provide the needed ounces of it in hopes of defraying anticipated pounds of cure. Historically though, we have been unsure just how to go about this, especially with older adults. We've been confused about whether the focus should be on saving lives or saving money. (How about both?!) On the policy level, we have been asked to make sense of conflicting recommendations and shifting priorities. In practice, we have encountered other hurdles, such as inadequate or no reimbursement, lack of time, and lack of motivation (our own and our clients).

Clear, compassionate, and enlightened policies are needed to:

- Shift some of the emphasis of our healthcare system from illness care to health management, particularly for older adults.
- Increase access to and participation in programs that both improve quality of life and reduce overall costs.
- Strengthen and protect the older adult's role in making medical decisions
- Encourage all older adults, in any physical condition and living arrangement, to help themselves live the most healthful and fulfilling lives possible.

This expanded second edition of David Haber's book points us in positive directions to achieve these goals. He presents a conceptual model for integrating key components for a healthy life: assessment, education, behavior management, social support, community health, and advocacy. And underlying these key components is a sturdy foundation for better health outcomes: true collaboration and improved communication between older adults and their health professionals.

Haber champions the notion that it is far better for older adults, and their health, to engage with health professionals as partners on the journey to health and wholeness, rather than reacting passively or noncompliantly.

Research into the "art of patienthood" bears this out. Being passive in the medical encounter is as much as a risk factor for poor health as is smoking or high blood pressure. And while the current cohort of older adults do appear to be somewhat more passive and unengaged in medical decision-making, a whole new crop of activated, involved, and demanding medical consumers are rising through the ranks to change the fundamental way in which health professionals and consumers interact.

*Health Promotion and Aging,* second edition, prepares us for how to help these consumers to better health. Haber offers far more than rationales and verifying research for doing the right thing. Useful tools, such as sample health contracts, personal checklists, and activity guides are salted through-out the book to help lend specific practicality to the subject. Of particular interest to students and practitioners will be the questions for discussion at the end of each chapter. These open-ended questions will encourage the reader to stop, digest, and reflect what has been read. Examine these questions—this is important stuff and merits thoughtful evaluation.

Also laced throughout the book are Haber's personal beliefs and biases, with the author noting when it is personal opinion you are reading, and not necessarily doctrine. And, without having to look too hard, you'll be treated to some easy humor.

Take this book into the next millennium with you. Older adults—we—will have a major impact on the healthcare system. Empowering older adults to practice health promotion and to participate in their healthcare decisions will make the healthcare system more relevant to their—our—needs.

Molly Mettler, MSW
Senior Vice President, Healthwise, Incorporated
and coauthor of *A Healthy Old Age* and *Healthwise for Life*

# Preface

As we enter the new millennium, research is providing convincing evidence that health promotion works—no matter what our age and even after many decades of practicing unhealthy habits. The findings are also providing specific ideas on what we need to do and how we ought to go about doing it. In some areas, like exercise and nutrition, the strategies for improving our health are a lot less onerous than we thought they had to be.

These positive research findings are contributing to the idea that in this early stage of managed health care, we ought to be making health promotion and disease prevention a more significant part of health care. Although there is still more talk than action among managed care potentates, there is undeniably a lot more action than there used to be.

This is not all the good news. As this book goes to press, the tobacco industry, despite one last media blitz in mid-1998, continues to lose both public and congressional support. The smart political strategy of the Clinton administration to focus on teenage smokers will eventually lead to legislation and public education that will help Americans of all ages to resist or to quit smoking.

And, despite the scary—in my opinion—Dietary Supplement Health and Education Act of 1994 that eliminated premarket safety evaluations for many herbs, vitamins, minerals, and hormones, we are quickly learning through research that many dietary supplements have extraordinary benefit, and many others have extraordinary promise.

Before you discount me as a Pollyanna, I am not blinded to the many health problems that not only remain but seem to be getting worse. The most obvious problem is that the percentage of Americans who are overweight has steadily increased over the past three decades, until now two thirds of the population is overweight and, even more alarming, one third is obese.

Nonetheless, one of the main reasons for our expanding waistlines—as the title of this book, *Health Promotion and Aging* suggests—is that we are an aging population. Aging persons who are not vigilant about their health habits will gradually gain weight. However, I am encouraged by the amount of attention that has been given to nutrition and exercise in the media, and also by the frequency with which new health behaviors are adopted by older adults in later life.

In addition, I predict that the next generation of older adults—the baby boomers—will not continue to be content with accepting their expanding waistlines. Any cohort that was able to exert its collective will and reduce the escalation of the war in Vietnam can also exert its will to reduce the escalation of their midlife weight gains. War and obesity can kill, but they are reversible as well.

There are many other roadblocks to a healthier society than just expanding waistlines, and many of these are identified in this book. Nonetheless, there is much to be optimistic about.

This second edition, therefore, is not just about updating data from 1994, though there are many changes of this nature. It is about examining new ideas that have emerged in the past 5 years on managed care, exercise, nutrition, smoking cessation, weight management, dietary supplements, and many other topics. Two of these topics—weight management and dietary supplements—have been converted into two new chapters for the second edition.

This book is unique from other health promotion and aging books in a few respects. It is, for instance, guided by a broad conceptual model with integrated components. The model begins with the importance of collaboration and communication between health professionals and their clients, and then explores the areas of health assessment, health education, social support, behavior and psychological management, and community health education and advocacy.

Also, the book is not only research driven and linked to theory and current issues, but practical as well. There are checklists, health contracts, assessment tools, illustrated techniques, resource lists, model programs, Internet addresses, and discussion questions at the end of each chapter.

The basic premise of this book is that every health professional ought to be a health educator. Health education can be provided directly to a client—though the reality in health care today is that it must be done in a time-efficient manner. Or it can be provided through referrals—though even referrals require knowledge of appropriate and successful community health programs and awareness of other qualified and competent health professionals who promote health. Or it can be provided through the training of office staff members who play specific health education roles.

I think it is an exciting time for students in the health professions— nursing, medicine, occupational therapy, physical therapy, physician's assistant studies, pharmacy, nutrition, and health education—who in the coming decades will have an opportunity to strengthen the *health* component of health care.

The goal of this book is to provide hope, ideas, and techniques in health promotion and disease prevention for not only students in the health professions but for practicing health professionals who have remained open to change within a health care system that is itself undergoing tremendous change. And no change will create more upheaval than the aging of Americans.

# Acknowledgments

I dedicate this book to all the people who have brought humor into my life. I want to especially thank my wife, Jeanne St. Pierre; my children, Benjamin and Audrey Haber; my sister, Bonnie Glazer; my boss, David Chiriboga; my old friend, Stephen McConnell; and my favorite pros, beginning with Sid Caesar and Groucho Marx and continuing to Jim Carrey and Michael Richards (once known as Kramer).

# 1
# Introduction

[T]o increase years of healthy life remaining at age 65 from 12 (1980 estimate) to 14 years (a public health goal from the U.S. Public Health Service's Healthy People 2000 Initiative). (American Association of Retired Persons [AARP], 1991)

As of 1993, healthy life remaining at age 65 is still 12 years, and the "data indicate movement away from the targets for Blacks and Hispanics." (*Healthy People 2000 Midcourse Review: 1995 Report on Progress*, DHHS, OPHS)

## SOCIODEMOGRAPHIC TRENDS

It has seemed almost obligatory to begin a gerontological article or book with comments about the rapid aging of society over the past quarter-century. About 1985, we began to see a slight variation of the ritual; many writings began with comments about the aging of the aged. About 1995, a spate of writings appeared on the coming onslaught of 50-year-olds (i.e., the aging baby boomers born between 1946 and 1964).

The aging population is not only increasing in numbers but in breadth. It has become more difficult to examine the topic of aging Americans. Fifty-year-olds are eligible for membership in the AARP, but they are quite different from 70-year-olds who, in turn, are significantly different from 90-year-olds. Conversely, 90-years-olds—a few of them, anyway—are pumping iron and throwing away their canes (Fiatarone et al., 1990).

What aging Americans have in common, be they 50 or 90 years old, robust or frail, is a future with an intensified demand for health care and

*1*

the escalation of health care costs. Driving these demands and costs are the increasing numbers of aging persons with chronic medical conditions and a high-tech medical system (though technology in some instances can lower medical costs).

Colliding with this demand for abundant, high-quality, and sophisticated medical care is the new era, beginning in 1998, of expecting the federal budget to be balanced. The collision generates considerable media and legislative attention, much of it in the form of an examination of managed care (see chapter 12). Also sneaking on to center stage over the past several years has been the topic of disease prevention/health promotion. The media has allocated considerable time and space to its merits including its potential for cost savings.

Joining the media are the federal and state governments that have strongly endorsed disease prevention/health promotion; the health professions that have proclaimed its importance in education and training; the business community that has firmly supported it; and individuals who have often discussed their attempts at it, both successful and otherwise.

If disease prevention/health promotion has been vying for center stage, though, it has been the stage of a not very prosperous community theater. The federal government plays a limited role in disease prevention and will not subsidize health promotion. State governments have been more concerned about new expenditures that the federal government continues to pass along to them (welfare reform among them) rather than on new health initiatives that need funding.

Health professionals have given more in the way of lip service to health promotion because they have not been reimbursed for it. Health science students have received only a modicum of health promotion information and practically no experience in applying it (Haber et al., 1997).

The business community has devoted resources to health promotion but has stopped short of focusing on the employees who need it most— older and more sedentary employees.

Individuals have spent more time and money on health promotion, but they also have spent more time at restaurants eating larger portions and higher fat content, and more money on computers, in front of which they have sat for an increasing number of hours.

Perhaps the disparity between attention on health promotion and the resources to support it has been due to the American value of individual responsibility. We know we are not able to prescribe medicine intelligently nor conduct surgery on ourselves and family members; however, we feel like we can walk briskly, eat healthfully, and refrain from smoking—if we choose—without the necessity of health programs that require taxpayer support. Thus, although most people are not doing that good of a job at promoting their health, we believe it is up to the individual to take responsibility for it.

This is true to some extent, but let us be realistic; human beings are imperfect. We need help. If we get support from government, business, the media, the community, health professionals, family, and friends, we are going to do much better at being active, energetic, and healthy. I hope the subsequent chapters of this book will provide the reader with sufficient ideas and data in this regard to justify some degree of optimism and to inspire additional initiatives—from the individual level to all the major institutions of society including family, work, government, religion, and education.

What follows are cautionary and hopeful sociodemographical data to suggest that aging adults may not only lead the way in escalating health care costs, but may also lead the way in the development of creative and cost-effective health-promoting strategies. The data reveal that the educational level of aging Americans has risen, that they are increasingly health conscious, and that they are active in community volunteer endeavors.

Much of the information in this section is taken from *Developments in Aging: 1996, Vol. 1* (Report of the Special Committee on Aging, U.S. Senate) and the Administration on Aging's *A Profile of Older Americans: 1996*. The profile can be accessed through the following World Wide Web site: http://www.aoa.dhhs.gov/aoa/pages/profil96.html#older).


## POPULATION GROWTH OVER AGE 65

The American population has been aging dramatically. Since 1900, the percentage of Americans age 65 and older has more than tripled, from 4% in 1900 to about 13% million in 1995, and the number has increased about 11-fold, from 3 million to almost 34 million. This trend will continue for several decades. Between 1995 and 2030, the number of people who are age 65 and older is expected to more than double—from about 34 million to 70 million.

Table 1.1 shows why the population "pyramid" is rapidly becoming shaped like a "rectangle."

**TABLE 1.1   Population Rectangle**

| Year | Under age 18 (%) | Over age 65 (%) |
|------|------------------|-----------------|
| 1900 | 40 | 4 |
| 1980 | 28 | 11 |
| 2030 | 21 | 22 |

## THE BABY BOOMERS

The baby boomers are the 76 million persons born between 1946 and 1964. They were largely conceived by the millions of soldiers, sailors, and marines who returned home from World War II and created a baby boom that started quickly—there were less than 2.8 million births in 1945 but more than 3.4 million in 1946—and lasted 18 years. The boomers challenged our hospital capacity when they were born, the school system a few years later, and society in general when they were draft age, and many did not agree with the politicians who wanted to expand the Vietnam War.

The baby boomers' impact as middle-aged persons (by the year 2010, the number of persons between ages 45 and 64 is projected to be more than twice as many as those age 65 and older—79 million versus 39.4 million) is uncertain, but their impact as retirees is not. When boomers retire, they will make enormous demands on both the Social Security and Medicare programs, which, at the same time, will be supported by a considerably smaller taxpaying workforce. By the time the last boomer turns age 65 in the year 2029, the retirees drawing Social Security and Medicare benefits will include one in five Americans.

## THE OLDER OLD

The older population itself is getting older. In 1995 the 65 to 74 age group (18.8 million) was eight times larger than in 1900, but the 75 to 84 group (11.1 million) was 14 times larger, and the 85+ group (3.6 million) was 29 times larger. The proportion of the population over age 65 will double between 1995 and 2030, whereas the proportion over age 85 will more than triple during this time. This demographic trend is significant, primarily because of the differences in functioning ability between the younger old and the older old.

Only 6% of persons aged 65 to 69 reported difficulties with at least one activity of daily living (ADL) task, whereas 35% of persons aged 85 and older had such difficulties. Similarly, only 1% of persons aged 65 were residents of nursing homes, but 22% of persons aged 85 and older were residents. The older-old person places more demands on family caregivers and societal resources, and at the end of the 20th century and beginning of the 21st century, the 85 and older group will be expanding rapidly (see Table 1.2).

## CHRONIC CONDITIONS, FUNCTIONAL STATUS, AND AGE

The leading chronic ailments of older adults in 1994 were arthritis (50%), hypertension (36%), heart disease (32%), hearing impairments (29%), cataracts (17%), orthopedic impairments (16%), sinusitis (15%), and diabetes (10%). The prevalence of each condition increases with age, and many older adults have multiple conditions.

By age 65, approximately 13% have difficulty performing an ADL (bathing, transferring, dressing, toileting, eating, or walking); about 18% have difficulty with an instrumental ADL (shopping, preparing meals, managing money, light housework, and getting around the community). The need for personal assistance with everyday activities increases from 9% of persons aged 65 to 69 to 50% of the age 85 and older group.

## MEDICARE

Medicare was enacted in 1965 to help persons age 65 or older pay for medical care. In 1996, Medicare covered 33 million older adults and 5

**TABLE 1.2  Older Old (population in millions)**

| Year | Under age 65 | 65 and older | 85 and older |
|------|--------------|--------------|--------------|
| 1995 | 229.8 | 33.6 | 3.6 |
| 2000 | 240.9 | 35.3 | 4.3 |
| Increase | 5% | 5% | 20% |

Source: U.S. Census Bureau (1992).

million younger disabled persons. Medicare is a major payer in the U.S. health care system, spending $200 billion in 1996 and accounting for 32% of hospital and 20% of physician payments.

Part A includes hospital care ($760 deductible in 1997), inpatient psychiatric care (190 day lifetime maximum), skilled nursing, rehabilitation or home care following a hospitalization, and hospice care for the terminally ill. Part B generally pays 80% of physician and outpatient services after an annual $100 deductible. Part B includes some medical screenings, but does *not* cover outpatient prescription drugs, routine physical examinations, dental services, hearing aides, eyeglasses, and most long-term care.

A little more than one fourth of the federal outlay for older adults is for Medicare, and Medicare expenditures have been rising (and continue to rise) rapidly. Between 1960, 5 years before the onset of Medicare, and 1990, the proportion of the federal budget spent on programs serving older adults has doubled, from 15% to 30% of the federal budget. Much of this increase occurred between 1975 and 1988, when personal health care expenditures under Medicare increased an average 14.4%, more than twice the rate of inflation.

Medicare spending increased from $7.5 billion in 1970, to $114 billion in 1991, and then to $200 billion in 1996. It is not surprising, therefore, that even though the single largest component of out-of-pockets costs for older adults is nursing home care—which has increased more than fourfold in inflation-adjusted dollars since 1961—the federal government has resisted overtures to include more long-term care coverage.

## HOSPITAL STAYS

In 1994, older adults accounted for 37% of all hospital stays and 47% of all days of care in hospitals, even though the average length of a hospital stay for older persons has decreased 3.3 days since 1980. Older adults are hospitalized more than three times as often as younger adults and stay 50% longer. Hospital expenses account for the largest percentage of health expenditures for older persons, followed by physician costs, and nursing home care.

## VISITS TO HEALTH CARE PRACTITIONERS

In 1994, adults age 65 and older averaged 11 visits to a physician a year compared with the general population average of five visits. It is estimated that older adults occupy 50% of the time of health care practitioners, and it is predicted that visits to health care practitioners will increase 22% by the year 2000 and 115% by 2030.

## MEDICATIONS

In 1995, older adults constituted 12% of the population but consumed 32% of all prescription drugs and 40% of over-the-counter drugs. Between 1980 and 1994, the rate of prescription drug inflation was more than 4% a year. One recent inroad into exerting influence on drug prices has been the use of formularies (list of drugs that organizations rely on to achieve financial objectives) by managed care organizations. Managed care organizations, however, then attempt to limit physicians and clients to the drugs listed on the formulary.

## HEALTH HABITS

On the brighter side, the health habits of older adults are, on balance, slightly superior to those of younger adults. People aged 65 and older are, for instance, less likely to smoke, drink, be obese, or report high stress. They eat more sensibly than do younger adults, are as likely to walk for exercise, and are more likely to check their blood pressure regularly. Conversely, the elderly are less likely than young people to engage in regular exercise, to be educated on medical matters like heart disease and self-examinations, and to take certain safety precautions. They are less likely to know how long, how often, or how intensely they should exercise. Older adults are also less likely than younger adults to use seat belts in their cars and smoke detectors in their homes (Haber, 1989).

## PERCEPTIONS OF HEALTH

Most elderly tend to view their health positively. About three of four community-based older adults describe their health as excellent, very good, or good. Conversely, 28% of older persons assessed their health as fair or poor in 1994 compared with 10% for all adults. Older Blacks were much more likely to rate their health as fair or poor (43%) than were older Whites (27%).

Income directly relates to perceptions of health. In 1994, about 49% of older people with incomes more than $35,000 described their health as excellent or very good, but only 29% of those with incomes below $10,000 did.

## VOLUNTEERING AND WORK

Many older adults are active and productive, choosing to engage in volunteer opportunities and work. In any given year almost one of every five older Americans engage in unpaid volunteer work for organizations (i.e., churches, schools, or civic organizations). In addition, an unknown number of older adults do other volunteer work, for example, helping a neighbor.

Participation in the labor force after age 65 is greater in the United States (17% for men and 9% for women in 1995) than in most other countries (e.g., France, Germany, Italy, Sweden, United Kingdom, and Canada), although it is considerably lower than in Japan (36% for men and 16% for women).

## EDUCATIONAL STATUS

Between 1960 and 1989, the median level of education among older adults increased from 8.3 to 12.1 years. Between 1970 and 1994, the percentage of older adults who has completed high school rose from 28% to 62%. About 13% of older adults in 1994 had a bachelor's degree or more.

By the year 2000, the median number of years of education of people who have reached age 65 will be equivalent to that of all adults age 25 and older (about 12.7 years). However, the percentage who had completed high school varied considerably by race and ethnic origin among older persons in 1994: 65% of Whites, 37% of Blacks, and 30% of Hispanics.

As the formal educational level of older adults continues to rise, this may well correlate with an increase in their interest in seeking out health information and joining health education programs.

## POVERTY

About 3.7 million, or 10.5%, of older adults, were below the poverty level in 1995, slightly less than the 11.4% rate for persons aged 18 to

64. Another 2.3 million or 7% were near-poor (up to 125% of poverty level), resulting in almost one fifth (18%) of the older population being poor or near-poor in 1995. The poverty rate was almost three times higher for older Blacks and Hispanics than for older Whites, and more than twice as high for older women than older men. The major source of income for older persons in 1995 was Social Security (42%), public and private pensions (19%), earnings (18%), asset income (18%), and all other sources (3%).

## RACIAL AND ETHNIC COMPOSITION

In 1995, about 15% of persons age 65 and older were either Black (8%), Hispanic (4%), Asian or Pacific Islander (2%), and American Indian or Native Alaskan (less than 1%). Minority populations are projected to increase to 25% of the older adult population in the year 2030. Between 1990 and 2030, older Whites are projected to increase 91%; older Blacks, 159%; and older Hispanics, 570%.

## COMPETITION FOR LIMITED HEALTH CARE DOLLARS

The demographical and economical circumstances reported in this chapter do not limit the future of disease prevention and health promotion in this country. Even in past years when federal and state funding in disease prevention and health promotion were lacking, there was still considerable leadership and accomplishments in these areas.

Future accomplishments in disease prevention and health promotion, however, are likely to be based on either (a) the continuation of creative initiatives among individuals, community groups, and community organizations; or (b) convincing federal and state government officials that allocating funds for disease prevention and health promotion is cost-effective rather than just providing an improvement in quality of life.

The claim that disease prevention and health promotion practices may be cost-effective, however, is unsubstantiated. It can be argued, in fact, that if health practices elongate life expectancy, social security payments will certainly be increased, and Medicare expenses may also. The final year of a longer life is likely to be more medically expensive than death at an earlier age (see following section on the compression of morbidity).

On a similar note, after proclaiming community-based long-term care a less expensive alternative than nursing home care, we were humbled to find that these claims were not well supported by research findings (Haber, 1989). Conversely, do we want to live in a nursing home even if it happens to be a cost-effective alternative? Do we want to be told when and what to eat, who to room with, whether to have a pet, and what our home should look like?

Likewise, good health practices feel good, and living in a healthy society is more satisfying, regardless of whether this lowers or raises our taxes. The real issue, therefore, is how to improve our own health and the health of our society given the many pressing medical, economical, and social problems that provide strong competition for the focus of our attention as well as our scarce tax dollars.

We should advocate for more support, financial and otherwise, from all sectors of society based on the promise of research findings in the areas of health promotion and disease prevention, and the desire for a higher quality of life.

## COMPRESSION OF MORBIDITY

"Although there is little hope for cure of chronic diseases through the traditional medical model, the onset of these diseases may be postponed through modification of risk factors, many of which are possible to control, either personally or socially. As the onset is delayed to older ages and approaches the limit of the human life span, we can envision a society where everyone can expect to live in vigorous health to close to the average life span and then die after a brief period of illness" (Fries & Crapo, 1986, p. 37).

The prospect of living almost two more decades after reaching one's 65th birthday is bittersweet. Although Americans are living longer today than ever before, we have greater fear of a prolonged period of disability and dependency in late life.

One definition of successful aging, then, is to be able to live life fully until death. According to one national study, however, only 14%, on average, of those who have died beyond age 64 were fully functional in the last year of their life (Lentzner et al., 1992). Unfortunately, the study did not identify the number of older adults who, despite the fact that they were not fully functional in the last year of life, lived active and fulfilling lives until the end.

Most of us are greatly concerned with the probability of being severely restricted for a long period in late life. The evidence is not encouraging in this regard in that the longer we live, the more likely we are to endure a prolonged period of disability before our death. Death after age 85 is almost four times more likely to follow a period of profound physical impairment than is death between the ages of 65 and 74 (Lentzner et al., 1992).

Examining the length of the dependency period before death, at age 65 we have about 17 years left to live, with 6.5 of those years in a dependent state (38% of our remaining years). Also, less than 6% are receiving help in the basic ADLs between the ages of 65 and 74. In contrast, at age 85 we have an average of seven years left to live, with 4.4 in a dependent state (63% of our remaining years). At age 85, more than one in four are receiving help in the basic activities of daily living (Guralnik, 1991).

Pessimists argue that the period of morbidity preceding death will increase in the future because of (a) limited biomedical research funds available to improve the physical and mental capacity of the very old; (b) the fact that some major diseases, like Alzheimer's disease and arthritis, do not have recognized lifestyle risk factors that we can modify; and (c) medical advances, such as dialysis and bypass surgery, will increase the life expectancy of individuals with disease rather than prevent the occurrence of disease.

Optimists, conversely, argue that there will be a *compression of morbidity* (see Figure 1.1) in the future because of (a) probable advances in biomedical research that will prevent or delay the occurrence of disease; and (b) the continued reduction in such risk factors as smoking, blood pressure level, cholesterol level, and sedentary lifestyles that will result in better health.

At the same time that the general population will be able to delay the onset of chronic disease because of these factors, the life *span* (the maximum number of years of the species) is fixed. Thus, argue the compressionists, we will not only delay morbidity; we will shorten it.

A study by Manton and colleagues (1993) that analyzed data from the 1982, 1984, and 1989 National Long Term Care Surveys—a federal study that regularly surveys almost 20,000 people aged 65 and older—arrived at the unexpected conclusion that the percentage of chronically disabled older persons grew at a much slower rate than forecast and, even more surprising, the percentage of those older than age 65 reporting no disabilities rose.

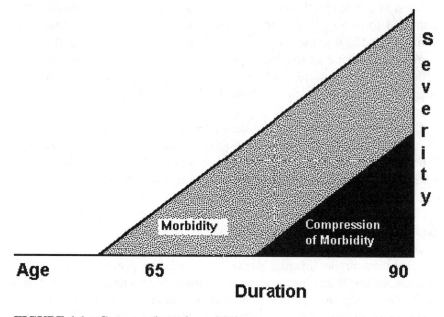

**FIGURE 1.1   Compression of morbidity.**

Data from the 1994 National Long Term Care Survey have just been analyzed (Kolata, 1996) and the annual decline in disability rate, though only about 1% or 2% a year, has continued unabated from 1982 to 1994. Moreover, every year there is a smaller percentage of older adults who are unable to take care of themselves, unable to comb their hair, feed themselves, or take a walk. At the same time, the percentage of older adults with chronic diseases like high blood pressure, arthritis, and emphysema has steadily declined.

These unexpected findings still need further examination, especially as to whether they are linked to improvements in diet, exercise, nonsmoking, and other lifestyle factors. One such attempt was made over a period of 32 years with 1741 alumni of the University of Pennsylvania who were born between 1913 and 1925 (Vita et al., 1998). Body-mass index, exercise patterns, and smoking were predictors of compressed disability at the end of life. Although promising and exciting, the conclusions must be qualified, as 90% of the subjects were still alive at the time of the data analysis and the length of their disability before death remain indeterminate.

# HEALTH PERSPECTIVES

## PERSONAL PERSPECTIVE ON GOOD HEALTH

Are people who are very happy with themselves and the way their lives are going, but who suffer from severe heart disease, in good health? Is a person who is in outstanding physical health, but is also depressed, in good health? I do not think good health can be viewed objectively, independent of the values of particular individuals.

Good health is primarily a psychological state, dependent on the unique values of an individual. Physical health, whether excellent or poor, is only one determinant of good health and not the most important one. Good physical health is appreciated as a means to an end and that end is likely to be a satisfying relationship, an achievement, or the independence to live as one chooses.

This is not to discount the importance of the strong reciprocal relationship between changes in physical health and changes in mental and emotional health. When our physical health is threatened, so typically is our mental and emotional health. The converse is equally true.

I do not believe the practice of good health habits should be taken from the medical arena and assigned exclusively to health educators and other practitioners on the periphery of medicine. I believe that the health habits of clients, both physical and mental, ought to be a major concern of medical personnel, many of whom currently view their role as disease oriented and exclusively biomedical in content.

## PROFESSIONAL PERSPECTIVE ON HEALTH AND AGING

Most health professionals subscribe to the notion that health is more than the absence of illness. Were this not the case, we would have to label most older adults, 90% of whom are coping with a chronic condition, unhealthy.

Moreover, as *aging* health professionals we have a greater aptitude for viewing good health from a broader perspective than we did when younger (Hanna, 1989). We are more likely to appreciate health's multiple dimensions rather than simply to perceive health as physical vitality.

Our broader perspective on good health may include such elements as a feeling of empowerment (which can be defined in many ways, one of which is the perceived ability to marshal resources to accomplish goals), loving relationships, zest for living, a strong social support network, a sense of meaning in life, or a certain level of independence. The psychosocial (Hanna, 1989) and functional dimensions (Duffy & MacDonald, 1990) of health become increasingly integral components of our definition of good health.

Regardless of our physical health or age, or that of our family, friends, or clients, we have the opportunity, if not to improve health, to delay the physical, mental, and emotional deterioration that may accompany chronic illness.

Older persons with chronic illness or functional impairment are continuously being challenged to attain or maintain a satisfying lifestyle. We, as health professionals, can help these clients identify the activities or strengthen the social interactions that will make their lives fulfilling.

It is incumbent that we avoid fixating on the medical aspects of chronic illness, even if our older clients are thus preoccupied. We should identify the psychological, social, and behavioral issues that are relevant to the chronically ill older person, and look for opportunities to foster new health habits.

It is not helpful to view health as a continuum, ranging from disability and illness at one end, to a high level of wellness, which includes health awareness, health education, and psychological growth, at the other (Kemper et al., 1987; Sarafino, 1990). In the middle, according to advocates of a continuum, resides a neutral point where there is no discernible illness or wellness.

The limitations of this health continuum concept can be summed up in a single sentence. A person who is functionally impaired, or even disabled, can still focus considerable attention on a high level of wellness, devoting considerable energy to health awareness, health education, and psychological growth.

## DISEASE AND HEALTH

Although most older persons must contend with chronic disease, that disease is a pathological state and may have no relationship with the individual's ability to perform daily activities. Disease, in fact, may not be evident, even to the person who has it.

The presence or absence of disease, therefore, may not be a source of great concern to older adults. The ability to perform ADLs, however, *is* of great concern to older adults who desire as much independence as possible (Duffy & MacDonald, 1990). The definition of health, especially among older adults, should not be linked with disease or its absence, as the medical model suggests, but with independence, the ability to accomplish one's goals, and the existence of satisfying relationships.

## BROAD DEFINITION OF HEALTH

The federal government's Public Health Service, through its 1990 Health Objectives for the Nation, encouraged the following broad definition of health:

1. Disease prevention, which includes strategies to maintain and improve health through medical care, such as high blood pressure control and immunization.
2. Health protection, which includes strategies for modifying environmental and social structural health risks, such as toxic agent and radiation control, and accident prevention and injury control.
3. Health promotion, which includes strategies for reducing lifestyle risk factors, such as avoiding smoking and the misuse of alcohol and drugs, and adopting good nutritional habits and a proper and adequate exercise regimen.

## HEALTH DEFINED AS EXTRAORDINARY ACCOMPLISHMENT

At age 99, Mieczyslaw Horszowski, a classical pianist, recorded a new album, and twin sisters Kin Narita and Gin Kanie recorded a hit single in Japan; at age 92 and 91, Paul Spangler completed his 14th marathon, and Hulda Crooks climbed Mount Whitney, the highest mountain in the continental United States (Wallechinsky & Wallace, 1993). At age 63, a California woman lied about her age (she said she was 59) to become eligible for a fertility program where she was implanted with an embryo from an anonymous donor. She is now the proud mother of twins. At age 77 John H. Glenn Jr. prepares to become the oldest space traveler in history.

Although I marvel at these examples of unusual achievement by aging adults, I do not use them as inspiration for older clients. These models are astonishing, but they do little to enhance the confidence of older adults who do not believe they can—and oftentimes do not want to—come close to similar achievement. As Betty Friedan noted in her popular-selling book, *The Fountain of Age* (1993), older adults "attempt to hold on to, or judge oneself by, youthful parameters of love, work and power. For this is what blinds us to the new strengths and possibilities emerging in ourselves."

Perhaps health professionals should be more cautious about setting standards for, or even defining, good health for older adults. This is the message delivered by Faith Fitzgerald, M.D., in an editorial in *The New England Journal of Medicine* (Fitzgerald, 1994, pp. 197–198). "We must beware of developing a zealotry about health, in which we take ourselves too seriously and believe that we know enough to dictate human behavior, penalize people for disagreeing with us, and even deny people charity, empathy, and understanding because they act in a way of which we disapprove. Perhaps [we need to] debate more openly the definition of health."

## HEALTHY AGING: ONGOING CHALLENGE

As we age, it becomes increasingly more difficult to take our health for granted. It seems like some part of life is always out of balance or on the verge of getting out of equilibrium. Slowly but surely, for instance, we may reach a sense of dissatisfaction with our weight. Or someone moves out of state and weakens our social support system. Or a death has us questioning our spiritual resolve. Or increasing arthritic pain makes exercise no longer appealing. Or we relapse in our effort to stop smoking.

In my experience as a health educator, people often set health goals that are difficult to achieve and wind up feeling disheartened and discouraged when they fall short. Many stop making health goals. It is important, therefore, to be modest with our goals and to build into them an allowance for occasional slips in behavior, to choose to take legitimate detours, to expect occasional failure, to set new goals, and to try again.

## HEALTH EXPECTANCY VERSUS LIFE EXPECTANCY

Those who live to the age of 65 are likely to live into their 80s. Of the remaining average of 17 years to live after age 65, 12 are likely to be healthy, and 5 will be years in which there is some functional impairment (National Center for Health Statistics, 1990a).

Place yourself in the shoes of the person who just reached age 65. Are you primarily interested in extending your life for more than the 17 years you are likely to live, or are you most interested in how many of your remaining years will be healthy and independent ones?

Your health expectancy, or the number of healthy years you can expect to have left, depends to a great extent on your physical activity, nutritional intake, social support network, access to good medical care, health education, and health services. Health expectancy is much more important to older adults than life expectancy (see Figure 1.2).

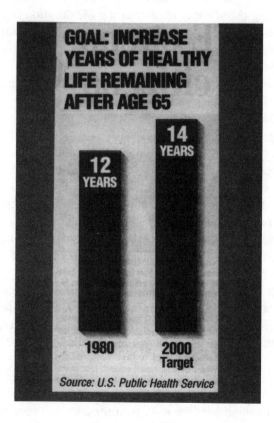

**FIGURE 1.2   Goal: Increase years of healthy life remaining after age 65.**

## PREVENTION

Prevention is often categorized as primary, secondary, or tertiary. Primary prevention focuses on an asymptomatic individual in whom potential risk factors have been identified and targeted. Preventive measures, such as regular exercise, good nutrition, smoking cessation, or immunizations, are recommended to decrease the probability of the onset of specific diseases or dysfunction. Primary prevention is almost synonymous with the term *health promotion.*

Secondary prevention is also practiced when an individual is asymptomatic, but actual (rather than potential) risk factors have been identified at a time when the underlying disease is not clinically apparent. A medical screening as secondary prevention is cost-effective only when there is hope of lessening the severity or shortening the duration of a pathological process. Blood pressure and cholesterol screenings at community health fairs or seminars have become the most widely implemented forms of secondary prevention.

Tertiary prevention, which occurs after a disease or disability becomes symptomatic, focuses on the rehabilitation or maintenance of function. Health professionals attempt to restore or maintain the maximum level of functioning possible, within the constraints of a medical problem, to prevent further disability and dependency on others.

Tertiary prevention corresponds to Phase 2 (rehabilitation of outpatients) and Phase 3 (long-term maintenance) of the cardiac rehabilitation of a cardiac patient (Phase I is the care of a hospitalized cardiac patient). A study of 10 randomized clinical trials involving more than 4,000 patients who had myocardial infarctions, revealed that patients who completed a program of tertiary prevention reduced their likelihood of cardiovascular mortality by 25% (Oldridge et al., 1988) (see Figure 1.3).

A focus on prevention may be more appealing to some older adults than an emphasis on health promotion. Older adults are likely to be coping with chronic conditions, and the prevention, delay, or reduction of disability and dependency is much more salient an issue for them than it is for most younger adults.

Moreover, among medical professionals the relevancy of prevention is enhanced because several prevention activities, like mammograms, are reimbursable through Medicare. Prevention has its "foot in the door" in the system of health care reimbursement, whereas the activities of health promotion have not.

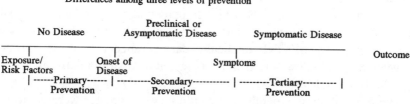

Differences among three levels of prevention

**FIGURE 1.3  Differences among three levels of prevention.**

One advantage of the use of the term *health promotion*, however, is that it encompasses mental and spiritual health concerns. Instead of clients and health professionals becoming fixated on risk factors and the prevention of disease or disability, health promotion can be viewed as a joyful process. As health professionals, for instance, we may want to encourage bird watching to a particular client and not concern ourselves with its direct relationship to physical health or illness.

*Health promotion* is also a more proactive term than *primary prevention*, which tends to imply a reaction to the prospect of disease. Directing a client's anger or frustration into political advocacy work, for example, is a proactive, health-promoting enterprise that benefits both the individual and society.

In one health study, however, in-depth interviews with older adults who declined to participate in a health promotion study, reported that they were less familiar and comfortable with the phrase *health promotion* than were those who eventually participated (Wagner et al., 1991). The topic of older adults' attitudes toward different terms remains largely unexamined, and this can reduce our effectiveness as health educators.

## HEALTH CARE VERSUS MEDICAL CARE

Although societal resources in general continue to be viewed as increasingly limited, health care (typically defined as the narrow domain of medical care) has maintained its status in this country as a very high priority. Spending for national health care has grown from 5% of the Gross National Product (GNP) in 1960 to almost 14% in 1992. This represents an increase from $27 billion in 1960 to $738 billion in 1992 (over $2 billion a day).

The United States spends a higher percentage of its GNP on health care than does any other country—14% in 1996. In 1989, Americans spent about 12% of GNP on health care; France and West Germany between 8% and 9.5%; and Britain, Japan, and Australia between 6% and 8% (Marmor & Mashaw, 1990).

These health care expenditures would be even greater were we to find a way to include the 43 million younger Americans who lack access to the health care system through insurance coverage and were we able to increase the coverage of an additional 50 million persons who have inadequate insurance.

Even the relatively affluent (medically speaking) older Americans covered by Medicare spend more than twice as much in out-of-pocket medical expenditures now (in inflation-adjusted dollars) than they did in 1965, before Medicare was instituted.

Ironically, health itself has not been a high priority for the health care dollar. At present, only 3% of the nation's health care costs are spent on health promotion and disease prevention. When rising costs are combined with limited access, the chances of attracting additional federal or state funds to health promotion and disease prevention are slim (see Figure 1.4).

Most of the 3% spent on health promotion and disease prevention goes either to the physician's office or other clinical settings for preventive measures, such as medical screenings and vaccinations (35% or more), or to health protection in the physical environment, such as toxic agent and radiation control (30% or more) (*American Medical News*, August 10, 1992). *Considerably less* than 1% of our health care dollars is spent on changing unhealthy behaviors.

Although there has been undeniable financial neglect at the federal level for unhealthy lifestyles or risk factors among the American people, increasing attention has been focused on these areas ever since the publication of the landmark document, *Healthy People: The Surgeon General's Report on Health Promotion and Disease Prevention* (United States Department of Health and Human Services [USDHHS], 1979). This report provided considerable credence for the idea that major gains in health and independence in the future are likely to come from personal lifestyle changes.

Dr. John Rowe, director of the MacArthur Foundation's Consortium on Successful Aging reports that "Only about 30% of the characteristics

# For every health care dollar:

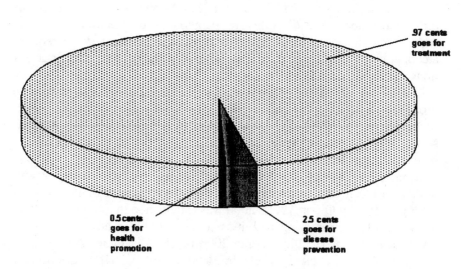

.97 cents goes for treatment

0.5 cents goes for health promotion

2.5 cents goes for disease prevention

**FIGURE 1.4   Health promotion: An ignored priority.**

of aging are genetically based; the rest—70%—is not (Brody, 1996). He concludes that how vigorous and healthy we are in old age is mostly a matter of how we live. A widely cited article in the *Journal of the American Medical Association* (McGinnis & Foege, 1993) suggests that we no longer should view death as being due to heart disease, cancer, stroke and COPD, but rather due to tobacco, inactivity, diet, alcohol, microbial and toxic agents, sexual behavior, motor vehicles, and illicit or inappropriate use of drugs.

## HEALTHY PEOPLE 2000

In 1979, an influential document, *Healthy People: The Surgeon General's Report on Health Promotion and Disease Prevention* (USDHHS, 1979), was published. This report has been widely cited by the popular media as well as in professional journals and at health conferences. Many attribute a seminal role in fostering health-promoting initiatives throughout the nation to the surgeon general and this particular document (McTernan & Rice, 1986; Willis, 1986).

A decade later, in 1990, a national follow-up effort, Healthy People 2000, was initiated by the U.S. Public Health Service in an effort to reduce preventable death and disability for Americans by the year 2000. The strategy announced by the secretary of health and human services required a cooperative effort by government, voluntary and professional organizations, businesses, and individuals.

During the 1990s, the Healthy People 2000 initiative focused on three broad public health goals for Americans: (a) to increase the span of healthy life, (b) to reduce health disparities, and (c) to achieve access to preventive services. Three hundred specific objectives, designed to help achieve these goals, were set in 22 priority areas (see Figure 1.5).

More than 25% of the 300 national objectives focused on or were related to the health of *older* adults. Therefore, as part of this national strategy, Healthy Older Adults 2000 was established to implement a wide array of health-promoting activities to benefit older adults. For more information about Healthy People 2000 or Healthy Older Adults 2000, contact: Healthy People 2000, Public Health Service, DHHS, Coordinator of ODPHP, 330 C Street SW, Washington, DC 20201.

Setting health care priorities is no longer a simple matter of tabulating the number of deaths from a few diseases and then organizing a campaign against the most prevalent ones, like heart disease and cancer. The Healthy People 2000 Initiative is health oriented, not disease oriented, and as such has recognized the complexity of the socioeconomic, lifestyle, and other nonmedical influences that impact on our ability to attain and maintain health.

Relying more on encouragement than direct financial support, it remains to be seen how effective our nation will be with achieving the Healthy People 2000 and Healthy Older Adults 2000 objectives. The rationale for such a highly publicized project, backed by limited funds, is that setting targets can clarify goals, identify opportunities, and generate action. Tracking progress will allow us to quantify our achievements, or lack of such.

Healthy People 2000 has the potential to establish an important framework for improving the nation's health. One issue that has yet to be resolved, however, is that "23% of the 1990 target objectives could not be evaluated because of lack of data to gauge results" (Miller, 1993).

In addition, the issue of accountability has not been addressed. Responsibility for accomplishing some of the Healthy People 2000 objectives,

```
┌─────────────────────────────────────────────────────────────────┐
│                    HEALTHY  PEOPLE  2000                          │
│            PRIORITY  AREAS  AND  LEAD  PHS  AGENCIES              │
│                                                                   │
│  1. Physical Activity ...........................President's Council on Physical │
│       and Fitness                         Fitness and Sports      │
│                                                                   │
│  2. Nutrition...........................................National Institutes of Health │
│                                           Food and Drug Administration │
│                                                                   │
│  3. Tobacco............................................Centers for Disease Control │
│                                                                   │
│  4. Alcohol and Other Drugs.................Alcohol, Drug Abuse, and │
│                                           Mental Health Administration │
│                                                                   │
│  5. Family Planning.............................Office of Population Affairs │
│                                                                   │
│  6. Mental Health and...........................Alcohol, Drug Abuse, and │
│       Mental Disorders                    Mental Health Administration │
│                                                                   │
│  7. Violent and Abusive Behavior........Centers for Disease Control │
│                                                                   │
│  8. Educational and...............................Centers for Disease Control │
│       Community-Based                     Health Resources and    │
│       Programs                            Services Administration  │
│                                                                   │
│  9. Unintentional Injuries....................Centers for Disease Control │
│                                                                   │
│ 10. Occupational Safety and Health....Centers for Disease Control │
│                                                                   │
│ 11. Environmental Health....................National Institutes of Health │
│                                           Centers for Disease Control │
│                                                                   │
│ 12. Food and Drug Safety...................Food and Drug Administration │
│                                                                   │
│ 13. Oral Health........................................National Institutes of Health │
│                                           Centers for Disease Control │
│                                                                   │
│ 14. Maternal and Infant Health...........Health Resources and     │
│                                           Services Administration  │
│                                                                   │
│ 15. Heart Disease and Stroke.............National Institutes of Health │
│                                                                   │
│ 16. Cancer.............................................National Institutes of Health │
│                                                                   │
│ 17. Diabetes and Chronic.....................National Institutes of Health │
│       Disabling Conditions                Centers for Disease Control │
│                                                                   │
│ 18. HIV Infection.................................National Aids Program Office │
│                                                                   │
│ 19. Sexually Transmitted Diseases....Centers for Disease Control  │
│                                                                   │
│ 20. Immunization and Infectious Disease.........Centers for Disease Control │
│                                                                   │
│ 21. Clinical Preventive Services ........Health Resources and     │
│                                           Services Administration  │
│                                           Centers for Disease Control │
│                                                                   │
│ 22. Surveillance and Data Systems....Centers for Disease Control  │
└─────────────────────────────────────────────────────────────────┘
```

**FIGURE 1.5   Healthy people 2000: Priority areas and lead PHS agencies.**

such as the reduction of obesity may be placed on individual initiative. Other issues, such as homicides, however, are clearly the responsibility of the federal and state governments. The homicide rate rose from 8.5 per 100,000 people in 1987 to 10.4 in 1991, whereas the target objective was 7.2 per 100,000 people (Miller, 1992).

Will Healthy People 2000 provide the leadership and the initiative to accomplish its goals? If unsuccessful, will policy makers inappropriately point the finger of blame primarily at individuals? The term *victim blaming* refers to when individuals are viewed to be primarily responsible for the status of their health, regardless of environmental circumstances or the efficacy of public policy.

*Healthy People 2000 Midcourse Review and 1995 Revisions* is a report from the Department of Health and Human Services to assess the progress made toward achieving the year 2000 targets and to summarize the challenges that remain (Public Health Service, 1995). The good news is that there has been progress in most priority areas. Particularly good progress has been made in the reduction in adult use of tobacco products and alcohol-related automobile deaths, and there has been a steady decline in deaths from coronary heart disease and stroke. "On the other hand, there has been no decline in the proportion of people who lead essentially sedentary lifestyles, and there have been increases in the share of the population that is overweight" (McGinnis & Lee, 1995, p. 1125).

Twenty-six percent of the priority areas have no baseline data or baseline data with no new data with which to evaluate progress. Scanning the data from the *Healthy People 2000 Midcourse Review* reveals a particular problem with obtaining new data on the progress of older adults.

## HEALTH PROMOTION AND AGING MODEL

It may not be feasible to incorporate the health promotion model that provides the conceptual framework for this book, in its entirety, into the health science classroom or the clinician's office. The health science curriculum is very concentrated; the introduction of new material is a highly competitive process (Haber et al., 1997). And the clinician's propensity for health education, no matter how much the health professional wishes to engage in health promotion, is limited by lack of reimbursement (Haber, 1992c, 1993a).

Nonetheless, much of this model can be incorporated into the classroom and into practice in a time-efficient manner. It is hoped that the material will have irresistible appeal for the teacher and the practitioner. The model summarized in this chapter is elaborated on in succeeding chapters.

## AGING COMPONENT OF HEALTH PROMOTION MODEL

The health promotion and aging model presented in this second edition focuses primarily on older adults in general. Unfortunately, a scarcity of data still exists on the *young-old* and the *old-old*, two groups that will become increasingly important to practitioners and policy makers in the coming years.

The young-old are in their 50s and 60s, people who in all likelihood are not enthusiastic about an oxymoronic label that includes the dreaded term *old*. Nonetheless, the cutting edge of the baby boomers turned 50 years of age on January 1, 1996, with another boomer being added to the ranks every eight seconds until about the year 2010. And just as the boomers were difficult to ignore as babies, and later as Vietnam War protesters, they will be hard to ignore as adults who are eligible for AARP.

People in their 50s and 60s are not old in the sense of physical vitality, mental acuity, or occupational productivity. But none has escaped diminished hearing and vision; few have overlooked the fact that more of their life is behind them then ahead; and most have given considerable thought to their retirement years.

It is during these years that the incidence of major chronic conditions like arthritis, hypertension, and obesity rises significantly. At the same time, more than 4 million Americans between the ages of 50 and 64 are without health insurance. These persons are too young for Medicare, not poor enough for Medicaid, and not very well protected by the Age Discrimination in Employment Act.

Given the substantial number of years remaining to persons in this age group, and the potential to defer or prevent chronic impairments, it is imperative that an aging model of health promotion follow the lead of AARP and begin to include the aging baby boomers.

The old-old are persons 85 and older. Probably half of them are physically frail, mentally diminished, or societally disengaged. These older adults have a challenging and diverse set of problems to solve to remain independent. At the same time, their problems are likely to be costly to resolve and bedeviling to future cohorts of politicians to solve. In this new era of the balanced budget, how do you provide necessary home care, programs to strengthen muscles that are in danger of becoming too weak to maintain independence, vital over-the-counter medications, and meaningful opportunities to allow the old-old to engage themselves fully in society?

On the bright side, some of the nonagenarians are pumping iron for the first time. And the potential to strengthen the old-old, to keep them independent in a home setting, to engage them in society, has never been more promising. This potential continues through the dying process, when the ability to die in comfort with family and friends visiting in a home environment is also, thanks to the hospice movement, more promising than it has been in decades.

It is fine to support the value that individuals are responsible for promoting their own health. But given our imperfections, and especially given our vulnerabilities in late life, it is insufficient. All the components of the health model to follow need to be supported by all segments of society, from the federal government to the average citizen, and by all the institutions in between: the business community, the religious institutions, the health professions, and the voluntary associations and neighborhood groups.

## COLLABORATION AND COMMUNICATION

A fundamental assertion of this health promotion and aging model is that it is better for older adults to collaborate with health professionals than to take a passive, compliant (or, equally likely, noncompliant) role or to engage in health-promoting activities on their own.

This assertion is based on two facts: (a) that most older adults have medical conditions that require professional supervision, and health-promoting activities can affect these medical conditions; and (b) that health professionals who keep up with the health promotion field can make vital contributions to the health-promoting efforts of older adults.

Also, effective communication between the client and the health professional can be enhanced through the shared adoption of a core of knowledge, skills, and motivation. Improved communication leads to better results and more satisfied clients.

## HEALTH ASSESSMENT

Health assessments help determine where best to focus one's limited time, energy, and resources. Crucial to this process is to select the area that the individual (or group, organization, or society) is most ready to change. Within this priority area, select goals that are relatively easy to achieve to increase the likelihood of success in future endeavors. This is best done by selecting a desired behavior and dividing it into small, graded tasks that can be accomplished in short time periods, until the ultimate goal is achieved.

## HEALTH EDUCATION

Health education has advanced considerably beyond the idea that knowledge inspires change. First, given the plethora of information that pours out of the media, bookstores, libraries, and the mouths of people, it is difficult for individuals to sort out accurate, up-to-date information that is pertinent to their particular health needs.

Second, older adults learn best in andragogical (adult-oriented learning; see chapter 2) situations in which new ideas are presented through collaborative relationships and in small participative groups where they have control of the situation.

Third, education by itself is often insufficient to inspire behavior change. It is far more effective to add behavior and psychological management techniques to the transmission of knowledge as well as to infuse the educational process with social support.

## SOCIAL SUPPORT

Social support should be an integral ingredient of all the other components of the health promotion and aging model, including client-health professional encounters, health education classes, and behavioral and psychological management techniques.

Social support enhances a client's motivation to practice good health habits on an ongoing basis. The most familiar sources of social support are family members (spouses, children, and other relatives), friends, and neighbors. A rapidly growing source of support is peer support, to be found in community health education programs and mutual help groups. The medical profession, because it tends to slight behavioral, psychological, and social interventions, is probably the least used of all sources of support.

## BEHAVIOR AND PSYCHOLOGICAL MANAGEMENT

Behavior and psychological management encompass a wide variety of techniques for bringing about and maintaining change. These techniques include such activities as health contracting, self-monitoring, stimulus control, response substitution, stress management, and cognitive restructuring. It is important for health professionals to learn multiple techniques to adapt specific ones to the special needs of older adults and to deal effectively with the unique problems of individual clients.

## COMMUNITY HEALTH EDUCATION AND ADVOCACY

Health professionals have limited time, knowledge, and skills. It is vital, therefore, that they be as informed as possible about the community options that are available for improving the health of clients.

The past two decades have witnessed a proliferation of low-cost or free educational and health promotion opportunities within the community. To make more effective referrals to meet their clients' needs, health professionals need to identify and then visit educational programs, support groups, advocacy groups, and other community health resources and services.

Until utopia comes to America, however, the health care system will never work for all of the people all of the time. In fact, in recent years the managed care health system has become more challenging to access at a time when a growing number of health, medical, and social needs are being recognized more clearly.

By dramatizing their particular plight to community leaders, media representatives, and state and federal legislators, older adults can be effective change agents in ways that health professionals can not. Therefore, when health professionals mobilize their clients to political or community action, they may help to bring about a more responsive health care system—not only for clients but also for themselves.

## QUESTIONS FOR DISCUSSION

1. Do you believe research supporting the claim that health promotion and disease prevention *save medical dollars* is a necessary incentive

for obtaining support for such activities from our federal and state governments? Explain your answer.

2. Are you optimistic or pessimistic about the occurrence of a compression of morbidity?

3. What is *your* definition of health?

4. Why do we call medical care "health care"?

5. How important is it that we set national health objectives through the Healthy People 2000 initiative, considering the constraints imposed by the limited financial support of our government?

6. As a health professional, how can the Healthy People 2000 initiative be of use to you and your clients?

7. Can you think of ways to improve on the health promotion and aging model in this chapter (and as further details are provided in subsequent chapters)?

# 2

# Health Professionals and Older Clients: Collaboration and Communication

> The art of medicine consists of amusing the patient while nature cures
> the disease. (Voltaire, French physician and author)

Voltaire knew that most medical conditions are self-limiting, and that amusing the patient benignly is oftentimes all that is needed. However, other than for perhaps a unique problem with stress management, benign amusement is not enough help for clients who are collaborating with health professionals on health promotion or disease prevention goals.

## COLLABORATION BETWEEN HEALTH PROFESSIONALS AND OLDER CLIENTS

The commonly used terms *patient compliance* and *patient adherence* imply that a patient is responding passively to the decision of a professional. Collaborating clients (I prefer the term *client* because *patient* implies passivity), however, participate in the decision-making process. To do so, clients must understand the treatment choices available to them. These choices may be profound, such as deciding whether to combine chemotherapy with visualization techniques, or mundane, such as deciding on the timing of the treatment. Research has shown that client participation, even in mundane choices, such as the timing of chemotherapy treatment, can result in fewer side effects (Spiegel & Bloom, 1983).

Similarly, nursing home residents receive health benefits when encouraged to make choices about their environment. Residents who make decisions become more sociable, show improvement in their mental health, and even live longer than do residents who continue to live a passive lifestyle (Rodin & Langer, 1977).

Another example of the benefits of decision making is demonstrated by the client whose compliance with his or her drug regimen improves after participating in the choice of medication. The client may be able to live more easily with the side effects of one medication than with those of another (Lorig, 1992). A client taking multiple medicines may desire a less challenging medication schedule to comply with a busy calendar or a faulty memory.

## CLIENT WILLINGNESS TO COLLABORATE

In a 1992 national survey by the Gallup organization, 63% of the 1,514 randomly selected adults said doctors did not involve patients enough in treatment decisions (*American Medical News*, June 1, 1992, p. 16). A survey sponsored by the American Board of Family Practice (May 1987) reported that earlier cohorts of *older* persons have been less likely to take an active role in the professional-client relationship, but present and future cohorts of older adults have significantly higher educational levels than do their predecessors. Educational levels correlate with client willingness to collaborate with a health professional.

Even older adults with less formal education are more likely than previous cohorts of older adults to encounter health information from television, radio, newspapers, and magazines. This type of informal health education also correlates with client willingness to collaborate with a health professional.

Nonetheless, clients will differ significantly in the degree to which they want to collaborate in an active way in a health care encounter. Some clients may want to give up all responsibility to the practitioner; others may want an active part in the decision-making process (Haug & Lavin, 1981).

The same is true of practitioners. Some health practitioners want the relationship to be "professional centered." They want to be in total control of the interaction and prefer brief responses to their questions. This professional-centered approach is guided by structured questions to elicit simple (oftentimes yes or no) answers.

Others are more "client centered." They ask open-ended questions, restrict the use of jargon, and encourage clients to participate in the decision-making process (Sarafino, 1990). Questions that will elicit the client's perception of the health problem are desired, and the psychosocial aspects of the problem are valued.

A middle position is to assess the client's willingness to be active in his or her health promotion and medical care, and then match the strategy with the level of participation desired by the client. Although this approach may reduce client stress levels and enhance communication, it may be difficult to assess accurately our client's willingness or potential to be active in their health decisions.

We may, therefore, wish to encourage our clients to be more involved in their health care regardless of their initial enthusiasm toward this prospect. We may base this stance on the belief that, in this age of managing chronic health problems and promoting health over long periods, it is in the best interests of the clients to be informed and involved.


## CLIENT EMPOWERMENT VERSUS THE PASSIVE PATIENT

From the client's perspective, empowerment means having the opportunity to learn, discuss, decide, and act on decisions. From the perspective of the health professional, empowerment of the client means not only to provide service but to collaborate, to encourage the client's decision-making ability.

In addition, both the client and the health professional can empower themselves through health advocacy activities, that is, engaging in activities to change the health care system to make it more responsive to health consumers and health providers.

The role of the *passive patient* evolved from the belief that health care is too complex to be understood or controlled by the layperson, that "the doctor knows best." In the past, when acute care medicine reigned supreme, the patient only came to the physician when seeking a cure, and this attitude merited validity.

Today, however, acute care diagnosis and treatment are but two of many important health care activities. Other high-priority health activities include health maintenance, rehabilitation, disease prevention, health promotion, and health advocacy. The one common element among these areas is persistence; one cannot maintain, rehabilitate, prevent, promote, or advocate successfully except on a long-term basis. The *passive patient role*, extended over time, can be dangerous to one's health.

We, as health professionals, frequently encounter older clients who could benefit were they more assertive about improving their health and the health care system in which they participate. Following are some typical examples:

- An older client with unhealthy lifestyle habits expresses the desire to eat less and get more exercise, but no health professional has galvanized this client to action.
- A chronically impaired older client, or a member of this client's family, is disgruntled by the lack of some service, such as home care or respite, that could enhance the client's independence or the family caregiver's mental health; however, this service is not covered by Medicare or a medigap insurance policy, and the family cannot afford it.
- A client who is recovering from a stroke or heart attack or coping with cancer or some other chronic disease appears to be isolated and discouraged. This client could benefit from interacting with people who are coping with similar challenges.
- An older client who takes multiple medications on an ongoing basis is having trouble complying with the medication regimen and needs help in managing her medication schedule and monitoring possible interactive effects.

The passive client or family member has little hope of rectifying any of the aforementioned situations, and health professionals cannot solve all problems for all clients. We can, however, motivate, educate, refer, and follow up. These interventions can empower the older client or family member.

## HOW TO COLLABORATE

The U.S. Preventive Services Task Force (1996) recommendations for patient education and counseling are applicable to how to collaborate with a client. They are (liberally) paraphrased as follows:

1. Consider yourself a consultant and help clients remain in control of their own health choices.

2. Counsel all clients, and reach out to those who differ from you in age, educational level, gender, and ethnicity.
3. Make sure your clients understand the relationship between behavior and health. Understand, though, that knowledge is necessary, but not sufficient to change clients' behaviors.
4. Assess clients' barriers to change including their lack of skills, motivation, resources, and social support.
5. Encourage clients to commit themselves to change, involving them in the selection of risk factors to eliminate.
6. Use a combination of strategies including behavioral and cognitive techniques, the identification and encouragement of social support, and appropriate referrals.
7. Monitor progress through follow-up telephone calls and appointments, and activate your health care team including the receptionist.
8. Be a role model.

## How to Change a Medical Encounter into a Health Encounter

Although some persons may enthusiastically discuss health issues with their nurse, physician, or other health professional, many do not. Often, people simply wish to resolve the immediate medical problem. They may not view health promotion as a personal priority, much less an issue to be discussed during an illness-related visit to a health professional. Those who are interested in health-promoting practices may not think of their health professional as an authority in this area.

Health professionals who *are* interested in health promotion should inform clients at their first visit that health issues are part of their job. It helps to have an ample supply of health-related materials readily available: health articles posted on bulletin boards, a stock of health education materials in the waiting area, relevant materials given directly to clients. And office personnel, such as receptionists, need to be trained to distribute and explain health information and assessment forms to waiting clients.

The likelihood that a nurse, physician, or other health professional will turn an office waiting room into an environment that is conducive to health education is not great. A survey of 150 South Carolina physicians, for instance, found that most thought the office waiting area a potential place for health education, but few had purchased any health education materials. In contrast, most spent more than $100 a year on commercial magazine subscriptions (Taylor et al., 1982).

A 1996 Kaiser Permanente survey found that many of their patients were dissatisfied with the current state of patient education. As one physician noted: "Who can blame them? In most cases, patient education consists of an out-of-date brochure, pulled from the back of a drawer, dusted off and handed to the patient following diagnosis" (Hutchinson, 1998).

## OFFICE SYSTEM FOR IMPLEMENTING A HEALTH PRACTICE

A report by the American Cancer Society Advisory Group provides an office system for organizing preventive services (Leininger et al., 1996). The report includes such ideas as writing a practice policy for preventive care and setting performance goals, auditing charts for baseline performance, implementing a plan with office staff for efficient delivery of preventive care, choosing a staff member to be the coordinator of the plan, and monitoring progress.

Every medical intervention can include a brief health assessment of the client, conducted either by a health professional or a front office person. The assessment may begin with an evaluation of progress on a health contract or another type of intervention plan and end with a notation on the client's progress on the medical record along with a reminder system to ensure timely follow-ups and reinforcements.

There are a variety of effective tracking systems, including chart inserts, flow sheets, and office computer systems, that facilitate systematic follow-up of client's attempts to change or maintain health habits. The most effective strategy is to include health issues at each client visit, to keep up-to-date health data, and to make telephone calls to the client (by clinician or office designee) as follow-ups that are preferable to impersonal written reminders (McDowell et al., 1986).

The more intense a client's behavior change (e.g., stopping smoking as opposed to including more fruit and vegetables in a diet), the more frequently should follow-up contact be made (Sennott-Miller & Kligman, 1992). The more consistent the follow-up, the more influential it will be. The clinician can also encourage the client to view a relapse as a temporary slip rather than a permanent set-back.

## PERSONALITY CHARACTERISTICS OF A HEALTH
## PROFESSIONAL "COLLABORATOR"

Certain personality characteristics, such as patience, tolerance, and a positive attitude, enhance the health professional's chances for collaborating successfully on a health goal. Encouraging health change requires *patience*; client progress tends to be slow, incremental, and characterized by lapses or reversals. Health professionals are unrealistic if they expect to achieve health goals with their clients in the same period required for the reversal of most acute care problems.

*Tolerant* health professionals are nonjudgmental about the poor health habits of clients. These habits should no more be viewed as character weaknesses than a physical illness would be. If a client senses self-righteous rejection on the part of a health professional, even though it may not be verbally expressed, any mutual health endeavor is doomed to fail.

Health professionals with a *positive attitude* begin any health endeavor by identifying the personal assets of clients that will facilitate a change in health behavior. If, for instance, a client has a receptive attitude toward health, the professional should acknowledge it. It is also important to acknowledge past successes in a health area; positive personality traits, like persistence or a sense of humor; the support of a spouse or friend; or the educational and financial resources that will help the client access community health education programs.

## COMMUNICATION BETWEEN HEALTH
## PROFESSIONALS AND CLIENTS

Effective collaboration between health professionals and clients is dependent on good communication. Open-ended inquiries and empathic listening skills are important aids to the health professional, increasing the likelihood of good communication with clients. Taking the time to explore the values and beliefs of clients can help the professional overcome communication barriers erected by differences in educational attainment, cultural beliefs, socioeconomic status, religion, gender, and age.

One small study in Albuquerque, New Mexico, brought family medicine residents and older patients together to examine provider-client discrepancies in medical encounters (Glassheim, 1992). The elders said they wanted health providers to "listen to us more." The providers, in contrast, said they wanted their older patients to "focus, tell us what you want."

Communication takes time. The client may need to focus more precisely to help busy health professionals be more effective. But busy health professionals need to be part of a team effort, and some member of the team (e.g., office staff, peer support group members, or trained paraprofessionals) need to allow the client adequate time to communicate.

Time and caring work together: "the quality of the relationship also may be enhanced through the use of appropriate touch and the acceptance of patient reminiscences during the medical exchange" (McCormick & Inui, 1992, p. 222). Health professionals who are unable to communicate warmth and unwilling to spend time with older clients put themselves at a severe disadvantage for motivating and encouraging behavior change.

## COMMUNICATION SKILLS

A health professional's message can be viewed as a therapeutic agent comparable to a prescription of medicine or a surgical intervention. The positive expectations and good communication skills of a person considered to be trustworthy, expert, and powerful should not be underestimated as a therapeutic tool.

The following questions are designed to help assess communication skills. About half were influenced by a discussion with Kate Lorig, RN, health educator at Stanford, or borrowed from an article by McCormick and Inui (1992). The rest are based upon my personal experience with health education in the community.

### INTERPERSONAL EFFECTIVENESS

1. Do you make eye-to-eye contact?
2. Do you have a caring but not condescending tone of voice?
3. Are you and your clients comfortable with touching? If so, will this enhance rapport and communication?
4. Do you engage in reciprocity of information, and, if necessary, are you willing to self-disclose?
5. Do you let your clients talk enough, provide someone who will, or refer to a support group that will listen?

6. Are you well informed about clients' religious or cultural restrictions regarding privacy, touching, speaking to a woman alone, or other types of intimate interactions that are applicable to your clients?

7. Cross-cultural issues are not just racial, religious, or ethnic issues. We all interpret our health and diseases uniquely (i.e., we try to make sense of things within our belief system). Do you try to be sensitive to everyone's "cultural interpretations"?

8. Are you able to resist countering client beliefs that are not harmful and instead just add to them? "Yes, astrology [or, acknowledge to yourself, preordained circumstances] can cause pain, but pain is also caused by other factors." Give clients power; don't take it away. Just add extra data.

9. Is it possible to gain insight into your client's lifestyle by making a home visit or getting feedback from someone who has?

## INFORMATIONAL PROCESSING

1. Do you know if your clients understand what you said? Can they paraphrase it back to you? If you think you understand what your clients said, can you paraphrase it back to them?

2. Do you supplement your verbal instructions and encouragements with clear, unambiguous written instructions?

3. Do you ask your clients to write down their questions between office visits and bring them on their next visit?

4. Do you encourage your clients to bring along a helpful family member or friend to help with communication? Do you talk directly to your client and not, primarily, with their support person?

5. If appropriate, have you screened for cognitive impairment?

6. Are you aware of the impact that medication side effects may have on your client? Do these side effects interfere with the adoption of healthy behaviors?

7. Do you share medical records and laboratory findings with your clients?

8. Do your clients have any interest in the science (anatomy, physiology, etc.) of their medical problem, or are they just interested in practical skills and knowledge? Do you provide data in a manner that is easily understood or refer clients to a suitable source?

9. Do you have an adequate reminder system to support the healthful behaviors of your clients or to help them avoid health risks?

## SOCIAL AND BEHAVIORAL SUPPORT

1. Do you motivate through positive incentives rather than rely exclusively on fear topics like warning your clients of a probable increase in morbidity or mortality?
2. Do you rely exclusively on talk to change client behaviors, or do you combine talk with other strategies?
3. Do you employ behavioral techniques with clients including the most basic one: praising desired behaviors and suggesting alternatives to undesirable behaviors?
4. Do you involve the social support system of family or friends in behavior change and maintenance?
5. Do you make appropriate referrals when necessary, and do you follow up with your client referral?
6. When making referrals, do you consider programs and resources that are offered at culturally relevant sites, such as neighborhood churches?
7. Do you ascertain client goals, see their underlying importance even if seemingly trivial, help your client redefine goals until they are do-able?
8. Do you encourage your client to seek support from other health professionals to achieve behavior-changing goals?
9. If you refer clients to support groups with lay leaders, do you know if they are receiving appropriate information from peers? Do they invite professional expertise, and are you interested in contributing information?
10. When you refer a client to a community program or service, do you ask them to write their reaction to the program or service, and share their written response with other clients interested in a similar program or service?

## HOW TO COMMUNICATE ABOUT HEALTH GOALS

Effective communication between health professionals and clients about health goals entails three steps (Haber, 1991):

1. *Client readiness.* Clients may have troublesome medical symptoms or physical difficulties that need to be addressed first. Clients may

lack confidence—a situation that may be responsive to an expression of empathy: "I know how difficult exercise is. I also find it hard to do it regularly." Or "I know that we all struggle to eat correctly. How do you feel you have been doing with your eating behaviors?" Clients may be responsive to your enthusiasm and confidence, converting them from contemplating change to action. Or you could be contributing an important step in that direction, even if the success of your effort is not immediately apparent.

2. *Selection of a health goal.* Clients may want *you* to set their health goals. Make sure they know that health goals are more likely to be achieved if *they* take responsibility for choosing them. Conversely, client goals may be unrealistic, inappropriate, or vague, which necessitates a collaborative approach to goal setting. A *mutually* acceptable plan of action should be developed.

   a. Make the plan of action specific—the client needs to know what to do and by when.
   b. Set goals that are modest and doable.
   c. List the benefits to be gained.
   d. Identify prior barriers and engage in problem-solving discussion.
   e. Employ a combination of behavior-changing strategies, such as a professional-client health contract, identification of strong social support, and appropriate referrals to community health programs or health professionals.
   f. Allow for occasional slips.

3. *Follow-up.* Behavior change is an *ongoing* challenge. Are modifications in the plan of action necessary? Is the client getting adequate support from spouse or significant others? Is the health professional or office staff providing reinforcement through telephone calls, subsequent office visits, and letters of support or commendation?

## REFERRALS TO COMMUNITY HEALTH EDUCATION PROGRAMS

Communicating about an appropriate health goal and developing an effective plan of action ought to be an important component of the professional-client relationship, but the amount of time available for this endeavor is severely limited. It is important, therefore, for the health professional to learn more about the health resources and programs available in the community, and to make appropriate referrals.

The past decade has witnessed a proliferation of low-cost or free educational opportunities for older adults within the community. Except in isolated rural areas, many health education opportunities for older persons are available.

These opportunities may include programs sponsored by the YMCA/YWCA or senior center, hospital and church-based senior health education programs, AARP programs, health education events sponsored by professional associations, health advocacy groups and mutual help groups, community college programs for older adults, Elderhostel programs, town hall meetings sponsored by state or local elected officials, shopping center mall walker programs, or corporate retiree wellness programs.

Once having identified community health organizations or resources, additional considerations come into play. Cost, transportation access, and instructor competency with older students are important factors in referring clients to community health education programs.

Community health programs are likely to be more successful if organized "andragogically." Andragogy is the art and science of teaching adults based on a set of assumptions about learning that are different from traditional pedagogy. These assumptions, which have received only limited empirical examination (Brookfield, 1990), are twofold:

1. *Active involvement.* Active involvement on the part of older students is preferable to the more traditional, passive student role. Older adults learn best when actively participating in an experience, such as setting goals and planning instruction.
2. *Peer interaction.* Participation of older adults is encouraged by peer support, information, and assistance. Community health education programs that allow for peer interaction are more effective than those that rely primarily on didactic educational techniques.

Finally, besides being knowledgeable about community health services and programs, and referring clients to them, it is important to get feedback on the effectiveness of community health programs. Do your clients recommend the program to others? Forms can be distributed to clients to elicit their responses systematically on the effectiveness of the programs and then made available to your other clients.

## CRUISING THE NET

Face-to-face communication with health professionals has become increasingly limited during this new era of managed care. Consumers, therefore, need other sources of health information. A 1998 Roper survey (Kleyman, 1998) of Americans found that television is their primary source of health information (40%), followed close behind by physicians (36%) and magazines and journals (35%).

The fastest growing source of health information, however, is the World Wide Web, also referred to as the Internet. Moreover, the fastest-growing age segment using the Internet is the 50-plus category. Merely 7% of online users were aged 50+ in 1996; however, that increased to 25% in 1997.

Not only are older net surfers proliferating but so are health-related Web sites. On the burgeoning World Wide Web there are now an estimated 10,000 consumer health information sites (Schwartz, 1997). One of the more important and trustworthy sites is Healthfinder, a new entry launched by the U.S. government on April 15, 1997. Healthfinder is an entry point for a vast collection of publications, clearinghouses, databases, Web sites and self-help or support groups.

Vice President Gore, however, stressed that the wealth of online consumer health information is "a mixed blessing because finding high-quality information that is accurate, timely, relevant and unbiased is a daunting challenge to even the most experienced Web surfer" (Schwartz, 1997). It is important to know the credentials of contributors to Web sites, whether the contributor has a financial stake in the products or information discussed, and if there are other sources of information with competing points of view.

A survey of 160 randomly selected health information sites found that more than half might have contained biased information (Laurence, 1997). Bias was not defined as accuracy but awareness as to whether the site's owner stood to gain financially from the products or services mentioned.

Other cautions with using the Internet are lack of privacy, inefficiency (a search using the key words seniors brings up 57,600 sites, and senior centers turned up 275,992 sites), and high traffic causing delays (*"A World of Information Beckons,"* 1998). Problems aside, however, more and more health consumers are finding the Internet to be an incredibly useful tool.

Free online health information is available in all forms including continuing education, consumer education, bulletin-board discussion groups, prescription and over-the-counter drug information, health news, regularly scheduled chats, in-depth feature articles, book reviews, Web reviews, databases, and so forth. I have attempted to categorize below a few of the more interesting Web addresses that I have collected from dozens of sources. To access the Web sites listed subsequently, it is necessary to first type in "http://www.".

## Government

healthfinder.gov, nci.nih.gov (National Cancer Institute), nlm.nih.gov (National Library of Medicine—free access to MEDLINE, a database of articles published in 3,800 biomedical journals), fda.gov (Food and Drug Administration), odphp.osophs.dhhs.gov (Office of Disease Prevention and Health Promotion), and aoa.dhhs.gov (Administration on Aging).

## General

healthanswers.com, healthy.net, healthtouch.com.

## Professional Associations

cancer.org (American Cancer Society), amhrt.org (American Heart Association), diabetes.org (American Diabetes Association), lungusa.org (American Lung Association), nof.org (National Osteoporosis Foundation), ama-assn.org (American Medical Association), ana.org (American Nurses Association), geron.org (Gerontological Society of America), nho.org (National Hospice Organization).

## Exercise

dhhs.gov/progorg/ophs/index.html (President's Council on Physical Fitness and Sports), aahperd.org (American Alliance for Health, Physical Education, Recreation, and Dance), acsm.org (American College of Sports Medicine), and pitt.edu/~pahnet (Physical Activity and Health Network).

### Nutrition

eatright.org (American Dietetic Association), refdesk.com/health.html, usda.gov (U.S. Department of Agriculture), spectre.ag.uiuc.edu/~food-lab/nat/ (do-your-own nutritional analysis), and wheatfoods.org (grain products).

### Smoking Cessation

cdc.gov/nccdphp/osh/tobacco.htm.

### Alcohol and Drug Abuse

niaaa.nih.gov/, nida.nih.gov, samhsa.gov, well.com/user/woa.

### Mental Health

cmhc.com, samhsa.gov (Substance Abuse and Mental Health Services Administration).

### Older Consumers

aarp.org (American Association of Retired Persons), seniornet.org (Seniornet teaches older adults how to use computers), thirdage.com, senior.com, cmhc.com/selfhelp (American Self-Help Clearinghouse-best list of support groups).

## MISCELLANEOUS COMMUNICATION ISSUES

### CROSS-CULTURAL COMMUNICATION

Many managed care organizations are recognizing the importance of improving communication with minority patients. In Southern California, for instance, Kaiser Permanente has a medical anthropologist on staff to help health professionals communicate more effectively with minority patients and to develop special programs for minority members.

Cross-cultural communication, however, is not simply an issue of race or nationality. Many cultural differences that emerge between health professionals and clients are based on differences in age, gender, religion, ethnicity, socioeconomic class, and education. Every health professional must deal with cross-cultural issues. Open-ended questions can help the health professional understand the client's viewpoint: How would you describe your health problem? Why do you think this problem occurred? Do you have sources of relief that I don't know about? Apart from me, who do you think can help you get better? Has anyone made recommendations to you? Did you try any of them?

Following is a list of videotapes designed to improve communication between the health professional and client: Miles Inc., Pharmaceutical Division in West Haven, Connecticut (203-498-6464): on communication skills with problem patients; American Academy of Family Physicians (800-274-2237): on racial and cultural biases; Boston Area Health Education Center of Boston City Hospital (617-534-5258) on geriatric bilingual medical interviews; and the National Coalition of Hispanic Health and Human Services Organizations (202-387-5000) on preventive health care for Hispanic patients.

## END-OF-LIFE COMMUNICATION

Some health care professionals believe that discussing end-of-life care issues upsets their clients. The data suggest, however, that few older adults are upset by such a discussion (Finucane, 1988). It is important that people's views be clearly recorded before an unexpected crisis develops. Clear thinking is more likely when a patient is relatively healthy and not suffering from anxiety.

Unfortunately, however, this type of communication is the exception rather than the rule. For instance, more than 90% of older adults do not clearly understand cardiopulmonary resuscitation (CPR) (Shmerling et al., 1988). Eighty-seven percent of older respondents thought CPR should be discussed routinely with health professionals, but only 3% had engaged in such discussions with them.

Another common example of a serious failure to communicate is the fact that most older adults understand the idea of a Living Will, but most have neither signed one nor discussed the issue with a health professional (Gamble et al., 1991). Geriatrician Joanne Lynne, director of George Washington University's Center to Improve Care of the Dying, reported on the importance of clear communication between health professionals and clients. She examined 569 advance directives, but only 22 of them were specific and clear enough to help physicians and family members decide what to do (Lynne, 1997).

## COMMUNICATING TO CLIENT COMPANIONS

Older men are less likely than women to bring a companion when visiting a doctor but more likely to bring a companion into the examining room to help them communicate with the doctor. Older women tend to bring companions primarily for transportation or companionship, visiting with the doctor alone (Beisecker, 1990).

A client's companion can provide a vital service to both the health professional and the client, serving as an independent monitor of a person's condition and providing helpful feedback on client collaboration with treatment regimens. A companion can make sure questions are asked and answers understood. Conversely, health professionals can be seduced into communicating with companions and ignore their clients. Problems that may stem from coalition formation (between two of three participants) have not been examined as yet.

## PHYSICIAN COMMUNICATION AND AGEISM

The satisfaction of older clients is positively associated with the length of their visits with a physician and with the physician's support of topics initiated by the clients (Greene, 1991). Using audiotapes of medical encounters, however, researchers have found that doctors seem reluctant to discuss psychosocial issues with older clients and are less receptive to these issues when raised by older clients than when raised by younger ones (Greene, 1991; Greene et al., 1987).

Another study reported that older clients are less likely than younger clients to agree with their physicians on the main goals of their visit (e.g., to discuss medication side effects, physical symptoms, etc.), and the topics that ought to be discussed (Adelman et al., 1989). An exception was with personal habits (e.g., diet, exercise, smoking, and drinking). These topics, however, are infrequently discussed with physicians, regardless of a client's age (Greene et al., 1989).

A study of older diabetic clients reported that 42% were unable to discuss the symptoms that concerned them (Rost, 1990). Physicians were much less responsive to topics raised by their older clients than to those raised by themselves (Adelman et al., 1989; Greene, 1991).

Physicians give older clients considerably less cardiac risk reduction advice (regarding diet, exercise, weight control, smoking, stress management, and work) than they give younger clients (Young & Kahana, 1989). Thus, older clients are systematically denied the opportunity to lessen their risk of future heart problems by adopting the behavioral advice of their physician.

## JARGON

A study of lower class clients' comprehension of 13 terms used by their physicians found, not surprisingly, that each term was understood by only about one third of the clients (McKinlay, 1975). What *was* surprising was the fact that physicians expected these clients to have even *less* comprehension than was reported.

Sarafino (1990) points out some obvious reasons why physicians persist in using incomprehensible language: habit; the belief that accurate comprehension of a medical problem might increase the client's stress level; the fact that difficult-to-understand terms may be conversation stoppers, making more time available for seeing other clients; the belief that the use of big words elevates the status and the authority of the practitioner; and the belief that lack of comprehension may make errors more difficult to detect and litigation less likely.

Clients, however, prefer health professionals who are willing to listen, communicate clearly, and show warmth and concern. When these expectations are met, clients offer more significant diagnostic details, keep more appointments, and litigate less (Sarafino, 1990).

## FOUR COMMON REASONS NOT TO INITIATE HEALTH EDUCATION

1. *I do not think most of my clients want it.* This may be true, given the dry way in which health education is often presented. But many clients

become more enthusiastic about health when they are encouraged to identify benefits that are meaningful to them; benefits like more energy, less arthritic pain, better sleep, slimmer waist, better relationships, or more strength. Clients also need help with finding a way to accomplish the health goal of their choice.

2. *I am not skilled in doing it.* With a few exceptions in nursing (Wold & Williams, 1996) and allied health (Haber et al., 1997) health science students do not receive adequate knowledge, skills and, especially, practice in providing health promotion and education to clients during the course of their student training. Given the wealth of continuing education opportunities available, however, the major barrier to becoming more skilled at practicing health promotion and education with clients is insufficient motivation.

3. *I do not have the time for it.* This is a major concern that permeates the managed care environment. Conversely, many ideas and techniques can be presented to clients in a brief period, or the health professional can make an educated referral to an appropriate and effective community health program.

4. *I am not paid to do it.* True—health professionals rarely benefit monetarily from offering health promotion and education to clients. But they do receive the gratitude of clients who stop smoking, start exercising, lose weight, or reduce stress. And this, in turn, provides most health professionals with tremendous mental health benefits, not to mention more clients from the family and friendship networks of satisfied clients.

## QUESTIONS FOR DISCUSSION

1. Think about an occupation that you wish was more health oriented (like a nursing home or hospital administrator, a physician, or a minister); how could you transform that job to generate more health-promoting activities with older adults?
2. Three important personality characteristics of a *health* provider are mentioned in this chapter. Can you add a fourth? Why do you think it is important?
3. Can you provide any examples of ageism that you witnessed in a health professional-client or teacher-student encounter?
4. The term *empowerment* can easily be viewed as a buzzword (i.e., thrown around a lot, signifying much, but meaning little). How can

(or have) you become a more empowered student/teacher/practitioner (choose one), or do you see this term as a buzzword yourself?

5. Suppose you have encountered a 70-year-old client or a student who prefers an authoritarian health provider or teacher. As a clinician or teacher, should you accept this person's attitude, or should you encourage more initiative? If you choose to encourage this type of person, how would you go about it?

# 3
# Medical Screenings and Health Assessments

[T]o increase from 67% to (no target percentage) routine check-ups for adults 65 years and over.

[T]o increase from 14% to 60% pneumococcal pneumonia immunizations, and from 30% to 60% influenza immunizations for adults 65 years and over.

[T]o increase from 51% to 60% breast exams and mammograms in past 2 years for women 50 years and over; and from 43% to (no target percentage) for women 65 years and over.

[T]o increase from 51% to (no target percentage) Pap tests in last 3 years for women 65 years and over. (Public health goals from the U.S. Public Health Service's Healthy People 2000 Initiative [AARP, 1991])

As of 1994, routine check-ups for adults 65 years and older have declined to 62%; pneumococcal pneumonia immunizations have increased to 32% and influenza immunizations to 58%; breast exams and mammograms have increased for women 50 years and older, to 56%; and Pap tests have increased to 57%. (*Healthy People 2000 Midcourse Review: 1995 Report on Progress*, DHHS, OPHS)

## MEDICAL SCREENINGS

It is well known that the incidence of stroke and heart attack can be reduced by increased screening for and treatment of hypertension. And we know that cervical cancer mortality dropped substantially during the 1970s and 1980s because of the Pap smear test. Nevertheless, despite considerable support and, in some instances, universal acclaim, medical screenings are neither systematically nor uniformly implemented by clinicians.

This behavior is due to both clinicians and researchers failing to agree on the effectiveness of screenings among the population at large, that is, the relative benefits versus the risks (medical and financial) to individual patients at a particular age and frequency rate.

Inconsistent recommendations for medical screenings have also been due, in part, to the lack of reimbursement for patients without health insurance or who were poor (Dawson et al., 1987). Not only did these patients receive few preventive services, but they have had little opportunity during visits to discuss screening options or other health education matters resulting from the physician's large patient loads and subsequent time constraints (Gemson et al., 1988).

Although these controversies and inconsistencies persisted into 1998, that year marked the biggest change to prevention services offered through Medicare since the health insurance program was founded more than 3 decades ago. These changes amount to $4 billion over the next 5 years and $8.5 billion over the next 10 years. We will describe and evaluate these changes in the section on "Medicare Prevention."

## GUIDE TO CLINICAL PREVENTIVE SERVICES

Routine annual medical screenings are no longer recommended. Health professionals, therefore, must take the time to inform themselves about the unique health risk factors of individual clients. Because the collection of research data on which to base medical decisions is an ongoing process, health professionals have an ongoing need to educate themselves on current screening recommendations.

To simplify and standardize this task, in 1976 the Canadian Task Force on the Periodic Health Examination initiated the first comprehensive effort to assess the effectiveness of a wide array of preventive services. They began by developing explicit criteria for assessing the quality of the evidence from published clinical research. Decision rules were then developed to guide clinicians.

In a similar effort in 1984, the U.S. Preventive Services Task Force developed recommendations for clinicians on the basis of a comprehensive review of the evidence of clinical effectiveness. The conclusions were published in the *Guide to Clinical Preventive Services* (U.S. Preventive Services Task Force, 1989), which cataloged 60 preventable diseases and conditions and provided guidelines to help health professionals select the primary, secondary, and tertiary preventive interventions that were most appropriate for their clients. In 1996 the second edition of the *Guide* was published, and the number of topics expanded to 70.

The *Guide* reinforces the need to select screening tests according to the unique risk profiles of individuals rather than the traditional annual physical. Its authors conclude that education and counseling—not medical screenings—are the most effective forms of prevention (see Table 3.1).

To order the *Guide to Clinical Preventive Services*, contact Williams and Wilkins, P.O. Box 1496, Baltimore, MD; 800-638-4007 or 800-638-5298. A similar book with more practical guidelines for clinicians is the *Clinician's Handbook of Preventive Services*, 2nd ed., 1998, Office of Disease Prevention and Health Promotion; call toll-free 800-358-9295.

**TABLE 3.1 Medical Screening Schedule for Persons Age 65 and Over**

| Interventions Considered and Recommended for the Periodic Health Examination | Leading Causes of Death |
|---|---|
| | Heart disease |
| | Malignant neoplasms (lung, colorectal, breast) |
| | Cerebrovascular disease |
| | Chronic obstructive pulmonary disease |
| | Pneumonia and influenza |

**Interventions for the General Population**

**SCREENING**
Blood pressure
Height and weight
Fecal occult blood test[1] and/or
 sigmoidoscopy
Mammogram ± clinical breast exam[2]
 (women ≤69 yr)
Papanicolaou (Pap) test (women)[3]
Vision screening
Assess for hearing impairment
Assess for problem drinking

*Injury Prevention*
Lap/shoulder belts
Motorcycle and bicycle helmets*
Fall prevention*
Safe storage/removal of firearms*
Smoke detector*
Set hot water heater to <120–135°F*
CPR training for household members
*Dental Health*
Regular visits to dental care provider*
Floss, brush with fluoride toothpaste
 daily*

## COUNSELING

### Substance Use

Tobacco cessation

Avoid alcohol/drug use while driving,
swimming, boating, etc.*

### Diet and Exercise

Limit fat & cholesterol; maintain caloric
balance; emphasize grains, fruits,
vegetables

Adequate calcium intake (women)

Regular physical activity*

### Sexual Behavior

STD prevention: avoid high-risk sexual
behavior; use condoms*

## IMMUNIZATIONS

Pneumococcal vaccine

Influenza[1]

Tetanus-diphtheria (Td) boosters

## CHEMOPROPHYLAXIS

Discuss hormone prophylaxis (women)

### Interventions for High-Risk Populations

| POPULATION | POTENTIAL INTERVENTIONS |
|---|---|
| Institutionalized persons | PPD (HR1); hepatitis A vaccine (HR2); amantadine/rimantadine (HR4) |
| Chronic medical conditions; TB contacts; low income; immigrants; alcoholics | PPD (HR1) |
| Persons ≥75 yr, or ≥70 yr with risk factors for falls | Fall prevention intervention (HR5) |
| Cardiovascular disease risk factors | Consider cholesterol screening (HR6) |
| Family h/o skin cancer; nevi; fair skin, eyes, hair | Avoid excess/midday sun, use protective clothing* (HR7) |
| Native Americans/Alaska Natives | PPD (HR1); hepatitis A vaccine (HR2) |
| Travelers to developing countries | Hepatitis A vaccine (HR2); hepatitis B vaccine (HR8) |
| Blood product recipients | HIV screen (HR3); hepatitis B vaccine (HR8) |
| Health care/lab workers | PPD (HR1); hepatitis A vaccine (HR2); amantadine/rimantadine (HR4); hepatitis B vaccine (HR8) |
| Persons susceptible to varicella | Varicella vaccine (HR11) |

[1]Annually. [2]Mammogram q 1–2 yr, or mammogram q 1-2 yr with annual clinical breast exam. [3]All women who are or have been sexually active and who have a cervix: q ≤ 3 yr. Consider discontinuation of testing after age 65 yr if previous regular screening with consistently normal results.

*The ability of clinician counseling to influence this behavior is unproven.

*continued*

**High Risk Definitions**

HR1 = HIV positive, close contacts of persons with known or suspected TB, health care workers, persons with medical risk factors associated with TB, immigrants from countries with high TB prevalence, medically underserved low-income populations (including homeless), alcoholics, injection drug users, and residents of long-term care facilities.

HR2 = Persons living in, traveling to, or working in areas where the disease is endemic and where periodic outbreaks occur (e.g., countries with high or intermediate endemicity; certain Alaska Native, Pacific Island, Native American, and religious communities); men who have sex with men; injection or street drug users. Consider for institutionalized persons and workers in these institutions, and day-care, hospital, and laboratory workers. Clinicians should also consider local epidemiology.

HR3 = Men who had sex with men after 1975; past or present injection drug use; persons who exchange sex for money or drugs, and their sex partners; injection drug-using, bisexual, or HIV-positive sex partner currently or in the past; blood transfusion during 1978–1985; persons seeking treatment for STDs. Clinicians should also consider local epidemiology.

HR4 = Consider for persons who have not received influenza vaccine or are vaccinated late; when the vaccine may be ineffective due to major antigenic changes in the virus; for unvaccinated persons who provide home care for high-risk persons; to supplement protection provided by vaccine in persons who are expected to have a poor antibody response; and for high-risk persons in whom the vaccine is contraindicated.

HR5 = Persons aged 75 years and older; or aged 70–74 with one or more additional risk factors including: use of certain psychoactive and cardiac medications (e.g., benzodiazepines, antihypertensives); use of ≥ 4 prescription medications; impaired cognition, strength, balance, or gait. Intensive individualized home-based multifactorial fall prevention intervention is recommended in settings where adequate resources are available to deliver such services.

HR6 = Although evidence is insufficient to recommend routine screening in elderly persons, clinicians should consider cholesterol screening on a case-by-case basis for persons ages 65–75 with additional risk factors (e.g.. smoking, diabetes, or hypertension).

HR7 = Persons with a family or personal history of skin cancer, a large number of moles, atypical moles, poor tanning ability, or light skin, hair, and eye color.

HR8 = Blood product recipients (including hemodialysis patients), persons with frequent occupational exposure to blood or blood products, men who have sex with men, injection drug users and their sex partners, persons with multiple recent sex partners, persons with other STDs (including HIV), travelers to countries with endemic hepatitis B.

HR9 = Persons who exchange sex for money or drugs and their sex partners; persons with other STDs (including HIV); and sexual contacts of persons with active syphilis. Clinicians should also consider local epidemiology.

HR10 = Persons who continue to inject drugs.

HR11 = Healthy adults without a history of chickenpox or previous immunization. Consider serologic testing for presumed susceptible adults.

ACCURACY, RELIABILITY, AND EFFECTIVENESS OF SCREENING TESTS

Accuracy refers to the sensitivity and specificity of screening tests. The sensitivity of a screening test is defined as how many people who actually had the disease tested positive when screened. A test with poor sensitivity will miss persons with the condition and produce a large proportion of false-negative results. Persons who receive false-negative results will experience delays in treatment.

Specificity refers to the proportion of persons without the condition who correctly test negative when screened. A test with poor specificity will result in healthy persons being told that they have the disease and produce a large proportion of false-positive results. Persons who receive false-positive results may experience expensive follow-up tests or unnecessary treatment.

Even if the test is sensitive and specific, it may not be reliable or effective. Reliability refers to the ability of a test to obtain the same result when repeated. The reliability of mammograms and Pap smears have been increased recently because of federal certification and annual state inspections of facilities. Effectiveness refers to whether the test is worth the cost, time, and bother, that is, whether there is a subsequent clinical intervention for a positive finding that can prevent or delay the disease.

Comments about accuracy, reliability, or effectiveness will be included when describing the following screening tests.

CHOLESTEROL

Clinicians need to check the accuracy of blood cholesterol screening tests obtained either by venipuncture or finger stick because, for a variety of reasons, the result of a single reading is not reliable. Each individual normally undergoes substantial physiological fluctuations, for instance, and a single blood test may not be representative. Misclassification resulting from laboratory error is also common. Some tests produce systematic or consistent bias, whereas others are subject to a lack of precision in the interpretation of results (United States Preventive Services Task Force, 1996).

If a second measurement by an accredited laboratory is also normal, retesting is recommended once every 5 years. Should an abnormal result be confirmed by a second reading, more frequent screenings are recommended.

A total blood cholesterol level of 240 mg/dL or higher is considered abnormal because it has a substantial association with coronary heart disease (United States Preventive Services Task Force, 1996). About 27% of U.S. adults have total blood cholesterol levels of 240 or higher.

Between 1983 and 1988, the percentage of adults who had their cholesterol checked rose from 35 to 59% of the population (AARP, 1991). Although this achievement, inspired by widespread media attention and public education, is impressive, the recommendation for cholesterol screening has not been uniformly taken to heart by all sectors of the general public. Only 35% of Hispanics, for instance, and 39% of blacks have been determined to know their blood cholesterol levels.

Controlled trials indicate that each 1% reduction in serum cholesterol level is matched by a 2% reduction in the risk of death by heart disease (Kottke et al., 1988), which reinforces the importance of treatment when blood cholesterol levels are elevated.

However, the wisdom of recommending cholesterol screenings after the age of 70 remains unresolved. It has not yet been determined whether the association between higher cholesterol concentrations and atherosclerotic coronary artery disease, for instance, may weaken *or* strengthen with age (Ettinger et al., 1992). Should the association remain the same or strengthen with age, it is an important and modifiable risk factor among older persons. Should it weaken with age, cholesterol testing with older adults would not be effective.

An informal survey of several hundred physicians revealed that most considered 70 the approximate threshold age for effective treatment of an elevated cholesterol level. Most expressed some concern about initiating treatment through drugs or diet with patients over 70.

Concerns regarding the use of hypolipidemic drugs relate to their cost, side effects, potential interaction with other medications, and the 2 or more years "between the onset of drug treatment and the beginning of reduced morbidity and morality" (Hazzard, 1992, pp. 98–100).

Dietary therapy and follow-up by physicians, dietitians, or nutritionists can be effective in reducing dietary fat intake and serum cholesterol in adults of all ages (Insull et al., 1990). Unfortunately, dietary recommendations, which typically consists of reducing fat intake to less than 30% of total calories, saturated fat (fat that is solid at room temperature, e.g., butter, cheese, and fat in red meat) to less than 10% of total calories, and cholesterol intake to less than 300 mg/day (Report of the National

Cholesterol Education Program, 1988), may foster malnutrition in highly compliant older clients (see Figure 3.1).

Malnutrition is a not uncommon issue when it comes to older adults, and cholesterol or fat avoidance that triggers malnutrition is a legitimate concern. Conversely, three in four patients report that there was *no discussion* at all on the topic of eating proper foods during a visit to a doctor or other health professional during a routine visit (National Center for

**FIGURE 3.1   Elizabeth "Grandma" Layton, popular artist from Wellsville, Kansas, focused her artistic attention on her own aging process and that of her husband, Glenn, who is pictured on a bathroom scale, concerned about his loss of weight.**

Health Statistics, 1988). (For additional information on cholesterol, see chapter 5 on nutrition.)

## HIGH BLOOD PRESSURE AND HYPERTENSION

Measurement error should be the first consideration of a health professional assessing elevated blood pressure levels. Errors can result from manometer dysfunction, difficulty in hearing the Korotkoff sounds or in reading the manometer, posture variations (lying, standing, or sitting), and changing physical factors (anxiety, last meal eaten, exertion, etc.).

In addition, "white coat hypertension" (Pickering, 1988) refers to the consistent overestimation of the blood pressure of certain patients in the physician's office. It is commonly recommended that to counteract low reliability "the average of multiple measurements of blood pressure over several different visits is more likely to approximate a person's true blood pressure" (Applegate, 1992, p. 107).

A few years ago, clinicians distinguished between hypertension, or readings over 160/95, and high blood pressure, readings over 140/90. This is no longer the case. Statistical evidence now indicates that blood pressure readings above 140/90 increase the risk for disease and premature death, prompting the American Heart Association to revise its standards. Hypertension is now defined as blood pressure levels that are equal to or greater than 140 mmHg systolic or 90 mmHg diastolic. Many experts believe that it is best for older adults to not only reduce their readings to below 140/90 but to the standard level of 120/80 (see Figure 3.2).

Based on 1996 estimates by the American Heart Association, 50 million Americans were hypertensive (Hoeger & Hoeger, 1997). Because of the likelihood of measurement error, however, this figure has not been universally accepted. "Instead of the more commonly cited 50% of all elderly persons having high blood pressure, the prevalence rate may be closer to 33% of whites and 40% of blacks over age 65" (Applegate, 1992).

It is estimated that three out of four adults and perhaps 90% of older adults have had their blood pressure measured within the preceding year. Among those with accurately measured high blood pressure, only one third remain in treatment and consistently take their medication in sufficient amounts to achieve adequate blood pressure control (Haynes et al., 1980). In addition, some older persons "may actually experience side effects that are so serious that antihypertensive therapy is not warranted" (Applegate, 1992, p. 107).

**FIGURE 3.2** **Nursing student teaching older adult to take a blood pressure reading in one of the author's health education classes.**

The effectiveness of nonpharmacological therapies, such as exercise, sodium restriction, weight reduction, decreased alcohol intake, smoking cessation, and stress management, on the other hand, is promising (National Heart, Lung and Blood Institute, 1988) but complicated by biological factors (e.g., hypertensives who are not salt sensitive) and behavioral factors (e.g., ability to maintain weight loss or sustain an exercise program).

## PNEUMOCOCCAL AND INFLUENZA IMMUNIZATION

Pneumococcal vaccine should be administered at least once during a lifetime and the influenza vaccine annually to all persons aged 65 and older. Health care providers for high-risk patients should also receive influenza vaccine.

Pneumonia is three times more prevalent among those age 65 and older than among younger persons. Pneumonia accounts for an average of 48 days of restricted activity per 100 people aged 65 and older (National Center for Health Statistics, 1990a). Nonetheless, only 10% of older adults in the community had received the pneumococcal vaccine in 1989 (Center for Infectious Diseases and Center for Prevention Services, 1990). By 1995, however, 32% of older adults had received the vaccine, due in large measure because of the onset of Medicare reimbursement.

Immunization against influenza is also recognized as a standard preventive medicine intervention for older adults. Between 1972 and 1982, the death rate during six flu epidemics was 34 to 104 times higher among older adults than younger persons. Yet only 20% of older adults in the community received influenza vaccines in 1989 (Center for Infectious Diseases and Center for Prevention Services, 1990). This percentage, however, increased to 58% by the end of 1995, after Medicare began paying for influenza shots for the nation's elderly and disabled populations (Health Care Advisory Board, 1997).

Although vaccination rates are improving, they are still well below optimal levels. Part of the problem is that 91% of physicians agree that older adults should be vaccinated, but only 24% offer the vaccine. In addition, 22% of seniors refuse the influenza vaccination, primarily because they believe flu shots will make them sick (Health Care Advisory Board, 1997). The older adults who are at risk, however, are only a very small number of people who are allergic to the vaccine, those who are allergic to eggs, and those who have a current fever.

Another immunization shot is recommended for all adults including older adults. After a primary series of three doses of the tetanus-diphtheria toxoid, a booster shot should be administered at least once every 10 years.

## BREAST CANCER SCREENING

Breast cancer is the leading cause of cancer among women, accounting for 46,000 deaths in 1997. In 1995, an estimated 182,000 new cases of breast cancer were diagnosed in women, with 48% of new breast cancer cases and 56% of breast cancer deaths occurring in women age 65 and older (United States Preventive Services Task Force, 1996).

The three screening tests for breast cancer are breast self-examination, clinical examination, and x-ray mammography. Breast self-examinations have never been proved to reduce breast cancer deaths, but many physicians and the American Cancer Society still encourage their use because the procedure is simple, safe, and free. One meta-analysis, however, reported that although larger tumors are more likely to be discovered through self-examination (Hill et al., 1988), the sensitivity of self-examination is quite low and specificity remains uncertain (United States Preventive Services Task Force, 1996).

Regarding annual clinical breast examinations, there is consensus that all women older than 40 should receive them. However, the age at which annual mammographic screenings should begin does not inspire such consensus. The National Cancer Institute, for instance, changed its guidelines in March 1997 and joined the American Cancer Society in recommending regular mammograms beginning at age 40. This guideline, however, departs from the advice of the National Institutes of Health's consensus panel, which recommended that decisions about mammograms before age 50 be left up to each woman and her physician. The American Medical Association's Council on Scientific Affairs took a middle position—mammograms every 2 years between the ages of 40 and 49; and annually beginning at age 50.

It is unclear whether this controversy involving the middle-aged baby boomers is bringing desirable attention to breast cancer screening in general, or whether it is shifting attention and resources away from the women with the highest incidence of breast cancer—those age 60 and older (Stapleton, 1997).

The discontinuance of mammographic screenings is recommended at age 75 in asymptomatic women who have had consistently normal results on previous examinations (United States Preventive Services Task Force, 1996).

Breast cancer mortality can be reduced by 30% among women aged 50 and older if they are screened by mammography and clinical breast examination (Shapiro et al., 1985). Nonetheless, in 1987, only one in four women older than age 50 had received a clinical breast examination and mammography within the preceding two years (AARP, 1991).

A national survey found in 1985 that most primary care physicians never recommended mammography screening to their female patients, though by 1988, 96% reported having done so (*Report on Medical Guidelines*, 1991). A national study of primary care physicians by the American Cancer Society in 1988 found that 80% of physicians did more screenings than 5 years ago.

The importance of the recommendation of a mammogram by a physician was confirmed in a study of mostly older white women, two thirds of whom had mammograms within the past year (Brimer et al., 1991). Education and affordability might also have been factors in this study, but such was not the case for two samples of older black women, of whom 60% complied when specifically offered a mammogram. Once again, the recommendation of a physician was a key factor (Brimer et al., 1991; Burack & Liang, 1987, 1989).

In 1992, Medicare began offering partial coverage for mammograms conducted every 2 years, in addition to the coverage of mammograms recommended for at-risk women. (These benefits improved in 1998—see Medicare Prevention, p. 67.) Also, in 1992 Congress approved the Mammography Quality Standards Act, which regulates equipment and personnel, including technologists and physicians, and requires federal certification and annual state inspections of facilities. It is anticipated that the reliability of mammography screenings will improve as a result.

The specificity of mammograms, however, still leaves much to be desired. Fifty percent of women who have 10 mammograms will have one false positive result, which will require further testing, and more unnecessary stress and expense. As many as 20% of these false alarms will lead to a breast biopsy in which tissue is removed from the suspected tumor (Elmore et al., 1998).

To enhance the likelihood that older women will get a mammogram screening, up to 50 free copies of a pamphlet titled, "Chances Are . . . You Need a Mammogram" (No. D14502) can be ordered from: AARP Fulfillment, 601 E. Street NW, Washington, DC 20049 (no telephone orders).

## CERVICAL CANCER SCREENING

Until the 1940s, more American women died of cervical cancer than any other type of malignancy. However, the Papanicolaou test, named for its creator, reduced the death rate from cervical cancer by 70%. Pap testing is recommended for women beginning at the age at which they first engage in sexual intercourse and should be repeated every 1 to 3 years, depending on risk factors. Pap smears may be discontinued at age 65 if previous smears have been consistently normal.

Many older women, however, have not had adequate screening; nearly half have never received a Pap test, and 75% have not received regular screening. Older women are least likely to have had Pap smears, in part because they no longer visit gynecologists, the specialists most likely to recommend the test (Jones, 1992).

Even many gynecologists, though, do not routinely alert women to the need for Pap smears. Many physicians habitually respond to patients' requests rather than initiate advice (Jones, 1992). A possible solution to this dilemma for physicians might be tagging and monitoring patient files and routinely sending out reminder postcards.

Screening of older women is important and cost-effective. Recognizing this fact, Congress, in 1990, mandated that Medicare cover Pap smears triennially. In 1992, however, Medicare paid a maximum of $7.89 per Pap smear, despite the fact that new federal clinical laboratory regulations increased the cost of Pap smears. Benefits improved considerably in 1998 when the full claim for Pap smears became reimbursable (see Medicare Prevention, p. 67).

## COLORECTAL CANCER SCREENING

Colorectal cancer is the second most common form of cancer, accounting for 55,000 deaths in 1997. Recent studies have prompted the United States Preventive Services Task Force (1996) to revise its 1989 guidelines and to recommend annual fecal occult blood testing and sigmoidoscopy for all persons aged 50 and older. On the down side, however, proctoscopic tests remain uncomfortable, embarrassing, and expensive, and both client noncompliance and physician reluctance to perform the procedure on asymptomatic patients has been reported (United States Preventive Services Task Force, 1996).

It should be noted that digital rectal examinations are of limited value because few colorectal cancers can be detected by this procedure, and fecal occult blood testing still produces a high percentage of false positives. For asymptomatic older adults, colonic polyps discovered by routine sigmoidoscopy will not develop clinically significant malignancy during their lifetime.

## CANCER SCREENINGS

The risk of cancer increases rapidly with age, especially between the ages of 65 to 69, when cancer incidence is almost double that for persons age 55 to 59 (Newell, 1989). More than 80% of deaths from cancer occur in the population aged 55 and older (List, 1987).

Despite the demographical reality, most older adults in one sample did *not* believe that older persons are more likely to get cancer than younger ones are (Rimer et al., 1983). This ignorance was compounded by fear. Most people in this sample of older adults believed cancer treatments to be worse than the disease.

Despite a significant amount of ignorance, denial, and fear among older adults, there usually comes a time when information about cancer screenings and treatment is sought. Free information on cancer screenings and treatments is available to clients in a booklet titled "Cancer Tests You Should Know About: A Guide for People 65 and Over," and a toll-free telephone number (800-4-CANCER) provides the caller with the latest information on cancer treatments from the Cancer Information Service. Confidential information is provided by a trained staff person.

## OSTEOPOROSIS

Osteoporosis is a condition in which the bones are thin, brittle, and susceptible to fracture. During menopause, there is a rapid loss of bone over a period of several years and an age-related bone loss thereafter. About half of all postmenopausal women are affected by osteoporosis, with about 25% of women over age 60 having spinal compression fractures and 15% sustaining hip fractures during their lifetime.

Older women should be screened for osteoporotic risk factors. The risk factors in addition to age include female gender, Caucasian or Asian race, slender build, bilateral oophorectomy before natural menopause, early-onset menstruation, smoking, alcohol abuse, physical inactivity, inadequate calcium intake, or excess caffeine, protein, and salt in the diet.

Densitometry is a type of x-ray that is a safe (very low levels of radiation), noninvasive, imaging technique that can help determine whether intervention is recommended. In 1997, however, the technique was still relatively unknown, expensive (the most accurate test is dual-energy X-ray absorptiometry [DEXA] and ranged from $125 to $350 in 1997) and not widely available (the National Osteoporosis Foundation, 800-464-6700, can send a list of DEXA locations). Private insurance remains uncertain, but beginning in 1998 Medicare reimbursement began.

Interventions for reducing or reversing bone loss include dietary calcium supplementation and weight-bearing exercise (these two topics will be examined in the chapters on nutrition and exercise), estrogen replacement, and Fosamax.

*Routine* postmenopausal hormone replacement (HRT) is not yet recommended, despite its proven long-term protection against not only osteoporosis, but heart disease as well (Grodstein et al., 1997). Two reasons HRT has not garnered universal support among postmenopausal women are unpleasant side effects and a higher risk for breast cancer among those who use it for more than a decade (Persson et al., 1997). Consequently, only 15% of women who were eligible for hormone replacement therapy in 1997 were receiving it.

One study reported, however, that starting HRT after age 60 rather than at menopause may significantly reduce the risk of breast cancer and heart disease, and offer almost as much protection against osteoporosis (Schneider et al., 1997). Another study reported that half the usual dose of estrogen may be sufficient to protect bones from thinning as well as offer some protection from heart disease, while posing a lower breast cancer risk (Genant et al., 1997).

Also, a new drug Evista (raloxifene), approved by the Food and Drug Administration (FDA) in 1997, appears to lower the risk of osteoporosis (Mestel, 1997) and heart disease (Walsh et al., 1998) without an increased risk of breast cancer. Conversely, this potential replacement drug was about only half as effective as estrogen in reducing the risk of osteoporosis, and its ability to protect the heart as effectively as estrogen remains unproved.

Fosamax (alendronate sodium) is an alternative approved by the FDA in 1995 that can actually reverse osteoporotic bone loss. It increased bone density 3% to 9% in one sample of postmenopausal women, whereas a placebo group lost bone (Liberman et al., 1995). That study also reported that women with osteoporosis who took Fosamax were only half as likely to break a hip as women who did not take it.

The major drawback to Fosamax at this time is that it is a tablet that must be swallowed without chewing, and it can linger in the esophagus and cause serious ulcers if not taken exactly as directed: on an empty stomach, with a full glass of water, half an hour before the first meal of the day, and standing or sitting upright for at least 30 minutes. Many patients have problems complying with these recommendations (DeGroen et al., 1996). A nasal spray called Miacalcin (calcitonin) is easier to use, but only half as effective.

## OTHER SCREENINGS

A variety of other screenings may be of use to older adults. It is conserva-tively estimated, for instance, that one in four persons between the ages of 65 and 74, one in three between 75 and 84, and one in two aged 85 and older are hearing impaired. Only 10% to 15% of patients who could benefit from a hearing aid actually use one (Office of Disease Prevention and Health Promotion, 1998). Medicare and most health insurers do not pay for hearing aids. However, the Better Hearing Institute (800-EAR-WELL) may help you locate financial aid in your area, and Hear Now (800-648-HEAR) may provide hearing aids if your income level qualifies you for assistance.

Although less common than hearing impairment, blindness is one of the most feared disabilities (Gallup, 1988). About 13% of persons aged 65 and older and 28% of those aged 85 and older have some form of visual impairment. Many older adults are unaware of decreased visual acuity, and up to 25% of such persons may have the wrong corrective lens prescription (Office of Disease Prevention and Health Promotion, 1998). Common visual disorders affecting older adults are cataracts, glau-coma, diabetic retinopathy, and macular degeneration. Macular degenera-tion, the loss of central vision, is the leading cause of blindness among older adults and can be detected by oneself by looking at a grid (the Amsler grid) with a dot in the middle of it. Though damage from macular degeneration and other vision and hearing problems cannot be reversed, early detection may help slow the progression of several types of sen-sory diseases.

Although there has been a decline in the level of edentulism (loss of all teeth) one third of persons aged 65 and older had lost all of their teeth in 1988 (National Center Institute, 1989). One contributing factor was a lower use of dental services with age. Although nearly two thirds of the population between the ages of 35 and 44 visited the dentist during 1986, only 42% of people aged 65 and older visited a dentist that year.

Type II diabetes, previously called adult-onset diabetes, afflicted more than 14 million Americans in 1997, but half of them did not know it. Moreover, the number of Americans developing diabetes surged by 5 million during the last 12 years (Eastman, 1997). This growth is due to an increase in obesity, and to an increase in minorities (Asians, Hispanics, and African-Americans) that have higher incidence rates.

The 1996 *Guide to Clinical Preventive Services* reports that there is insufficient evidence to recommend for or against routine screening for diabetes mellitus in asymptomatic adults. However, at its 1997 national meeting the American Diabetes Association, with the endorsement of the National Institutes of Health, recommended that Americans over age 45 have their blood sugar screened every 3 years and that the blood sugar threshold be lowered from 140 to 126 milligrams of glucose per deciliter of blood. This new level can detect many more cases when diet and exercise can prevent or delay the disease.

At least half of all men older than age 50 are bothered by benign prostatic hyperplasia, a gradual enlargement of the prostate that occurs with age and a disease that is second to lung cancer in accounting for cancer deaths in men. Despite the increase in the use of the prostate-specific antigen (PSA) screening test, routine screening for prostate cancer is not yet recommended. Although autopsy studies indicate that prostate cancer is present in about 30% of men over age 50, a large proportion of these cancers may be latent—unlikely to produce clinical symptoms or affect survival (United States Preventive Services Task Force, 1996). Thus, prostate screening is not yet deemed effective (i.e., can lead to treatment that reduces the mortality rate) (Sox, 1997).

Treatment options for prostate cancer vary, and include drug therapy, surgery, heat, freezing, and herbs. Regarding drug therapy, Proscar (finasteride) reduced symptoms and the need for surgery in 53% of study participants with abnormally enlarged prostates (McConnell et al., 1998). The increasing use of saw palmetto, a plant-based remedy for prostate problems, is *not* yet supported by controlled clinical trials (*The Johns Hopkins Medical Letter*, 1997).

## MEDICARE PREVENTION

Nearly 40 million older adults and disabled persons covered by Medicare were eligible for new prevention benefits in 1998. Mammogram screenings, for instance, increased to annually for all Medicare-eligible women ages 40 and older, and the Part B deductible was waived.

The United States Preventive Services Task Force, however, noted that the more frequent annual mammogram screenings will be expensive and may not result in reduced mortality compared with 2-year screenings. The task force also raised the prospect of more false-positive results and additional biopsies.

New bone mass screening procedures were approved for high-risk individuals as of July 1998 for women age 65 and older. High risk was defined as estrogen-deficient women at clinical risk for osteoporosis—which includes practically all women in that age category. Although the National Osteoporosis Foundation hailed the new benefit, opponents argued that it is an expensive test and provides redundant data that a good medical history conducted at that age would provide.

New benefits were also provided for colorectal cancer screenings of all individuals age 50 and older. Two of the modalities covered—fecal-occult blood tests and flexible sigmoidoscopy—were endorsed by the Preventive Services Task Force. Two other modalities—colonoscopy and barium enema screening—were less clear-cut. Colonoscopies are very expensive and pose a small risk of perforation; barium enemas are safer and less expensive, but less accurate and often require a follow-up colonoscopy.

There will also be new coverage of annual prostate cancer screenings to become available to men over age 55 on January 1, 2000. This coverage will be provided despite the lack of evidence that early detection improves survival and the fact that prostate screening carries a strong risk of false-positive results that can lead to expensive interventions against growths that pose no harm.

There were also new Medicare benefits in 1998 that were not controversial. There was new coverage for 3 million Medicare beneficiaries with diabetes: outpatient self-management training services, and coverage for blood glucose monitors and testing strips for type II diabetics without regard—for the first time—to whether insulin was being used.

Other noncontroversial additions to the 1998 Medicare prevention benefits were a new coverage of screening pelvic examinations, an enhanced coverage of Pap smears with the Part B deductible waived, and the extension of coverage for influenza and pneumococcal vaccination through the year 2002.

## FINAL WORD

Medical screenings and immunizations are undeniably important tools for disease prevention, but the data collected by the United States Preventive Services Task Force (1989) resulted in a surprising conclusion, "among the most effective interventions available to clinicians for reducing the incidence and severity of the leading causes of disease and disability in the United States are those that address the personal health practices of patients" (p. xxii).

Stated another way, "clinician counseling that leads to improved personal health practices may be more valuable to patients than conventional clinical activities such as diagnostic testing" (United States Preventive Services Task Force, 1996).

The task force recommends that in this era of prevention and health promotion (as well as chronic impairment) the traditional health professional-client relationship be altered significantly. Professionals need to shift from their role as authorities transmitting information to passive patients to a relationship in which they collaborate with their clients.

## HEALTH RISK APPRAISALS

Health risk appraisals (HRA) became popular in the 1970s and have continued to be widely used (Wellness Councils of America [WELCOA], 1997). During the 1970s and 1980s, the HRAs were used primarily by employers who gave feedback to their employees on their major health risks. Some companies demonstrated cost savings through the use of HRAs (Uriri & Thatcher-Winger, 1995). By the late 1980s, this technique was adapted to health programs for older adults in the community, though effectiveness was rarely evaluated (Uriri & Thatcher-Winger, 1995).

An HRA is an intermediate step in client involvement between a medical screening and a health assessment. It requires more client participation than consenting to (or, less frequently, asking for) a medical screening, but it is not as effective an educational tool as a health assessment instrument, which encourages people to set priorities for changing their health habits.

HRAs generally determine the probability of death or disability from selected causes within a given time for individuals with specific characteristics and health behaviors (i.e., risk factors). In a typical HRA, data on individual risk factors, such as medical history, age, gender, blood pressure level, smoking, exercise, and diet, are gathered and used to determine the likelihood that a given disease, condition, or death will develop or occur within a particular period. A major goal of the HRA is the motivation of an individual to change undesirable health behaviors to reduce specific risk factors.

It should be noted that the population data on which health risk appraisals are based do not necessarily apply to the risk profiles of particular individuals. The HRA is simply a statement of probability determined by comparing specific individual data to general age-specific demographic and epidemiological data.

In 1986, at least 44 HRA versions were available (Green & Lewis, 1986), an increasing number of which were designed to be computer scored. Three sources of health-risk appraisal instruments for older adults (Sennott-Miller & Kligman, 1992) and office employees are The Society of Prospective Medicine, P.O. Box 5510, Indianapolis, IN 46205-0110; Health Institute of New England Medical Center, 750 Washington Street, P.O. Box 345, Boston, MA 02111; and Health Risk Appraisal Activity, Carter Center of Emery University, One Copenhill, Atlanta, GA 30307.

Free health-risk appraisals are beginning to appear on the Internet, especially ones that target specific health areas. A fitness profile is available, for instance, which assesses your fitness level ranging from inactive to athlete, and provides information on how you can exercise and at what pace, based on your profile: www.fitnesszone.com/profiles. A nutrition profile is available that assesses the nutritional content of foods that you have consumed: www.spectre.ag.uiuc.edu/~'food-lab/nat/nat.cgi.

An HRA alone, without supportive education and guidance, may be ineffective in eliciting behavior change. A disappointing score, in fact, can lead to anxiety or depression, especially among older clients, who may believe it is too late to do anything about the risk factors identified.

A computer- or self-scored HRA that approximates the number of years remaining is of far less value to older adults than a discussion of the importance of reducing specific risk factors. Most older adults are concerned about and will respond favorably to specific ways to avoid future dependency.


APPRAISALS BY WRITTEN CORRESPONDENCE


Nonetheless, sometimes the only option is through the mail. An innovative HRA program, titled Senior Healthtrac, is based in San Francisco and reaches out to 300,000 individuals aged 55 and older, nationwide, through Blue Cross and Blue Shield plans and Medicare supplemental coverage programs. Periodically, the program distributes a Senior Vitality Questionnaire and follows up with a Personal Vitality Report that includes an individual's "vitality age," which may be younger or older than an individual's chronological age. The report notes an individual's risk for cancer, heart disease, emphysema, cirrhosis, and arthritis compared with that of other persons of the same age and sex, and suggests lifestyle changes to reduce specific risk factors.

Although this assessment tool is not nearly as effective as a personal health assessment conducted on a one-to-one basis, it appears to be a state-of-the-art mass-mailing appraisal program. For more information contact: National Program Manager, Healthtrac, Blue Shield of California, 2 North Point, San Francisco, CA 94133.

Another innovative health risk appraisal instrument that is implemented through written correspondence was developed by the Mercy Medical Center in Denver, Colorado (Fried et al., 1985). The developers of this instrument were resourceful in asking respondents, after completing it, to check the categories that interest them (smoking, exercise, etc.), and to send this information to the National Health Information Clearinghouse, P.O. Box 1133, Washington, DC 20013, to receive additional health education material.

## HEALTH ASSESSMENT INSTRUMENTS

At the end of this section are the health assessment tools that I use before conducting a community health education program. These differ from more commonly used health risk appraisal instruments in that they focus on the respondents' motivation for changing health behavior rather than on the recommendations of the health professional. Another difference is that they are not concerned about the number of years that risk behaviors reduce life expectancy, nor any other quantifiable measure. These health assessment tools are educational devices, designed to stimulate thinking on a variety of health topics and to assess the readiness of older adults to change their health behaviors.

### WELLNESS CHECKLIST

Before, or during, a health education program with older students, I administer a general health assessment tool similar to the one in Appendix A. Its purpose is to focus client awareness on health behaviors that they might wish to change. The topics are linked to a 7-week, 2- or 3-times-weekly, health education program that I typically offer.

## SELF-EFFICACY

I have used a second health assessment tool the past 3 years when my classes have been primarily focused on exercise. The instrument was developed from ideas by Bandura (1977) and later adapted by Garcia and King (1991) (see Appendix B). Lack of confidence is a major barrier to adopting or sustaining an exercise routine (Bandura, 1995; Holman & Lorig, 1992; McAuley, 1993). The lower the confidence levels of the older adults, the greater the need to be exposed to the three components of self-efficacy described by Bandura (1977, 1986): guided mastery experiences, modeling, and persuasion.

Guided mastery experiences involve learning and practicing appropriate behaviors through the assignment of small, graded tasks that are accomplished in a short period. These tasks must be achievable and done in an environment of enjoyment and ongoing feedback.

Modeling involves teaching and leadership responsibilities by persons who are as much alike the clients being taught as possible in terms of age, race, gender, and physical limitations. Appropriate role models enhance self-efficacy because clients can relate realistically to them. The ideal role modeling occurs when older adults teach exercise to their peers. However, increasing responsibility and confidence can be enhanced in other ways as well including peers who help set up the classroom, lead small group discussions, and identify and bring in health professionals with specific expertise.

Persuasion focuses on convincing older adults about the validity of three health beliefs: (a) sedentary people are at risk for disease and functional impairment; (b) exercise can reduce this risk; and (c) I (the older adult) am capable of adopting a regular exercise routine to reduce this risk. These cognitions are more likely to be believed and heeded in a trusting environment, like a church (Ransdell & Rehling, 1996), where there is considerable social support.

## PHYSICIAN WELLNESS PRESCRIPTION

An instrument that I always use before beginning a health education class is the Physician Wellness Prescription form (Appendix C), which asks the physician to help set parameters on the health behaviors (exercise, diet, stress management, etc.) of their clients who have enrolled in my health education class. On rare occasions older students choose health goals that exceed the parameters set by their physician. In these cases, additional communication between the older adults and their physicians is required.

In addition to the obvious advantage of having physician guidelines for safety purposes, physicians are one more source of motivation and support for changing health habits. Because the instrument that the physicians complete needs to be time efficient, I use one that takes only 5 minutes. I enclose a stamped, self-addressed envelope with the form, which I ask the older adults to deliver to their physicians who, in turn, mail it back to me. (Sending the form directly to the physician—without the older adult's direct request—results in a lower response rate). I have never had an older student report that their physician charged them for completing the form.

## HEALTH CONTRACTS

A health assessment tool that I find to be most effective with older adults who have higher educational levels is a health contract (see Figure 3.3a, b, c). A health contract is based on a self-management version of social learning theory (Bandura, 1977) and operant conditioning (Skinner, 1953), theories that will be examined in more detail in the chapter on behavior and cognitive management.

The self-management version of these theories states, in essence, that clients can select and monitor health behavior and can provide the discipline and motivation to achieve their goals.

Although it is always the client who is in charge of accomplishing the goal, the health contract is most likely to be effective when it represents the collaborative effort of a client and a health professional. A health contract is alleged to have several advantages over verbal communication alone. The advantages of a health contract, which still need additional empirical testing, are that it

1. Is a formal commitment that enhances motivation
2. Clarifies goals and behaviors and makes them explicit
3. Requires the active participation of the client

**MY GOAL:** In keeping with my doctor's recommendations for the benefit of my good health, I will_____

_____

_____

**Good Health Contract**

MY SIGNATURE          DATE          DOCTOR'S SIGNATURE          DATE

**THE BENEFITS I WILL GET FROM ACHIEVING THIS GOAL ARE:**
1.
2.
3.
4.

**THESE ARE SOME BARRIERS THAT WILL INTERFERE WITH ACCOMPLISHING MY GOAL:**
1.
2.
3.
4.

**THIS IS MY PLAN OF ACTION FOR ACHIEVING MY GOAL:**
*Specific steps*
1.
2.
3.
4.
5.
6.
7.
8.
9.
10.

**FIGURE 3.3a   Good Health Contract.**

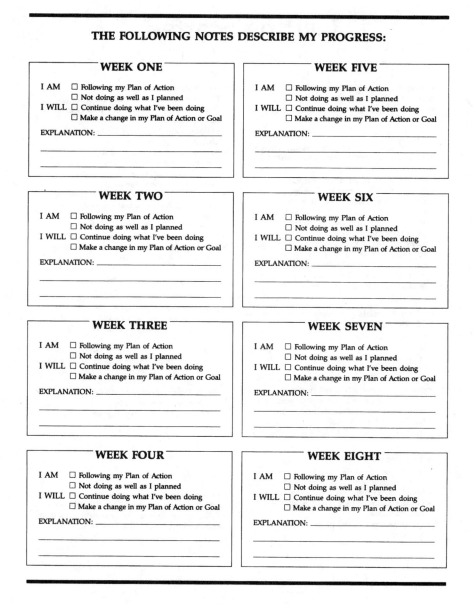

## THE FOLLOWING NOTES DESCRIBE MY PROGRESS:

### WEEK ONE

I AM ☐ Following my Plan of Action
☐ Not doing as well as I planned
I WILL ☐ Continue doing what I've been doing
☐ Make a change in my Plan of Action or Goal

EXPLANATION: _____

### WEEK FIVE

I AM ☐ Following my Plan of Action
☐ Not doing as well as I planned
I WILL ☐ Continue doing what I've been doing
☐ Make a change in my Plan of Action or Goal

EXPLANATION: _____

### WEEK TWO

I AM ☐ Following my Plan of Action
☐ Not doing as well as I planned
I WILL ☐ Continue doing what I've been doing
☐ Make a change in my Plan of Action or Goal

EXPLANATION: _____

### WEEK SIX

I AM ☐ Following my Plan of Action
☐ Not doing as well as I planned
I WILL ☐ Continue doing what I've been doing
☐ Make a change in my Plan of Action or Goal

EXPLANATION: _____

### WEEK THREE

I AM ☐ Following my Plan of Action
☐ Not doing as well as I planned
I WILL ☐ Continue doing what I've been doing
☐ Make a change in my Plan of Action or Goal

EXPLANATION: _____

### WEEK SEVEN

I AM ☐ Following my Plan of Action
☐ Not doing as well as I planned
I WILL ☐ Continue doing what I've been doing
☐ Make a change in my Plan of Action or Goal

EXPLANATION: _____

### WEEK FOUR

I AM ☐ Following my Plan of Action
☐ Not doing as well as I planned
I WILL ☐ Continue doing what I've been doing
☐ Make a change in my Plan of Action or Goal

EXPLANATION: _____

### WEEK EIGHT

I AM ☐ Following my Plan of Action
☐ Not doing as well as I planned
I WILL ☐ Continue doing what I've been doing
☐ Make a change in my Plan of Action or Goal

EXPLANATION: _____

**FIGURE 3.3b   Good Health Contract** *(continued).*

# Getting Started

Making changes in behaviors we have had for many years is not easy, but sometimes it is necessary. Use the guidelines below to help you succeed.

### Set your goal — state the change which you and your doctor agree you should make

- Are you ready to make this change?
- Are you specific—how much change by when?
- Start with small steps over a two-month time period.
- Be modest—most people tend to expect too much from themselves.
- Allow yourself an occasional "slip." If you admit ahead of time that you're not perfect, a slip won't turn into a major setback.
- Write your Health Contract in pencil. You may want to revise it later on.

### List the benefits you want to get from achieving your goal

- Record the most important benefits. Typically these will have to do with health, energy level, appearance, self-esteem, medical costs and relationships.
- Post your contract on the refrigerator with the enclosed magnet so you can read this list every day; or, if you prefer, post your contract in a private place such as inside a closet door.
- Making this list will reinforce your commitment to your Goal and build your confidence.

### Know your barriers

- Be aware ahead of time of those things which could interfere with your achieving your Goal.
- Record the excuses you might make.
- List the names of people who might not support your Goal.
- List situations that can trigger negative behavior.

### State your plan of action

- The more detailed your plan, the more likely it will work to help you achieve your Goal in the desired time period.
- Problem solve around the barriers you listed above.
- Set the scene: you may need to buy something, set aside time, arrange for help, etc., to make sure your Goal is do-able.
- Record your activities on a calendar.
- Keep reminders of your Goal in conspicuous places, such as on the bathroom mirror, the dashboard of your car, etc.
- Keep telling yourself, "I'm worth it."
- Plan to reward yourself for successes.
- You may need a support buddy. It's especially helpful when you can give support to one another.

### Evaluate your progress regularly

- It is up to you to determine how often you should review and evaluate your progress.
- Also, arrange for regular evaluation by your doctor's office.
- You may need to revise your Plan of Action.
- Are you getting pleasure from pursuing your Goal? If not, think of ways to make it more enjoyable.
- Be sure to pat yourself on the back for your successes or even for trying.
- If you're not succeeding, regroup and try again.

Don't get bogged down wondering if you're doing the contract "right." The only right way is what works for you. The important thing is to begin working toward your Goal now.

**FIGURE 3.3c   Getting started on a health contract.**

4. Enhances the therapeutic relationship between provider and client
5. Provides a structured means for involving significant others (family, friends, etc.) in a supportive role
6. Provides a structured means of problem solving around barriers that previously interfered with the achievement of a goal
7. Provides incentives to reinforce behaviors

The health contract includes a set of instructions that encourage older adults to state a clear, specific, and measurable goal; describe the tasks participants are committed to in order to achieve the stated goal; reinforce accomplishments, if only by verbal praise, in a timely fashion; and periodically evaluate progress. The signatures on the contract of both a health professional and the older client are desirable (see Hill & Smith [1985] for additional information on health contracts).

Health contracts are effective in reinforcing individual commitment to a wide variety of behaviors, such as appointment keeping; knowledge retention; cessation of drug abuse, smoking, or overindulgence in alcohol consumption; weight reduction; and exercise (Leslie & Schuster, 1991). A cardiac rehabilitation program in Canada reported that participants who signed contracts adhered to their 6-month program more faithfully (65%) than did members of a control group (42%) or people who were asked to sign an agreement but did not (20%) (Cooper & Cooper, 1988).

Although these results are promising, research on health contracts is often marred by a lack of random assignment and control groups (Janz et al., 1984). In addition, there are several uncertainties about the effectiveness of health contracts in terms of separating out the effects of the health contract from accompanying strategies like health education, social support, and the professional-client relationship; determining whether contracts work with different types of persons, especially those not volunteering for a study; determining whether contingency contracts are more effective than noncontingency contracts; and assessing how much training is required for health professionals to administer health contracts effectively.

Nevertheless, even without a definitive body of research, health contracts are widely used. They are simple to administer and can be time efficient for health professionals who are willing and able to assign an office worker or paraprofessional to work with clients. In my community health education classes with low-income, minority older adults, however,

I sometimes employ verbal health goals in place of formal, written health contracts.

## OTHER HEALTH ASSESSMENT TOOLS

There are two other health assessment tools that I do not use, but they have achieved widespread acceptance in the literature. Although both tools have taught me useful ideas and strategies, I find the first one (PRECEDE) too multifaceted and unwieldy, and the second one (Stages of Change) would lead me to give up temporarily on people who turn out to be very ready for health behavior change.

## PRECEDE

The PRECEDE framework, developed by Laurence Green and colleagues (1980), offers a conceptual guideline for assessing the readiness of older adults in general for a health education program. PRECEDE is an acronym for predisposing, reinforcing, and enabling causes in the diagnosis and evaluation of educational readiness.

*Predisposing* factors are the knowledge, attitudes, or beliefs a person holds about a health behavior. For instance, if an older woman believes exercise will aggravate her arthritis or cause her unnecessary fatigue, exhortation to exercise will be difficult. Because older adults, especially minority older adults or those over age 75, frequently have lower formal educational levels than adults in general and may be prone to act on less information or on misinformation, it is necessary that health professionals ascertain the barriers to changing health behaviors.

Oftentimes it is not necessary to change a belief, just to add a new one. If older persons believe, for example, that God will take care of their health, the health professional can agree with this assertion and then simply add Sophocles' declaration, "Heaven never helps the man who will not act" (Lorig, 1992).

Older adults may believe (or espouse) that, because of their age, it is too late to change or to do themselves any good. It may be helpful to respond with specific data on how rapidly health improvements can occur after the age of 65. A significant number of older adults may believe they get all the exercise they need when, according to indicators of exercise frequency, intensity, and duration, they actually do not (DiGilio & Howze, 1984).

Predisposing factors can be determined by finding out what the clients know about the health area of concern, whether they believe they have a problem, whether they have cultural habits that need to be taken into consideration, and whether they believe behavior changes will help (Green et al., 1980).

*Enabling* factors are those resources necessary for engaging in health-related activities, specifically, access and skill level. Before making recommendations to their clients, health professionals need to determine whether there are appropriate programs with leaders who are experienced with and trained to work with older adults, whether these programs are accessible to those with limited transportation and financial means, whether their clients have the necessary skills for modifying their behavior, whether recommended foods for older adults are affordable and available, and whether their clients perceive their neighborhoods to be safe enough to implement walking programs.

Practitioners need to be resourceful; it may be necessary to help older adults find accessible programs or gain necessary skills. It is also important that health professionals facilitate ways in which older persons can help themselves rather than solve problems for clients and thereby foster dependency.

*Reinforcing* factors refer to the peers, significant others, and professionals who can support the continuation of new health behaviors. Older adults may be widowed, uninvolved in former occupational groups, and relatively isolated from other persons interested in maintaining health. Practitioners primarily ought to consider whether their clients have family, peer support, and professional support to reinforce health behavior changes.

It is best that clients have more than one source of support rather than overburden a single person. A team approach can be useful. Supportive spouses of clients, for instance, can attend health programs with them. Receptionists in the offices of health professionals can play supportive, follow-up roles for clients changing health behaviors. Many health professionals believe they are too busy to be involved in health education, but there are time-efficient means for them to play a role (see chapter 10 on behavior management).

Green and colleagues have added an additional step, called PROCEED, to their PRECEDE model (Green & Kreuter, 1991). The newest edition of this model focuses on policy, regulatory, and organizational barriers to health education and is targeted toward policy makers and resource allocators.

## STAGES OF CHANGE

Prochaska and colleagues (1988, 1992, p. 271) have conceptualized a model of the "stages of change" that may help health professionals assess an individual's readiness to change a health habit.

1. *Precontemplation*—no intention to change behavior in the foreseeable future
2. *Contemplation*—awareness that a problem exists but no commitment to action
3. *Preparation*—intention to take action in the next month and, typically, unsuccessful action taken in the past year
4. *Action*—modification of behavior, experiences, or environment for a period of from 1 day to 6 months to overcome a problem
5. *Maintenance*—an indeterminate period, perhaps a lifetime, in which people work to prevent relapse

Because relapsing and recycling through some or all of the stages of change is the rule rather than the exception, this process should be viewed as a spiral rather than a linear model. If individuals were more aware of the norm (i.e., recycling through the stages several times precedes the achievement of long-term maintenance), the perception of repeated failure and the feeling of guilt or embarrassment following each unsuccessful attempt might be redefined and reduced. If we are educated to understand the phases most of us—health professionals and clients—go through, we may be more accepting of and patient with the change process.

Because most persons are likely to be in the precontemplation stage, it has been suggested that action-oriented programs may not be useful for these types of persons (Prochaska & DiClemente, 1992). In contrast to this, I have found many individuals who have been too ambitious in prior undertakings and just need assistance in selecting meaningful and achievable goals (Haber, 1996). I have found others to be somewhat apathetic at first, but who quickly shift from a seemingly precontemplation stage to a contemplation or action stage when I uncover a health benefit that motivates them.

One behavioral scientist has even questioned the ethics of ignoring precontemplators, or postponing interventions with them, when they constitute sections of the population in greatest need. She suggests that this model may lead to discrimination against the poor, the less educated, and the frail (Whitehead, 1997). I believe that few people are precontemplators all the time regarding all health behaviors. I recommend, therefore, that the health professional and client identify several health behaviors that need to be changed, and then let the client identify the one behavior that she or he is most motivated to change. Thereupon, the professional and the client choose one modest and measurable goal that is likely to lead to a high probability of success.

## QUESTIONS FOR DISCUSSION

1. If you were a government policy maker or a managed care administrator, how would you encourage health professionals to routinely conduct medical screenings? How would you encourage them to stay current with the literature?
2. Conduct a health assessment with an older person using one of the instruments in the appendix. Evaluate the instrument as a health education tool with this particular person, and find ways to improve it.
3. Do you think encouraging most precontemplators is, for the most part, an inefficient waste of valuable time and resources; or do you think you can help a significant number of precontemplators by assisting them with setting more appropriate health goals, and finding ways to accomplish them?
4. Write a health contract for yourself to be conducted over a two-week period. What steps do you propose to make sure you will complete it successfully?

# APPENDIX A

## Health Assessment

Name _____

Address/phone _____


## *Weight/Nutrition*

1. Do you eat six or more servings of bread, cereal, rice, and pasta per day?
   usually/always _____ sometimes _____ rarely/never _____
   (One serving consists of 1 slice of bread, 1/2 a hamburger bun, a small roll or biscuit, 1/2 cup of cooked cereal, rice, or pasta, one ounce of breakfast cereal, etc.).
2. Do you eat five or more servings of vegetables and fruits per day?
   usually/always _____ sometimes _____ rarely/never _____
   (One serving consists of 1/2 cup of cooked or chopped raw vegetables, one cup of leafy raw vegetable, such as spinach or lettuce, a piece of whole fruit, 3/4 cup of juice, 1/2 cup of cooked or canned fruit, 1/4 cup of dried fruit, etc.).
3. Do you limit foods high in fats, such as red meat, pork, sausage, butter, whole milk, and cheese?
   usually/always _____ sometimes _____ rarely/never _____
4. Do you limit foods high in salt or sodium, such as luncheon meats, bacon, canned foods, and potato chips?
   usually/always _____ sometimes _____ rarely/never _____
5. Do you limit your intake of sweets?
   usually/always _____ sometimes _____ rarely/never _____
6. Do you eat the right amount of food?
   usually/always _____ sometimes _____ rarely never _____
7. Do you have difficulty chewing food to the degree that it interferes with your getting proper nutrition?
   yes _____ no _____

  8. weight _____ height _____ (body mass index _____)
  9. Are you satisfied with your weight?
     yes _____ no, I'm underweight _____
     no, I'm 10 lb. or less overweight _____
     no, I'm more than 10 lb. overweight _____
  10. Has there been a significant change (either direction) in your weight
      (i.e., 10 or more lb) over the past year?
      yes _____ no _____
      (If yes, why _____)


## Fitness

  1. Do you participate in a regular exercise program, such as walking,
     calisthenics, swimming, or biking at least three times a week, for
     20 minutes or more each time?
     yes _____ no _____
  2. Do you have trouble lifting or carrying things, things that you need
     to have lifted or carried, like a bag of groceries?
     yes _____ no _____
  3. Do you have trouble with turning, stretching, or bending because
     of stiffness, aches or pains, or other reasons?
     yes _____ (specify _____)
     no _____
  4. Do you participate in any type of bending, stretching, or turning
     activity, at least three times a week, to improve your flexibility,
     balance, or agility?
     yes _____ no _____
  5. Do you participate in any type of strength-building program at least
     twice a week?
     yes _____ no _____


## Stress

  1. Do you have headaches _____ fatigue _____ or forgetfulness _____?
     usually/always _____ sometimes _____ rarely/never _____
  2. Do you feel anxious or tense?
     every day or almost every day __ sometimes __ rarely/never __

3. In the past year, how often have you experienced repeated or long periods of feeling sad or blue?
   usually/always _____ sometimes _____ never _____

4. Do you have a close friend or relative with whom you can share your experiences, someone you can really talk to about things that matter, whether it's good news or something that's really troubling you?
   yes _____     no _____

5. How satisfied are you with your present level of socializing?
   very satisfied _____ somewhat satisfied _____ not at all satisfied _____

6. Do you practice any type of relaxation activity to help with hassles or stress?
   yes _____     (specify _____)
   no _____

7. Do you agree or disagree with the following statement: I have a positive attitude toward myself (after asking "agree or disagree," ask "strongly or not").
   strongly agree _____ agree _____ disagree _____ strongly disagree _____

8. Are you currently: living alone _____
   living with spouse, or with spouse and others _____
   living with someone other than spouse _____

9. Are you widowed less than 1 year _____
   more than 1 year _____ or never widowed _____

## Habits/Medications

1. Do you currently smoke? yes _____ no _____

2. Do you drink alcohol? yes _____ no _____
   If yes, have you ever felt the need to cut down on your drinking of alcohol?
   yes _____     no _____

3. Are you using tranquilizers _____ sleeping pills _____ medication for constipation problems _____ or medication for pain _____ ?
   (put checkmark for a "yes" answer, then note which ones/how often _____).

4. Do you know the purpose of each medicine you are taking?
   I am not taking medicine _____ yes, I know the purpose of each _____ no, I do not know the purpose of each _____

## *General Health and Miscellaneous*

1. Do you agree or disagree: I'd rather have doctors and nurses make the decisions about what's best for me than for them to give me a whole lot of choices (after asking "agree or disagree," ask "strongly or not").
   \_\_\_ strongly agree \_\_\_ agree \_\_\_ disagree \_\_\_ strongly disagree
2. How would you rate your own overall health at the present time?
   poor \_\_\_\_ fair \_\_\_\_ good \_\_\_\_ excellent \_\_\_\_
3. Is your health better, about the same, or worse than it was 8 weeks ago?
   \_\_\_\_ better \_\_\_\_ about the same \_\_\_\_ worse
4. Has a health professional recommended to you that you change a health habit (diet, nutrition, exercise, stress management, other)?
   yes \_\_\_\_ (specify) _____
   no \_\_\_\_
   If *yes*: Did the health professional provide you specific guidelines on how to change this health habit? yes \_\_\_\_ no \_\_\_\_
   Did you comply with the recommendations? yes \_\_\_\_
   some \_\_\_\_ no \_\_\_\_
5. Did you have a major physical set back or surgery this past year?
   yes \_\_\_\_ (specify _____)
   no \_\_\_\_

# APPENDIX B

### SELF-EFFICACY

Name _____ date _____

Self-Efficacy for Exercise

Using the 0% to 100% scale as a yardstick, please answer the following: How confident are you that you could exercise under each of the following conditions over the next 6 months? Please circle one number for each of the situation below:

0%   10%   20%   30%   40%   50%   60%   70%   80%   90%   100%

I cannot do it          Moderately certain that          Certain that I
at all                  I can do it                      can do it

a. When I am tired
b. During or following a personal crisis
c. When feeling depressed
d. When I am feeling anxious
e. During bad weather
f. When slightly sore from the last time I exercised
g. When a favorite show of mine is on television
h. When I have a lot to do
i. When I do not receive support from my family/friends
j. In general, I believe I could exercise regularly (at least 2 times a
   week, for 20 minutes or more) over the next 6 months

## APPENDIX C

### PHYSICIAN PRESCRIPTION AND CONSENT FORM

date

Dear Dr. ———————————————————————————— ,
This brief form pertains to your patient ——————— who
wants to participate in our Healthy Aging Program. The program will be
cotaught by faculty from the Departments of Physical Therapy, Occupational Therapy, and Health Promotion and Gerontology. The health program begins October 30, 1999, and consists of exercise, nutrition, and
stress management.

I am providing consent for you to release this information.
———————————————————————— (patient signature)

Please indicate the limits of your patient's participation by checking the
categories you do *not* want your patient to comply with, adding appropriate
parameters wherever necessary.

## Exercise (Please check only *inappropriate* activities)

_____ 1. Seated position with gentle twisting, turning, stretching on a daily basis

_____ 2. Standing position with gentle twisting, turning, stretching on a daily basis

_____ 3. Leisurely walk on a daily basis

_____ 4. Aerobic walk or other aerobic activity

     _____ 60% Target heart rate

     _____ 75% Target heart rate

_____ 5. Strength building

     _____ Elastic band (low resistance, medium repetitions)

Additional comments: _____

_____

### *Nutrition/Diet*

(If your patient is on a special diet, please check which one[s] and note additional information.)

_____ 1. Salt _____

_____ 2. Fat/cholesterol _____

_____ 3. Sugar _____

_____ 4. Calcium _____

_____ 5. Caloric intake _____

_____ 6. Other _____

### *Stress Management*

(Please check only *inappropriate* activities)

_____ 1. Daily diaphragmatic breathing

_____ 2. Daily progressive muscle relaxation

_____ 3. Meditation

_____ 4. Other _____

Is there anything else you would like us to know about your patient?

_____

Please check one of the following three options, sign your name, and return the completed form in the enclosed, stamped envelope. *Thank you!*

1. ____ This patient may participate in your program without restrictions.
2. ____ This patient may participate in your program but is limited in the following ways as indicated on this form.
3. ____ This patient should not participate in your program.

Please sign your name:

_____ MD    _____ date

# 4
# Exercise

To reduce from 43% (baseline, 1985) to 22% the proportion of persons age 65 and older who engage in no leisure-time physical activity.

To increase from 22% (baseline, 1985) to 30% the proportion of persons age 18 to 74 years who engage in moderate physical activity 5 or more times per week. (Public health goals from the U.S. Public Health Service's Healthy People 2000 Initiative [AARP, 1991])

From 1985 to 1991 sedentary lifestyle for persons age 65 and older has reduced from 43% to 29%; from 1985 to 1991 moderate physical activity 5 or more times per week for persons age 18 to 74 has increased from 22% to 24%. (*Healthy People 2000 Midcourse Review: 1995 Report on Progress*, DHHS, OPHS)

## 1996 SURGEON GENERAL'S REPORT ON PHYSICAL ACTIVITY AND HEALTH

In her exercise video *Shopping for Fitness*, Joan Rivers espouses walking the malls for aerobics, hefting shopping bags for weight training, and trying on jeans that are one size too small to motivate oneself for weight reduction. According to Rivers, "Everybody's got a tape out, Buns of Steel, Breasts of Iron and Bunions of Teflon. They just don't get it, that it should be fun." Although many of her comments are satirical, much of the *Surgeon General's Report* supports what she espouses.

The July 11, 1996, *Report* represented a 2-year collaborative effort of the Centers for Disease Control and Prevention and the President's Council on Physical Fitness and Sports. It is the most comprehensive review of the research on the effects of physical activity on people's health. In short, 60% of adults do not achieve the recommended amount of physical activity, and 25% of adults are not physically active at all. Inactivity increases with age; by age 75 about one in three men and one in two women engage in no physical activity. Inactivity is also more common among women and people with lower income and less education.

Previous reports of the Surgeon General on national health risks, such as the health hazards of tobacco published in 1964, have had a major influence on public awareness and the policies of government and business. Acting Surgeon General Audrey F. Manley, MD, states, "This report is nothing less than a national call to action. Physical inactivity is a serious nationwide public health problem, but active and healthful lifestyles are well within the grasp of everyone."

The report agrees with Ms. Rivers in that most sedentary Americans are not going to rigorously pursue buns of steel, and among those who do, all will fall short of the goal. Instead, it is important to make the first step for most Americans achievable and to do so requires a large degree of modesty in setting goals and at least a small degree of enjoyment. Hence, the emphasis on being more active, like shopping while walking briskly, than adherence to a rigid exercise regimen.

*The basic premise of the Surgeon General's report is that Americans should get at least 30 minutes of physical activity each day.* This statement provides a major perspective shift from previous recommendations by government and exercise leaders. In summary, this new message is that Americans should be more concerned about total calories expended through activity or exercise than about intensity level or continuity. Regarding intensity level, the report stresses the importance of raising respiratory and heart rate—physiological changes that are apparent to the participant—but to not be too concerned about raising intensity level to a target heart rate, particularly if you are sedentary or have a not-too-active lifestyle.

Regarding continuity, it is no longer deemed essential to obtain 20 to 30 consecutive minutes of exercise. For Americans, most of whom are not too active, accumulating shorter activity spurts throughout the day is effective. Got a spare few minutes? Then briskly walk the shopping malls with Joan or climb a few stairs. A review of the research literature concludes that accumulating several 5 or 10 minute bursts of physical activity over the course of the day provides beneficial health and fitness effects (DeBusk et al., 1990; Jakicic et al., 1995; Pate et al., 1995). One study reported that if you time these bouts of activity right, you may gain the added benefit of replacing junk food snack breaks (Jakicic et al., 1995).

Finally, regarding exercise itself, it is difficult for adults to go from inactivity to an exercise routine. Thinking about how to accumulate short bouts of activity is a useful way to get started on better health and fitness. For example, briskly wax your car or wash your floor (even if it means doing it in segments throughout the day), put a little more energy into your leaf raking or lawn mowing, garden with enthusiasm, or dance. And try to be active every day or most days of the week, and not just three times per week.

## MOST POPULAR ACTIVITY OF ALL: WALKING

Several recent studies have indicated that older adults need not become triathletes or engage in other high-intensity activities, to reap the benefits of exercise. For most older adults, a walking program will provide sufficient intensity for a good aerobics program. An 8-year study of more than 13,000 people has indicated that walking briskly for 30 to 60 minutes every day is almost as beneficial in reducing the death rate as jogging up to 40 miles a week (Blair et al., 1989). The authors of a study of 1,645 older adults reported that simply walking 4 hours per week decreases the risk of future hospitalization for cardiovascular disease (LaCroix et al., 1996).

The National Center for Health Statistics reports that walking has much greater appeal for older adults than high-intensity exercise. A national survey indicated that a smaller percentage of persons age 65+ (27%) in comparison with the general adult population (41%), engage in vigorous activities, whereas people of all age groups (41%) are equally likely to walk for exercise (National Health Interview Survey, 1985).

As the acting surgeon general emphasized in her report, most Americans can benefit from activities like brisk walking and not concern themselves about target heart rates. Brisk walking is the most popular aerobic activity for older adults. Many older adults, though, abandon their walking routines in unfavorable weather. Prolonged hot or cold spells may sabotage a good walking program. Rather than discontinue this activity because of the weather, adults should consider walking indoors at their local shopping malls. Many shopping malls—about 2,500 nationwide—now open their doors early, usually between 5:30 and 10:00 a.m., for members of walking clubs. To find the nearest club, contact the National Organization of Mall Walkers at P.O. Box 191, Hermann, MO 65041; 573-486-3945.

Traveling to another city can also be an excuse to not exercise. Recommend to your clients that they join a walking tour for an enjoyable way to get exercise and a unique way to learn offbeat aspects of a city's history. If the chamber of commerce or the local paper's weekend entertainment section is not helpful, try some of these unique walking tours: in Los Angeles, tour theaters on foot (213-623-2489); in Atlanta, tour Druid Hills where the Oscar-winning *Driving Miss Daisy* was filmed (404-876-2041); in Oak Park, Illinois, tour Frank Lloyd Wright homes (708-848-1976); and in New York City tour multiethnic restaurants (212-439-1090).

Walking is so popular that it has spawned many magazines, newsletters, and books. It may appear that there is not much to walking—we have been doing it, after all, since we were toddlers—but proper technique improves benefits and reduces injuries. Good walking technique involves proper posture (head erect, chin in, shoulders relaxed, and back straight), a bent-arm swing, and a full natural stride. Good walking shoes should have flexible soles, good arch supports, and roomy toe boxes.

## EXERCISE

The preceding data drive home the point that activity like brisk walking is very good for your health and fitness. And for sedentary older adults it is the perfect place to begin. Nonetheless, engaging in a regular exercise routine is even better for you, provided it is done correctly and safely. Through regular exercise we can achieve greater cardiovascular fitness, strength, and flexibility benefits that enhances the quality of our life (Williams, 1997b).

According to the *Surgeon General's Report*, regular exercise and physical activity improves health in the following ways:

- Reduces the risk of dying prematurely
- Reduces the risk of dying from heart disease
- Reduces the risk of developing diabetes
- Reduces the risk of developing high blood pressure

- Helps reduce blood pressure in people who already have high blood pressure
- Reduces the risk of developing colon cancer
- Reduces feelings of depression and anxiety
- Helps control weight
- Helps build and maintain healthy bones, muscles, and joints
- Helps older adults become stronger and better able to move about without falling
- Promotes psychological well-being

In 1992, for the first time in nearly 20 years, the American Heart Association added a new risk factor to the list of those already implicated in the onset of acquiring coronary heart disease. Joining hypertension, smoking, and high blood cholesterol levels was physical inactivity. Routine screening of all patients for inactivity is now recommended by the American Heart Association. If the physician is inhibited from exercise counseling by time constraints, it should be coordinated through a nurse, an allied health professional, or some other health educator (Fletcher et al., 1992).

Inactive persons have five to eight times as great a risk of developing cardiovascular disease as those who are physically fit, yet 35 to 50 million American adults are inactive. As several gerontologists have noted, if exercise could be encapsulated in a pill, it would be the single most powerful medication a physician could prescribe.

## THREE TYPES OF EXERCISE PROGRAMS

### AEROBICS OR CARDIOVASCULAR ENDURANCE

Aerobic means "with oxygen." Any activity that moves large volumes of oxygen, employs large muscle groups (like the arms and legs), and is sustained at a certain level of intensity over a period of time, is aerobic. Aerobic exercise is rhythmic, repetitive, and continuous, and includes such popular activities as brisk walking (about twice as fast as one normally walks), swimming, and bicycling.

Anaerobic ("without oxygen") activities that depend on short bursts of energy (like a 50-meter sprint or barbell press), quickly deplete energy resources, and have limited cardiovascular benefit. This type of activity is, however, essential for strength-building purposes.

Aerobic capacity, or maximum oxygen uptake ($VO_2$ max), is the maximum amount of oxygen that an individual can use during strenuous exertion. Aerobic capacity is considered to be the best measure of cardiorespiratory fitness; although it tends to decrease with age, it can be increased through a regularly practiced aerobic regimen.

Most aerobic exercise programs are designed to stimulate the heart and lungs for a sufficient period (generally, a minimum of 20 to 25 minutes) to produce an increased and sustained heart rate. Traditional programs encourage the participants to gradually raise the normal heart beat, about 60 to 80 beats a minute, to the "target zone" of the individual, the upper and lower limits of which are based on age (see Table 4.1).

The target zone refers typically to between 60% and 75% of the estimated maximum heart rate, which is calculated by subtracting a person's age from 220, and multiplying it by 60% and 75%. The target for the beginning exerciser should be near the 60% level (or less if the person has been sedentary), and gradually increase to the higher level over succeeding months.

Individuals can assess the intensity of their aerobic exercise program by counting their pulse beats for a 10-second period and multiplying by

**TABLE 4.1 Aerobic Target Zone**

| Age | Target Zone For Heartbeats During Exercise (60–75% of Max. Heart Rate) | Average Maxium Heart Rate (100%) |
|---|---|---|
| 50 years | 102–127 beats per minute | 170 |
| 55 years | 99–124 beats per minute | 165 |
| 60 years | 96–120 beats per minute | 160 |
| 65 years | 93–116 beats per minute | 155 |
| 70 years | 90–113 beats per minute | 150 |
| 75 years | 87–108 beats per minute | 145 |
| 80 years | 84–105 beats per minute | 140 |
| 85 years | 81–101 beats per minute | 135 |
| 90 years | 78–97 beats per minute | 130 |

Source: Exercise and Your Heart, National Heart, Lung and Blood Institute, National Institutes of Health, USDHHS, 1981, NIH Publication No. 81–1677.

6. Most aerobics instructors ask their students to conduct this assessment at periodic intervals.

## Low, Moderate, and Vigorous Intensity Levels

Walking, swimming, cycling, dancing, gardening, yard work, and other activities can be performed at low, moderate, or vigorous intensity levels. Activities of low to moderate intensity are generally performed at 50% to 65% of the maximum heart rate for one's age. For most people that would be walking a mile in about 15 to 25 minutes. This type of exercise is preferably conducted daily, though less frequent or intermittent activity can also provide health benefits (American College of Sports Medicine, 1988).

Several earlier studies have supported the surgeon general's report that activities of low to moderate intensity activities not only improve the aerobic capacity of older adults, but are less likely than more vigorous activities to result in injury and are more likely to be maintained over time (Agre et al., 1988; Buchner & Wagner, 1992; Gossard et al., 1986). And when low- to moderate-intensity activity is sustained over long periods, it may be more effective at burning fat-derived calories than higher intensity activity over shorter periods (Dunn et al., in press; Keim, 1995). This is because the slower workout will help heavier persons sustain a reasonable fat-burning rate.

On the other hand, it does not provide the fitness benefits of higher intensity exercise (Duncan, 1996), and the evidence on the ability of low intensity exercise to extend life is mixed (Kushi et al., 1997; Lee et al., 1995).

The definitions of low to moderate and high-intensity exercise vary according to fitness level. For the physically fit older adult, activities resulting in 60% of maximal heart rate may be considered low-intensity exercise. Frail or sedentary older adults, however, may find exercise that elevates their heart rates to 60% of maximum heart rate may quickly escalate beyond that and reach too great of an intensity level.

When a sedentary person begins to exercise, it is necessary to start with a mild activity, such as a short walk at low speed to avoid physical symptoms and discomfort. This type of low-intensity exercise can, and probably should, be performed daily. In contrast, older adults who seek a higher fitness level are better served by performing vigorous exercise with rest days between exercise days.

My own experience with exercise programs with older adults has led me to appreciate Fries's comment (1989): "We generally find this whole heart rate business a bit of a bother and somewhat artificial. There really are not good medical data to justify particular target heart rates. You may wish to check your pulse rate a few times to get a feel for what is happening, but it doesn't have to be something you watch extremely carefully" (p. 69). Bailey (1994) reports that the formula for the target heart rate (220 minus age, times the desired intensity range) is inappropriate for 30% to 40% of adults. These persons have hearts that beat faster or slower than the age-predicted maximum.

Typically, I implement periodic checking of target heart rates during the beginning weeks of class and then encourage those who are receptive to it to check their heart rate on their own. Also during the beginning weeks of class, we practice the Borg technique, a subjective assessment of how hard one is working, and we encourage this technique throughout the exercise program (see Figure 4.1).

Ideally, the inactive older adult should seek an intensity level of very light, a 9 or 10 on the Borg scale, or about 50% of maximum heart rate.

## BORG SCALE: HOW DOES YOUR EXERCISE FEEL

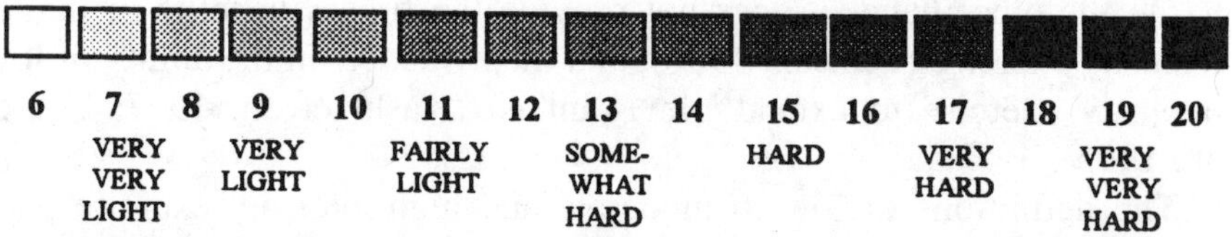

| 6 | 7 | 8 | 9 | 10 | 11 | 12 | 13 | 14 | 15 | 16 | 17 | 18 | 19 | 20 |
|---|---|---|---|----|----|----|----|----|----|----|----|----|----|----|
| | VERY VERY LIGHT | | VERY LIGHT | | FAIRLY LIGHT | | SOME- WHAT HARD | | HARD | | VERY HARD | | VERY VERY HARD | |

Studies have shown that people, whether beginning walkers or athletes in training, are really quite skillful at assessing how hard they are working doing aerobic exercise. Just ask yourself, "How does this exercise feel to me right now?" With practice, you will be able to keep both a comfortable and efficient hand on your throttle. **Try to keep your exercise between a 13 and a 15.** Be especially careful of letting your efforts drift past 15; activities that are very hard or very, very hard are seldom done daily over very long periods of time. Remember this scale can only be used by **you.** Your 13 may be another's 19. The Borg Scale only measures how the work feels for **you.**

**FIGURE 4.1    Borg scale. From Pathways: A Success Guide for a Healthy Life, Healthwise, Inc., P.O. Box 1989, Boise, Idaho 83705.**

The active older person should be in the 13 to 15 range on the Borg scale, or approximately 70% of maximum heart rate. Generally speaking, we tell participants that the exercise level should be of sufficient duration and intensity to break out into a sweat (indicating a rising internal body temperature) but not so intense that they are unable to conduct a brief conversation (if desired) while exercising.

Regardless of whether target heart rates or perceived intensity levels are used, exercise should be discontinued immediately if shortness of breath, chest pain, dizziness or light-headedness, confusion, or pain occur.

## MUSCULAR STRENGTH OR ENDURANCE

Muscular strength or endurance is the ability of the muscle to exert force (strength) or to repeat action over time without fatigue (endurance). This is frequently accomplished through a weight-training program.

Some experts do not believe strengthening exercises are as important for older adults as other components of exercise (Fries, 1989, p. 66), and many geriatric exercise manuals ignore strengthening exercises altogether (Switkes, 1982). I disagree with this perspective and with manuals that overlook strength as an important exercise factor.

In the spring of 1990, a strength exercise program for older adults captured the health headlines in the media, headlines that previously had been dominated by popular aerobic activities, or unusual aerobic accomplishments (like the exploits of Johnny Kelley, who completed the Boston Marathon race 58 times and ran his last one as an octogenarian).

This highly publicized strength exercise program involved 10 (including 1 drop-out) frail, very old nursing home residents who, after completing an 8-week training program, almost tripled their leg strength, expanded their thigh muscles by more than 10%, and were able to walk 50% faster (Fiatarone et al., 1990).

The participants ranged in age from 87 to 96 years. One 93-year-old participant reported, "I feel as though I were 50 again. Now, I get up in the middle of the night, and I can get around without using my walker or turning on the light. The program gave me strength I didn't have before. Every day I feel better, more optimistic. Pills won't do for you what exercise does!" (Evans et al., 1991)

Another resident who at first could not rise from a chair without the use of his arms was able to do so after the training, and two others no longer needed canes for walking (Fiatarone et al., 1990).

Arm strength, as well as leg strength, is an important benefit that may result from a program designed to increase muscle strength or endurance. Most older adults need to carry groceries, pick up household items, twist off jar lids, and make minor repairs.

As people age, lean muscle tissue tends to decrease, and the percentage of body fat increases. Thus, muscle strength tends to decline with age. Weight training, or isometrics, can reverse this trend. Strength training for increasing muscle mass and functioning ability also increases bone density. When the skeletal frame is strengthened, the likelihood of bone fractures resulting from osteoporosis is reduced (Jaglal et al., 1993).

To improve strength through weight training, an individual uses about 75% of maximum resistance for each muscle group and conducts one to three sets (i.e., groups) of six repetitions. To improve endurance, the individual uses 50% of maximum resistance and increases sets to 12 or more repetitions. The preferred schedule of activity for improving or sustaining strength or endurance for older adults is 2 or 3 days a week, with at least 1 day of rest between workouts.

A good alternative exercise for increasing strength in older adults with painful arthritic joints is isometrics, the contraction of a muscle without movement at the joint. The typical way to engage in isometrics is to pull or push against a stationary object, usually against a wall or against another body part. Each contraction should be held for about 5 seconds and repeated three times. Many exercise physiologists are reluctant to recommend isometric exercise for heart patients because of the increased likelihood of performing the Valsalva maneuver (i.e., holding ones breath). It is possible, however, to avoid this maneuver when doing isometrics.

Isometrics is an effective alternative to weight lifting or weight-resistance machines. Because there is no movement, you can do isometrics any place, any time, and at no cost. The muscle that you select tightens but does not change length, thus there is no movement of the joint or the bone to which the muscle is attached. Isometrics, therefore, has the advantage of allowing you to build muscle at a fixed angle, avoiding those joint positions that may be affected by arthritic pain. Conversely, unless you systematically alter the angle (at least 20 degrees) you do not develop strength over the range of motion.

There are several problems to avoid with all strength-building techniques but can be especially problematic with isometrics. To avoid the unhealthy Valsalva maneuver, for instance, count slowly out loud to trigger continuous breathing. To improve range of motion, it is not only important to vary the isometric angle but to develop opposing muscle groups. Finally, the Borg scale for estimating appropriate intensity level should be used frequently with isometric exercise.

A good resistance-training class for older adults would not only be designed to build strength and endurance but would include safety tips on lifting objects and moving one's body to avoid muscle strain, backaches, hernias, and the like. Although there are still few resistance-training programs available to older persons, components of strength-building increasingly are being incorporated into aerobic exercise classes.

Injury from weight lifting is not uncommon. In weight rooms around the country, you can observe many examples of incorrect technique that lead to injury. Men, typically, are hoisting too-heavy weights, arching their backs, holding their breaths (the Valsalva maneuver should be avoided at any age), swinging the weights or otherwise using momentum, and dropping the weights (free weights or machine weights) when done.

Instead, manageable weights and proper technique should be used. Lift slowly and smoothly and return the weights under full control, maintain the natural curve of your back, exhale on exertion, and inhale as you relax. If you break form, the weights are too heavy. Weight lifters who use correct form actually reduce injuries by strengthening joints and ligaments (Marcus, 1997). Machine weights are safer than free weights because they help foster proper technique and prevent the weight from falling on you (Hesson, 1995).

Sixty percent of weight lifters are males, but women are joining them at a very quick pace. Between 1987 and 1996 women strength builders more than doubled, from 7 to 17 million, to join the 26 million men (Marcus, 1997). Women have learned that they need not fear building bulging muscles because they have less testosterone and fewer cells that make up muscle fiber. In addition to working toward a better appearance, women weight lifters enjoy the benefits of improving strength and balance and preventing osteoporosis.

Rubber tubing is an alternative to free weights (which are more likely to lead to injury) and resistance machines (which are less accessible and affordable) that I use for strength-building programs for older adults. It is safe, portable, and cheap (about $1 per band) when bought in bulk through brand names like Theraband and Dynaband (Fitness Wholesale, 895A Hampshire Road, Stow, OH 44224; 800-537-5512).

The band fits easily into your pocket and is convenient to take on a trip. A potential disadvantage to bands is that they can be difficult to grip with arthritic fingers. This can be overcome by buying handles, or tying the band into a circle and exerting power through your wrists or forearms.

Another potential disadvantage is that the band will eventually wear out, and this could occur when in use, with the rubber snapping in the direction of your body or someone else's. Also, although the bands can be purchased in four or five different levels of intensity, they are still less precise than free weights or weight machines for measuring improvement.

Two research leaders who extol the benefits of resistance exercise (free weights, machines, isometrics, and rubber tubing), exercise physiologist William Evans and physician Maria Fiatarone, believe that strength building may be even more important for older adults than aerobic exercise. Although many physicians recommend walking because they think it is the safest activity, people who are weak have poor balance and are more subject to fall. Prescribing resistance exercise can give older adults the strength and confidence they need to begin aerobic activity in the first place.

## FLEXIBILITY EXERCISE

Different types of exercise activities for older adults result in different types of benefits. A study by King and associates (1997) reports that although programs emphasizing aerobics and strength building provide an array of benefits for older adults, flexibility exercises may be particularly well suited for improving range of motion and reducing pain.

Ballistic stretching, using quick and bouncy movements, works against the protective reflex contraction and can result in muscle tears, soreness, and injury. Static stretching is preferred and uses slow and smooth movement through a muscle's full range of movement until you feel resistance or the beginning of discomfort. The maximum position is held 10 to 30 seconds, which allows for reduction of the protective reflex contraction.

Stretching should always be preceded by a brief aerobic warm-up to increase heart rate, blood flow, and the temperature of the muscles, ligaments, and tendons. Stretching while muscles are cold may sprain or tear them.

Stretching may affect ones mind as well as body and is one reason why the Eastern traditions of yoga and Tai Chi are ancient and gentle practices that still attract people of all ages, especially older adults. Sadie Delaney (who reached age 108 on September 19, 1997), for instance, reported in her book that she began her yoga practice in her 60s and has continued it for 40 years, the last several of which she followed a yoga program on television. She also reported that when her sister Bessie turned 80 she decided that Sadie looked better than her and began doing yoga too (Delany et al., 1993).

The most popular yoga activity is hatha yoga, a sequence of stretching, bending, and twisting movements that causes each joint to move slowly through its maximum range of motion, then is held for several seconds and repeated (see Figure 4.2). These practices improve body awareness, reduce stress, improve balance and coordination, and increase the maximum range of motion by expanding joint mobility (Christensen & Rankin, 1979).

Hatha yoga and other types of stretching, twisting, and bending exercise programs, possess two characteristics that make them highly desirable for older adults. They are well suited to all adults, even the very frail elderly (Haber, 1979, 1988), and are exceptionally easy to incorporate into a daily routine. The movements of a stretching program, for instance, can be performed easily while one is watching television or talking on the telephone. For people who engage in regular aerobic or strength-building activity, the warm-up or cool-down period can easily include a 10- to 15-minute flexibility routine.

Performing yoga-type exercises in a group setting has become very popular with older adults. For more than a decade, I worked with older adults through the Easy Does It Yoga for Older People program (Christensen & Rankin, 1979), a widely used yoga program for older persons. I implemented these programs at senior centers (Haber & George, 1981–1982), congregate-living facilities (Haber, 1986), nursing homes (Haber, 1988), churches (Haber & Lacy, 1993), and other sites. Without exception, the programs have been enthusiastically received, and individual benefits have been demonstrable.

## OTHER EXERCISES

Tai chi consists of slow, graceful movements that are derived from a martial arts form in oriental cultures. It is gentle in nature and well suited to young and old. Persons of all ages in China can be observed in groups practicing Tai Chi in urban parks and in front of congregate housing (Haber, 1979). The movements are becoming increasingly popular in the

**CHAIR EXERCISES**

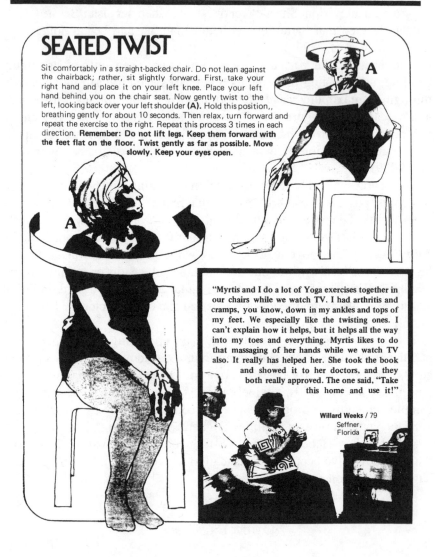

# SEATED TWIST

Sit comfortably in a straight-backed chair. Do not lean against the chairback; rather, sit slightly forward. First, take your right hand and place it on your left knee. Place your left hand behind you on the chair seat. Now gently twist to the left, looking back over your left shoulder **(A)**. Hold this position,, breathing gently for about 10 seconds. Then relax, turn forward and repeat the exercise to the right. Repeat this process 3 times in each direction. **Remember: Do not lift legs. Keep them forward with the feet flat on the floor. Twist gently as far as possible. Move slowly. Keep your eyes open.**

"Myrtis and I do a lot of Yoga exercises together in our chairs while we watch TV. I had arthritis and cramps, you know, down in my ankles and tops of my feet. We especially like the twisting ones. I can't explain how it helps, but it helps all the way into my toes and everything. Myrtis likes to do that massaging of her hands while we watch TV also. It really has helped her. She took the book and showed it to her doctors, and they both really approved. The one said, "Take this home and use it!"

**Willard Weeks** / 79
Seffner,
Florida

**FIGURE 4.2    Seated twist. From *Easy Does It Yoga for Older People*, Copyright 1979 by The American Yoga Association, Harper & Row, San Francisco.**

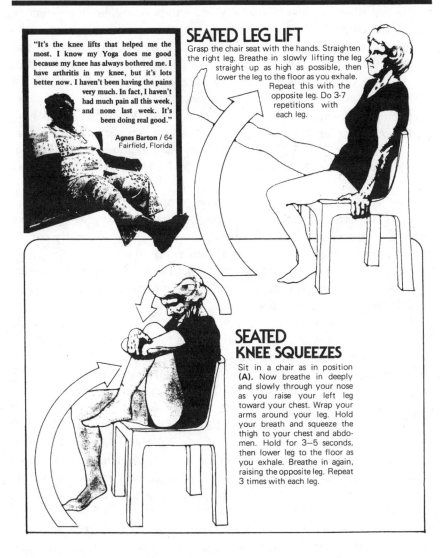

"It's the knee lifts that helped me the most. I know my Yoga does me good because my knee has always bothered me. I have arthritis in my knee, but it's lots better now. I haven't been having the pains very much. In fact, I haven't had much pain all this week, and none last week. It's been doing real good."

**Agnes Barton** / 64
Fairfield, Florida

## SEATED LEG LIFT

Grasp the chair seat with the hands. Straighten the right leg. Breathe in slowly lifting the leg straight up as high as possible, then lower the leg to the floor as you exhale. Repeat this with the opposite leg. Do 3-7 repetitions with each leg.

## SEATED KNEE SQUEEZES

Sit in a chair as in position (A). Now breathe in deeply and slowly through your nose as you raise your left leg toward your chest. Wrap your arms around your leg. Hold your breath and squeeze the thigh to your chest and abdomen. Hold for 3–5 seconds, then lower leg to the floor as you exhale. Breathe in again, raising the opposite leg. Repeat 3 times with each leg.

**FIGURE 4.2    Seated twist.** (*continued*)

United States as well. In addition to improving flexibility, tai chi is conducted with a lowered center of gravity (knees and hips held in flexion) and can contribute to lower extremity strength building, body awareness, and balance control.

In terms of balance control two rigorously controlled studies—part of a $2.9 million, eight city, 3-year exercise research project sponsored in 1990 by the National Institute on Aging and the National Institute for Nursing Research—support the contention that Tai Chi has favorable effects on the prevention of falls (Wolf et al., 1996; Wolfson et al., 1996). One tai chi group endured 48% longer than a comparison group before a first fall (Wolf et al., 1996). By practicing the tai chi movements, older participants learn to stabilize their balance and regain it before they begin to fall.

Power yoga (an Americanized version of astanga yoga) is a blend of flexibility and strength building that has become popular mostly in New York and California. It was introduced into America by the aptly named Beryl *Bender* Birch (1995). Power yoga differs from traditional stretching programs that encourage you to relax into a pose while stretching, in that proponent's advocate for isometrically tensing specific muscles while relaxing the opposing muscles.

Pilates (pronounced pi-LA-tees) is a technique that uses specially made exercise equipment with pulleys and springs to stretch and to strengthen your midsection. Trained instructors guide you through breathing exercises and a routine to help you move in a balanced way. To find a Pilates instructor in your city, call 800-474-5283. The Alexander technique also attempts to promote balance and to retrain your body to carry itself properly, with particular attention to head and neck alignment. To see if there is a program near you, call 800-473-0620. The Feldenkrais method is a third alternative to train your body to move with efficiency and ease. A trained practitioner gently manipulates your muscles and joints to find the most comfortable ways to use your body. For more information, call 800-775-2118.

As the following chart (see Table 4.2) of five different exercise activities indicates, there is considerable variation in the types of benefits that can accrue, suggesting the importance of engaging in a balanced approach to exercise. It should be noted that each of the exercises below can be performed in such a way as to improve its ranking in each of the three categories (e.g., power yoga increases strength, high repetition weight lifting improves endurance, etc.).

**TABLE 4.2   Exercises Emphasize Different Benefits**

| Exercise | Aerobic Endurance | Strength | Flexibility/Agility |
|---|---|---|---|
| Swimming | High | Low | Medium |
| Brisk Walking/ Jogging | High | Low | Low |
| Yoga | Low | Low | High |
| Tai Chi | Medium | Medium | Medium |
| Weightlifting | Low | High | Low |

## ACTIVITY PYRAMID

Most people have heard of the U.S. Department of Agriculture's food guide pyramid (see chapter 5 on nutrition), and several organizations have developed an *activity* version of it. Not having seen one that I like as much as my own, I offer Figure 4.3.

A sedentary lifestyle, like the junk food at the top of the food pyramid, should be considerably restricted. It is acceptable to watch television, and even to eat junk food while doing it, but doing it to excess is dangerous

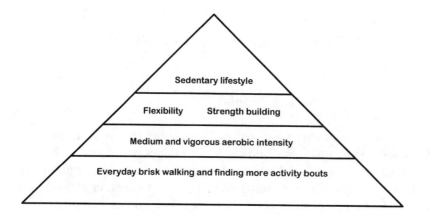

**FIGURE 4.3   Activity pyramid.**

to your health. I recommend slothfulness every now and then—it is an excellent antidote for self-righteousness.

Two to three "servings" of flexibility routines and strength-building exercises per week are recommended (similar to the daily recommendations for the dairy and the meat/beans group in the food pyramid). A regular routine of medium or vigorous aerobic intensity, like jogging and some recreational activities, can be done three or four times a week for those who have left the ranks of the sedentary. Light exercise, such as brisk walking, and finding additional activity bouts can be done everyday.

Incorporating additional activity bouts into your everyday routine can be done in a variety of ways. Park your car further away from the store; use stairs instead of escalators; walk the dog and work in your garden more; and, the most devious of all, do not use the remote control when watching television. Persons who are sedentary need to focus their attention on the base of the pyramid.

The activity at the base of the pyramid is different from the exercise above it. Activity can be defined as any body movement produced by skeletal muscles that results in energy expenditure. It is in this sector of the pyramid that we emphasize spontaneity and enjoyment.

Exercise, conversely, is planned, structured, and repetitive body movement (Jones & Jones, 1997). It is in these sectors of the pyramid where maintaining a routine, rather than spontaneity, is desirable. Exercise too can be enjoyable though, for me anyway, the highlight is when I am done with it, and I can savor the way my body feels for several hours afterward.

## BARRIERS TO EXERCISE AND ACTIVITY

### JOYS OF AGING

"I have become quite a frivolous old gal. I'm seeing five gentleman every day. As soon as I awake, Will Power helps me get out of bed. When he leaves I go see John. Then Charley Horse comes along, and when he is here, he takes a lot of my attention. When he leaves, Arthur Ritis shows up and stays the rest of the day. He doesn't like to stay in one place very long, so he takes me from joint to joint. After such a busy day, I'm really tired and ready to go to bed with Ben Gay. What a day!" (Anonymous).

## ARTHRITIS

The major barrier to performing resistance training, yoga, calisthenics, aerobics, and other types of exercise is arthritic stiffness and pain. Osteoarthritis (degenerative joint disease), the most common type found among older people, ranges in intensity from occasional stiffness and joint pain to disability. This disease is affected by genetics, obesity, injuries, and overuse of joint movement. Rheumatoid arthritis is less common but can be more disabling. Although the cause is unknown, scientists believe it may result from a breakdown in the immune system.

Many people with arthritis think that any type of exercise will be uncomfortable (i.e., cause joint or muscle pain or swelling of the extremities), or be downright harmful and lead to decreased functional abilities. These indicators of exercise intolerance, however, will typically *not* occur if exercise is performed properly. In fact, it is *more* likely that the joints will stiffen, the muscles will weaken, and the ability to function will decline if regular flexibility exercises are *not* performed. To counteract arthritic stiffness, it may be necessary to engage in flexibility exercises at least once daily, and three or four times a day may be preferable.

It also may be necessary to engage in strength-building exercise to strengthen the muscles that surround and support the joints and to force lubricating fluid into the cartilage that helps keep it nourished and healthy. Rall and colleagues (1996) found that even people with severe rheumatoid arthritis could safely increase their strength almost 60% in a 12-week progressive resistance-training program. A randomized trial comparing aerobic exercise and resistance exercise on older adults with knee osteoarthritis concluded that both types of programs are effective (Ettinger et al., 1997).

The advice of a physical therapist, occupational therapist, or nurse can be especially helpful when developing an individualized exercise program that balances exercise and rest. One way to minimize aches and pains is to relax joints and muscles before exercise by applying heat (or soaking in a warm bath) or ice packs, and gently massaging muscles. Weight control can also help keep unnecessary stress from joints.

Another technique for conquering the challenge of aches and pains that may prevent exercising is to choose a time of day when one is subject to the least amount of discomfort, stiffness, and fatigue. People who are on medication may find that their optimal time coincides with the period during which their medicine is having its maximum effect (Lorig & Fries,

1986). Many persons with arthritis depend on anti-inflammatory drugs to alleviate aches and pains, and to allow them to exercise.

Many others hold out hope for a miracle medication that will not only alleviate their arthritic pain but reverse the disease process. The latest prospect discovered by the public in this regard coincided with the publication of *The Arthritis Cure* (Theodosakis, 1997). The book touts two supplements, glucosamine and chondroitin sulfate that stimulate the growth of cartilage and keep it from wearing down. Although these supplements may be promising to some, the research evidence for a cure for arthritis is still inconclusive.

Another option for avoiding arthritic discomfort is finding a more appropriate exercise routine (Buchner & Wagner, 1992), like water exercise. An older adult, for instance, who believes she is aggravating an arthritic knee during her walking program may find an aquatic program more desirable than a land-based exercise program. Water provides buoyancy and will relieve some of the stress and strain of exercise on land where gravity and weight are greater influences. Body weight in water is less than 10% of its weight on land (Corbin & Metal-Corbin, 1997). Also, if the water is sufficiently warm, it will allow greater range of motion because muscles stretch better when they are warm.

A free brochure from the Arthritis Foundation explains how to set safe exercise limits and includes tips for easing into exercises, such as taking a warm shower before engaging in land-based exercise to loosen up. To obtain, contact the foundation at 800-283-7800 or its Web site: www@arthritis.org.

## OTHER BARRIERS AND CAUTIONS

There are several barriers to exercise besides the belief that it is unenjoyable or harmful. Some older adults, for instance, engage in a level of exercise that is inadequate or lacks the proper intensity to meet their needs while under the mistaken belief that they are sufficiently active (Fiatarone et al., 1990; Sidney & Shephard, 1977). Others have a problem with over exuberance, tackling an exercise program too strenuously and too quickly, and suffering the consequences of injury (Kannus et al., 1989).

It is necessary to begin and end an exercise routine with an adequate warm-up and cool-down period consisting of gentle aerobics and stretching. It is important that the warm-up period begin with aerobics (walking or a slow version of the exercise to be engaged in) and not stretching as the latter can create damage to the muscles and joints if the body temperature is not warmed up first. The cool-down period prevents blood from pooling in lower muscles, which reduces blood flow to the heart and brain, and can cause faintness or worse. Cool-down stretching also prevents muscle stiffness and soreness by restretching muscles that are shortened during exercise.

Another inhibitor of activity is the fear of falling. More than one third of community dwelling elderly fall each year (Speechley & Tinetti, 1991). The potential for falling has been used as a justification for physical restraints in the nursing home (Evans & Strumpf, 1989). Fear of falling, imposed by a caregiving spouse, may be a significant barrier to exercising. Some risk may have to be tolerated. However, the propensity for falling often can be reduced dramatically by exercising in a seated or lying position or by a change in medication (Ray et al., 1989).

Medications may require that exercise participants modify their exercise routine by decreasing the duration and intensity of an exercise, increasing fluid intake, or foregoing exercise for a period (Kligman & Pepin, 1992).

To treat injury to a muscle or ligament in the form of a strain, sprain, or tear, and keep it from becoming worse, the most commonly recommended guideline is the acronym RICE, for rest, ice, compression, and elevation. Rest the injured area immediately to cut down on blood circulation to that part of the body. Apply ice immediately, which shrinks blood vessels and reduces swelling. Compress the injured area with an elastic bandage or cloth to also help reduce swelling. Elevate the damaged part to a level higher than the heart.

Other barriers to exercise may include lack of transportation to an exercise facility, limited financial resources for joining a program, medical concerns, lack of access to consultation with a health professional, lethargy, inability to identify a pleasurable exercise that can sustain one's interest over time, and lack of time. Persistent and creative problem solving can overcome most barriers.

Some health professionals erroneously believe that older adults have considerably more discretionary time than younger adults (Haber, 1993a). A perceived lack of time, however, is as likely to be a problem among older adults as among younger adults (Dishman et al., 1985). In fact, a common response among older adults is that they lack the time for exercise because they provide care for a frail family member. other older adults may also have a busy schedule that consists of sedentary hobbies, family events, and volunteer obligations.

In general, exercise is a safe activity. "Indeed, a remarkable aspect of research on exercise in the elderly has been the virtual absence of reports of serious cardiovascular or musculoskeletal complications in any published trials. . . . Thus, exercise should be viewed as safe for most older adults" (Elward & Larson, 1992, p. 45). This is not to suggest that exercise is hazard free. Walkers and joggers oftentimes share a path with persons on bicycles, and rare collisions do occur. Overexertion in hot weather can lead to heat exhaustion (with symptoms of dizziness, and a rapid or weak pulse) or potentially fatal heat strokes. High humidity is dangerous because the air is saturated with moisture, which prevents heat from leaving the body through perspiration.

Occasionally, older persons with unsuspected heart problems embark on exercise programs. To avoid this problem, individuals, in addition to a medical examination, may undergo an exercise stress test before beginning an exercise program. This test (consisting of treadmills, cycle ergometers, and steps) is designed to identify individuals without symptoms who may be at high risk of suffering a medical complication during exercise because of undetected heart disease.

At-risk individuals are identified through such measurements as an electrocardiogram, heart rate, and blood pressure. Abnormal responses to a stress test may consist of a failure of the blood pressure level to increase as work intensity increases; or a slow recovery of ventilation and heart rate; or an excessive shortness of breath, chest pain, or electrocardiogram changes, like dysrhythmias.

A major barrier to taking a stress test is its cost, typically more than $300 in 1998. Another problem is its unusually high percentage of false positives (abnormal stress-test results and no heart disease) and false negatives (normal results for persons with heart disease). Moreover, persons most in need of a stress test (those with two or more risk factors for coronary artery disease and those with cardiovascular or lung disease or a metabolic disorder like diabetes) should be informed that the test itself involves a health risk ("Starting to Exercise? Do You Need a Stress Test?," 1998).

## EXCUSES

AARP's Staying Healthy After Fifty Program (SHAF) (Kane-Williams et al., 1986) lists the most common excuses for not exercising: fatigue; fear of heart attack or hypertension; trouble catching breath; need to relax; too old; bad back; and arthritis. Each of these excuses is examined during the SHAF program and exposed as myths or general misunderstandings that can keep older adults inactive.

Some examples of responses to these excuses are improved strength makes daily tasks easier and less tiring; an exercised heart is stronger, works easier, and can lower blood pressure; heart, lungs, and muscles become more efficient through exercise and make breathing easier; it is never too late to exercise, even nonagenarians benefit; bad backs are commonly caused by inadequate exercise, improper lifting, and poor posture; and exercise can alleviate the pain and stiffness of arthritis.

## BENEFITS

A negative attitude also can be a barrier to exercise. When motivating someone to exercise, it is important to shift the emphasis from the nega-tive—what will happen if you do not exercise—to the positive—how you will benefit if you do. The SHAF program lists benefits of exercise that are likely to motivate old and young alike: "having fun, sleeping better, feeling more energetic, controlling body weight, feeling more relaxed, feeling stronger, increased joint flexibility, maintaining an independent lifestyle, improving heart, arteries and lungs, new social contacts, im-proved morale and confidence, enhanced agility and mobility" (Kane-Williams et al., 1986).

If these benefits do not appeal, Erma Bombeck offers a particularly unique advantage to those who exercise. "The only reason I would take up jogging is so that I can hear heavy breathing again."

## HEALTH CLUB OR HOME SETTING

The number of health club members over age 55 increased by an aston-ishing 75% from 1987 to 1995 (*The Johns Hopkins Medical Letter*, 1997). Nearly half of all health clubs now offer special exercise classes for members over age 50. Baby-boomer membership in health clubs has grown almost as fast during this time, with a 61% gain in health club membership among persons aged 45 to 54. In a 7-year period, from 1988 to 1995, health club members age 45 and over increased from 18% to 29%.

There are many advantages to membership in a health club. Most clubs offer at least one free session from a qualified trainer as part of the membership fee. Weight machines are excellent for beginners because they are easy to use, and they reduce injury by controlling your form and preventing a weight from falling on you. Most health clubs arrange machines in a logical order to promote a balanced approach to strength building. Free weights are offered as an alternative and, although more injury producing, they involve stabilizing muscles that help you progress faster. Finally, aerobic and yoga classes are commonly offered at health facilities.

The down side is that a fee of $400 a year per individual is typical. Also, many older adults may feel shy or inadequate in a health club with a preponderance of young, fit participants. Finally, if motivation is marginal, sometimes all it takes is the prospect of a 15- to 20-minute drive to put you off.

Before joining a health club, it is wise to visit more than one; be sure you go the same time of day that you intend to exercise, ascertain the qualifications of staff, determine if the classes are reasonable for your level of fitness, and find out if personal training advice is available when you need it.

Exercising in the home setting, on the other hand, is as convenient as it gets. You do not have to worry about how you look, and you do not have to adapt to other people's musical tastes. The investment is a one-time expense consisting of weights or a weight machine, and music for aerobic conditioning. If even a one-time expense is too expensive, an excellent exercise routine can be devised from using the floor, wall, chair, or your own body weight, or by placing a household item in a container that offers a grip.

The down side is that you may be distracted by a ringing phone, the television set, or a family member. You also lack the peer support of an aerobics class or role models doing strength building. Home exercise lacks the variety of a health club.

If you are going to buy a piece of exercise equipment, consider the low-tech treadmill. One study (Zeni et al., 1996) reported that the walking or jogging machine outperformed a rowing machine, a cross-country skiing simulator, a stationary bicycle, and a stair stepper when it came to burning calories. Regardless of the home exercise equipment you purchase, try out the equipment before you buy; check a consumer magazine for recommendations; and remember that flimsy, uncomfortable, or noisy equipment is likely to wind up as a clothes rack.

Is it worth $50 to $75 an hour for a personal trainer? If you can afford it, the answer is yes—both in terms of expertise and motivation. The

Fitness Connection is a company that provides free referrals to certified personal trainers in your area (800-318-4024). Want to make sure that an instructor is certified? Ask about their certification, and call to check on their credentials. Most qualified trainers have been certified by at least one of the following organizations:

American College of Sports Medicine (317-637-9200)
National Strength and Conditioning Association (719-632-6722)
National Academy of Sports Medicine (312-929-5101)
American Council on Exercise (619-535-8227)
Aerobics and Fitness Association of America (800-446-2322)
International Association of Fitness Professionals (800-999-IDEA)
Cooper Institute for Aerobics Research (972-701-8001)
National Association for Fitness Certification (209-448-0232)
Arthritis Foundation PACE Instructor Training (800-364-8000)

Most certifications are not specific for exercises for older adults. Make sure that your personal trainer is experienced with persons who are of comparable age to you.

## ROLE OF THE HEALTH PROFESSIONAL

The percentage of inactive older adults would likely decrease if health professionals knew more about the benefits of exercise and were more inclined to recommend it to clients (Elward & Larson, 1992). Eighty-five percent of adult respondents report that a physician's recommendation would help motivate them to engage in regular exercise (Harris et al., 1989).

Yet, in 1983, less than half of the primary care physicians surveyed reported routinely asking patients about their exercise habits (Wechsler et al., 1983). A more recent survey indicated that the problem persists. Almost half of a convenience sample of 491 women 55 years and older reported that they have *never* been advised to exercise by their health care provider (Jones & Jones, 1997). Results from seven surveys of primary care physicians suggest that an estimated 30% of all sedentary patients receive counseling about exercise (Lewis, 1988).

Two factors correlate with the likelihood that physicians will counsel their patients to exercise: the physicians' training backgrounds (United States Preventive Services Task Force, 1996) and their personal levels of physical activity (Lewis & Wells, 1985). Many health care professionals either fail to recommend exercise for their clients (Wechsler et al., 1983) or recommend it in such a way as to be intimidating (Elward & Larson, 1992). Older adults are most likely to be motivated to exercise by a positive, personal approach, for instance, one that indicates that exercise may give them "more energy for grandchildren" or help bring about a "faster recovery from illness." Although telling older clients about their need to achieve a "training effect" may be positive, it probably is not the best method of motivation.

Nurses have been particularly creative with reaching out to persons and encouraging them to exercise. Two nurses have reported that posting a sign by the office elevator giving directions to the nearest stairs is a good way to promote physical activity (Jones & Jones, 1997). This technique works in shopping malls also (Andersen et al., 1998). Other nurses have been creative with implementing exercise programs for even the most physically and mentally compromised individuals (Colangelo et al., 1997).

## QUESTIONS FOR DISCUSSION

1. A client reports to you that friends of his have been injured while exercising, and he heard about one older person who had heat stroke while walking briskly and died. He has decided that it is safer to not exercise. How would you respond?
2. Is it essential that older persons seek physician approval before participating in all exercise programs?
3. Role play with a partner. Can you counter every excuse your partner offers for not exercising by suggesting an idea that will encourage your partner to exercise?
4. A client calls you and complains that the surgeon general only recommended moderate exercise like brisk walking, and she is doing a pretty rigorous aerobic class, with strength building included. She wants to know if she should exert this extra energy if it does not seem to matter.

# 5
# Nutrition

[T]o reduce dietary fat intake from an average of 36 percent (baseline, 1976–80) to 30 percent of calories, and average saturated fat intake from 13 percent (baseline, 1985) to 10 percent.

[T]o increase complex carbohydrate and fiber-containing foods in the diets of adults from 2 1/2 daily servings (baseline, 1985) to 5 servings of vegetables (including legumes) and fruits, and from 3 daily servings to 6 servings of grain products.

[T]o increase from 74 percent (baseline, 1988) to 85 percent the proportion of persons who use food labels to make nutritious food selections.

[T]o increase (no baseline data) to 80 percent the receipt of home food services by people age 65 and older who have difficulty in preparing their own meals or are otherwise in need of home-delivered meals. (Public health goals from the U.S. Public Health Service's Healthy People 2000 Initiative [AARP, 1991]). (*Healthy People 2000 Midcourse Review: 1995 Report on Progress*, DHHS, OPHS)

One national study reported that older people are more conscientious about managing their diets than those who are middle age (Harris et al., 1989). In this sample, a higher percentage of those over age 65 (approximately two thirds) than of those in their 40s (one half) reported trying "a lot" to limit sodium, fat, and sugar; eat enough fiber; lower cholesterol; and consume enough vitamins and minerals.

One can only speculate that, if this sample is representative, the better nutritional habits of older adults may be motivated by more immediate feedback (heartburn, constipation, and so forth), or feelings of greater

*115*

vulnerability (higher risk of impairment from disease and of institutionalization).

The next cohort of older adults, today's baby boomers, may add a few new wrinkles to a healthy diet. Middle-aged boomers, for instance, are once again eating Kellogg's Frosted Flakes because of the clever television commercials in 1997 that targeted them. Apparently, boomers paid less attention to the high-sugar content on the nutritional label and paid more attention to the statement on the cereal box proclaiming that "This product meets the American Heart Association's food criteria for healthy people over age 2 when used as part of a balanced diet."

The preceding statement, however, applies more to Kellogg's healthy "bran" cereals. In fact, the Kellogg company has petitioned the FDA to allow a new health claim on its bran cereal boxes: that the bran in these cereals helps prevent cancer, especially colon cancer. Rival Quaker Oats received FDA approval in 1997 to state that the fiber in oatmeal may reduce the risk of heart disease.

Middle-aged boomers and older adults are influenced not only by clever advertising and an interest in reviving earlier eating habits but also by the nutritional content of food products. Sometimes, however, it is difficult to ascertain the nutritional value of food. In 1993, for instance, newspaper headlines and television news announcers proclaimed the importance of bran in the diet but reversed those claims when the findings of a single research project with a small sample size indicated that the importance of bran was questionable.

Before the year was out, a new announcement declared, once again, that bran was an important component of the diet. By 1996 several controlled research studies supported the finding that bran and other forms of fiber reduced the risk of colon cancer and heart disease ("End of Debate: Fiber's Great," 1996).

The frequent controversies can be confusing and sometimes amusing, but they should not detract from the sensible advice that guides most educated adults. The best recipe for good nutrition is moderation and balance including plenty of fiber in the diet and avoiding excessive fat and sugar.

## FOOD PYRAMID

Not too long ago, the conventional recipe for a sensible diet included plenty of protein, such as meat and eggs; plenty of milk; and limited amounts of "fattening" bread, potatoes, and other starches. It is uncertain what percentage of older adults continue to adhere to this outdated advice. It is now recommended that the complex carbohydrates we consume daily (including previously maligned starches like breads and potatoes) constitute 55% to 60% of our diet and that protein make up no more than 10% to 15% of the diet.

Complex carbohydrates are good sources of energy that are completely digested or eliminated without taxing the digestive organs. In addition, they provide roughage or fiber that acts as a natural laxative and absorbs fat (which is associated with colon cancer risk). Conversely, Americans generally eat twice the recommended amount of protein (20%–30%), which can result in dehydration. Extra protein requires extra water, yet thirst declines with age. Thus, high-protein diets, which are associated with inadequate water intake, place an extra burden on our kidneys and liver. Moreover, high-protein diets tend to be high-fat diets despite the fact that an increasing number of low-fat meat and dairy products are now available.

In the spring of 1991, this perspective led to health-related headlines questioning whether the long-standing "circle" that depicted the four food groups should be changed to a "pyramid." This was not merely a question of geometrical aesthetics. The equally divided circle implied that the four food groups—bread/cereal, vegetable/fruit, milk, and meat—were equal in value, whereas the pyramid better portrays the desirable balance of foods we need to eat, that is, less fat and protein, and more complex carbohydrates.

The pyramid also implies a hierarchy of value, with greater emphasis (i.e., space in the triangle) at the base, which is devoted to bread and cereal. Higher up are vegetables and fruits; followed by dairy products and meat; and, at the narrow apex, the sinful fats, oils, and sweets (see Figure 5.1).

After only a few weeks of national publicity, the U.S. Department of Agriculture dropped the pyramid and returned to the circle diagram. Some accused the government of caving in to the dairy and meat industries. Supporters of the retraction, though, claimed the pyramid concept overlooked the recent surge of low-fat dairy products and leaner meats that made these foods more acceptable. Also, because we still have to worry about anemia, malnutrition, and calcium deficiency, we should not cut back on milk and meat.

The pyramid concept, beginning in 1992, has been growing in acceptance once again. Registered dietitians and nutritionists, for instance, have

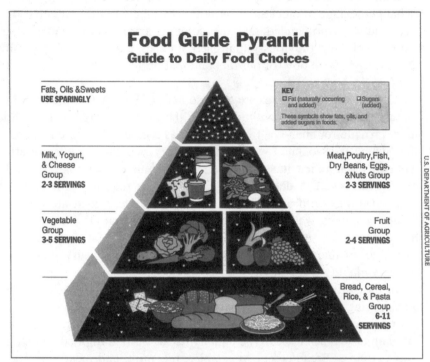

Remember the old food wheel that implied all foods were nutritionally equal? The USDA's new pyramid shows clearly which foods should be eaten most—and least.

**FIGURE 5.1   Food guide pyramid.**

been recommending more daily selections from the bread and cereal group (6–11) and the vegetable and fruit group (5–9), and fewer daily selections from the milk (2–4) and meat (2–3) groups than they previously did (Moore & Nagle, 1990). The pyramid design is being used in school systems and appears frequently on shopping bags in supermarkets.

Most Americans fall short of achieving the recommended number of servings in the important bottom part of the pyramid (grains, cereals, breads, rice, pasta, vegetables, and fruit). However, it is not as difficult to achieve the recommended number of servings in these food groups as many adults think.

It should be noted that a pyramid serving is typically smaller than the "average helping," which is depicted on nutritional labels (to be examined later in this chapter). One slice of bread or half a bagel, for instance, is a pyramid serving; so is one-half cup of cooked cereal, pasta, rice, most vegetables, and cut or canned fruit. The servings on a nutritional label, therefore, often represent more than one serving within a food pyramid group.

## BULL'S EYE

Nutritionist Covert Bailey developed an important adjunct to the food pyramid and called it the Smart Eating Food Target or the bull's-eye (see Figure 5.2) (Bailey & Gates, 1996). Like the food pyramid, Bailey has divided the target into four basic quadrants that correspond to the basic food groups: breads and cereals, fruits and vegetables, milks, and meats.

Unlike the food pyramid, however, Bailey makes important distinctions within food categories. Foods that are low in fat and sugar, and high in fiber, are listed in the bull's-eye; foods that are higher in sugar and fat, and lower in fiber are in the outer circles of the target. The goal of the food target, therefore, is to help consumers aim for the nutritious foods listed in the bull's-eye.

Whole-wheat products, for instance, are in the bull's-eye, whereas refined white-flour products with added sugar are placed in the outer circles. Fresh fruits and vegetables are in the bull's-eye, but juiced vegetables and fruit that lose fiber and concentrate sugar are, therefore, placed in a ring farther from the bull's-eye. Skim milk, low-fat and non-fat cottage cheese, and part-skim mozzarella go in the center ring, whereas whole milk and most cheeses are in the outer circles of the target.

## GOOD NUTRITIONAL HABITS

The principles of moderation, selectivity, variety, and balance are the keys to healthy eating: reduce the size of portions; consume less sugar, animal fats, and salt; and consume more fiber including a balance of vegetables, fruits, and whole grain breads and cereals.

Although 95% of the American people believe good nutrition to be based on these principles (American Dietetic Association, 1990), they

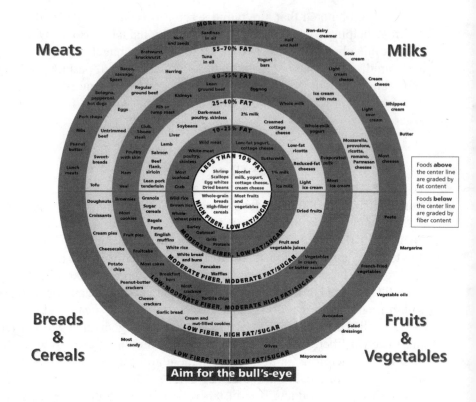

**FIGURE 5.2**

find them easier to endorse than to practice. However, in recent years, some progress has been made. The Department of Agriculture reports that people are consuming less sugar, switching from whole to low-fat milk, replacing red meat with fish and poultry, and eating fewer eggs (Sarafino, 1990).

Diet is only one component in the development of disease (heredity, environment, and lifestyle also play a part), but eating and drinking habits have been implicated in 6 of the 10 leading causes of death—heart disease, cancer, stroke, diabetes, atherosclerosis, and liver disease as well as in several debilitating disorders like osteoporosis and diverticulosis ("Are You Eating Right?" 1992).

# BASIC NUTRIENTS

Nutrients are substances in food that build and maintain body tissues and are necessary for bodily function. Nutrition education helps us learn how to provide our bodies with the more than 40 nutrients they need. Good dietary habits help us feel energetic, whereas poor nutrition contributes to feelings of fatigue and weakness. In addition, good nutrition helps us to avoid obesity and other health problems.

The basic categories of nutrients are fats, carbohydrates, proteins, fiber, water, vitamins, and minerals. Carbohydrates—sugars (simple carbohydrates) and starches (complex carbohydrates)—are our main source of energy. Fats provide a reserve of energy. Proteins are needed for the growth and repair of tissues. Fibers aid in the regulation of bowel function. Water—the main ingredient in the body—provides the proper environment for the body's processes, which vitamins and minerals help to control and regulate (Hurley, 1992). Large quantities of fat, carbohydrates, proteins, fiber, and water, and small quantities of vitamins and minerals, are needed by the body.

## FAT

The highest percentage of doctor visits, short-stay hospital visits, and bed disability days can be attributed to cardiovascular diseases like heart disease, hypertension, atherosclerosis, and angina. Ischemic heart disease is the leading cause of death in the U.S., accounting for 490,000 deaths in 1993 (National Center for Health Statistics, 1994).

Between 1970 and 1985, the annual number of deaths from heart disease declined by 39% (*Medical Tribune*, 1989). Public education has been given much of the credit for this decline; Americans have not only become more knowledgeable about the risk factors for heart disease—smoking, high blood pressure, sodium, obesity, cholesterol, and fats—but began to do something about them.

The American public has become particularly well informed about fat. In 1984, 8% of Americans considered fat their greatest dietary concern; by 1992, 48% designated it their major concern. Many Americans mistakenly believe cholesterol to be the chief health problem in their diet, yet only fat, not cholesterol, has been implicated in both heart disease and cancer (Hurley, 1992).

Fat has a stronger effect than dietary cholesterol in raising blood cholesterol and increasing vulnerability to heart disease. Dietary cholesterol inhibits to some extent the amount of cholesterol our bodies produce, a compensatory mechanism that helps keep blood cholesterol levels in check. Only 20% of the population is very sensitive to cholesterol-rich diets ("Are You Eating Right?" 1992).

Fat is an essential part of our diet and a major source of energy, but most Americans consume too much of it. According to data from the U.S. Department of Agriculture's food consumption survey, the average consumption of fat was 33% of total calories in 1994, down from 40% in the 1970s but above the recommended limit of 30%. In recent years, nutritionists have been recommending a daily fat intake of 20% to 25% (Hoeger & Hoeger, 1997).

Strong evidence indicates that high-fat diets cause obesity and increase the risk of heart disease and cancer. Yet food manufacturers are not in the business of helping us reduce the fat in our diet. They may, in fact, even be willing to fool us. Foods labeled cholesterol free, for instance, may still be high in fat; examples are peanut butter, cookies, nuts, granola, vegetable shortening, and oils.

Another way to fool the public is through hydrogenated fats or trans–fatty acids, which are similar to saturated fats in that the hydrogenation process makes the fats artificially hard at room temperature, and in the fact that they raise blood cholesterol about as much as saturated fats ("Trans: The Phantom Fat," 1996). The way the public gets fooled is that this type of fat does not have to be listed on food labels. The only way to determine trans–fat content is through a chemist in a laboratory.

The advantage of margarine over butter, for instance, was seriously compromised when it was discovered that margarine relied heavily on trans–fatty acids. Although it is pretty clear that both butter and margarine are bad for you, it is unclear at this time which is worse ("Trans: The Phantom Fat," 1996; Willet et al., 1997). The Center for Science in the Public Interest has been petitioning the FDA to count trans-fat as saturated fat on food labels, and to ban claims of low-cholesterol and low-saturated fat on foods that are high in trans–fatty acid ("Trans: The Phantom Fat," 1996).

## NOT ALL FATS ARE CREATED EQUAL

In 1997 the Mediterranean diet became very popular as Americans discovered that the countries along the Mediterranean had among the lowest rates of coronary heart disease and many common cancers in the Western world. This near-vegetarian diet was high on bread, potatoes, fruit, vegetables, wine, and olive oil, and low on meat, fish, cheese, butter, and margarine.

Surprisingly, the diet was not low in fat, with more than 35% of calories coming from fat—primarily olive oil, which consists mostly of monounsaturated fat. Thus, Americans began to extol the virtues of olive oil and other monounsaturated fats like canola and nut oils.

Monounsaturated fats are the best types of fat because they slightly lower low-density lipoprotein (LDL) (bad cholesterol) but leave the beneficial high-density lipoprotein (HDL) (good cholesterol) in tact or may even raise it a little (U.S. Department of Agriculture, 1997). Polyunsaturated fats, like sunflower and safflower oil, lower LDL, but are less desirable because they slightly lower HDL as well. Saturated fats, solid at room temperature and contained in butter, cheese, and meats, are more damaging than the liquid fats.

Some researchers, therefore, are beginning to suggest that we should be less concerned about overall fat content and more concerned about what types of fat we eat (Hu et al., 1997). Wolk and colleagues (1998), in fact, conducted animal studies and reported that monounsaturated fat lowered the risk of breast cancer by 45%, and polyunsaturated fat raised it by 69%.

However, most nutritional experts fall far short of suggesting that total fat content is now irrelevant, provided we obtain most of it from monounsaturated fats. They point out that Mediterranean-style cooking is healthy not primarily because it emphasizes monounsaturated fats, but because it relies heavily on vegetables, grains, and beans. Moreover, the people in the Mediterranean countries also have benefited from being traditionally much more active than Americans are and burning off excess fat (Brody, 1998).

In 1996, the American Heart Association summed it up best when it amended its advice on dietary fat by suggesting that Americans emphasize monounsaturated fats but also pay attention to total fat. Every tablespoon of olive oil, for instance, supplies 120 calories—and excessive weight raises the risk of heart disease, cancer, and diabetes.

## CALCULATING FAT CONTENT

Fat is more fattening than protein or carbohydrates; each gram of fat contains 9 calories compared with 4 in protein and carbohydrates. Although fat substitutes, like NutraSweet's Simplesse and Procter & Gamble's Olestra, may eventually overcome their unpleasant side effects, the major strategy for controlling weight today remains the limitation of total fats consumed, to 30% or less of total calories.

The formula for computing the percentage of total calories in foods that come from fat is as follows:

1. Multiply the number of grams of fat in a food by 9 (each gram of fat in a food contains 9 calories).
2. Then divide the result by the number of calories per serving.

Thus, a food that is advertised as being 97% *fat free* can be much fattier than it implies, depending on the percentage of calories per serving that consist of fat (Hurley, 1992). A cup of whole milk with 8 grams of fat, for instance, may be advertised as 97% fat free. Using the preceding formula, however, 8 grams is multiplied by 9 (72) and then divided by the number of calories per serving (150). Thus, 48% of the calories in whole milk come from fat. In 2% milk, 38% of the calories come from fat (still a high-fat food, despite the low-fat label on the carton), and in 1% milk, 18% of the calories come from fat.

The 30% rule does not forbid specific high-fat products every time we eat. Occasionally, we can indulge in high-fat milk or ice cream, as long as we balance them with low-fat foods that lower our average fat intake to 30% of daily calories. This can be accomplished by eating more fruits and vegetables (which have practically no fat) and fewer foods that are all fat (butter and margarine, for instance). The same is true of special days, like birthdays and holidays, when high amounts of fat are likely to be consumed. A steady diet that stays within the guidelines for fat consumption on other days will help to average out "exceptional" days.

Using low-fat products can lower fat intake. Many of these products may not be to our taste, but others probably are. In 1990 alone, nearly 1,000 new food products were introduced to the American public ("Are You Eating Right?" 1992). If appetizing low-fat foods cannot be found, we can lower fat content by avoiding deep-fried foods; choosing lean cuts of meat; trimming visible fat from meat; and baking, broiling, or roasting rather than frying food.

The number of allowable grams of fat per day can be calculated by estimating the *number of calories consumed per day* (2,000 calories, for example), *multiplying by .3* (to reach the goal of 30% of total calories, in this instance, 600), and *dividing by 9* (because each gram of fat contains 9 calories), producing the number of grams (approximately 67 in this example) of allowable fat. A much simpler technique (and much rougher approximation) is dividing your ideal weight (let's say 160 pounds) in half and allowing yourself that number (80) of grams of fat.

## CHOLESTEROL

Cholesterol received a great deal of public attention during the 1980s. The Multiple Risk Factor Intervention Trial added to this attention by evaluating a program that included lowering cholesterol and blood pressure levels among its goals. After 6 years, the men in the treatment group of this sample of 350,000 had lower cholesterol levels than did those in the control group (Stamler et al., 1986). More significant, the risk of mortality for heart disease or stroke was three to four times higher among the study subjects who had cholesterol levels over 245 mg than among those with levels under 180 mg.

In 1985, the National Heart, Lung and Blood Institute (NHLBI) set up the National Cholesterol Education Program (NCEP). The NCEP reported that 60 million American adults, including 24 million aged 60 and older, have borderline or high cholesterol levels. Because heart disease and stroke rise sharply with the cholesterol count, a federal campaign to lower the cholesterol level was launched.

The implications of the research findings on cholesterol for older adults were still far from clear during the 1990s. One major limit to the studies that linked heart disease risk to cholesterol level was the lack of evidence determining whether data on middle-aged men can be extrapolated to older persons (and women in general), who have been studied much less extensively.

Some experts, like P. J. Palumbo, MD, director of clinical nutrition at the Mayo Clinic in Rochester, Minnesota, endorse the popularly held belief of many health professionals that older persons can tolerate a higher level of cholesterol than the general adult population (*AARP Bulletin,* 1990).

Other experts, like William Castelli, MD, director of the Framingham Heart Study in Massachusetts, believe that older adults may be even more vulnerable than others to the effects of a high cholesterol level, and the standards should be more, not less, stringent (*AARP Bulletin,* 1990).

The Cholesterol Reduction in Seniors Program, sponsored by the NHLBI, is a study-in-progress that will attempt to resolve the issue. Meanwhile, older adults should follow the advice of their physicians.

Cholesterol is a lipid, a waxy, white, fatty substance that is manufactured by the liver and supplemented through the diet. Excess cholesterol can cling to the interior walls of the arteries and restrict the flow of blood to the heart. Eventually, it can narrow the passage sufficiently so that a heart attack results.

Two types of proteins, called lipoproteins, carry LDL and HDL. Researchers believe that LDL carries cholesterol toward the body cells, leading to plaque build-up and that HDL carries cholesterol away from the cells to the liver to be further processed and excreted (Sarafino, 1990). Exercise and smoking cessation will increase the good HDL lipids in your blood.

The definition of an acceptable blood cholesterol level in older persons has engendered considerable controversy. It is not known whether high cholesterol levels in late life should be lowered and, if so, how much and by what means. In the absence of definitive research, cholesterol levels of 240 mg/dL or higher should not be taken lightly.

The first step after obtaining a high cholesterol score should be a repetition of the test. Cholesterol scores, even from reliable labs, vary, and many laboratories measure cholesterol levels inaccurately. If the score on a second test is also high, the HDL and LDL levels should be examined. HDL and LDL levels are better predictors of heart disease than is total cholesterol level.

The recommended ratio between the total cholesterol level and the HDL level should be 4.2 or less for middle-aged and older persons, with an HDL goal of 45 or above and an LDL goal of 130 or below (Cooper, 1988–1989). A dietary change that reduces cholesterol and saturated fat can lower harmful LDL cholesterol, but only exercise and a reduction in body fat (as well as quitting smoking) can raise the HDL cholesterol (Evans et al., 1991).

Researchers at the Lawrence Berkeley National Laboratory are working on the latest iteration of cholesterol analysis. Pattern B (small dense LDL particles) has been identified and appears to be much more dangerous than pattern A (mostly large LDL particles). The more compact pattern B particles are more efficient at dumping their fat inside your arteries and, consequently, increasing the risk of triggering coronary disease threefold. Pattern B can be lowered by exercise, a reduction in refined carbohydrates and saturated fat, or medication.

Although the research is still in progress, a physician can mail samples of a client's blood to the Berkeley HeartLab (800-432-7889) for analysis. Typical health insurance covers half of the $300 fee.

## CARBOHYDRATES AND FIBER

Carbohydrates are the starches (complex carbohydrates) and sugars (simple carbohydrates) in our diet. Complex carbohydrates are found most commonly in breads, dry beans, potatoes, grains, pasta, carrots, peas, and corn. Many older adults have subscribed for years to the myth that complex carbohydrates, especially bread and potatoes, are fattening. In fact, they are moderate in calories and rich in nutrients.

Currently, 46% of the current American diet consists of carbohydrates; nutritionists recommend that this be increased to 55% to 60%. We can calculate our carbohydrate needs by multiplying our estimated daily caloric intake by 55% and dividing by 4 (4 calories are derived from each gram of carbohydrate versus 9 calories from each gram of fat). Thus, if 2,000 calories are consumed per day, 1,100 calories (55%), or 275 grams (divide by 4), of carbohydrates are needed.

Grains are the seed-bearing fruits of edible grasses. Each kernel of grain has a nutritionally dense "germ" or seed at its core, and a layer of bran surrounds the kernel itself. When grains are refined into white flour, white rice, and so forth, a process that began in the 1940s, the bran and germ of the whole-wheat kernel are removed through the milling process, losing fiber, vitamins, and minerals, but not fat content.

The term *whole grain* means that the kernels are unrefined, still containing the germ and the protective bran coating. The germ provides fiber, B vitamins, and vitamin E; the bran contains fiber. The most familiar whole grains are wheat, barley, oats, rye, rice, and corn, and the uncooked grains can be added to boiling water or simmering soup. When whole grains are a regular part of the diet, the risk for colon cancer and heart disease declines (Blumenthal et al., 1996; Rimm et al., 1996).

Conversely, when grains are ingested exclusively in the form of mashed potatoes, white rice, and other processed foods that have little of their fiber left, the starch converts quickly to sugar. Thus, it is important to pay attention to Covert Bailey's (1996) smart eating bull's-eye. Just as all fats are not created equally, the same holds true for carbohydrates and other nutrients.

Vegetables and fruits are complex carbohydrates that are low in fat and high in fiber, vitamins, and minerals. The exceptions are items like olives, avocados, salads with high-fat dressing, and vegetables that are fried or seasoned with margarine or butter. Unfortunately, the most popular vegetable is french fries. Americans of all ages tend to eat less than half of the recommended amount of fruits, vegetables, and whole-grain cereals and breads.

Fiber is the indigestible residue of food (e.g., the husk, seeds, skin, stems, and cell walls) that passes through the bowel and is eliminated in the stool. It appears to have a positive effect on cholesterol reduction, though scientists do not know exactly how this works. Fiber is a natural laxative that promotes regularity, adds bulk to stool, absorbs water, and reduces the amount of time stool is in the bowels. A diet that is high in fiber is especially important in later years when constipation is likely to be a problem.

Older adults, in general, have increased the fiber in their diets because it is known to increase the regularity of bowel action. Nonetheless, only about 5% of American adults overall follow the National Cancer Institute's recommendation and eat at least 20 grams of fiber a day.

Some older adults still rely on laxatives that are costly and in the long run self-defeating because they create a "lazy bowel." Fiber supplements like Metamucil do not contain the essential nutrients found in high-fiber foods, and their anticancer benefits are questionable ("The Many Benefits of Fiber," 1996). Although laxatives and supplements are not effective complements to fiber, fluid intake is. In fact, fiber needs fluid to be effective, and about 64 ounces of water daily is recommended ("The Many Benefits of Fiber," 1996).

## SUGAR

Sugars (also referred to as fructose, glucose, dextrose, maltose, lactose, honey, syrup, and molasses) are carbohydrates. Some are naturally present in nutritious foods, such as fruit and milk, but a good many are added to foods. Added sugar provides calories that have no nutritional value (i.e., empty calories) while increasing the likelihood of dental caries. Natural sugar in fruit, vegetables, and dairy products differs from added sugar in that vitamins, minerals, and fiber accompany it.

Much of the sugar we ingest is hidden; 29% of Heinz Tomato Ketchup, 30% of Wishbone Russian salad dressing, 65% of Coffee-mate nondairy creamer, 51% of Shake and Bake, and a certain percentage of some unlikely foods like soups, spaghetti sauces, frozen dinners, yogurts, and breads, is sugar (Hurley, 1992).

Although it is recommended that the American population reduce its intake of added sugar from the current average of 11% of its calories to 5% ("Are You Eating Right?" 1992), the chief culprit in obesity is fat, not sugar. Fat has more calories than sugar (36 vs. 16 calories per teaspoon) and whereas obese people tend to eat more fat than thinner people do, they eat *less* sugar! In fact, if you maintain low-fat levels in your food and high complex carbohydrates levels, eating moderate amounts of sugar is not hazardous to your health unless you are a diabetic.

Consuming artificially sweetened foods or low-fat food products (that still have high sugar and high calorie content) is not as effective as many people think. Most of these individuals are just adding these foods to their diet and not lowering their overall caloric intake.

## PROTEIN

Proteins form antibodies, which help the body to resist disease and enable the growth and repair of body cells—organs, muscles, skin, bones, blood, and hair. Amino acids, the units from which proteins are constructed, are the end products of protein digestion. Complete protein foods contain, in proper amounts for adults, eight essential amino acids that must be available simultaneously for the body to synthesize protein properly. Fish, dairy products, and eggs (complete protein foods) contain all the essential amino acids.

Proteins from legumes, nuts, and cereals are incomplete; that is, they lack one or more essential amino acids. Vegetarians, therefore, must combine food sources (such as rice with beans) to meet their need for complete proteins.

Protein should account for an estimated 12% to 20% of the total calories in the diet (Moore & Nagle, 1990), and Americans tend to get at least that much. Older adults who are ill, however, are the most likely segment of society to experience protein deficiency. They suffer loss of appetite and oftentimes eat little, if any, meat because of the cost, denture problems, lack of ability or desire to cook, or philosophy. Protein deficiency in older adults can result in a lack of vigor or stamina, depression, poor resistance to infection, impaired healing of wounds, and slow recovery from disease.

WATER

Although we can get by without most nutrients for several weeks at a stretch, we cannot survive without water, even for a few days. Water is the medium in which all the reactions in cells occurs. Water lubricates joints, infuses digestive juices, and regulates body temperature. Nevertheless, adults tend to drink less than half the water they need, only about 3 cups a day. Aging reduces thirst perception and consequently water intake, resulting in constipation and fatigue. Therefore, it is important that older adults drink approximately 8 cups of fluids per day, regardless of thirst.

Dehydration in the elderly was responsible for an estimated 1.8 million days of hospital care at a cost to Medicare of at least $1.1 billion in 1991 (Weinberg & Minaker, 1995). The American Medical Association's Council of Scientific Affairs recommends that undergraduate, graduate, and continuing education programs for nurses, allied health professionals, and physicians include the importance of hydration in older adults ("AMA Urges Awareness of Dehydration in Elderly," 1995).

Water, juice, and milk meet hydration needs, but alcohol, caffeinated tea, coffee, and soft drinks do not; these beverages increase water output, resulting in little fluid gain.

Additional water required by the body is obtained from foods. More than 80% of many fruits and vegetables, more than 50% of meat, and about one third of bread consists of water.

## VITAMINS AND MINERALS

There are 13 vitamins: 4 fat soluble (A, D, E, and K) and 9 water soluble (C and 8 B vitamins). Surplus water-soluble vitamins are excreted in urine, but surplus fat-soluble vitamins are stored in body tissue, and excessive amounts can become toxic. The body is especially sensitive to too much vitamin A and D. Vitamins in the right amounts are needed for normal growth, digestion, mental alertness, and resistance to infection. The body also needs 15 minerals that help regulate cell function and provide structure for cells.

The National Research Council of the National Academy of Science provides Recommended Dietary Allowances (RDAs) for most vitamins, minerals, and proteins that we require. Originally published in 1943, these recommendations are updated every few years based on ongoing research findings.

Unfortunately, the RDAs are determined for only very broad age categories, with all people age 51 and older in a single group. Although we know that increasing age alters nutritional requirements, the council concluded that insufficient data were available to establish separate categories for older adults. Consequently, the RDAs, although revised and updated in 1989, failed to identify specifically the needs of older persons. The new guidelines, which appeared in 1998, have corrected this deficiency only in regard to vitamin D (see chapter 7 on dietary supplements).

The U.S. RDAs of vitamins and minerals (1989) are shown in Table 5.1.

To increase vitamins and minerals, Table 5.2 (Covert & Bailey, 1996) identifies the best food group source.

**TABLE 5.1   U.S. RDAs for Vitamins and Minerals**

| Vitamin/mineral | RDA | Vitamin/mineral | RDA |
|---|---|---|---|
| Vitamin A | 5000 IU | Riboflavin (B-2) | 1.7 mg |
| Vitamin C | 60 mg | Niacin (a B vitamin) | 20 mg |
| Vitamin D | 400 IU | Pantothenic acid (B) | 10 mg |
| Vitamin E | 30 IU | Vitamin B-12[a] | 6 mcg |
| Iron | 10 mg | Biotin (B) | .3 mg |
| Thiamin (B-1) | 1.5 mg | Magnesium[a] | 350 mg |
| Phosphorus[a] | 800 mg | Zinc[a] | 15 mg |
| Calcium[a] | 1200 mg | Vitamin B-6[a] | 2 mg |
| Folacin[a] (B) | .4 mg | | |

[a]Most likely to be *inadequately* supplied in the diets of older adults, according to a review of 90 dietary surveys of the noninstitutionalized (Horwath, 1991). In 1998, it was revealed that vitamin D has been inadequately consumed as well (see chapter 7 on Dietary Supplements).

**TABLE 5.2   Best Food Group Source**

| To increase vitamins and minerals | Eat more from this food group |
|---|---|
| Protein, iron, niacin | Meats and beans |
| Calcium, riboflavin, protein | Milks |
| B vitamins | Breads and cereals |
| Vitamin C and A | Fruits and vegetables |

Two minerals of particular nutritional importance for the aging body are sodium chloride (salt) and calcium.

## SODIUM AND HIGH BLOOD PRESSURE

Sodium keeps muscles and nerves working properly and attracts water, thereby helping us retain the proper amount of body fluid. However, too much sodium in the system causes the body to retain excess water, increases the blood pressure level, and makes the heart work harder.

Americans consume twice the recommended amount of sodium (about 2,400 mg, a single teaspoon of salt) each day. Because many foods already contain high levels of sodium (such as potato chips, processed meats, frozen dinners, ketchup, most sauces, and canned foods), and it is hidden in a wide variety of other foods as well, we get plenty of salt (40% sodium and 60% chlorine) in our diet without adding more.

Adding salt to foods, although widely practiced, is unhealthy. Nonetheless, about half the women who prepared meals used salt when preparing food, and about one third used salt at the table (AARP, 1992). Because sensitivity to flavor and odors decrease with age, the desire to use salt to counteract blandness may increase with age.

Most Americans associate sodium intake with high blood pressure, yet the percentage of Americans whose high blood pressure can be attributed to salt sensitivity is unknown. In the absence of definitive research findings, many registered dietitians recommend that sodium reduction be practiced widely. Nevertheless, because it is difficult to determine unequivocally whether an individual is salt sensitive, it may be useful to alternately restrict salt and remove salt restrictions, for specified periods, to assess its impact on blood pressure levels.

Salt restriction is recommended for the elderly, for people whose blood pressure is elevated significantly (Grobbee & Hofman, 1986), for people with a family history of high blood pressure, and for Blacks, who are more likely to be highly sensitive to excess sodium (Public Health Service, 1988).

The amount of salt used in cooking should be reduced for many people and the salt shaker removed from the table. Some foods, which contain large amounts of salt, should be avoided altogether. Labels should be read for sodium content, and people should be made aware that sodium content may be indicated by complex names (e.g., monosodium glutamate).

From 1996 to 1998, the leading medical journals published several articles that offered contradictory conclusions. *The British Medical Journal* (Elliot et al., 1996) and *JAMA* (Whelton et al., 1998) concluded that the traditional association between salt intake and blood pressure is accurate, and monitoring salt intake is still important. Moreover, the relationship appears to be stronger in middle-aged persons than in young adults. In addition, other evidence indicates that salt increases calcium excretion, which raises the risk of osteoporosis (Devine et al., 1995).

*The Lancet* (Alderman & Cohen, 1998) and *JAMA* (Midgley et al., 1996), however, concluded that low-salt diets had virtually no effect on people with normal blood pressure, making low-salt diets irrelevant to most of the population. This finding supports the skepticism of many physicians. In a study of 418 primary physicians in Massachusetts, only 13% considered decreasing dietary salt to be very important for the average person in 1994, versus 40% in 1981 (Wechsler et al., 1996). The study did not, however, survey physicians on whether they recommended other strategies that may be more effective for keeping blood pressure in check, such as weight reduction, exercise, increasing potassium intake from fruits and vegetables, and reducing alcohol consumption.

## CALCIUM AND OSTEOPOROSIS

Calcium is essential for maintaining bone strength. If the amount of calcium contained in the diets of older adults is inadequate, the body takes calcium from the bones and uses it for other purposes. When people lose calcium from their bones, or their body's ability to absorb calcium is reduced (a process associated with age, and exacerbated by the excess use of such products as mineral-oil laxatives, caffeine, and alcohol), bones become more brittle and fragile.

This condition, characterized by low bone mass, which increases the risk of fracture from ordinary skeletal stress, is known as osteoporosis. Over the years, the bones of a person who has osteoporosis gradually thin, until some break, causing pain and disability. This process increases around menopause because of falling hormone levels.

One in four women over age 60, and nearly half of all people over age 75, suffer from osteoporosis. In addition to age and gender, other risk factors for osteoporosis include being female, being White or Asian, experiencing early menopause, having a family history of osteoporosis, having fair skin or a small frame, smoking, and inadequate weight-bearing exercise or calcium intake.

Approximately 1.3 million fractures each year may be attributable to osteoporosis (National Institute of Arthritis and Musculoskeletal and Skin Diseases [NIAMSD], 1991), a condition that affects older adults, especially women (4 to 1 over men), disproportionately. Osteoporosis most frequently affects the vertebra (of about 500,000 people, yearly), hip (250,000), or wrist (170,000).

Of all fractures, a fracture of the hip is one of the most devastating. A person's expectations for survival are reduced, overall, by 12% to 20% during the 6 months following a hip fracture. Twenty percent of the individuals who fracture their hips need to enter long-term care institutions shortly afterward (NIAMSD, 1991). A third of all women sustain hip fractures by age 75 (Sainsbury & Hanger, 1991).

Adult women consume about 500 mg/day of dietary calcium, considerably less than the 800 mg/day recommended for postadolescent females (Moore & Nagle, 1990). Postmenopausal women are advised to increase calcium intake to 1,500 mg/day (Heaney, 1993; "Calcium and Vitamin D," 1996), an amount difficult to achieve without a supplement. One doctor (personal communication) recommended taking Tums or Rolaids in lieu of a standard calcium supplement because they are essentially pure calcium carbonate and may be cheaper, more palatable, and less apt to produce uncomfortable side effects like nausea than other calcium supplements.

Five antacid tablets daily (well below maximum daily dosage warnings on the label) provides 1,000 mg of elemental calcium, leaving only 500 mg needed from the diet. Taking two tablets at a time *between* meals is preferable as the fiber and starch in vegetables and whole wheat bread will bind the calcium, making much of it unavailable.

The most common sources of calcium are dairy products, fortified foods, and dark green leafy vegetables (kale and broccoli, but not spinach). Older adults who are lactose intolerant may need to use lactose-free milk products, take a lactase pill with milk products, or decrease their intake of milk products and take a calcium supplement.

Weight-bearing exercise also helps to maintain strong bones by increasing bone mineral density and reducing calcium loss. The positive effect of exercise, however, appears to be lost within a relatively short period if the exercise program is discontinued (Fiatarone et al., 1990).

For information and resource materials on osteoporosis that is targeted to health care professionals or to the public, contact the National Osteoporosis Foundation, 2100 M Street NW, Suite 602, Washington, DC 20037; 202-223-2226.

## MALNUTRITION, UNDERWEIGHT, AND NUTRITION SCREENING

Approximately 30% of Americans older than age 65 ("Malnutrition, Food Intake in Elderly Studied," 1995; "Your Elderly Patients May Be Hungry or Malnourished," 1993) are underweight or malnourished. These older adults take 40% longer to recover from illness, have two to three times more complications, and have hospital stays that are 90% longer. Risk factors include inappropriate food intake, poverty, social isolation, chronic disease or condition, chronic medication use, and advanced age.

The link between malnutrition, underweight, and lifestyle is strong and suggests that "encouraging participation in various activities and clubs, as well as sharing meals with friends or neighbors may be far more effective in improving dietary intake than simple dietary advice" (Horwath, 1991).

Men living alone consume fewer fruits and vegetables and have a much greater propensity for selecting easy-to-prepare foods that are high in fat and low in complex carbohydrates than do those who have companions (Horwath, 1989). Loneliness, bereavement, and social isolation are associated with poor dietary intake in late life (Horwath, 1991).

About 5% of men and 9% of women who are age 65 or older report difficulty in preparing meals; the percentage increases fourfold after age 85 (Davis et al., 1985). Many elderly individuals depend on meals prepared at the congregate nutrition sites or Meals-on-Wheels programs. As the demand for services of this type increases along with the number of frail, very old adults, the number of services will also need to increase—but are unlikely to do so.

Nutrition screenings examine characteristics known to be associated with dietary and nutritional problems to identify high-risk individuals. One such screening initiative, a collaborative project by the American Academy of Family Physicians, the American Dietetic Association, and the National Council on the Aging, Inc., resulted in the production of a manual that begins with a "DETERMINE Your Nutritional Health" checklist. DETERMINE is the acronym for the characteristics known to be associated with dietary and nutritional problems. These characteristics are included in Figures 5.3 and 5.4.

The manual includes a variety of screening tools on nutrition and related topics, including body mass index, eating habits, functional status,

*The Warning Signs of poor nutritional health are often overlooked. Use this checklist to find out if you or someone you know is at nutritional risk.*

# DETERMINE YOUR NUTRITIONAL HEALTH

Read the statements below. Circle the number in the yes column for those that apply to you or someone you know. For each yes answer, score the number in the box. Total your nutritional score.

|  | YES |
|---|---|
| I have an illness or condition that made me change the kind and/or amount of food I eat. | 2 |
| I eat fewer than 2 meals per day. | 3 |
| I eat few fruits or vegetables, or milk products. | 2 |
| I have 3 or more drinks of beer, liquor or wine almost every day. | 2 |
| I have tooth or mouth problems that make it hard for me to eat. | 2 |
| I don't always have enough money to buy the food I need. | 4 |
| I eat alone most of the time. | 1 |
| I take 3 or more different prescribed or over-the-counter drugs a day. | 1 |
| Without wanting to, I have lost or gained 10 pounds in the last 6 months. | 2 |
| I am not always physically able to shop, cook and/or feed myself. | 2 |
| **TOTAL** | |

## Total Your Nutritional Score. If it's —

**0-2**    **Good!** Recheck your nutritional score in 6 months.

**3-5**    **You are at moderate nutritional risk.** See what can be done to improve your eating habits and lifestyle. Your office on aging, senior nutrition program, senior citizens center or health department can help. Recheck your nutritional score in 3 months.

**6 or more**    **You are at high nutritional risk.** Bring this checklist the next time you see your doctor, dietitian or other qualified health or social service professional. Talk with them about any problems you may have. Ask for help to improve your nutritional health.

*These materials developed and distributed by the Nutrition Screening Initiative, a project of:*

AMERICAN ACADEMY OF FAMILY PHYSICIANS

THE AMERICAN DIETETIC ASSOCIATION

NCOA NATIONAL COUNCIL ON THE AGING, INC.

**Remember that warning signs suggest risk, but do not represent diagnosis of any condition. Turn the page to learn more about the Warning Signs of poor nutritional health.**

**FIGURE 5.3   Determine your nutritional health.**

**The Nutrition Checklist is based on the Warning Signs described below.
Use the word DETERMINE to remind you of the Warning Signs.**

# Disease

Any disease, illness or chronic condition which causes you to change the way you eat, or makes it hard for you to eat, puts your nutritional health at risk. Four out of five adults have chronic diseases that are affected by diet. Confusion or memory loss that keeps getting worse is estimated to affect one out of five or more of older adults. This can make it hard to remember what, when or if you've eaten. Feeling sad or depressed, which happens to about one in eight older adults, can cause big changes in appetite, digestion, energy level, weight and well-being.

# Eating Poorly

Eating too little and eating too much both lead to poor health. Eating the same foods day after day or not eating fruit, vegetables, and milk products daily will also cause poor nutritional health. One in five adults skip meals daily. Only 13% of adults eat the minimum amount of fruit and vegetables needed. One in four older adults drink too much alcohol. Many health problems become worse if you drink more than one or two alcoholic beverages per day.

# Tooth Loss/ Mouth Pain

A healthy mouth, teeth and gums are needed to eat. Missing, loose or rotten teeth or dentures which don't fit well or cause mouth sores make it hard to eat.

# Economic Hardship

As many as 40% of older Americans have incomes of less than $6,000 per year. Having less--or choosing to spend less--than $25-30 per week for food makes it very hard to get the foods you need to stay healthy.

# Reduced Social Contact

One-third of all older people live alone. Being with people daily has a positive effect on morale, well-being and eating.

# Multiple Medicines

Many older Americans must take medicines for health problems. Almost half of older Americans take multiple medicines daily. Growing old may change the way we respond to drugs. The more medicines you take, the greater the chance for side effects such as increased or decreased appetite, change in taste, constipation, weakness, drowsiness, diarrhea, nausea, and others. Vitamins or minerals when taken in large doses act like drugs and can cause harm. Alert your doctor to everything you take.

# Involuntary Weight Loss/Gain

Losing or gaining a lot of weight when you are not trying to do so is an important warning sign that must not be ignored. Being overweight or underweight also increases your chance of poor health.

# Needs Assistance in Self Care

Although most older people are able to eat, one of every five have trouble walking, shopping, buying and cooking food, especially as they get older.

# Elder Years Above Age 80

Most older people lead full and productive lives. But as age increases, risk of frailty and health problems increase. Checking your nutritional health regularly makes good sense.

**The Nutrition Screening Initiative, 2626 Pennsylvania Avenue, NW, Suite 301, Washington, DC 20037**

© The Nutrition Screening Initiative is funded in part by a grant from Ross Laboratories, a division of Abbott Laboratories.

**FIGURE 5.4   DETERMINE.**

cognitive status, and depression. To order copies of this manual, contact: Nutrition Screening Manual for Professionals Caring for Older Americans, Nutrition Screening Initiative, 2626 Pennsylvania Avenue NW, Suite 301, Washington, DC 20037.

When clients lose their appetite, suggest the following: eat smaller, more frequent meals; take advantage of times when you feel good and are hungry, regardless of the time; eat higher-calorie foods or consider taking a nutritional supplement; postpone beverages toward the end of a meal; create a pleasant eating atmosphere, and find company to enjoy the meal with; and see a physician to either change a medication that is affecting appetite, or add a medication that relives nausea, heartburn, or other symptoms that occur when you eat ("Loss of Appetite," 1997).

## PROFESSIONAL INVOLVEMENT

Although convincing data on nutrition counseling of clients by health professionals is lacking, the Healthy People 2000 Midcourse Review suggests that about 30% of health professionals offered such counseling to clients in 1992, with no indication that this percentage increased by 1995.

Some advocates believe the percentage is much lower than 30% and question whether federal assessments really measure serious attempts by health professionals to analyze clients' diets, or whether they include the offer of a passing comment or two. Michael Jacobson (1992), director of the Center for Science in the Public Interest, estimates that only 5% of physicians offer genuine nutrition counseling.

Dietary counsel by nurses, physicians, allied health professionals, registered dietitians, and nutritionists can be effective in reducing the fat intake of clients and, subsequently, their serum cholesterol levels (Caggiula et al., 1987). Yet only one in four clients reported occasional discussions of "eating proper foods" during routine visits to a doctor or other health professional (National Center for Health Statistics, 1988).

Physician referrals to qualified nutritionists or dietitians for counseling are also not common (Lewis, 1988). The importance of referrals is substantiated by a survey of Massachusetts's primary care physicians. Only 35% reported being "very prepared" to counsel patients in nutrition themselves, and only 7% reported feeling "very successful" (Wechsler et al., 1983). Wechsler and colleagues (1996) did a follow-up survey 13 years later and found that physicians are even less attentive to their patients' diet than they were in the past.

If diet or health advice is provided by a visibly overweight doctor, nurse, or dietitian, almost half of the Americans (45%) surveyed in a national Gallup poll would either fail to take the advice seriously or be inclined to ignore it (Hurley, 1992).

The *Physician's Guide to Outpatient Nutrition* (Moore & Nagle, 1990) provides a simple nutritional guide for the busy health practitioner (non-physicians as well) to administer to clients. The first step is the administration of a simple survey to determine what the client eats during a particular day. The second step is a quick analysis of what the client eats in the four food groups, plus sweets, fats, and beverages. The third step is writing a nutrition prescription and discussing it with the client. The fourth step is follow-up and assessing progress on subsequent visits.

The *Guide* provides a "Guide to Healthy Food Choices," and a "Nutrition Prescription" form for the practitioner to duplicate and use (see Figures 5.5 and 5.6).

## QUACKERY

The following list of the characteristics of good nutritionists should help in distinguishing them from quacks. Good nutritionists individualize a plan and make sure that fat is limited, and complex carbohydrates and fiber emphasized. Good nutritionists encourage lifelong changes that include regular exercise, ongoing behavior management techniques, and identification of sources of emotional support to help clients sustain changes in their eating habits. Good nutritionists advocate consumption of a wide variety of foods and suggest supplements primarily when needs cannot be met through diet. Good nutritionists do not promise cures and do consult with physicians on medical matters. Good nutritionists are likely to have earned a degree from a 4-year accredited college or university; are registered dietitians (RD), which requires passing a national examination; and have enrolled in the requisite number of continuing nutrition education credits on an ongoing basis.

Quacks, conversely, rely on testimonials, are not shy about promising to cure a disease, typically foresee quick results, often emphasize one or two food groups, encourage megadoses of vitamins, and denigrate other people's ideas—even those based on scientific evidence.

Want a qualified nutritionist to design a healthy eating plan for you or your client? Call the National Center for Nutrition and Dietetic's Consumer Hotline, at 800-366-1655, to find an adviser in your area.

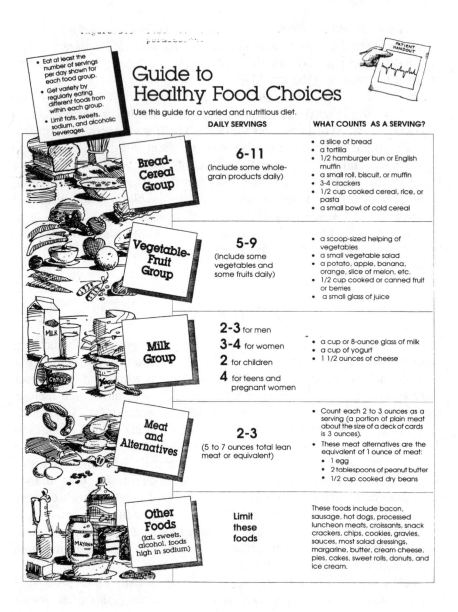

**FIGURE 5.5   Guide to healthy food choices.**

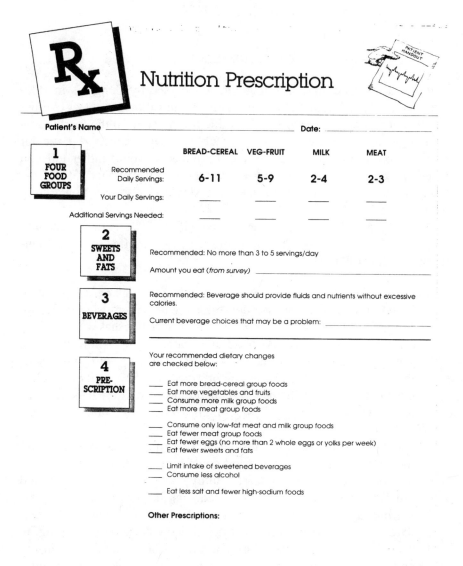

FIGURE 5.6   Nutrition prescription.

## MISCELLANEOUS

### NUTRITION LABELS

The Nutrition Labeling and Education Act passed by Congress in 1990 requires that the FDA make food labels more educational and less confusing. The major controversy regarding this law arose from the food industry's reluctance to include the percentage of a daily value for particular nutrients on a label. In other words, the industry would rather tell you that a frozen pizza contains 20 g of fat than that it contains 25% of the total fat that you should consume in a single day ("Are You Eating Right?" 1992).

After 2 years of debate and controversy (1990–1992), consumers won out over the food industry. The following rules were drafted for implementation in May 1994:

1. Terms like *low fat*, *reduced calorie*, *light*, and *high calorie* must be based on federally imposed definitions, with serving sizes uniform. Many food labels implied positive characteristics that were, in fact, meaningless (e.g., "lite," "natural," "pure," and "whole grains"). The term *light* could refer to color or flavor, or something other than fat, such as salt. Now, "light" means a 50% reduction from that which existed in the original product. Additional definitions are provided for "free," "low," "high," "source of," and "reduced" or "less."

2. Health or medical claims must be backed by solid research. In 1996, the FDA reported that any food containing 13 g of oat bran or 20 g of oatmeal can carry a heart-healthy claim provided that the food did not have other unhealthy ingredients like lots of fat or salt.

3. All packaged foods must have a standard nutrient chart, with standardized portions to make nutritional and calorie data meaningful. The chart must include information on calories, calories from fat, and the amounts of fat, saturated fat, cholesterol, carbohydrates, protein, and sodium. The label must include percentage of the total that someone on a 2,000- or 2,500-calorie diet should have for the day.

Despite the labeling law, there are still serious gaps in the area of nutritional labels, especially when it comes to ground beef. In 1997, ground beef accounted for 45% of the meat sold in the United States. This product added more saturated fat to the average American's diet than any other single food. Yet a package of ground beef, which can provide *14 g of fat in a single serving*, can have an "85% lean" label on it. This label falsely implies that the product is, for the most part, lean.

## ENRICHED AND FORTIFIED FOODS

When nutrients lost through processing are replaced, the food is labeled "enriched." When nutrients normally present are added to exceed the natural amount, the food is labeled "fortified." Enriched and fortified foods are not necessarily good substitutes for the foods or drinks being replaced. The label may emphasize what is enriched or fortified (vitamin C in orange drink, for instance), but fail to say what nutrients from a more nutritious counterpart (like orange juice) are not being replaced.

## FAST FOODS

On any typical day, one in every five Americans eats at a fast-food restaurant (*Survival Guide*, 1988). Sixty percent of these diners worry about the nutritional value of the food, but an equal percentage believes that fast food is better than it was 10 years ago. One reason for this is the advent of salads in fast-food restaurants. McDonald's introduced salads in 1987, and salads accounted for 7 cents of every dollar spent at McDonald's throughout the year that followed.

Now, many fast-food restaurants offer healthy options, like a salad bar (though many consumers are not cautious when it comes to adding salad dressing), and the choice of broiled instead of fried meat. At Mexican restaurants, soft corn tortillas can be substituted for hard taco shells (0 versus 6 g of fat), and consumers can fill up with beans, salsa, and low-fat sour cream. At Chinese restaurants, health-conscious customers can choose stir-fry fresh or frozen vegetables served over brown rice.

Older adults often opt for the convenience of prepared, frozen microwavable meals. These foods can be high in fat, sodium, and cholesterol. Healthier options have been made available by Con Agra's chief executive officer, Mike Harper, who, after a heart attack, created Healthy Choice

Dinners. Stouffer's followed with a similar line of prepared microwavable meals, labeled Right Course.

## CONTAMINATED FOODS

Public health officials are concerned about pesticides and other contaminants in the foods that we purchase because they interfere with hormones that regulate how the body functions. Fruits and vegetables are the most likely foods to contain pesticides, with about half of those tested having pesticide residues on or in them ("Pesticide Exposure," 1997). Strawberries are by far the most contaminated fruit or vegetable. When it comes to lettuce and cabbage, washing, peeling skins, and removing the outer leaves are helpful in reducing residues. A shopper's guide to pesticides in produce is available on the World Wide Web (www.ewg.org).

Wheat, bread, and other grain products tend not to have residues because the milling process removes them. Pesticides are more likely to accumulate in fatty meats, fish, and dairy products than in their leaner counterparts. The biggest seafood hazard by far is raw or undercooked shellfish, which accounts for more than 90% of seafood poisoning cases ("Fishing for Safe Seafood," 1996). Contaminated seafood causes about 113,000 *reported* cases of food poisoning each year in the United States, according to the FDA, and countless unreported cases. To find out about meat and poultry food safety issues call the hotline—202-720-3333—weekdays 10:00 a.m. to 4:00 p.m., ET (DC residents call 202-720-3333).

## CAFFEINE

According to the *Mayo Clinic Health Letter* (July 1997), if you are going to have a vice, coffee is probably one of the least harmful—as long as you drink it in moderation. Caffeine is the stimulant that gives coffee its kick. Evidence that the caffeine in coffee causes serious health problems like cancer, cardiovascular disease, osteoporosis, and fibrocystic breast changes is weak and, if health problems are found in the research at all, at only very high levels of coffee consumption.

Less harmful, but nonetheless very annoying, problems like irritability, heartburn, and bladder or stomach ulcer irritations tend to occur when only large quantities of coffee, perhaps eight cups or more, are consumed during the day. If you want to reduce consumption, do it gradually or suffer short-lived withdrawal symptoms like headaches, or even nausea or depression.

Want to try a really bad idea? Drink caffeine-spiked water like $Krank_2O$, Aqua Blast, Aqua Java, and Water Joe, or caffeine-spiked juice drinks like Java Juice and Energy Booster, which range from 60 to 125 mg of caffeine and cost about a dollar a bottle. An 8-ounce cup of coffee has 135 mg of caffeine.

### SENSORY DECLINE

An age-related decline in the sense of smell (not taste) directly affects a person's ability to taste or enjoy food (Greeley, 1990). Older persons have more trouble identifying pureed foods, for instance, than do younger persons. If younger persons held their noses while eating, their ability to identify foods would drop to the level of older adults.

To enhance food aromas for older adults, herbs and spices should be encouraged. Adding flavors and sweeteners also can enhance taste. Another technique for stimulating appetite is a combination of different textures, for example, adding granola to yogurt.

Several simple ideas can make eating more appealing. Take TV dinners from their containers and place them on a dinner plate, sit beside a window, and enjoy the view while eating. Eat with a friend at least twice every week.

### SOCIOECONOMIC AND CULTURAL SENSITIVITY

In addition to the physiological changes that occur with age, health professionals need to be sensitive to the socioeconomic and cultural factors that influence their clients. For example, health professionals ought not to try to increase the protein consumption of low-income clients by recommending diets that contain expensive lean meat, fish, or poultry. Nor should health professionals recommend diets that completely ignore the food preferences of members of particular ethnic groups. Ethnic foods are a source of pride, identity, and fond memories. Every effort should be made to incorporate food preferences in nutritional planning.

### PROGRAMS

Diet Improvement and Nutrition Evaluation Systems, Inc. (DINE) produced a software program called DINE Right. After clients complete a

7-day food intake record, the software analyzes their diets to determine what foods they eat too much or too little of and suggests dietary changes based on age, height, gender, and activity level. The software was developed over a decade, with $3 million in grants from the National Institutes of Health. It can be purchased through the American College of Preventive Medicine, 1015 15th Street NW Suite #403, Washington, DC 20005.

At a lot less cost to consumers, individuals can log on to the World Wide Web and use, for free, the Nutritional Analysis Tool provided by the University of Illinois. Type in what you eat, click on the nutrients that interest you, identify your age and gender, and receive a free breakdown of your diet. The Web address is: www.spectre.ag.uiuc.edu/~food-lab/nat/.

The Farmer's Market Coupon Program for Low-Income Elders in Boston, Massachusetts, provides coupons that are redeemable for fresh fruits and vegetables at outdoor farmers' markets. The program promotes the consumption of fresh fruits and vegetables by elders, who traditionally are without access to them, and at the same time supporting direct marketing opportunities for small farmers. By 1991, the program served 16,000 older adults. For more information, contact the Division of Elderly Health, Massachusetts Department of Public Health, 150 Tremont Street, Boston, MA 02111.

The Center for Science in the Public Interest (CSPI) is an educational and advocacy organization. Its educational component consists of the *Nutrition Action Healthletter*, published monthly, and informs more than 800,000 subscribers, including this author. The organization is best known, however, for its advocacy accomplishments, under the leadership of its executive director and cofounder (in 1971), Michael Jacobson.

Jacobson and CSPI staff, for example, led the fight for nutrition labels on food items in the supermarket; for exposing the hidden fat in Chinese, Mexican, Italian, and delicatessen food; and for pressuring movie theaters to stop cooking popcorn in artery-clogging coconut oil. Current advocacy efforts are against Procter & Gamble's fake fat, Olestra, which Jacobson claims interferes with the absorption of nutrients and can cause loose stools and cramping, and for more accurate labeling of ground beef in supermarkets.

For more information, contact the Center for Science in the Public Interest, 1875 Connecticut Avenue, NW, Suite #300, Washington, DC 20009; 202-265-4954 (fax); www.cspinet.org.

## MATERIALS

The Society of Nutrition Education promotes nutrition education, collects and disseminates information and research findings about nutrition education, and publishes the *Journal of Nutrition Education*. Contact the Society of Nutrition Education, 1700 Broadway, Suite 300, Oakland, CA 94612.

The Agricultural Extension Service provides educational programs on nutrition, food safety, and food purchasing. Contact the U.S. Department of Agriculture, Extension Service, National Program Leader, Room 3443, Washington, DC 20250-0900.

To obtain newsletters on nutritional topics, contact the following:

Center for Science in the Public Interest, *Nutrition Action Health Letter*, 1875 Connecticut Avenue NW #300, Washington, DC 20009

*Environmental Nutrition: The Professional Newsletter of Diet, Nutrition and Health*, 2112 Broadway, New York, NY 10023

Mayo Foundation for Medical Education and Research, *Mayo Clinic Nutrition Letter*, 200 1st Street SW, Rochester, MN 55905

Diet, Nutrition and Cancer Prevention: The Good News, National Cancer Institute, Building 31, Room 10A24, Bethesda, MD 20892; 800-4-CANCER

National Center for Nutrition and Dietetics, 216 W. Jackson Boulevard, Suite 800, Chicago, IL 60606-6995

Consumer Nutrition Hotline: 800-366-1655

*Tufts University Health and Nutrition Letter*, P.O. Box 57857, Boulder, CO 80322-7857; 800-274-7581

*University of California Berkeley Wellness Letter*, P.O. Box 420148, Palm Coast, FL 32142.

## QUESTIONS FOR DISCUSSION

1. What are some important differences to consider when attempting to motivate an older versus a younger adult to change an eating habit?
2. Generally speaking, older adults are more conscious of their nutritional habits than younger adults. Conduct your own survey of five older and five younger adults, asking persons to rate how much attention they pay to eating what is good for them, using a scale of 1 (not very often) to 10 (all the time). Does your convenience

sample corroborate the positive relationship between age and good nutritional habits?

3. Can you list five examples in which changing a dietary habit may provide an acceptable alternative to taking a medication for a health problem?

4. Do you think the Nutrition Labeling and Education Act has had a significant impact on the dietary habits of Americans? Why?

# 6

# Weight Management

[T]o reduce obesity among adults age 20 to 74 from a prevalence of 26 percent (baseline, 1980) to 20 percent (Public health goals from the U.S. Public Health Service's Healthy People 2000 Initiative) (AARP, 1991)

From 1980 to 1992, obesity prevalence for adults age 20 to 74 *increased* from 26% to 34%. (*Healthy People 2000 Midcourse Review: 1995 Report on Progress*, DHHS, OPHS)

In 1995, the Louis Harris poll reported that an astonishing 71% of the American population over the age of 25 was overweight. Moreover, according to the national Harris surveys, the percentage of overweight adults in America increased during every survey over a 12-year period (1983–1995). This surprising epidemic has escalated despite the fact that excess weight was widely known to be a risk factor for disease and death; that obesity has been a social stigma in our society and has continued to offend most people's personal vanity; and that a health revolution supposedly occurred in America during the past 15 years.

It does appear that some type of health revolution has occurred in America during the past 15 years. Cigarette smoking declined significantly during that time; alcohol abuse was identified as a common risk factor, and steps were taken to curtail it, especially among automobile drivers; seat-belt use has risen steadily; brisk walking, jogging, aerobic dancing, and other exercises have attracted tens of millions of new participants;

and the use of low-fat food alternatives has proliferated. How could the nation have grown fat while all of this was happening?

Some health analysts believe that the fitness revolution was limited to only a segment of the population, with most Americans still sedentary. Others theorize that significant numbers of Americans have been responding to the computer age by relying on computers rather than physical activities for entertainment as well as work. Another theory is that many people, in this highly stressful era, have been using food as a coping device to combat the anxiety and depression caused by widespread violence, job reductions, divorce, and so forth. One social scientist proclaimed that we have become more afraid to go out at night because of crime, and, in its place, we have become a nation of cable channel-surfing couch potatoes. It has also been suggested that many Americans are preoccupied with fat reduction but are not as vigilant with calorie reduction. In addition, we eat out at restaurants more frequently, and one of the ways that restaurants compete is through bigger and bigger servings. Yet another theory is that legions of ex-smokers have turned to overeating.

Each of these ideas contains some elements of truth, yet I favor still another theory. Our society is aging. The familiar population pyramid, with a few old people at its top and many young people at its base, is fast becoming a rectangle. This population rectangle, which has been taking shape over the past 20 years, will complete its metamorphosis over the next three decades. In 1980, nearly three times as many persons were under age 18 as were over age 65 (28% vs. 11%). By 2030, slightly more persons will be over age 65 than are under age 18 (22% vs. 21%).

As we age our metabolism—the chemical processes that build and destroy tissue—gradually slows. When it comes to eating, our fat oxidation or fat-burning rate slows down about 30% with age (Roberts et al., 1996). The metabolism that breaks down food components, therefore, releases them in the form of energy and heat more slowly. Thus, the number of calories that were required to maintain our weight when we were young no longer maintains our weight but increases it.

Also, chronic conditions—most notably arthritis—that accompany the aging process place limitations on our ability to stay active. Activity, however, is a crucial factor in weight management.

According to the Harris poll and the National Health and Nutrition Examination Survey, obesity reaches a peak among people in their 50s. More specifically, obesity peaks between the ages of 45 and 55 for men, and 55 and 65 for women (Van Itallie & Lew, 1990). Between the ages of 25 and 55, the average American gains 30 pounds of weight, about a pound a year. Moreover, during this period most Americans are sedentary and *lose about 15 pounds of muscle mass*, so the 30-pound weight gain actually translates into a 45-pound *fat* gain.

Around age 70, there tends to be an inclination to lose weight. Unfortunately, this weight loss is due more to lost muscle than lost fat, and older persons not only become thinner, but weaker and less functional as well.

Obesity is even more prevalent among low-income populations, especially low-income minority women. In 1980, 25% of women above the poverty level were overweight, whereas 37% of women with incomes below the poverty level were overweight (Public Health Service, 1988). In 1997, the Centers for Disease Control and Prevention reported that Mexican-American and African-American women were 16% more likely to be overweight than women in general.

## DEFINITION OF OBESITY AND OVERWEIGHT

The terms commonly used to refer to people who weigh more than recommended are *overweight* and *obese*. People who exceed the desirable range by 10% are classified as overweight, and by 20% or more, obese. It is questionable whether overweight is associated with disease risk, but obesity is definitely associated with late-onset diabetes, heart disease, hypertension, hypercholesterolemia, gallbladder disease, cancers of the breast, colon and prostate, and osteoarthritis of the weight-bearing joints (Public Health Service, 1988).

The body mass index (BMI) provides a simple and roughly accurate method for determining obesity. BMI can be easily calculated by multiplying weight in pounds by 700, divided by height in inches, and then dividing by height again—or if you have a pocket calculator, divide body weight (kg) by height squared (m²). Persons who have a BMI above 27 (120% or more of desirable body weight) are obese. According to this criterion, about one third of the adults in the United States are obese.

An additional 29 million adults were defined as overweight in June of 1998 by an expert panel from the National Institutes of Health. Based on an evaluation of several large-sampled obesity studies, the panel recommended lowering the BMI cut-off point from 27 to 25. In other words, a 5'5" woman who weighs 150 pounds is now deemed overweight by the NIH—and at risk for developing a long list of ailments; whereas this same woman a day before this pronouncement would not have been so designated until she reached 162 pounds.

The BMI is a useful tool to screen the general population but, similar to height/weight charts, fails to differentiate fat from lean body mass—an athlete with a large amount of muscle mass can fall into the high-risk category (see body composition section). It also fails to differentiate between the centrally obese apple-shape body (a heart risk factor) from the pear-shape body (less of a risk factor).

## GENETICS

Although genes do not destine you to become fat, a family history of obesity increases your chances of becoming obese by about 25 to 30% ("Weight Control: What Works and Why," 1994). Moreover, if you carry the extra weight primarily around your waist (apple shaped), you are at higher risk for heart disease, hypertension, stroke, and diabetes than the noncentrally obese (pear shaped) (Young & Gelskey, 1995). A reasonably accurate way of gauging central obesity is to divide the measurement of your waist at the narrowest point by the measurement of your hips (over your buttocks) at the widest point. If you are a woman, a waist-to-hip ratio greater than .85 indicates a health risk and if you are a man, above 1 (American College of Sports Medicine, 1995).

The set-point theory states that the body has what amounts to a genetic thermostat for body fat, which maintains a fairly constant weight. If body weight decreases through dieting, the set point either triggers appetite or makes the body conserve energy (lowers basal metabolic rate) to maintain the fat cells and a set weight. Set-point theory has received support from research conducted at Rockefeller University (Leibel et al., 1995). Researchers found that the body burns calories more slowly than normal when weight is lost. In other words, when fewer calories are consumed, the thermostat is lowered to conserve energy. This is a useful compensation when future sources of food are unpredictable or possibly scarce.

This theory needs more empirical support as does its corollary. Although the thermostat setting for fat cells and weight is resistant to dieting, exercise appears to speed up metabolism and lower the set point. Muscle has a higher metabolic rate than fat tissue, and exercise increases the muscle-to-fat ratio (Wood et al., 1988).

In summary, although genetics is a major contributor to the development of obesity, the primary reason that an individual becomes overweight or obese is related to lifestyle (Howley & Franks, 1997). By limiting the types of food and how much one eats, and increasing daily energy expenditure through physical activity and exercise, one has the ability to make a significant impact on body weight.

## LIFESTYLE

The National Weight Control Registry is an ongoing study of 800 persons, average age 45, who shed at least 30 pounds and kept the weight off for at least 5 years (Klem et al., 1997). Weight loss was confirmed in a variety of ways including documentation from physicians, interviews with family members or friends, and photographs. The researchers concluded that persistence was probably the most important component of successful weight loss. The average person failed half a dozen times before success was obtained.

Moreover, there was no single magic way to achieve success, unless you count the modification of eating and exercise habits as magic. Half the participants lost weight on their own; the other half consulted with a physician, a psychologist, or a nutritionist. About 44% limited their food portions, 40% counted calories, 33% limited fat intake, and 25% kept track of fat grams. Only 4% relied on diet drugs as the study occurred before the new wave of diet drugs.

Most of the registry's participants had been overweight since childhood, nearly half had one overweight parent, and more than a quarter had two overweight parents. Genes may predispose some toward obesity, but apparently lifestyle changes can sustain weight losses. On average, they reduced their body weight by 29% and successfully moved into the normal weight range.

A similar study on a smaller sample size ($n = 160$) was conducted earlier by Anne Fletcher (1994), a registered dietitian, and published in her book, *Thin for Life*. Fletcher distills 10 strategies for success from persons who kept off at least 20 pounds (average weight loss was 63 pounds) for a minimum of 3 years (most over 5 years). The strategies included focusing on what you can eat, not what you cannot eat; not denying yourself your favorite food and not worrying about periodic slip-ups; identifying and then avoiding high-risk situations and emotional eating; finding a way to incorporate exercise into your weekly routine; and identifying when you need to seek outside help. Her findings were later corroborated by the National Weight Control Registry study with its larger sample size.

## BODY COMPOSITION

Body composition is a better measure of health and fitness than body weight. Improving your fat-to-muscle ratio helps protect you from serious ailments as well as improves your fitness. Middle-aged and older women with more than 31% body fat, and men with more than 24%, are at increased risk for heart disease, stroke, various cancers, high blood pressure, diabetes, and degenerative joint disease (Howley & Franks, 1997).

There are several ways to measure body fat. The gold standard is hydrodensitometry, or underwater weighing, and is based on the principle that fat is less dense than water, and overweight individuals weigh less in water. After air is exhaled from the lungs, the body is submerged in a tank of water, and the under-water weight is registered on a scale. This technique is very accurate but expensive and time-consuming (about 30 minutes).

Skin-fold caliper is the most commonly used method because it is quick and reasonably accurate. Fat is pinched and measured in several areas including the triceps, suprailium, and thigh for women; and chest, abdomen, and thigh for men. Using fewer sites or employing technicians with inadequate training lowers the accuracy.

Bioelectrical impedance is about as accurate as the caliper technique when it is administered by a trained technician. One electrode is attached to an individual's foot and another to the hand, and a weak electrical current (that is safe and painless) is sent from one electrode to the other. The technique is based on the premise that the signal will travel faster through muscle because water conducts electricity and muscle is 70% water. Fat, in comparison, is about 9% water.

The newest technique is the Bod Pod, which works on the premise that a muscular body is denser and takes up less space than one that has more fat. The pod has a built-in computer that uses your weight and how much volume you take up and converts it into what percentage of your body is fat. Preliminary tests report that the technique may be as accurate as underwater measurement but not as demanding on the participant. To see if there is a Bod Pod in your area, the manufacturer's telephone number is 510-676-6002.

## SHOULD WE GAIN WEIGHT WITH AGE?

Although the answer to this question is controversial, many argue that gaining a few extra pounds with age may not only be common but healthy. Dr. Reubin Andres, clinical director of the National Institute on Aging, conducted a series of long-term studies and found that people in their 60s who are somewhat overweight—according to the Metropolitan Life Insurance charts—but not grossly obese had a better chance of living into their 80s and 90s than those whose weight is "normal." Thus, he created age-specific weight tables that generally have upper-weight limits that are 10 to 20 pounds higher than the insurance-based tables (Salon, 1997) (see Table 6.1).

A study by the Cooper Institute for Aerobics Research (Shapiro, 1997) appears to support Andres's contention that we need to be more lenient with recommended weight ranges. Men who gained significant amounts of weight over time but remained moderately or very fit had lower death rates than men who were in the average rate group but were unfit.

The chief opponent of Dr. Andres's theory, Dr. Roy Walford at University of California at Los Angeles School of Medicine, practices what he preaches and has placed himself on a lifelong diet of 1,500 calories a

**TABLE 6.1   Recommended Weights**

### RECOMMENDED WEIGHTS

| Metropolitan Life Insurance Co. | | | | | | Gerontology Research Center | | |
| Men | | | Women | | | Men and Women | | |
| Height | Small frame | Medium frame | Large frame | Small frame | Medium frame | Large frame | Height | 50-59 yr | 60-69 yr |
|---|---|---|---|---|---|---|---|---|---|
| 4'10" | --- | --- | --- | 102-111 | 109-121 | 118-131 | 4'10" | 107-132 | 115-142 |
| 4'11" | --- | --- | --- | 103-113 | 111-123 | 120-134 | 4'11" | 111-139 | 119-147 |
| 5'0" | --- | --- | --- | 104-115 | 113-126 | 122-137 | 5'0" | 114-143 | 123-152 |
| 5'1" | | | | 106-118 | 115-129 | 125-140 | 5'1" | 118-148 | 127-157 |
| 5'2" | 128-134 | 131-141 | 138-150 | 108-121 | 118-132 | 128-143 | 5'2" | 122-153 | 131-163 |
| 5'3" | 130-136 | 133-143 | 140-153 | 111-124 | 121-135 | 131-147 | 5'3" | 126-158 | 135-168 |
| 5'4" | 132-138 | 135-145 | 142-156 | 114-127 | 124-138 | 134-151 | 5'4" | 130-163 | 140-173 |
| 5'5" | 134-140 | 137-148 | 144-160 | 117-130 | 127-141 | 137-155 | 5'5" | 134-168 | 144-179 |
| 5'6" | 136-142 | 139-151 | 146-164 | 120-133 | 130-144 | 140-159 | 5'6" | 138-174 | 148-184 |
| 5'7" | 138-145 | 142-154 | 149-168 | 123-136 | 133-147 | 143-163 | 5'7" | 143-179 | 153-190 |
| 5'8" | 140-148 | 145-157 | 152-172 | 126-139 | 136-150 | 146-167 | 5'8" | 147-184 | 158-196 |
| 5'9" | 142-151 | 148-160 | 155-176 | 129-142 | 139-153 | 149-170 | 5'9" | 151-190 | 162-201 |
| 5'10" | 144-154 | 151-163 | 158-180 | 132-145 | 142-156 | 152-173 | 5'10" | 156-195 | 167-207 |
| 5'11" | 146-157 | 154-166 | 161-184 | 135-148 | 145-159 | 155-176 | 5'11" | 160-201 | 172-213 |
| 6'0" | 149-160 | 157-170 | 164-188 | 138-151 | 148-162 | 158-179 | 6'0" | 165-207 | 177-219 |
| 6'1" | 152-164 | 160-174 | 168-192 | --- | --- | --- | 6'1" | 169-213 | 182-225 |
| 6'2" | 155-168 | 164-178 | 172-197 | --- | --- | --- | 6'2" | 174-219 | 187-232 |
| 6'3" | 158-172 | 167-182 | 176-202 | --- | --- | --- | 6'3" | 179-225 | 192-238 |
| 6'4" | 162-176 | 171-187 | 181-207 | --- | --- | --- | 6'4" | 184-231 | 197-244 |

day. Dr. Walford's animal research has shown that underfed rats live one third longer than well-fed rats. Critics of his research, however, are concerned not only with his extrapolation from rodents to humans, but also with whether longer life on an "eat less" diet, even among the rats Dr. Walford studied, is associated with stunted growth and lower energy levels (Finn, 1988).

Although Dr. Andres's extra-weight theory has been supported by some studies (Finn, 1988), it has not been corroborated by others (Tayback et al., 1990; Van Itallie & Lew, 1990). Critics note that Andres's sample is biased toward the affluent elderly who can pass life-insurance medical examinations, and that he ignores health problems like diabetes, hypertension, and hyperlipidemia that are often unfavorably influenced by weight gain.

The Nurses' Health Study also suggests that the increasingly permissive U.S. weight guidelines may be unjustified. The researchers tracked the health status of 115,000 female nurses for 16 years and discovered a direct correlation between weight and susceptibility to stroke (Rexrode et al., 1997). Women whose BMI score rose into the 27 to 31 range during the 16-year period were 1.7 times more at risk for stroke; women who rose to a BMI of at least 32 more than doubled their risk.

## EXERCISE

It has been said that man does not live by bread alone. It can also be said that man does not control his weight by nutrition alone. Restricting the number of calories consumed without exercising tends to result in quick, dramatic weight loss. Unfortunately, it tends also to result in quick, dramatic weight gain. About half the weight loss will be water, which will be regained, and muscle, which will make us weaker. Dieting without exercise also lowers our metabolic rate (the amount of energy used for physiological processes), causing a reduction in our fat-burning capacity. This not only slows weight loss, but when the dieting ends, the weight is gained back faster than ever.

Exercise, in contrast, assures that weight loss will come primarily from fat, not water and muscle. Exercise also increases metabolic rate so that our body burns calories more efficiently and over a longer duration. Unfortunately, exercise as a weight reduction or weight maintenance strategy may become less effective as we age.

Researchers at The University of Texas Medical Branch (Klein, 1997a) monitored the fat and carbohydrate breakdown for older and younger participants who pedaled 60 minutes on stationary bikes. Measurement of oxygen consumption indicated how hard they were able to exercise. Then the study subjects pedaled at speeds that made them consume identical amounts of oxygen. Older participants oxidized less than a third as much fat as their younger counterparts. In other words, older adults appear to burn less fat doing equivalent exercise than younger adults.

Paul Williams (1997a) of the Lawrence Berkeley National Laboratory is in the midst of a study of 7,000 men and also tentatively concludes that men who run at a steady level between the ages of 20 and 50 will gain an average of 3.3 pounds each decade. He calculates that runners would have to increase their distance 1.4 miles a week each year to stay at the same weight.

The best exercises for weight control are a combination of aerobics and strength building. The aerobic activity should involve the large muscle groups like those in the legs. Longer durations and higher intensity levels accelerate progress, but are also likely to increase the likelihood of dropping out of an exercise routine. Strength-building increases muscle mass and boosts the metabolic rate, which allows the individual to burn calories throughout the day, not just when exercising.

Unfortunately, many Americans get their information from commercials and infomercials on television. Instead of accenting the effort it takes to lose weight, they learn that weight reduction is the consequence of buying a particular product. "Twenty minutes on a particular treadmill three times a week for two months will halve your body fat and reduce your weight into the desirable range." "The Ab (for abdominal) machine will reduce the size of your stomach" (even though there is no such thing as spot reducing).

The Federal Trade Commission is working on providing clearer legal standards for claims made on television. In the meantime, adults spent $2.5 billion on exercise equipment for home use in 1996 (Jackman, 1997). For a large, but unknown, percentage of obese television watchers who purchase exercise equipment, television viewing itself rather than exercising continues to be the leisure activity of choice (Buchowski & Sun, 1996).

## DIETING

Miracle diets, like the Rotation Diet, the Beverly Hills Diet, and the Scarsdale Diet, have been with us for many years, and there is no sign that their popularity is waning. The diets tend to reduce weight in the short run (primarily because of loss of water and high short-term motivation) but invariably prove ineffective in the long run. Typically, the diets are condemned by nutritionists and researchers because of lack of data from peer-reviewed studies to support them. But diets, in general, do not lose their popularity because, lo and behold, along comes another one that this time "really works!"

A recent diet craze (actually one that has resurfaced from before) is the high-protein, low-carbohydrate diet described in the best-selling books of Barry Sears (*Entering the Zone*, 1995; *Mastering the Zone*, 1997) and Robert Atkins, MD (*Dr. Atkins' New Diet Revolution*, 1997). These authors believe that obesity is increasing in America because we consume too many carbohydrates and too little protein. Sears, for instance, recommends that carbohydrates constitutes 40% of total calories, whereas mainstream health professionals recommend it to be 55%; and that proteins constitute 30% of calories, instead of the 15% to 20% recommended by nutritionists.

High carbohydrate and low-protein intake, according to the theory, cause our blood insulin level to rise, and this, in turn, leads to obesity. These claims, however, are untested by controlled studies (Liebman, 1997), and the more convincing explanation—that we consume too many calories and exercise too little—does not appear to be persuasive to these authors.

Why is this particular diet so popular? Because, like many other miracle diets, followers report that they are losing weight and feeling great. They are losing weight, however, but not because of a change in carbohydrate or protein consumption. The diet tends to be low calorie. Moreover, eating a low-carbohydrate diet builds up a chemical called ketones that curbs appetite, but also makes you nauseous and causes bad breath. After a while, though, the diet becomes monotonous, and the dieters become tired of being nauseous, woozy, fatigued, foul mouthed, and dehydrated despite immense thirst. Eventually, people go off the diet, regain weight, and wait for the next miracle diet to come along (which looks like it will be the Sugar Busters diet [Leighton, 1998]. It jumped to second place on the best-seller list as this is being written).

As the comedian and quasi-nutritionist Art Buchwald is fond of saying, the word *diet* comes from the verb to *die*. Or stated another way, the best diet is no diet. People who go *on* a diet, eventually go *off* a diet. Dieting becomes a never-ending cycle of activity that stresses the system with little to show for it.

# CALORIC INPUT AND EXPENDITURE

Lifestyle changes gradually implemented are the key to successful weight management. These changes should involve how much and what we eat, and activity level (Stunkard, 1987). People who successfully maintain or lose weight have a favorable balance between caloric input and caloric expenditure.

Calories are a measure of the energy contained in food. Calories tell us how much work our body can do with the energy it gains when we eat specific foods. If we consume more calories than needed for our particular activity level, we gain weight; if we consume fewer calories than needed for our activity level, we lose weight.

A nutritionist can prescribe a specific number of calories for an individual to consume each day that is based on size, age, and level of physical activity. An older adult woman, for instance, who is trying to lose weight, but is not physically active, might be prescribed a diet of 1,800 calories per day. This fairly rigid calorie limitation does not allow for many empty calories (i.e., junk or luxury foods that contain plenty of sugar, salt, or saturated fats, and not many important nutrients). The more this older person increases her physical activity, however, the more leeway she can have with her diet.

As a general rule of thumb, daily caloric intake should be 15 times your desired weight—10 times your weight if you have a light activity level or 20 times if you have a heavy activity level. Thus, if you engage in a moderate activity level and wish to weigh 160 pounds, your daily caloric intake will be approximately 2400.

It takes a reduction of 3,500 calories a week from the normal calorie level to lose a pound of fat. If you reduce food intake by 500 calories per day, a loss of 1 pound per week will result. If you reduce food intake by 200 calories per day, a loss of 2 pounds per month will result. These modest goals are more likely to lead to permanent changes in eating patterns than are more ambitious weight loss goals.

# EATING BEHAVIORS

Nutritionists contend that one of the main problems people have with maintaining or losing weight is portion control (Marston, 1996). The Center for Science in the Public Interest, for instance, investigated dinner house restaurants and discovered that many serving sizes are at least twice what is recommended by the U.S. Department of Agriculture (Liebman & Hurley, 1996). A side order of french fries or a muffin ordered at a restaurant, for example, is typically equivalent to two serving sizes.

To get the equivalent of a single drink serving, a customer must drink only two thirds of the soft drink can; instead, that person is more likely to find the 7-11 Double Gulp, which is equivalent to eight serving sizes. Steak portions are typically five times what is recommended. Tuna salad sandwiches are almost three times the recommended size.

Most adults have difficulty with portion control because they are unfamiliar with what constitutes an official serving size and underestimate what they eat. Even when told what an official serving size is, adults have trouble visualizing it. Many nutritionists compare a serving of meat, therefore, to a tape cassette rather than stating it is 3 ounces. They compare a cheese serving to a pair of dice, instead of stating it is 1 ounce. Other visual comparisons are a small fistful of french fries; a baseball of salad with 2 tablespoons of salad dressing; and a fist of pasta, rice, or mashed potatoes.

Complicating the problem of portion control is not only the fact that restaurant serving sizes have gotten increasingly large but, between 1955 and 1996, Americans doubled the number of meals eaten at restaurants (*Food and Nutrition Research Briefs*, 1996; Marston, 1996).

In addition to portion control difficulties at restaurants, adults are typically uneducated about low-fat alternatives. The CSPI, however, offers many restaurant suggestions in their *Nutrition Action Healthletter*. Suggestions for Mexican food: bean burritos and chicken fajitas instead of quesadilla and chile relleno, and substitute the salsa for the guacamole dip. For Italian food: avoid cream-based sauces. For Chinese food: avoid fried rice, breaded dishes, and items loaded with nuts; ask for vegetables steamed or stir-fried with less oil. For deli sandwiches: ask for mustard, ketchup, or horseradish, instead of mayonnaise.

A lawsuit by CSPI has resulted in regulations that make restaurants more accountable for low-fat menu claims. Low-fat foods on the menu cannot have more than 3 g of fat per standard serving (bearing in mind, though, that restaurant serving sizes are far from standard). If a food is described as light or lite, it must disclose why. Foods advertised as cholesterol free cannot have more than 2 g of saturated fat in a *standard serving*. Sugar-free foods that are not low-calorie, must state that on the menu.

# TEN QUICK TIPS BY HEALTH PROFESSIONALS
# TO CLIENTS

Following are some popular tips for losing weight:

1.  Exercise is essential for sustained weight loss. Exercising before meals decreases appetite for most people. Exercising or physical activity between meals or after dinner can take your mind off eating.

2.  Focus on your body fat, not your weight on a scale. If you exercise and limit calories in your diet, you will replace body fat with lean muscle mass. It is more important to measure body composition (perhaps through a fitness instructor at the local YMCA) than weight on a scale that can reflect loss of water and muscle.

3.  Focus on calories, not just fat. As the number of low-fat foods proliferate, the percentage of Americans who are obese goes up. This may not be a coincidence. Low-fat foods have calories (sometimes a substantial amount from sugar), and the more low-fat foods eaten, the more calories consumed. (The average consumption of fat was 33% of total calories in 1994, down from 40% in the late 1970s; however, people ate 6% more calories per day in 1994 [$n = 1,949$] than they did 17 years ago [$n = 1,837$]) (*Food and Nutrition Research Briefs*, 1996).

4.  Shop after you have eaten so you will not be tempted by junk food. Use a list and plan for the week so you don't need to keep returning to the store. Avoid purchasing quick snack foods, except for the low-calorie kind like fruit, yogurt, carrots, celery, salads, and so forth.

5.  If cooking is an enjoyable hobby, prepare less food, serve smaller portions, and do not overlook "tasting" as a source of calories. Perhaps chew gum while preparing the meal.

6.  Eat slowly, and put your fork down between bites. It takes a while for the stomach to signal the brain that it is full. If we eat rapidly and wait for our body to tell us it has had enough, we have probably had too much.

7.  Put smaller portions on your plate, and wait 5 minutes before deciding on seconds. Wait 15 minutes before having dessert. Waiting allows you the time you need to feel satisfied with the food you have already eaten. Still hungry? Brush your teeth; the toothpaste aftertaste may squelch your desire.

8.   For a calorie-free snack, enjoy a large glass of ice water or hot tea, and garnish with a twist of lemon or lime. Sip slowly. Have low-calorie snack foods, like fruit, yogurt, carrots, and celery, available.

9.   Keep a list of enjoyable activities (e.g., a cross-word puzzle, letter-writing, organizing a photo album, etc.) in a strategic location as a substitute for snacking.

10.   Eat out less. Most meals served at restaurants are high in fat and calories.

Fifteen behavior and psychological management strategies for weight management are described in chapter 10.


## MEAT AND MILK

The two largest contributors of fat in the American diet are hamburger meat and milk. Unfortunately, extra-lean and low-fat versions of these products are neither lean nor low fat. Using the formula for calculating percentage of calories from fat (grams of fat × 9/total calories), extra-lean ground beef is really 51% fat calories, and low-fat 2% milk is really 38% fat calories.

Why is there confusion on this matter? Because expressing fat as a percentage of the overall weight of the food product disregards the fact that more than half of the content may be water. Take 90% *lean* meat, for example. Sounds healthy, right? Wrong! Remove the 50+% water content, which has no calories, and we find that 51% of calories comes from fat. Eighty percent *lean* meat? A staggering 69% of calories comes from fat.


## FAT SUBSTITUTES

In 1995 the FDA approved a fat substitute called Olestra (manufactured by Procter & Gamble and sold under the brandname Olean). Olestra tastes like fat and, in fact, really is a fat-based product made from vegetable oil and sugar. It is engineered, though, so that it is too large to be absorbed and passes right through the digestive tract. The downside, however, is that it is associated in some people with cramps, gas, and diarrhea.

In addition, although olestra is fortified with the vitamins (A, D, E, and K) that it removes from the foods it is eaten with at the same time, it is not fortified with the carotenoids it removes because its nutritional role is not clear. Some studies, however, have suggested a relationship between high blood levels of carotenoids and low rates of some cancers and heart disease ("Olestra-Fried Snacks Fat-Free, But Not Free of Concerns," 1996).

By 1999, it is expected that the next generation of fat substitutes will be on the market. Z-trim is an insoluble natural fiber made from the hulls of oats, corn, or soybeans. The U.S. Department of Agriculture researcher who developed it, George Inglett, claims that it will not produce the side effects of olestra.

## COMMERCIAL WEIGHT LOSS PROGRAMS

Americans spend about $40 billion dollars a year attempting to lose weight (Hoeger & Hoeger, 1997). Despite this investment, 95% of people who lose weight regain the weight in 5 years ("Weight Control: What Works and Why," 1994), and the percentage of American adults who are overweight continues to increase. Repeatedly losing and gaining weight, or yo-yo dieting, may increase the risk of coronary artery disease and a higher death rate.

About 8 million Americans enroll in some kind of commercial weight-loss program each year. In 1993, *Consumer Reports* completed the first large-scale survey ($N = 19,000$) of people who joined one or more of the nation's five largest diet programs: Diet Center, Jenny Craig, Nutri/System, Physicians Weight Loss Centers, and Weight Watchers. Three-fourths of the participants in these commercial diet programs were *not* able to keep off the weight they had lost for 2 years.

Respondents reported, on average, that they stayed in a program for 6 months, lost 10% to 20% of their starting weight but gained back half of it in 6 months. Almost half of Jenny Craig and Nutri/System participants (but only 7% of Weight Watchers) reported higher costs than they were led to believe.

*Consumer Reports* (1993) also surveyed participants in three very low-calorie liquid diets: Optifast, Medifast, and Health Management Resources. Although the participants lost weight more rapidly than the regular diet programs, they regained it more quickly as well. Also, *less than*

5% of those who had tried over-the-counter appetite suppressants (e.g., Acutrim and Dexatrim) were very satisfied with how well these medications helped them to lose, and keep off, weight.

The authors of the *Consumer Reports* findings concluded that "None of the diet programs we investigated give top priority to increasing physical activity, a change that researchers now unanimously agree is critical to lasting weight loss. If you use one of these programs, you should be prepared to find a way to exercise on your own" (1993).

## RADICAL WEIGHT LOSS PROGRAMS

One radical weight-loss strategy is surgical modification of the gastrointestinal tract. Because of a high incidence of complications and subsequent dietary restrictions, this technique is usually reserved for clients who are more than 100% over their ideal body weight and have attempted nonsurgical weight loss without success. Gastric balloons are another option, but weight loss is usually regained after the removal of the balloon.

Crash diets or very-low-calorie diets depend on rapid weight loss resulting from loss of water and lean muscle tissue, and are usually regained quickly (Caterson, 1990; Stunkard, 1987) (see Figure 6.1). As the proportion of fat to muscle increases, we become fatter internally, even if we lose weight. In addition, because the metabolic rate has slowed, we easily regain weight that returns mostly as fat because it is easier to gain fat than lean body mass.

Dietitians and nutritionists, therefore, prefer that individuals consume sufficient calories (at least 1,200 for women per day and 1,500 for men) to prevent the metabolic rate from slowing.

In contrast to radical weight-loss programs, the aim of programs combining conservative changes in eating patterns with regular exercise is the cultivation of *lifelong* habits that will make it possible for individuals to lose and keep off fat rather than lose and regain water. Conservative weight-loss programs recommend a loss of about 1% or less of total body weight per week.

Combining techniques—changing food consumption, adopting an exercise routine, and seeking support through individual or group psychotherapy, mutual help groups, behavioral methodologies, hypnosis, or stress management—may help individuals maintain changes in eating patterns.

```
                     TEN CALORIE DIET

MONDAY     : Breakfast: Weak tea
             Lunch    : 1 bouillon cube in 1/2 cup of diluted water
             Dinner   : 1 pigeon thigh and 30 oz. of prune juice
                        (gargle only)

TUESDAY    : Breakfast: Scraped crumbs from burned toast
             Lunch    : 1/2 dozen doughnut holes
             Dinner   : 2 jellyfish skins

WEDNESDAY: Breakfast: Boiled out tablecloth stains
             Lunch    : 1/2 dozen poppy seeds
             Dinner   : Bee knees and mosquito sauteed in vinegar

THURSDAY  : Breakfast: Shredded egg shell skin
             Lunch    : Belly buttons from naval oranges
             Dinner   : 2 eyes from Irish potatoes

FRIDAY     : Breakfast: 2 lobster antennas
             Lunch    : 1 guppy fin
             Dinner   : 1 filet of soft shell crab claw

SATURDAY  : Breakfast: 4 chopped banana seeds
             Lunch    : Broiled butterfly liver
             Dinner   : Jellyfish vertebrae (Ala Book-Binder)

SUNDAY     : Breakfast: Pickled humming bird tongue
             Lunch    : Prime rib tadpoles
             Dinner   : Aroma of empty custard pie plate, tossed
                        paprika and 1 clover leaf

The first week you lose 50 pounds, the second week you lose another
50 pounds, and the third week we lose you.
```

**FIGURE 6.1   Ten calorie diet.**


## CHRISTIAN WEIGHT LOSS PROGRAMS

Christian diet books began in 1957 when Presbyterian minister Charles Shedd urged his readers to pray their weight away. During the 1990s, Christian diet books began to proliferate, combining evangelical theology, psychology, and nutrition education. Critics have expressed concern about the accuracy of the nutritional advice and the questionable association between losing weight and gaining God's approval.

One of the more successful Christian diet books is Gwen Shamblin's (1997) *The Weigh Down Diet*. This book sold 200,000 copies in its first 2 months of release, and Shamblin also reports conducting more than 17,000 Weigh-Down Workshops. The only exercise her program requires is getting down on your knees to pray. A concern is that Shamblin, a registered dietitian with a master's degree in food and nutrition, advocates that even people with serious weight problems like anorexia should turn to God rather than to medical professionals.

## DIET DRUGS

In the 1960s and 1970s, the drugs of choice for desperate dieters were amphetamines, or speed, which promoted weight loss by boosting metabolism. Unfortunately, the drugs caused more problems than they solved, not the least of which were addiction and serious side effects. In the 1990s, two new drugs were introduced to Americans: fen-phen (fenfluramine and phentermine) and Redux (dexfenfluramine).

With one third of Americans seriously overweight and most of them unsuccessfully attempting to reduce to a healthier and more socially acceptable weight, it was not surprising when fen-phen and Redux became best-selling diet drugs. New prescriptions for fen-phen increased by 6,390% in the 4 years before fenfluramine was taken off the market in 1997, and similar statistics were unofficially estimated for Redux, which had been sold in this country for 16 months before its withdrawal from the market in 1997.

In total, these two diet drugs of the 90s were prescribed to more than 50 million people in the United States (60 million worldwide), with 18 million prescriptions filled in 1996 alone.

The drugs worked by curbing people's appetites, and studies reported the average weight loss to be about 20 pounds in a year's time. Unfortunately, the drugs had been linked to heart-valve abnormalities (Connolly et al., 1997), life-threatening pulmonary hypertension (Mark et al., 1997), and long-lasting brain cell damage in animals. Brain cell damage in human beings may also occur because short-term memory loss has been reported in 13% of the people who had taken fen-phen.

Defenders of the drugs proclaim that the hazards from serious obesity is a far greater risk, resulting in 300,000 deaths a year from heart disease, diabetes, kidney disease, and stroke. Many people who had taken the drugs, however, were not obese and were taking them from commercial weight-loss clinics without a physician's supervision.

The next generation of antiobesity drugs (like Meridia, Xenical, leptin, and neuropeptide-Y blockers) are moving from the strategy of appetite suppressant to absorption blockage. These drugs are on, or propelling closer to, the marketplace. Meridia, for instance, was approved by the FDA in 1997 and reached pharmacy shelves in February 1998. Trial results had indicated that dieters using this drug lost about 10 pounds more than mere dieters and, at the same, did not pose the risk of heart valve damage that forced the ban on Redux and fenfluramine. Meridia, however, can elevate blood pressure and pulse rate even as patients are losing weight. And it is also believed to be psychologically and physically addictive.

In the meantime, so-called diet herbs (see chapter 7 on dietary supplements) have grown popular since the diet drug ban. St. John's wort, taken for years in Germany to lift sagging spirits, is now being used for weight loss in America. Repackaged with names similar to the unavailable fen-phen, like Herbal Phen Fuel and Diet Phen, this herb has not been tested for weight loss.

The herbal mixture used at Nutri-System weight loss centers is called Herbal Phen-Fen, a combination of St. John's wort and ephedra. Ephedra, an herb that is also known as ma huang, is a major constituent in many herbal weight-loss products and appears to work in the short run. But ephedra is also the likely culprit in approximately 800 health problems reported to the FDA including more than 40 deaths ("Are Natural Fen-Phens Safe?" 1998).

Yet another popular alternative to fen-phen is phen-pro, a mixture of phentermine and Prozac. Although the makers of Prozac, Eli Lilly and Company, once considered marketing this antidepressant for weight loss, the data was never strong enough to win the approval of the Food and Drug Administration. Officials of Lilly wrote the Nutri/System Weight Loss Centers warning them against their use of Prozac for weight loss ("Lilly Issues Warning on Use of Prozac for Weight Loss," 1997).

## MENTAL HEALTH AND DIETING

A study of 183 overweight older adults reported that those individuals who exhibited the most effective dieting behaviors might also be particularly vulnerable to an emotional vacuum that can worsen with the loss in their diet of desired foods (Rosendahl & Kirschenbaum, 1992). Dieting may be especially difficult for *older* adults, who may become discouraged by the inevitably slow progress that results from slow metabolic rates.

Encouraging older dieters to add aerobic exercise and social support to the changes undertaken in their eating patterns may help to offset emotional distress and discouragement (Mellin et al., 1997).

Aerobic exercises may not only enhance their ability to achieve dieting goals but may also improve their mood, reduce depression, decrease somatic symptoms, and reduce muscle tension (deVries and Hales, 1974; McNeil et al., 1991). The evidence, to date, on the impact of exercise on psychological and neuropsychological function—although mixed—is promising (Albert et al., 1995; Blumenthal et al., 1991).

Social support may be especially important to older dieters who are vulnerable to emotional distress while dieting. The positive and independent effects of exercise and social contact on depressive symptoms was reported by McNeil and colleagues (1991). Social support may be provided by sharing experiences with peers, or support may need to be solicited from a spouse or health professional.

## QUESTIONS FOR DISCUSSION

1. Should we gain a little extra weight with age?
2. For an older person with a moderate activity level, how many grams of fat should be consumed with an average daily caloric intake of 2,100 kcal?
3. A 68-year-old woman has been unsuccessful with losing weight, despite watching her caloric intake and increasing her activity level. She wants to try a diet pill or a high-protein/low-carbohydrate diet. What is your advice, and how would you persuade her to your viewpoint?
4. Why is exercise essential for losing weight?
5. Develop an outline for a presentation on weight reduction and maintenance, using the Food Guide Pyramid and Covert Bailey's Bull's-Eye.

# 7
# Dietary Supplements

## NUTRITIOUS FOODS VERSUS DIETARY SUPPLEMENTS

The controversy over whether a balanced diet is sufficient to achieve all nutritional goals or whether there is a need for dietary supplements continued during the 1990s. Although the issue is far from being resolved, the advocates for dietary supplements have gained ground among health professionals, researchers, the lay public, and Congress.

For many years, the conventional wisdom in the nutritional sciences has been that a balanced diet is sufficient to achieve all nutritional goals. Horwath (1991), for instance, reported that purchasing healthy foods within the context of a balanced diet is more effective and less costly than purchasing supplements. She also noted that "most of the nutrients identified as being the least adequately supplied in the diets of elderly persons (i.e., zinc, potassium, folate, vitamin $B_6$) were rarely being used as supplements" (1991). In addition, she notes that the suspected value of any particular dietary supplement is subject to change with each new research finding.

Horwath's conclusion: It is best to rely on the *variety* of good foods provided by nature.

### MULTIVITAMIN

In an essay in the *Journal of the American Medical Association*, however, Ranjit Chandra (1997)—a physician twice nominated for a Nobel Prize in medicine—reported that deficiencies in vitamins and trace elements have been observed in almost one third of analyzed elderly. Because it is expensive and impractical to analyze the blood levels of various nutrients in all individuals, Chandra encourages older adults to take a multivitamin containing modest amounts of vitamins and minerals as good preventive medicine practice.

A placebo-controlled double-blind trial with older adults also came up with the recommendation that low to moderate doses of a daily multivitamin made a significant difference in immune response among the participating older adults (Bogden et al., 1994).

Robert Butler, MD, Pulitzer Prize–winning author and former chair of the Department of Geriatrics and Adult Development at New York's Mount Sinai Medical Center, agrees with the practice of taking a multivitamin. Butler once considered vitamin and mineral supplements to be a rip-off, but his concern about the methods of food production and processing led to the recommendation that older adults consume an inexpensive multiple-vitamin supplement on a daily basis (unpublished communication).

However, although a significant percentage of older adults are deficient on several nutrients, it is unclear when these deficiencies begin. There is less evidence, therefore, on the benefits of dietary supplements for baby boomers. Ranjit Chandra recommends that middle-aged people take a good multivitamin once a week and slowly increase the frequency until they are taking it daily by their late 60s ("Building Immunity," 1997).

## CHANGING RESEARCH

One of Horwath's other claims, that the suspected value of a particular supplement is subject to change with each new research finding, is well taken. It is not a good idea to be the first one on your block to take a newly touted supplement. Conversely, when research findings are consistent and persuasive it *is* a good idea to change. Just a few years after Horwath noted that adults rarely took two nutrients that were probably being inadequately consumed—folate and zinc—additional research supporting these supplements led to a surge in consumption.

The RDA (recommended dietary allowance) for folate, in fact, doubled in 1997, and the FDA required manufacturers of breads, cereals, pasta, and other grain products to fortify their products with it by January 1998. Also, after a 1996 study published in the *Annals of Internal Medicine* showed that dissolving a zinc lozenge in your mouth can reduce the severity and duration of a cold, and another study reported that zinc may increase immune response in older people, consumption of zinc skyrocketed ("Vitamin and Nutritional Supplements," 1997).

## CAUTIONS

Horwath's comment that the value of a supplement is subject to change with each new research finding, however, applies to zinc as well because the methodological soundness of the *Annals* study appeared to be flawed (*Consumer Reports on Health,* 1997). Besides the plethora of questionable research findings concerning dietary supplements in general, there are several other cautions when it comes to taking dietary supplements.

Most dietary supplements, for instance, are narrowly targeted while the nutrients in foods work in synergy. Phytochemicals are an example of this distinction. They are recently discovered chemical compounds found in abundance in fruits and vegetables that seem to exert a powerful synergistic effect in cancer prevention (Hoeger & Hoeger, 1997). These compounds, however, are presently impossible to replicate in pill form. Adults who eat a poor diet and try to compensate with a variety of specific supplements will not derive the same benefits as they would from healthy eating because of the inability to replicate synergistic chemical compounds in pill form.

Another caution with taking supplements is that they can be dangerous. An overdose of vitamin A can cause headaches, nausea, diarrhea, and liver and bone damage. Too much vitamin D can cause appetite loss, fatigue, nausea, and constipation; can lead to abnormal calcium deposits in the body; and can adversely affect the kidneys. An overdose of bran can lead to seriously reduced calcium absorption. Excess vitamin $B_6$ can cause numbness; vitamin E, bleeding; and niacin, gastric problems.

In addition, people on medication need to be careful with taking dietary supplements. A person taking coumadin, a blood-thinning medication, for instance, should avoid vitamins K and E, which can negate or exacerbate the effect of this medication.

Finally, people need to be cautious about the proclaimed benefits of dietary supplements that are often exaggerated. If consumers acquire a false sense of security regarding supplements, this may contribute to a failure to pay sufficient attention to the nutritive value of the foods they eat.

The evidence for dietary supplements is convincing in a few areas, such as when it comes to older adults taking a multivitamin or taking calcium with vitamin D. Good evidence is also rapidly accumulating on the effectiveness of vitamins E and $B_{12}$. However, many other supplements—vitamins, minerals, herbs, and nonherbal varieties—are promising, but the evidence is much less convincing.

## DIETARY SUPPLEMENT HEALTH AND EDUCATION ACT

Although researchers, health professionals, and the lay public are bullish lately on the prospects of dietary supplements, the FDA has logged more than 2,500 reports of side effects associated with dietary supplements including 79 deaths (Neergaard, 1998). Because the federal government has decided to take a caveat emptor, or buyer beware, approach to regulating supplements, there has been insufficient consumer guidance about what works, what does not work, and what are the potential side effects.

Before 1994, the FDA regulated nutritional supplements through premarket safety evaluations—similar to the procedure required for food and drugs. Most herbs and all vitamins that were sold in dosages exceeding 150% of recommended daily allowance were considered to be prescription drugs in 1993.

In 1994, however, the federal government created the Dietary Supplement Health and Education Act, which eliminated premarket safety evaluations for a wide variety of dietary supplements including many herbs, vitamins, minerals, and hormones. The FDA can now only intervene after consumers complain about illnesses from supplements; even then, the FDA can only restrict the product if it can be proved that the specific supplement caused the harm. This is difficult to accomplish because it is hard to separate out those people who just did not take the supplement as directed, or who exceeded the recommended dose, or who took different types of supplements simultaneously, or who engaged in some other confounding practice.

The 1994 legislation also allows advertisers to make unproved claims, like their product "reverses aging," as long as the product is not being sold at the same time. The only legal restriction on the product's label is that it not be promoted as preventing or treating disease. To circumvent this, manufacturers proclaim to "promote prostate health" or to "promote leg vein health."

Even false claims on product labels, which are illegal, are not being sanctioned because government agencies lack the resources for enforcement. Moreover, the public has to contend with the lack of regulation over product purity (i.e., the amount of active ingredient in a supplement). Two packages of the same product may have vastly dissimilar amounts of active ingredients. Some "all-natural" products are contaminated and the consequences are lead poisoning, impotence, blood clots, abnormal heart rhythms, nausea, vomiting, diarrhea, or disorientation (Angell & Kassirer, 1998).

Without safeguards against grandiose claims, it is not surprising that dietary supplements became a $6 billion business in 1996. Thirty percent of Americans took a daily vitamin supplement, 33% of people with chronic disease took herbal remedies on occasion for help, and 70% took nutritional supplements on at least an episodic basis ("Vitamin and Nutritional Supplements," 1997).

Given widespread public use and limited government regulation, it is important to examine the research on the most popular vitamins, minerals, herbs, hormones, and other supplements being taken. Unfortunately, most research studies have been conducted outside of the United States because many dietary supplements are naturally occurring substances and cannot be patented in the United States, thereby reducing the incentive for individual manufacturers to invest money in research.

## VITAMIN AND MINERAL SUPPLEMENTS

### CALCIUM AND VITAMIN D

In 1997 the Food and Nutrition Board of the National Academy of Sciences increased the recommended intake of calcium for adults over age 50 by 50%, to 1,200 mg of calcium daily. There is widespread recognition, however, based on research findings, that even this amount for postmenopausal women may not be sufficient, and 1,500 mg/d is recommended ("Calcium and Vitamin D," 1996).

Current calcium intake, however, is only 600 mg/d. Most people cannot drink 3 or 4 glasses of milk every day, or eat other calcium-rich foods like broccoli on such a repetitive basis. Moreover, calcium can be a difficult mineral to absorb; it clings tightly to wheat bran, for instance, making the calcium in your cereal milk go largely unabsorbed. Other foods that inhibit calcium absorption are spinach, green beans, peanuts, and summer squash. Also, high levels of protein, sodium, or caffeine in the diet have each been associated with the excretion of high levels of calcium in the urine (Atkinson, 1998).

Thus, a calcium supplement is recommended for most postmenopausal women by geriatricians who keep up to date on nutrition research. Several cautions do apply, however. It is important not to take the supplement in one dose as the body absorbs best when smaller amounts are ingested throughout the day. Doses of 500 mg or less are ideal. Also, not all pills contain the same amount of calcium. Calcium carbonate (e.g., Tums) is 40% calcium and calcium phosphate is 38%, but calcium citrate is only 21%.

Vitamin D enhances the absorption of calcium, and its recommended intake recently doubled to 400 IU daily for people ages 51 to 70 and tripled to 600 IU daily for those 71 and older. This is the first time that the Food and Nutrition Board of the National Academy of Sciences has made recommended daily allowances for adults over age 70—making official that the nutritional needs of baby boomers and the young-old are different from those for older adults.

Older adults are deficient in vitamin D for a variety of reasons, such as their inability to absorb the vitamin from foods as efficiently as when they were younger. Older adults also tend to be outside less where vitamin D can be produced from exposure to the sun. Although 15 minutes a day outside is sufficient for younger persons, the skin becomes less effective at absorbing vitamin D as we age.

During the colder months in the northern climate, it is almost impossible to receive the ultraviolet light needed for vitamin D production (Sharp, 1997). It is even more important at that time to eat fish, eggs, liver, and meat, which naturally contain vitamin D, or drink fortified vitamin D milk. Perhaps the best idea, though, is to take a multivitamin that contains D, checking the label because not all varieties include it.

For the first time the Food and Nutrition Board has set upper limits for some vitamins and minerals. The upper intake level for calcium is 2,500 mg/d and for vitamin D is 2,000 IU. Too much calcium can contribute to kidney stones; too much vitamin D can actually cause bone loss.

The final word on calcium and vitamin D is that even if you take supplements, it will not be sufficient protection for your bones. If you want to preserve bone density, it is essential to engage in regular weight-bearing exercise like walking. This type of exercise stresses the bone in such a way as to allow it to retain calcium.

## VITAMIN E

The evidence for taking a vitamin E supplement is not as strong as it is for calcium and vitamin D but quite promising. As we age, we produce fewer T cells and antibodies that help us attack viruses and cancers, and fight infection. Studies of older adults taking vitamin E supplements of 200 IU/d (significantly higher than the 30 currently recommended) reported improved T-cell function and other immune function tests (Chandra, 1997; Chandra, 1992; Meydani et al., 1997).

Vitamin E also appears to be important in the reduction of risk for heart disease. It seems to be a potent antioxidant that attaches directly to LDL cholesterol to prevent damage from free radicals. A study in the *New England Journal of Medicine* (Kushi et al., 1996) reported that older women who eat more food rich in vitamin E reduce their chance of heart disease by almost two thirds. A study in *Lancet* (Stephens et al., 1996) reported that adults who were given 400 or 800 IU of vitamin E a day for 18 months had a 77% lower risk of heart attack.

Vitamin E supplementation also reduced prostate cancer incidence and mortality in male smokers in Finland, and provided some protection against colorectal and lung cancer (Heinonen et al., 1998). This study, however, did not include nonsmokers or people of other ethnic backgrounds. Yet another study reported that 1,000 IU of vitamin E twice a day slowed the progression of Alzheimer's disease, though it did not stop or reverse it (Sano et al., 1997). It is not clear, however, what the recommended amount of vitamin E consumption per day should be nor what is the relative effectiveness of a vitamin E supplement versus vitamin E obtained through diet.

Researchers have been testing primarily between 60 and 400 IU of vitamin E a day with promising results. Even 60 IU of vitamin E, twice what is currently recommended, is very difficult to acquire through diet alone. Simin Meydani, chief of the Nutritional Immunology Laboratory at the U.S. Department of Agriculture's Human Nutrition Research Center on Aging reports that once the ideal amount is determined "we're pretty close to making a recommendation for a vitamin E supplement" ("Vitamin E," 1996). In the meantime, large supplements of vitamin E are not recommended for individuals on anticoagulant therapy as vitamin E is an anticoagulant in itself.


## VITAMIN B-12

The National Academy of Sciences, which advises the federal government on nutrition, recently urged people over age 50 to take a vitamin $B_{12}$ supplement or eat cereals fortified with $B_{12}$ ("Take Vitamin B-12, New Study Advises," 1998). The academy reviewed several research studies and concluded that up to 30% of persons older than age 50 cannot absorb $B_{12}$ in food, primarily because of the onset of atrophic gastritis—a reduction in the ability to secrete stomach acid that allows us to separate and use vitamin $B_{12}$ in our food.

Researchers are beginning to recommend, therefore, that persons older than age 50 increase the recommended daily allowance for vitamin $B_{12}$ in their diet from 6 mcg to 25 mcg ("Vitamin B-12," 1998). Although most multivitamin supplements have only 6 mcg, Centrum Silver and other supplements for older people typically have 25 mcg.


## ANTIOXIDANTS

Oxygen is used during metabolism to change carbohydrates and fats into energy. During this process, oxygen is converted into stable forms of water and carbon dioxide. Some oxygen, however, referred to as free radicals, end up in an unstable form with a normal proton nucleus but a single unpaired electron. The unpaired electron seeks to steal a second electron from a stable molecule, and in so doing it damages proteins and lipids, which likely contributes to heart disease, cancer, and other diseases. This chain reaction among unpaired electrons continues until antioxidants help stabilize the free radicals so they will not be as reactive.

Antioxidants are found in food, especially fruits and vegetables. Unfortunately, only 9% of Americans eat the recommended minimum of five daily servings of fruits and vegetables ("Vitamin Report," 1994). Among those who recommend antioxidant supplementation (such as Kenneth Cooper, 1994; and experts who contribute to the *University of California at Berkeley Wellness Letter*, 1995), there are standard *cocktail* guidelines that range from 250 to 1,000 mg of vitamin C (no more than 500 mg at one time); 200 to 800 IU of vitamin E; and 10,000 to 25,000 IU of beta-carotene.

Based on more recent research, however, the editorial board of the *University of California at Berkeley Wellness Letter* modified the cocktail recommendation and suggested that the beta-carotene be obtained from natural food sources rather than through dietary supplements ("Beta Carotene Pills: Should You Take Them?" 1997). This can be accomplished through the consumption of one medium raw carrot, which contains 20,000 IU of beta-carotene. Several well-designed studies have found that beta carotene supplements offer no protection against cardiovascular disease and that two studies even found an increased risk of lung cancer in smokers who took the supplements ("Vitamin and Nutritional Supplements," 1997).

The other two components of the antioxidant cocktail, vitamin E (which was examined previously) and vitamin C, have received more research support. The National Institutes of Health and the National Cancer Institute, for instance, have proposed raising the current RDA for vitamin C from 60 to 200 mg/d ("Vitamin and Nutritional Supplements," 1997). Two hundred milligrams per day can be achieved through five servings of fruits and vegetables a day, but only about 10% of Americans consume the recommended five servings.

Vitamin C supplements may prevent cataracts. Cataracts are thought to result from the oxidation of lens protein, and vitamin C may prevent this oxidation. One study of long-term vitamin C supplement use of at least 500 mg daily reported that there were 77% fewer early-stage cataracts among the women who took the supplements for more than 10 years. These study results corroborated an earlier report that linked 10-plus years of vitamin C supplements with far fewer cataract surgeries (Jacques et al., 1997). Researchers urge caution, however, when taking large doses of vitamin C supplements (Podmore et al., 1998).

## OTHER VITAMIN AND MINERAL SUPPLEMENTS

Advocates for other vitamin and mineral supplements are basing their beliefs more on anecdotal evidence and less on rigorously controlled studies. The vitamin and mineral supplements receiving the most attention are niacin, chromium, iron, selenium, and zinc. None has received consistent support from well-controlled research studies. Conversely, all have detrimental effects if taken in excess.

Niacin at doses higher than 2,000 mg can cause liver damage, high blood sugar, and irregular heartbeats; as little as 50 mg can cause headaches, cramps, and nausea. Iron may be beneficial to young children, early teenagers, menstruating women, and people with internal bleeding. Iron deficiency in healthy older adults, however, is rare, and high iron levels have been associated with a wide variety of risk factors. Excessive amounts of selenium causes hair and nail loss, whereas immoderate quantities of zinc may weaken the immune status of older adults, interfering with the absorption of iron and copper, and lower HDL ("good") cholesterol levels.

## HERBS

The medicinal benefits of plants are undeniable. Herbs, for instance, are the basis for aspirin, morphine, digitalis and many other medicines. Most of the $700 million that consumers spend on herbal remedies, however, do not produce effective outcomes, and a not insignificant number create health risks. Even among those products that appear to be helpful, the consistency of ingredients is unregulated and uncertain.

The regulation of herbs in Europe, where they are treated almost like drugs, sharply contrasts with America. In Europe, herbal labels warn people with diseases or conditions that might leave them susceptible to bad outcomes. Germany's widely respected Commission E of the Federal Department of Health has tested hundreds of herbs, approving those with absolute proof of safety and reasonable proof of efficacy. These well-researched, clearly labeled herbal medicines outsell prescription drugs in most European countries. In contrast, Americans must rely on books for information (a good one is *The Honest Herbal* [1993] by Varro Tyler), or they need to contact the American Botanical Council by telephone at 512-331-8868, or through the World Wide Web sites: www.herbalgram.org, or www.usp.org/did/mgraphs/botanica.

### EPHEDRA

Ephedrine-containing compounds, sold under such names as Ephedra, Ma Huang, and Ultimate Xphoria, stimulate the heart and central nervous system, and are sometimes used for weight control. Not only is the efficacy of these drugs unproved, they can cause heart palpitations, seizures, hypertension, heart attacks, and stroke. Given that bottles standing side by side may supply doses varying from 1 to 110 mg of ephedrine, it is not surprising that they have been linked to 36 deaths ("Ephedrine's Deadly Edge," 1997).

## Ginkgo Biloba

Ginkgo biloba is the best studied and most popular herb in Europe. Numerous studies in Europe show that an extract from the leaves of the ginkgo biloba tree dilates blood vessels and can improve blood flow in the brain and the extremities. It may also alleviate vertigo and ringing in the ears. In addition, a placebo-controlled, double-blind, randomized trial in the United States reported that ginkgo biloba is safe and appears capable of stabilizing and, in a substantial number of cases, improving the cognitive performance and the social functioning of demented patients for 6 months to 1 year (LeBars et al., 1997). This study, however, was limited by a high drop-out rate and small differences between treatment and control groups.

## Ginseng

Ginseng products are notorious for containing little or none of its active ingredient. *Consumer Reports* tested ten ginseng products and found that one contained almost none of the active ingredient, and the remainder varied by 1,000%. It is debatable whether ginseng is more likely to increase immunity or blood pressure. Only one well-controlled experiment with ginseng has ever been reported, and its results were equivocal (Tyler, 1993).

If you are avoiding alcohol, be aware that the Bureau of Alcohol, Tobacco, and Firearms tested 55 ginseng extracts in 1998 and found that 48 of them contained alcohol. To find out about a particular brand of ginseng, call the bureau's public information office at 202-927-8500.

## St. John's Wort

Though the evidence is still incomplete, one of the most promising new herbs is St. John's wort (botanical name *hypericum perforatum*), a weed native to the western United States and parts of Europe and named for St. John the Baptist, whose birthday is celebrated on June 24, about the time the plant puts forth its yellow blooms.

St. John's wort appears to be an effective treatment for mild to moderate depression. The herb is the most popular antidepressant in Germany, where 66 million daily doses of it were prescribed in 1994 and where one brand alone outsells Prozac 7 to 1. In Germany, the research results have been consistent: St. John's wort is two times more effective than a placebo for mild and moderate depression, and has fewer side effects than drugs ("A Natural Remedy for Depression," 1997).

Although Prozac costs, on average, $80 a month, a regimen of St. John's wort costs about $10 a month. Researchers warn, however, that the German studies involved small numbers of patients, the trials were brief, the diagnosis of depression was not standardized, and the potency and dosages studied varied. Clinicians warn about the adverse effects from stopping prescribed antidepressants on one's own, or the danger of taking the herb along with other medications.

## SAW PALMETTO

Saw palmetto is being touted as an herb that may improve urinary flow in men with noncancerous enlarged prostate (benign prostatic hypertrophy). The potential market is huge, with half of all men older than the age of 50 having enlarged prostates. Moreover, prescription prostate drugs have substantial side effects. Saw palmetto is definitely not a substitute for conventional medical treatment. In fact, it does not actually shrink the prostate but may relieve the symptoms of enlargement such as the frequent urge to urinate. Although the efficacy of the herb is unproved, it appears to have few side effects (Smith et al., 1986). Saw palmetto is definitely not effective when the dried berry or extract is made into a tea.

## GARLIC

There have been widespread reports that garlic pills or whole garlic can substantially lower elevated blood cholesterol levels. Consequently, garlic is one of the most popular herbal supplements in the United States. Americans spent $71 million on garlic supplements in 1997, up 11% from 1996. A rigorously controlled study in 1998, however, reported that the overall effect of garlic on cholesterol is zero (Berthold et al., 1998).

To a much lesser extent, garlic is known for lowering blood pressure, killing germs, and slowing the growth of cancer cells. These results, however, are also unproved.

# HORMONE SUPPLEMENTS

## DHEA

DHEA (dehydroepiandrosterone) is a hormone secreted by the adrenal glands, and the body converts it into estrogen and testosterone. By age 70, DHEA levels are only 25% of the peak reached by most people between the ages of 18 and 30. DHEA was banned before the Dietary Supplement Health and Education Act of 1994. Since then it has been promoted as an anti-aging remedy that improves strength, energy, and immunity as well as a treatment for heart disease, cancer, impotence, and Alzheimer's disease. The benefit of reviving the vigor and strength of youth through DHEA has been anecdotal, and the risks with taking large amounts range from acne and increased facial hair and deepened voice in women, to an increased risk of breast, ovarian, and prostate cancer, and liver damage.

Although DHEA or one of its components could have a bright future (Morales et al., 1994), buying pills or getting shots (that can cost more than $15,000 a year) is unwarranted at this time.

## MELATONIN

Melatonin is a hormone produced in the brain by the pineal gland, and it is believed to set the body's sleep cycle. It became the first best-selling hormone supplement with 20 million new melatonin users in 1995 in the United States. Adults appear to reduce the effects of jet lag when melatonin is taken in the right amount and dose (0.5 mg when you awake; if traveling westward, in midafternoon, if heading east, beginning the day before you travel and continued on the same schedule according to your home-town clock).

However, the more popular reasons for taking the hormone—to aid sleep, increase immune function, or slow the aging process—have not demonstrated much support. To induce sleep, the herb valerian is much more popular than melatonin or sleep medications in Europe. In 1997 the

National Institute on Aging warned that melatonin may decrease fertility or sex drive; increase headaches; increase the risk of temporary depression; and, in tests with rats, restrict arteries in the brain.

For free fact sheets on melatonin, DHEA, human growth hormone, estrogen, and testosterone, call the National Institute on Aging 800-222-2225.

# OTHER DIETARY SUPPLEMENTS

## GLUCOSAMINE AND CHONDROITIN

Glucosamine and chondroitin in the human body is used to make cartilage, and have been touted as a way to reverse the effects of arthritis in *The Arthritis Cure* (Theodosakis, 1997). In supplement form, these compounds come from crab shells and cow cartilage and appear to ease arthritic aches almost as well as medications, with fewer side effects ("Natural Relief from Arthritis," 1997), and over a longer period (Morreale et al., 1996).

However, the risk of long-term use of these supplements is unclear, ideal doses have not been determined, and the quality of ingredients varies tremendously. Moreover, the substances are not cheap (glucosamine at $0.50 to $1.50 a day for 1,500 mg; and chondroitin at $0.75 to $2.00 a day for 800 to 1,200 mg), and the claims to protect cartilage or rebuild it are as yet unproven. Finally, researchers have not looked at whether a glucosamine plus chondroitin combination is more effective than taking either one separately.

## NUTRITIONAL DRINKS

Ensure, Sustacal, Nutra Start, and Boost are liquid meal supplements touted to increase energy. The supplements were designed for elderly persons who have debilitating health conditions that make it difficult for them to eat or keep their food down. Advertisers, however, are promoting the product to baby boomers and the young-old who are still in good health but are seeking more vitality. For them, these supplements may be expensive and ineffective. Sometimes the nutrients in these supplements are not fully absorbed by the body and provide only a third of the calories (about 240 versus 750) of a meal if used as a substitute.

# QUESTIONS FOR DISCUSSION

1. An older client asks you what supplements you are taking, and do you recommend taking vitamin E. How do you respond to these two requests for information?
2. How would you change the Dietary Supplement Health and Education Act so that it maintains as much consumer freedom as possible, while protecting the safety of the public?
3. Because many dietary supplements are naturally occurring substances and cannot be patented, how do you provide incentives to individual manufacturers in the United States to conduct more research?

# 8

# Other Health Education Topics

[T]o reduce cigarette smoking from a prevalence of 29% (baseline, 1987) to 15%.

[T]o increase the routine advisement of smoking cessation to patients and to provide assistance and follow-up from 52% (baseline, 1986) of internists to more than 75% of their smoking patients.

[T]o reduce deaths among people aged 85 and older from falls and fall-related injuries from 131 (baseline, 1987) to 105 per 100,000 people.

[T]o reduce hip fractures among people aged 65 and older so that hospitalizations for this condition are reduced from 714 (baseline, 1988) to 607 per 100,000. (Public health goals from the U.S. Public Health Service's Healthy People 2000 Initiative) (AARP, 1991)

Cigarette smoking for adults was reduced from a prevalence of 29% (baseline, 1987) to 25% in 1995; the routine advisement of smoking cessation to patients and to provide assistance and follow-up increased from 52% (baseline, 1986) by clinicians to 56% of their smoking patients in 1994; fall-related deaths among people aged 85 and older increased from 133 (baseline, 1987) to 150 per 100,000 people in 1993; hip fractures among people aged 65 and older (per 100,000) increased from 714 (baseline, 1988) to 815 in 1994.(*Healthy People 2000 Midcourse Review: 1995 Report on Progress*, DHHS, OPHS)

## SMOKING

### PREVALENCE

Although most health educators proclaim the three leading causes of death to be heart disease, cancer, and stroke, others view these diseases as pathological diagnoses rather than as causes (McGinnis, 1992). The latter group cites the three leading causes of death to be smoking (400,000 deaths per year), diet, and activity patterns (300,000), and alcohol (100,000). From the perspective of these experts, the number one cause of death is smoking tobacco. And the Americans who are most likely to die as a result of smoking are over the age of 60.

Tobacco is a worldwide problem, the leading cause of premature death in all developed countries (Peto et al., 1992). Each year, 20% of the more than 1.25 billion deaths worldwide can be attributed to tobacco. Individuals whose deaths are tobacco-related lose an average of 15 years of life expectancy.

The prevalence of smoking in the United States, in contrast to that in the rest of the world, is declining. In the early 1960s, 41% of American adults smoked; in 1987, 29% smoked; and in 1990, 25.5% smoked (Fiore, 1992). By 1995, however, smoking had leveled off at 25% of the population.

## ASSOCIATED DISEASES

Cigarette smoke irritates and inflames lungs and air passages and produces excess mucus. Over time, these effects lead to or exacerbate a variety of lung diseases, including cancer and COPD. The incidence of coronary heart disease and the risk of sudden death among smokers are about three times greater than for nonsmokers (United States Preventive Services Task Force, 1996).

More deaths occur from lung cancer than from any other cancer, yet lung cancer is rare among those who have never smoked (Office on Smoking and Health, 1989). Smokers with a two-pack (or more)-per-day habit have lung cancer rates about 20 times greater than those who have never smoked (American Cancer Society, 1990).

Cigarette smoking accounts for more than 60,000 of the 80,000 deaths each year that are due to chronic obstructive pulmonary disease (COPD) (Office on Smoking and Health, 1989). Moreover, death from COPD usually is preceded by an extended period of disability owing, in most cases, to chronic bronchitis or emphysema (National Center for Health Statistics, 1988).

## QUIT RATIO

I phoned my dad to tell him I had stopped smoking. He called me a
quitter. (Steven Pearl)

It's not that difficult to quit. I did it 1,000 times. (Mark Twain)

The United States has approximately 48 million smokers, and 48 million
have quit since 1976. In 1991, 34 million people wanted to quit, 17 million
attempted to quit, but only 1.3 million did quit (Fiore et al., 1992). The
quit ratio (the ratio of former smokers to those who have ever smoked)
for the U.S. population increased from just under 30% in 1965, to 45%
in 1985 (Kottke et al., 1988), and 49% in 1990 (Centers for Disease
Control, 1992).

Age, race, and gender may have a small relationship to the quit ratio,
but it is formal educational level that is the most important factor. People
without a high school diploma, for example, are more than twice as likely
to smoke than those with a college degree (38% vs. 16%), and those
without a college degree are less likely to quit than are those with a
college degree (40% vs. 61%) (Fiore, 1992).

In general, older adults smoke less than do younger adults (USDHHS,
1990). The lower rate may be attributable to a higher quit rate (either
self-initiated or in response to advice from a health care professional) but
is more likely to be linked to a higher mortality rate. The 1988 *Surgeon
General's Report on Smoking and Health* (USDHHS, 1989), for instance,
cites that men in their 30s who smoke more than two packs a day lose,
on average, 8 years of life.

## AGE-BASED OBSTACLES TO QUITTING

Older smokers are likely to be pessimistic about their ability to quit as a
consequence of a longer history of unsuccessful quit attempts. Nonetheless, the number of failed attempts in the past appears to be unrelated to
success in quitting (Cohen et al., 1990).

Older smokers do, however, contend with a longer smoking history,
the tendency to be thoroughly addicted and to have a heavy smoking
habit, the absence of the nonsmoking norms and influences in the workplace, limited knowledge about the physical effects of smoking, a fatalistic
attitude regarding the benefits of quitting at their age, and a slimmer

likelihood than younger smokers that they will be told by their physicians to quit (Rimer, 1988).

## IT IS NEVER TOO LATE TO QUIT

Two stereotypical attitudes about smokers who survive into old age are (a) they must be resistant to the health hazards of smoking, and (b) because of their advanced age, they no longer have time to benefit from a reduction in risk by quitting.

In fact, older smokers continue to have an increased risk of morbidity and mortality. Conversely, "older smokers who quit have a reduced risk of death compared with current smokers within 1 to 2 years after quitting" (LaCroix & Omenn, 1992, p. 84). Within 2 years, the risk of heart attack returns to that of nonsmokers, and the risk for lung cancer is reduced by one third (Fries, 1989).

Another factor that motivates older adults to quit smoking is the improvement in the quality of their lives after they stop. "Continued smoking in late life is associated with the development and progression of several major chronic conditions, loss of mobility, and poorer physical function. Former smokers appear to have higher levels of physical function and better quality of life than continuing smokers" (LaCroix & Omenn, 1992, p. 84).

## GENDER

The prevalence of smoking among adults in general has declined over the past two decades. This decline, however, has been considerably lower among females; in fact, there has been a slight rise among female smokers who are age 65 and older. By 1987, the prevalence of female smokers (27% of adults including 14% of older women) had approached that of male smokers (32% of adults including 17% of older men).

If this trend continues, the prevalence of women smokers will equal that of men smokers by the turn of the century (LaCroix & Omenn, 1992). The American Cancer Society predicts that, as a consequence, women's deaths from smoking-related disease will exceed those of men in about two decades.

Lung cancer death rates are estimated to climb rapidly about 20 to 30 years after a large increase in the incidence of smoking. Men began smoking in large numbers after the turn of the century, and their death rate from smoking peaked during the first half of the century. Women's rapid rise in smoking began in the 1950s, and, by 1986, lung cancer had surpassed breast cancer as the leading cause of cancer death among women (Brown & Kessler, 1988).

In 1991, 45% of women who had ever smoked had quit versus 52% of men. Researchers believe that it is more difficult for women to quit smoking because they depend on cigarettes to control their weight. In fact, a nationwide survey of adults over age 35 revealed that women who gave up smoking gained an average of 11 pounds and men 10 pounds (Flegal et al., 1995). Although from a health perspective a modest weight gain is much more desirable than continued cigarette smoking, it is a difficult trade-off for many female American smokers to make because of the perceived stigma.

## PHYSICIAN IMPACT ON SMOKERS

About 70% of all adult smokers visit a physician each year, with almost 80% of the heavy smokers claiming that they would stop smoking if their doctors urged them to do so (American Cancer Society, 1994). Only half of all smokers, however, report having heard an antitobacco admonition from their physician (Morain, 1994).

When client readiness is combined with the authority of the physician, even *brief* smoking cessation counseling by primary care physicians— especially when reinforced by follow-up visits or telephone calls during the first 4 to 8 weeks—is effective in getting clients to quit (Davis, 1988; Glynn & Manley, 1989; Kottke et al., 1988; Lewis, 1988). An attempt to quit is "twice as likely to occur among smokers who receive nonsmoking advice from their physicians compared with those who are not advised to quit" (Glynn, 1990).

If every primary care provider offered a smoking cessation intervention to smokers, it is estimated that an additional one million would quit each year (Hypertension Detection and Follow-Up Program Cooperative Group, 1988; Lewis, 1988). Physicians either overestimate the percentage of smoking clients that they counsel to stop smoking on a regular basis, or their clients do not hear them (National Center for Health Statistics, 1988).

In one study only 40% of smokers reported that they received counseling from a physician, although most physicians reported that they counsel smokers on a regular basis (Horton, 1986). Other studies show that most physicians report that they routinely inquire about patients' smoking habits, but only 25% (Taylor et al., 1982) to 50% (Marcus & Crane, 1987) of smokers say their physicians have told them to quit.

Physicians are more likely to communicate effectively with smoking clients if they are well prepared for the task (Cohen et al., 1989; Ginzel, 1985; Ockene, 1987). One simple but effective smoking cessation intervention consists of asking whether patients smoke, motivating them to quit, setting a date, providing a written reminder or prescription, and using either a nicotine patch or gum as a supplement.

These principles have been incorporated into the Doctors Helping Smokers (DHS) system, which was developed by Minnesota physicians Thomas Kottke, MD, cardiologist, and Leif Solberg, MD, family physician, in 1989. The system has been implemented in 31 Minnesota clinics and reimbursed through Blue Plus, a health maintenance organization.

DHS is based on the four *As*: ask if patients smoke; advise them that smoking is harmful; assist them by providing self-help guides, education, and counseling; and arrange for a follow-up visit, mailing, or telephone call as the proposed quit date nears. Nurses and receptionists assist the physician in counseling and follow-up duties. In addition, follow-up audits allow the team to devise ways to improve the system (*American Medical News*, May 11, 1992).

It should be noted that more than 90% of successful quitters do not participate in organized smoking cessation programs. Nevertheless, some evidence suggests that heavier, more addicted smokers may be good candidates for formal smoking cessation programs (Fiore et al., 1990).

Because it is unusual for smokers to achieve success the first time they attempt to quit, they should be urged to consider failed attempts learning experiences and encouraged to try again.Even clients who are not ready to quit smoking can be moved toward greater readiness (Glynn, 1990).

## PATCH

It is estimated that more than 80% of smokers relapse after their first attempt to quit (Zajac, 1992). Withdrawal symptoms, such as irritability, anxiety, restlessness, and a craving for nicotine, are the major cause of relapse. Nicotine is the psychoactive drug that is primarily responsible for the addictive nature of tobacco use.

The nicotine transdermal delivery system, commonly referred to as the nicotine patch, was developed to combat withdrawal symptoms. In late 1991, the FDA approved three nicotine patches, Nicoderm, Habitrol, and ProStep. Nicoderm is the best-selling patch and employs a weaning process that releases 21 mg of nicotine a day, then dropping to 14 mg, followed by 7 mg over an 8- or 10-week period.

In 1996, Nicoderm became available over the counter as NicoDerm CO and soon thereafter increased its sales to about one half of the smoking-cessation aids market. Nicorette gum controls 40% of the market, followed by Nicotrol, another patch, at 10%. Thanks to relaxed FDA guidelines in 1997 making it easier to advertise prescription drugs on television, sales of the stop-smoking medication Zyban soared. The downside of over the counter medications and televised advertising is that it can undermine the authority of health professionals.

Both the patch and the gum manufacturers highly recommend that their aids be used as a component of a behavior modification and support group program. These educational programs typically include self-monitoring of daily living habits to determine which habits need to be changed to support a lifestyle without cigarette use. Other program components usually include a combination of breathing and other stress management exercises, nutrition education, assertiveness training, exercise, peer support, and tips for relapse prevention.

After reviewing all placebo-controlled, double-blind nicotine patch studies with at least 6 months' follow-up, Fiore and colleagues (1992) concluded that nicotine patches produced 6-month abstinence rates of 22% to 42%—higher percentages representing patches combined with education and support—while placebo patches produced quit rates of 5% to 28% (Fiore et al., 1992). Thus, education and support, in addition to the nicotine patches, appear to be significant factors in the long-term success of those who stop smoking.

## COMBINING INTERVENTIONS

The most effective behavior management strategy for stopping smoking employs a combination of approaches (Sarafino, 1990; United States Preventive Services Task Force, 1996). A health contract, which employs a variety of strategies (see chapter 3), such as social support, contingency contracting, problem-solving skills, and the involvement of a physician who signs the contract, is one effective technique.

Another strategy for clinicians is to have clients prepare ahead for smoking cessation. Clients should dispose of extra cigarettes and paraphernalia (ash trays, lighters); self-monitor how much they smoke, when, and with which mood states, and eliminate some cigarettes that are easy to omit; switch to a lower-nicotine brand of cigarettes; announce a quit date to their physician, family members, and friends; stock up on cigarette substitutes (celery and carrot sticks); spend less time with smokers, and avoid smoking situations.

For tips on how to remain a nonsmoker, see chapter 10 on behavior management. A wide range of strategies needs to be combined for maximum effect. An example follows:

1. *Solicit social support.* Engage the physician, spouse, friend, or support group.
2. *Employ response substitution.* Instead of smoking after dinner, quickly clean your mouth by brushing your teeth, taking a shower (where smoking will be difficult at best), or substituting a celery stalk or carrot stick for a cigarette.
3. *Activate a stress management routine.* Perhaps implement a daily deep-breathing regimen or progressive muscle relaxation.

It is wise to acknowledge the likelihood of relapses, and not to exaggerate or overgeneralize the implications of a failure or associate it with future attempts. Estimates of relapses within a year after stopping vary from 50% to 80% (Brownell et al., 1986). Techniques that were successful in initially helping an individual quit should be reapplied after a relapse.

## Taxes

In 1988, a California state referendum increasing cigarette taxes by $0.25 per pack required that 20% of the tax money be used for smoking cessation programs, especially for an antismoking television campaign. The state of Nevada also adopted a $0.25 per pack cigarette tax but did not institute a smoking cessation campaign.

The result? The reduction rate in cigarette smoking almost quadrupled in California but was not significantly affected in Nevada (*American Medical News*, February 8, 1993, p. 31). The decision to quit smoking, at least in Nevada, was not made on economic grounds alone. Moreover, antismoking media funding was reduced substantially in California in 1995–1996, and tobacco industry expenditures for advertising and promotion increased substantially. Not surprisingly, the intial effect of the antismoking television campaign did not persist (Pierce et al., 1998).

In addition, smokers will do what it takes to minimize economic disincentives. A study of taxes on cigarette consumption from 1955 through 1994 reported that state taxes are less effective than federal taxes because smokers will bootleg cigarettes across state lines to avoid state taxes (Meier & Licari, 1997).

## ATTACKING THE TOBACCO INDUSTRY

In January 1993, an Environmental Protection Agency report, widely publicized in the media, declared that passive tobacco smoke is a human carcinogen responsible for 3,000 lung cancer deaths annually among U.S. nonsmokers and that there is an increased risk of cancer, lower respiratory tract infection, and severe asthma symptoms among children. Subsequent research has also documented the link between secondhand smoke and heart disease (Kawachi et al., 1997).

This 1993 report contributed to the implementation of subsequent smoking restrictions. Restaurants and other public places imposed restrictions in response to the fear of legal action by patrons and employees. (California became the first state in 1998 to extend the smoking ban to bars, casinos, and even private clubs.) Excise taxes on tobacco were raised to fund educational programs for the public, especially targeted to nonsmoking children and the spouses of smokers, regarding the dangers of secondhand tobacco smoke.

About the same time, Michael T. Lewis, a personal injury lawyer from Clarksdale, Mississippi, developed a strategy for attacking the tobacco industry on the basis of secondhand tobacco smoke and tobacco-related illnesses. Realizing that smokers as plaintiffs had almost no chance of winning conventional lawsuits, this small-town lawyer convinced the Mississippi attorney general to sue the tobacco companies to recover money the state spent in Medicaid bills for cigarette-related illness. By April 1997, 25 states had filed copycat suits against the tobacco industry.

Also during the 1990s, the FDA commissioner, David Kessler, MD, became convinced that the smoking industry deliberately relied on nicotine to hook smokers and, moreover, that they intentionally marketed to minors. In 1996, in fact, daily smoking among 12th graders had reached its highest level (21.6%) since 1979. Dr. Kessler, therefore, unveiled a proposal to restrict the sale and marketing of cigarettes to minors, and, in 1996, President Clinton, realizing that youth-smoking curbs would be politically viable, allowed the FDA to enforce it.

Attacked on both economic and political fronts, the tobacco industry appeared ready to pay a $368.5 billion legal settlement for the Medicaid expenses associated with smoking-related illnesses. Other features of the settlement included FDA regulation of nicotine content, advertising and labeling restrictions especially as they related to minors, and tobacco company financial penalties if youth-smoking rates did not decrease. In exchange, the tobacco industry would receive immunity from lawsuits for punitive damage that their products cause, and a cap on other damages.

By early 1998, however, critics of the government, emboldened by economic and political successes, were contending that the settlement was not strong enough. Moreover, they argued, tobacco companies should not be allowed to shift their focus to exporting tobacco products to overseas markets. The World Health Organization reported that in 1997, cigarette consumption was decreasing in developed countries and increasing in developing nations. Americans accounted for only 4% of smokers world-wide, as the percentage of smokers in, for instance, China increased to 40%, and among Vietnamese men, to 70%.

It remains to be seen how well the tobacco industry will survive the attack by state and federal governments. In mid-1998 they decided that the best defense was a good offense. After a series of television and newspaper advertisements attacking "Big Government" (and reportedly spending 40 million dollars in 30 days), the tobacco industry managed to sway public opinion, resulting in an inundation of letters to Congress and a temporary standstill in the federal and state governments' war on tobacco.

### Additional Programs and Materials

Fresh Start is a group smoking-cessation program that is offered by many local chapters of the American Cancer Society. To locate your local chapter or to obtain several free publications on smoking cessation, contact the American Cancer Society, 1599 Clifton Road, Atlanta, GA 30329; 404-320-3333, or 800-227-2345 (Information Service).

Two booklets, *Clearing the Air—A Guide to Quitting Smoking* and *Guide to Quit Smoking for Your Health and Your Family* (the latter available in Spanish as well) offer strategies and suggestions for quitting and staying a nonsmoker. These booklets (up to 200 copies free) are available from the Office of Cancer Communications, National Cancer Institute, Building 31, Room 10A24, Bethesda, MD 20892; 800-422-6237.

*Freedom from Smoking* is offered by local affiliates of the American Lung Association. To locate your local chapter, or to obtain manuals, audio and video tapes, films, posters, and buttons, contact The American Lung Association, 1720 Broadway,New York, NY 10019-4374; 212-315-8700.

Local affiliates of the American Heart Association offer a series of 9-minute videos entitled, *In Control: A Video Freedom from Smoking Program* and a manual, *Calling It Quits*. To obtain copies, contact the American Heart Association, 7320 Greenville Avenue, Dallas, TX 75231; 214-373-6300.

The *Smoking and Health Bulletin*; a free guide entitled *Out of the Ashes: Choosing a Method to Quit Smoking*; a free bibliography on smoking and health, and materials on smoking-cessation techniques are available from the Office on Smoking and Health, Park Building, Room 1-16, 5600 Fishers Lane, Rockville, MD 20857; 301-443-5287. Smoking-cessation kits are available from the American Academy of Family Physicians; 800-944-0000.

# ALCOHOL

## DEFINITION

No consensus exists among alcohol researchers and other experts regarding what constitutes moderate drinking and what constitutes alcoholism (Dufour et al., 1992). The Department of Agriculture (1990) somewhat arbitrarily defined moderate drinking as no more than two drinks a day for men and one drink a day for women, with a drink defined as approximately 12 ounces of beer, 5 ounces of wine, or 1.5 ounces of spirits.

Dufour and colleagues (1992) conclude, however, that "given the dramatic increase in the proportion of body fat with aging and the concomitant decrease in volume of total body water," a maximum of one drink a day is advised for older men.

It may be best, when attempting to define alcoholism, to avoid associating it with a specific number of drinks. One definition states that alcoholism is "impaired control over drinking, preoccupation with the drug alcohol, use of alcohol despite adverse consequences, and distortions in thinking, most notably denial" (Morse & Flavin, 1992).

The diagnostic criteria for alcohol dependence used in the *Diagnostic and Statistical Manual of Mental Disorders* is the persistence, for a month or more, of three or more of the following nine criteria:

1. Drinking more or over a longer period than previously
2. Persistent desire or unsuccessful efforts to cut down or control use
3. Considerable time spent in obtaining, drinking, or recovering from the effects of alcohol
4. Intoxication or withdrawal when expected to fulfill major obligations
5. Important activities given up or reduced because of drinking
6. Continued use despite knowledge of having persistent or recurrent psychological or physical problems related to alcohol
7. Marked tolerance
8. Withdrawal symptoms
9. Drinking to relieve or avoid withdrawal symptoms

## TYPES OF ALCOHOLISM

About one third of elderly alcoholics are late-onset, reactive problem drinkers. Late-onset alcoholics are likely to be the product of a life-cycle crisis, such as the death of a spouse or the loss of a physical function. Once the precipitating event is identified and therapy is pursued, the condition may be reversible. In fact, a return to moderate drinking may be viable for late-onset alcoholics (Nathan, 1986).

Early-onset drinkers have had a drinking problem for many years and have either avoided or undergone unsuccessful treatment. Although the prognosis for successful treatment of chronic, lifelong problem drinkers is poor, they may be successfully treated. However, successful treatment requires sustained belief in the ability of the older person to recover and a refusal to be discouraged by the pessimism that characterizes many health professionals (Hans, 1990).

## ASSESSMENT

During the early stages of alcoholism, no physical signs nor symptoms signal the shift from health to disease. Often, though, behavioral problems, such as repetitive accidents or injuries or ongoing family or work problems, accompany alcohol misuse.

It may be especially difficult to detect alcohol problems among retired persons, who have few opportunities to experience problems in the work or community setting. It is estimated that physicians make the correct diagnosis of alcoholism in older adults in only 22% to 37% of actual cases seen in emergency departments or during hospitalizations ("AMA Reports Hidden Epidemic of Elderly Alcoholism," 1995). Even when alcoholism is recognized, the physician is less likely to initiate or recommend treatment for older clients than for younger clients (Curtis et al., 1989).

One of the most popular assessment tools for busy health professionals and one that has been tested with older clients is the CAGE questionnaire. It has good sensitivity and specificity for alcohol abuse in general, though is less sensitive to early problems or heavy drinking (United States Preventive Services Task Force, 1996). The four questions in this instrument ask:

Have you ever:

| Thought about | *C*utting down? |
| Felt | *A*nnoyed when others criticize your drinking? |
| Felt | *G*uilty about drinking? |
| Used alcohol as an | *E*ye opener? |

Two or more affirmative responses to the preceding questions suggest an alcohol problem.

Although the CAGE instrument is practical for the busy health care professional, more sensitivity and specificity can be obtained with longer questionnaires, especially the well-tested 25-item Michigan Alcohol Screening Test (MAST) (Selzer, 1971) that has been also tested with older adults (Schonfeld, 1993). The MAST, however, is too lengthy for routine screening. Both a brief version of the MAST and the CAGE lose sensitivity when used in a community where the base rate of alcoholism is low (Crowe et al., 1997).

A third commonly used assessment tool is the Alcohol Use Disorders Identification Test (AUDIT). The value of the AUDIT is that it also incorporates questions about quantity, frequency, and binge behavior (United States Preventive Services Task Force, 1996). Conversely, the AUDIT focuses on drinking in the previous year and is less sensitive for past drinking problems that can help the clinician distinguish between late-onset versus long-term drinking problems.

## PREVALENCE

The American Medical Association estimates that about 3 million Americans older than age 60 have a drinking problem. Moreover, at least 10% of patients who go to an emergency room with an alcohol-related problem are over age 60 ("Measuring Alcohol's Effect On You," 1996), though the prevalence of alcohol-related hospitalizations declines with age for both men and women (Adams et al., 1993).

Although problem drinking in late life is less than for younger adults, the risks of alcohol abuse for older drinkers are elevated: falls and accidents, dementias, medical problems, and interactions with prescription and over-the-counter drugs (Maddox, 1988; Schonfeld, 1993). Nutritional deficiencies are more common among older alcohol drinkers because of the increased inhibition of the absorption of many nutrients.

## ASSOCIATED DISEASES AND PROBLEMS

Our bodies absorb a higher percentage of alcohol consumed as we age because lean body mass has decreased and our volume of body water is smaller. Thus, in later years we become more vulnerable to malnutrition, liver disease, chronic obstructive pulmonary disease, peptic ulcers, and some forms of cancer (Schonfeld, 1993).

Although alcohol adds calories to the diet, it adds almost no nutrients; therefore, malnutrition becomes a problem. Other problems of excess alcohol consumption are an increased risk of injury or accident, especially when driving, and (along with excess caffeine and medications) an adverse affect on sleep.

At least 100 of the most commonly prescribed medications interact negatively with alcohol. This interaction effect along with the increased vulnerability of older adults to alcohol abuse accounts for the fact that older adults are hospitalized as often for alcohol-related problems as for heart attacks (Adams et al., 1993).

## INTERVENTION AND REFERRAL

Most patients with suspected drinking problems receive no counseling from primary care physicians. One study cited that about a third of physicians report having counseled patients on alcohol abuse (Rosen et al., 1984). However, the percentage is likely to appear much lower when patient records are examined. One study of patient records, in fact, revealed that only 18% of patients were counseled by physicians (Hayward et al., 1987).

Older adults often drink in response to depression and loneliness, whereas younger adults are likely to use multiple substances to assuage their anger, frustration, tension, interpersonal conflicts, and social pressure (Schonfeld et al., 1992). If interventions are to be effective, most older adults with alcohol abuse problems will need to be referred by their health professionals to groups or specialists who recognize the different needs of older and younger persons.

Some evidence indicates that persons referred to age-specific support groups remain in treatment longer and complete treatment more often than those in age-mixed groups (Atkinson et al., 1985; Kofoed et al., 1987). Problems such as widowhood and retirement, which are not of universal concern, may be particularly difficult for older people to share in support groups of mixed ages (Schonfeld, 1993). Borkman (1982) reports that older adults might also be reluctant to air their problems in AA groups with predominantly younger memberships.

About a third of those who attend meetings of Alcoholics Anonymous (AA) are older than age 50, and many communities operate programs specifically for older adults. Health professionals should be familiar with community resources before referring problem patients to other health providers or programs. It may be helpful to call the state alcohol or drug abuse agency for a list of the publicly and privately funded treatment programs and AA groups in the state (Kinney, 1989). Health professionals may need to help clients set up an appointment, and may wish to request reports from treatment providers.

## TREATMENT ALTERNATIVES

*Detoxification programs* focus on the drying-out process, providing medical supervision to addicted persons going through periods of withdrawal. Because withdrawal symptoms can be severe, most, but not all, detoxification programs are affiliated with hospitals and under the supervision of a physician.

AA employs a strategy that encourages public confession, intense social support, contrition, and a spiritual or philosophical awakening (Robertson, 1988). Founded in the 1930s, AA today has thousands of chapters throughout the United States and the world. Companion organizations have been set up for the spouses (Al-Anon), teen-age children of alcoholics (Alateen), and adult children of alcoholics.

Professionally led programs and support groups should be viewed as complementary rather than as competition for one another. The anonymous nature of membership in AA makes it difficult to compare these two types of interventions. Professionally run treatment programs may be more effective than AA groups for some individuals (Brandsma et al., 1980); for example, older alcoholics may be unprepared for the openness that characterizes these support groups or may not have access to a support group with other older alcoholics to whom they can relate.

Professionally led programs, however, whatever their advantages, are typically costly and time bound, whereas support groups can and do meet frequently (sometimes several times a week) on an ongoing basis.

The self-management strategies outlined under smoking cessation, and the vulnerability to relapse, are applicable to alcohol addiction as well. Behavior management techniques may need to be reapplied on multiple occasions.

## POSITIVE EFFECTS OF ALCOHOL USAGE

"Reasonably small and controlled alcohol intake may be of benefit to the elderly, as it may stimulate appetite, increase socialization, and may play a 'protective' role against coronary artery disease" (Lamy, 1988).

A survey of 490,000 adults, ranging in age from 30 to 104, concluded that taking an alcoholic drink a day provides a slight edge in longevity compared with nondrinkers (Thun et al., 1997). People who drank a small amount of alcohol on a daily basis reduced their incidence of heart disease and stroke, and modestly outweighed their increased risk of death from cancer (especially breast cancer) and accidents that are also associated with regular drinking. The study authors were not touting alcohol as the preventive therapy of choice for middle-aged people at higher risk of heart disease since one drink of alcohol daily is not the drinking pattern of many Americans.

Nursing homes, however, may be one type of facility where the introduction of alcohol can be an effective preventive therapy. Research findings indicate that moderate alcohol drinking in nursing home institutions improves mental health and functioning, although the effects of an increased opportunity for socialization have not been separated from such factors as increased personal control.

After a comprehensive review of the literature, two researchers concluded that "institutionalized senior citizens who are treated like adults and allowed to continue practices they pursued in independent life are more likely to have higher self-esteem and, therefore, better subjective feelings of well-being, regardless of whether or not they elect to consume alcohol" (Mishara & Kastenbaus, 1980).

## Resources

For written material and other resources on alcohol abuse, contact:

Alcoholics Anonymous, 475 Riverside Drive, 11th Floor, New York, NY 10115, or the Web site, www.aa.org; or the local chapter of Alcoholics Anonymous, Al-Anon and Adult Children of Alcoholics, listed in area phone books, or the Web sites, www.al-anon-alateen. org.

National Clearinghouse for Alcohol and Drug Abuse Information, P.O. Box 2345, Rockville, MD 20852; 800-729-6686.

National Council on Alcoholism and Drug Dependence, Inc., 12 West 21st Street, New York, NY 10010; 800-622-2255.

Hazelden's brochure on "How to Talk to an Older Person Who Has a Problem with Alcohol or Medications," and other materials, call 800-I-DO-CARE, or contact the Web site, www.hazelden. org.

## MEDICATION USAGE

More than 10,000 prescription drugs currently are available, about 2 billion prescriptions are dispensed, and countless over-the-counter medications are consumed. It is not unreasonable to suggest that most Americans consider taking medications a normal part of life.

Because vulnerability to chronic disease increases over time, medication usage becomes more typical with age. Although adults age 65 and older constituted 12.4% of the population, they accounted for more than 34% of outpatient prescription medications and nearly half of those purchased over-the-counter ("Protecting Yourself Against Prescription Errors," 1996). Older persons rely on drugs to alleviate pain and discomfort and to give them a sense of security and control in sometimes frightening health situations. Drugs, however, can make matters worse as well as better. The potential for serious adverse drug reactions is great.

About 50% of all prescriptions are not taken properly and, according to the National Council on Patient Information and Education an estimated 125,000 Americans die each year from prescription drug misuse. In fact, you are more likely to die from prescription medication than from an accident, pneumonia, or diabetes (Lazarou et al., 1998).

In addition, about 15% to 20% of hospital and nursing home admissions are the result of adverse drug reactions ("Protecting Yourself Against Prescription Errors," 1996). This percentage is probably underestimated because medical personnel are unwilling to file additional reports to the FDA (Lazarou et al., 1998). Adverse drug reactions probably affect older adults three times as often as the general population (Sloan, 1986).

To avoid adverse drug reactions, patients need to comply with their medication regimen, report unexpected side effects, and show caution with over-the-counter medications. Health professionals need to take a good drug history, carefully assess the dosage, communicate the rationale for the drug treatment and the expected response and common side effects, and monitor patient reactions.

Unfortunately, both professionals and patients tend to fall short of the ideal. Consequently, overmedication, drug interactions, and medication side effects are quite common.

## RISK OF POLYPHARMACY

"Even when nonpharmacological treatments are suitable for a given condition, physicians often prescribe medications. Predictably, the greater the number of drugs prescribed, the greater the risk of inadvertent or intentional misuse of drugs by the patient or caregiver" (Montamat & Cusack, 1992).

Polypharmacy is the use of more medication than is clinically indicated. Older adults are particularly vulnerable to polypharmacy because most of the chronic conditions associated with aging are potentially responsive to medications. This leads to the increased risk of multiple drug use among older adults, complicated by the fact that many older patients see more than one health care provider. With more than one provider, prescription and over-the-counter drug usage may not be coordinated, and older clients are vulnerable to potential interactions (drug-drug, drug-allergy, drug-food/drink, drug-disease) and therapeutic duplication.

This challenge has been met, to some extent, by the fact that almost all pharmacies in this country are using computers. Nonetheless, many pharmacies do not have complete computer records of all the medication usage of their clients.

The potential causes of polypharmacy or drug misuse are listed by Montamat and Cusack (1992).

## PATIENT-RELATED FACTORS

1. Expectation of physician to prescribe medication
2. Inadequate reporting of current medications
3. Failure to complain about symptoms, especially if related to medications
4. Use of multiple, automatic refills without visiting a physician
5. Hoarding prior medications
6. Use of multiple pharmacies or multiple physicians
7. Borrowing medications from family members or friends
8. Self-medication with over-the-counter drugs
9. Impaired cognition or vision
10. Economic factors, such as high drug costs

## PHYSICIAN-RELATED FACTORS

1. Presumption that patients expect a prescription
2. Drug treatment of symptoms without sufficient clinical evaluation
3. Treatment of conditions without setting goals of therapy
4. Communication of instructions in unclear, complex, or incomplete manner

5. Failure to review medications and their possible adverse effects at regular intervals
6. Use of automatic refills without adequate follow-up
7. Lack of knowledge of geriatric clinical pharmacology, leading to inappropriate prescribing practices
8. Inadequate supervision of medications in long-term care
9. Failure to simplify drug regimens as often as possible

## PREVENTION

One of the most effective prevention strategies against drug abuse is to avoid unnecessary medication. Many Americans unthinkingly take pills to alleviate constipation, insomnia, indigestion, headache, and other types of pain or discomfort. Diet, exercise, and stress management, however, may be effective alternatives that eliminate the danger of medication side effects.

Elderly clients with high blood pressure are susceptible to severe adverse drug reactions (Potter & Haigh, 1990); treating some patients with nonpharmacological alternatives to blood pressure medication may be appropriate. Older adults can be responsive to a reduction in sodium intake (Horwath, 1991), and exercise can reduce the risk of elevating blood pressure levels (Evans et al., 1991).

"Physician and patient must have an understanding of the . . . degree to which (the other) favors chemical or psychological coping devices" (Taylor et al., 1982, p. 299). Many patients, and some physicians, believe a productive medical encounter requires the writing of a prescription. In support of this assertion, about 75% of all physician visits result in the prescription of a drug (Kemper et al., 1985). Along with unnecessary prescriptions, older clients are likely to be the least knowledgeable about the drugs prescribed for them (American Board of Family Practice, 1987).

If prescriptions become the treatment of choice, more patients may be willing to participate actively in choosing among medication alternatives (type, dosage, and schedules) than the physician feels comfortable with (American Board of Family Practice, 1987). Yet active participation in choosing drugs is likely to lead to better compliance (Taylor et al., 1982).

## ADVICE FROM PHARMACISTS

Since January 1993, pharmacists have been required to give Medicaid patients advice about their prescription drugs. When the federal Health

Care Financing Administration implemented these rules, some state boards of pharmacies expanded them to cover all patients.

In addition to informing patients verbally and in writing, pharmacies must maintain files of patient information (including a list of the medicines and health care devices being used by the patient). The pharmacist must provide specific information about each medication, its common side effects, potential interactions, and contraindications, and must instruct patients on monitoring their responses, explaining what to do if a dose is missed, and how to store the medicine. Since 1995, pharmacies have been required to provide an area suitable for confidential patient counseling.

The only consumer who is still at a disadvantage, especially in monitoring potential interaction effects, is the one who pharmacy hops for either financial purposes or convenience. It is not uncommon for a patient to obtain prescription drugs from multiple sources, such as a community pharmacy, a hospital pharmacy, a mail-order pharmacy, and directly from the physician. In the future, however, a credit card system could be implemented to enable patients to carry prescription records with them wherever they go.

### PHYSICIAN'S EXPERIENCE

"Recently, I spoke to a group of older people. I told them that as a young doctor I had spent most of my time putting patients on drugs. But now that I'm an old doctor, I spend a lot of my time taking patients off drugs. I thought the remark might elicit a few smiles or chuckles. Instead, they rose as a body, cheering and clapping" (Morgan, 1993).

### RESOURCES

Many readily available booklets on medication provide a good consumer safety tool for today's cohort of older adults. These booklets remind consumers of important questions to ask their physicians and pharmacists about their medications, offer several ideas to improve daily compliance in taking medications, provide a listing of generic equivalencies, note commonly reported side effects of particular medications, and offer blank charts for listing all prescriptions and over-the-counter medications prior to visiting a physician.

Consumers who are vulnerable to psychological and emotional factors that may affect their use of medications, can obtain free copies of a booklet entitled, *So Many Pills and I Still Don't Feel Good: Suggestions for Preventing Problems With Medications.* The booklet helps individuals recognize times when they may be at risk for misuse of medications, suggests ways to manage medications, lists questions to ask the doctor or pharmacist about medications, and suggests things to do if there is a problem with medication usage. Up to 50 free copies are available from AARP Fulfillment, 601 E. Street NW, Washington, DC 20049 (Order No. PF 4767 [1091] D 14581).

Two other booklets that I recommend from having used them in community health education classes are provided free by AARP: *The Smart Consumer's Guide to Prescription Drugs* (Order No. PF 4297[389]-D13579) and *Using Your Medicines Wisely: A Guide for the Elderly* (Order No. PF 1436[1185]-D317). Contact AARP Publications, Program Resources, 601 E. Street NW, Washington, DC 20049.

To get questions answered about the drug approval process, drug reactions, and new and approved medications, contact the FDA, Center for Drug Evaluation and Research, CDER—Executive Secretariat (HFD-8), 5600 Fishers Lane, Rockville, MD 29857; 301-295-8012.

AARP's mail-order pharmacy is for members of AARP (who are age 50 and older and pay a small annual membership fee). This network of regional pharmacies provide information on common prescription drugs, their side effects, and cost differences between brand names and generic drugs: AARP Pharmacy Service, 500 Montgomery Street, Alexandria, VA 22314; 703-684-0244 or 800-456-2277.

Three sources of free information on older persons and medications are (a) FDA, Consumer Affairs Office, 5600 Fishers Lane, HFE 88, Rockville, MD 20857; 301-443-3170; (b) The Elder Health Program, School of Pharmacy, University of Maryland at Baltimore, 20 N. Pine Street, Baltimore, MD 21201; 410-706-3011; and (c) The National Institute on Aging, P.O. Box 8057, Gaithersburg, MD 20898-8057; 800-222-2225.

## INJURY PREVENTION

Injuries constitute the sixth leading cause of death for persons age 65 and older (USDHHS, 1990); their mortality rate from injuries is more than twice that of other age groups (Maddox, 1987). Two of the main antecedents of injuries are falls and motor vehicles.

Several physical and environmental factors contribute to the greater frequencies and seriousness of injuries as we age. Diminished vision and hearing, poor coordination and balance, slower reaction time, arthritis, and neurological disease all are intrinsic to the increased vulnerability to falls and motor vehicle accidents of older adults. In addition, medication use, which increases with age, can produce drowsiness, confusion, and depression, and increase the probability of accidents (Spirduso, 1995).

Other factors are extrinsic to the increased incidence of accidents among older people. Homes age along with people; uneven floor surfaces and the absence of safety equipment (like grab bars for bathtubs and showers) in older homes contribute to accidents. Other environmental culprits are throw rugs, inadequate lighting, steep stairs, and lack of railings on stairs.

Accidents increase as road repairs and improvements and law enforcement fail to keep pace with the increased demands of traffic. Transportation systems and cars are not designed with older people's capacities in mind. And few cities acknowledge the need to lengthen the duration of walk signals at crosswalks to accommodate older pedestrians.

## FALLS

Approximately 60% of persons who die from falls are age 65 or older, and more than half of the older adults who are hospitalized from a fall do not live more than one year (Rivara et al., 1997; Spirduso, 1995). People age 75 and older account for 59% of all fall deaths, even though they are only 5% of the population ("Accidents Don't Just Happen," 1995). Also, falls account for 87% of all fractures in older adults, and few older adults who have serious hip fractures ever regain their previous function (Rivara et al., 1997; Spirduso, 1995).

The primary risk factors for falling are balance abnormalities, muscular weakness, visual disorders, gait abnormalities, cardiovascular disease, cognitive impairment, medication, and environmental hazards (Spirduso, 1995). Many of these risks are preventable. Tai chi, for instance, improves balance and reduces falls (Wolf et al., 1996; Wolfson et al., 1996). Weight-bearing exercise reduces the risk of hip fracture and falls (Campbell et al., 1997; Paganini-Hill et al., 1991; Tinetti et al., 1993). Environmental changes (e.g., night lights, fluid limitation after supper, placement of objects and furniture) recommended by nurses can also lead to a reduction in the incidence of falls by older adults (Turkoski et al., 1997).

Regarding environmental hazards, up to 40% of older adults living in the community fall each year, and 75% of these falls occur within the home (Kiernat, 1991). It behooves the health professional, therefore, to recommend a home assessment to identify conditions that increase the risk for falling, to suggest environmental changes, and to educate their clients to reduce the risks.

Two thirds of all deaths resulting from falls in the home are preventable (Ferrini & Ferrini, 1989). Following is a list of simple precautions that can reduce the risk of falls within the home:

1. Provide proper illumination and convenient light switches—by the bed, at the end of the hall, and at the top and bottom of stairs. Older persons generally need two to three times as much illumination as younger persons do.
2. Install handrails, and place nonslip treads in strategic locations.
3. Tack down or remove loose throw rugs and repair torn carpet.
4. Install grab bars, and use adhesive strips in shower and bath. Only 6% of the dwelling units of older persons have grab bars in their bathrooms.
5. Eliminate such hazards as trailing electrical cords, sharp corners, slippery floors, and household items that require a step stool to reach.
6. Lower bed height for ease in getting in and out.
7. Wear footwear that provides adequate traction, such as supportive, rubber-soled, low-heeled shoes.
8. Exercise to improve balance, flexibility, strength, and coordination.
9. Avoid the misuse of medications and alcohol.

Several health conditions place older individuals at risk for falling. Some of these conditions are dizzy spells, osteoporosis, arthritis, alcoholism, structural diseases of the feet, stroke, visual or hearing impairments, gait and balance disorders, physical weakness, and the use of medications that impair coordination and balance or result in frequent trips to the bathroom at night. A multidisciplinary geriatric assessment can identify those at risk and thereby help to prevent serious injuries from falls.

An increasing number of departments of internal medicine and family medicine at university medical schools, as well as private practitioners, provide multidisciplinary geriatric assessments. Teams invariably include a physician and nurse; those that also include health professionals, such as occupational therapists, physical therapists, counselors, social workers, health educators, pharmacists, and dentists, are of enhanced benefit to consumers.

A telephone emergency alert system with a signaling device, worn around the neck or on the belt of older adults who have a tendency to fall, can ensure a prompt reaction to the situation.

Two guides that include summaries of innovative programs to prevent falls, short descriptions of research findings on the topic, a home safety/ fall prevention assessment tool, and educational strategies are provided by the AARP. For a copy of the 1992 booklet, *The Perfect Fit: Creative Ideas for a Safe and Livable Home*, or the 1993 booklet, *Fall Prevention Guide*, contact, AARP/Program Resources, 601 E. Street NW, Washington, DC 20049.

## MOTOR VEHICLE AND PEDESTRIAN ACCIDENTS

There were 24 million registered drivers at least 70 years of age in 1998 and that number will increase to more than 40 million by the year 2020. The rate of motor vehicle accidents for people age 65 and older is second only to that for young adults between the ages of 15 and 24. As older adults constitute a larger percentage of the population, they will account for an increasing share of the motor vehicle accidents each year. Once having been in an accident, older adults are more prone to serious injury and death.

Several physiological changes affect the driving of older adults. Arthritis makes it difficult to turn the head and directly observe cars coming up from behind. Slower reflexes make emergencies more dangerous to contend with. Susceptibility to glare, poor adaptation to dark, and the need for additional light make night driving riskier. Cognitive impairment rises with age and has been linked to higher motor vehicle crash rates in elderly individuals (Retchin & Anapolle, 1993). Medical conditions, and comorbidity in particular, are correlated with decreased driving amount and driving cessation (Forrest et al., 1997).

Driving in late life is not necessarily an all-or-none proposition. Older adults who find driving an automobile increasingly difficult can restrict their driving to areas with little traffic, avoid rush hours, and abstain from driving at night. In addition, older adults may need to be vigilant about restricting their driving to those periods when their medications are not slowing their reaction time or compromising their vision.

Measures to prevent motor vehicle accidents include the following:

1. Enroll in a driver safety class designed for midlife and older motorists, such as a course through AARP (55-Alive) or the state motor vehicle department.
2. Adjust to hearing and vision losses (e.g., keep radio, air conditioner, and heater noise low, and crack window open to hear warning signals; wear good-quality sunglasses, and keep windows clean inside and out).
3. Time trips to minimize the effects of medications.
4. Stop frequently to stretch muscles and rest eyes.
5. Limit driving to the safest times of day and to familiar areas.
6. Use seat belts all the time, even on short trips and in cars with airbags to prevent injury from side collision.
7. Keep the car in good working condition.
8. Avoid drinking while driving.
9. Lobby for state policies that are more responsive to the functional abilities of drivers, and the reporting responsibilities of physicians.

AARP's 55 Alive/Mature Driving Program is available around the country. It is an 8-hour, classroom-based, driver education refresher course for persons 50 and older, and is taught by instructors who are also 50 and older. In some states, drivers who complete the course are eligible for a discount on automobile insurance. For more information, contact the American Association of Retired Persons, 55 Alive/Mature Driving Program, Traffic and Driver Safety Program, 601 E. Street NW, Washington, DC 20049; 800-434-2277.

Older adults are more likely than members of any other age group to be injured by motor vehicles while crossing a street and experience the highest death rate from pedestrian accidents (USDHHS, 1985). A study of 1,249 residents aged 72 or older from New Haven, Connecticut, revealed that fewer than 1% of these pedestrians had a normal walking speed sufficient to cross the street in the time typically allotted at signalized intersections (Langlois et al., 1997).

The following measures to avoid pedestrian accidents are recommended:

1. Wear highly visible clothing, preferably of light-colored or even fluorescent material.

2. Do not assume moving vehicles see pedestrians.
3. Lobby local officials to install properly timed pedestrian traffic signals.
4. Start a pedestrian safety club in the neighborhood (Mockenhaupt & Boyle, 1992).

An excellent Web site is provided by the National Highway Traffic Safety Administration and covers traffic safety education, vehicle safety, and injury prevention for the older driver, contact: www.nhtas.dot.gov.

## SLEEP PROBLEMS

As many as 40% of older adults complain about sleep problems (Vitiello, 1997), and significant sleep disturbance impacts on quality of life. Insomniacs are 2.5 times more likely to have accidents than other drivers; are more likely to be anxious, depressed, or forgetful; and may recover more slowly from an illness (Mestel, 1997). Identifying the cause of sleeplessness, however, can be rather complicated.

Insomnia can result from arthritis, a hyperactive thyroid, sleep apnea, restless leg syndrome, too much caffeine, poor circulation, inadequate sleep hygiene, anxiety, and too little exercise. The first line of attack is lifestyle change, such as restricting caffeine, keeping a regular schedule, using relaxation techniques, and getting more exercise.

Regarding exercise, older adults with moderate sleep complaints slept almost an hour longer and cut in half the amount of time it normally took to fall asleep as a consequence of participating in a low-impact aerobic program (King et al., 1997).

Sleeping medication, conversely, may be effective in the short run, but in the long run individuals build up tolerance, the dosage must be raised, and the risk for memory impairment, hypertension, and more frequent accidents is increased. Many herbs are reputed to act as sedatives, like chamomile, exotic passionflower, and valerian extract (Mestel, 1997), but their effectiveness is supported by an inadequate amount of controlled research.

The same holds true for the popular hormone, melatonin, which is found in most health food stores and drugstores. There has been little research on its utility as a sleeping aid, and prolonged use may be unsafe.

Melatonin may be effective in only those elderly who are melatonin deficient.

If conventional solutions do not work, it may be necessary to contact an accredited sleep clinic, by writing to the American Sleep Disorders Association, 1610 14th Street, #300, Rochester, MN 55901. There is also a toll-free 24-hour hotline that provides information on sleep. Call 1-800-shuteye.

For a course syllabus on sleep education, contact Gregg Jacobs, PhD, an instructor in medicine at Harvard Medical School at 110 Francis Street, Suite 1A, Boston, MA 02215; 617-632-7369.

## QUESTIONS FOR DISCUSSION

1. You have been hired as a consultant by an alcohol abuse specialist and a smoking cessation specialist, both of whom have focused their practice exclusively on young adults. Each of these professionals is being confronted, for the first time, with older clients. What advice would you give each to help them become more responsive to the needs and interests of older clients?
2. Think about your classroom space, your professional office, or your neighborhood in terms of accident prevention. What, if any, steps can you take to reduce the chances that an older person will have an accident?

# 9
# Social Support

You need an experience with at least one person who cares about you. It doesn't matter at what age this person appears. If you didn't have a close relationship when younger, and you now have one close person in your life, that makes up for the early deficiency. That person can appear at any time in the life cycle, even on the day of death. One does not need to make up for lost time. (Weininger & Menkin, 1978)

Social support can be defined as the perceived caring, esteem, and assistance people receive from others. Support can come from spouses, family members, friends, neighbors, colleagues, health professionals, or pets. The literature is rife with elaborate taxonomies of social support (Eng & Young, 1992), yet it can be reduced to three basic types:

1. *Emotional support* provides people with a sense of love, reassurance, and belonging. When individuals feel they are being listened to, and valued, they develop a healthy sense of self-worth. Emotional support has a strong and consistent relationship to health status (Israel & Schurman, 1990).
2. *Instrumental support* refers to the provision of tangible aid and services that directly assist people who are in need. Examples are financial help and household maintenance. Good instrumental support has been correlated with a decrease in psychosomatic and emotional distress, and with greater life satisfaction (Revicki & Mitchell, 1990).

3. *Informational support* is the provision of advice, feedback, and suggestions to help a person address problems.

Social networks, unlike social support, are defined in terms of structural characteristics: number and types of social linkages, frequency of contacts, and so on. The characteristics of people's social networks do not correlate with the quality of their social support. Researchers have shown that support can come from a few confidants or from a large social network (Sarason et al., 1983).

Social support appears to boost the immune system, reduce the likelihood of illness, speed recovery from illness, result in clinical improvement that lowers required levels of medication, and reduce psychological strain and cognitive impairment (Koenig et al., 1997; Larson, 1995; Sarafino, 1990). Cohen and colleagues (1997), for instance, gave nasal drops containing viruses to a large sample of participants and discovered that those with more diverse social networks had greater resistance to upper respiratory illness.

Unfortunately, persons who provide social support can also set bad examples and offer poor advice. The correlation of negative relationships, such as those characterized by hassles and mistrust, with poor mental health is stronger than the association of social support with good mental health (Israel & Schurman, 1990).

## FAMILY, FRIENDS, CHURCH, AND OTHERS

Large-scale epidemiological studies have shown that membership in a network of family, friends, church, and other support structures is correlated with low mortality risk (Berkman, 1983; Rowe & Kahn, 1987).

The classic research endeavor in this area, led by the epidemiologist Lisa Berkman, was a study of the residents of Alameda County, California. The research team found that residents who were married, had ample contact with extended family and friends, belonged to a church, and had other group affiliations were half as likely to die over the course of the 9-year study as those with less adequate social supports (Berkman, 1983).

The results of research on the relationship between social support and mortality have been replicated in other large studies of both healthy and sick adults (Goodwin et al., 1987; House et al., 1988; Williams et al., 1992), most of which have been controlled for other factors that might affect mortality, such as lifestyle, socioeconomic status, age, race, and access to health care. House and colleagues (1988), in fact, have shown that social isolation has as strong an effect on mortality as does smoking or high-cholesterol levels.

Several studies report the importance of a spouse or supportive families in helping people adopt or sustain good health habits. One study reported that lifestyle interventions targeted at men and women as couples rather than as individuals resulted in a greater reduction in cardiovascular risk factors like cigarette smoking, systolic blood pressure, and cholesterol level (Pyke et al., 1997). The authors report that targeting the couple may strengthen outcomes through the mutual reinforcement of lifestyle changes.

Another study reported that women on insulin treatment were found to be more likely to experience metabolic control (i.e., a good fasting blood glucose level) if they were part of a supportive family (Cardenas et al., 1987). Supportive families were also found to be important in reinforcing eating behaviors, sustaining regular exercise, and helping individuals sustain weight loss (Stuart & Davis, 1972; Zimmerman & Connor, 1989). Men with supportive wives were twice as likely at those whose wives had neutral or negative attitudes to continue in a physical activity program (Heinzelmann & Bagley, 1970; Murphy et al., 1982).

Spouses as a source of support, however, are increasingly less common with age, particularly among older women. Although 84% of males and 67% of females live with their spouses during late middle age, the percentages drop to 65% of males and 21%(!) of females at age 75 and over (Senate Special Committee on Aging, 1985).

Considerable evidence suggests that adult children are the major alternative source of social support for older adults (Chiriboga, 1987). Parental support, however, often competes for time and energy with the adult children's own needs and those of their children.

Because of the limitations of spousal and child support, friendships take on increasing importance in late life (Wykle & Musil, 1993). In one sample, support from friends was found to be more important for preventing depression than support from children (Dean et al., 1990).

## LAY SUPPORT

"Professionals do not take the time to first gauge the ways that ordinary people help one another and then try to strengthen the helping processes that work for them" (Gottlieb, 1985). Different terms and definitions are used to describe lay support, but commonalties cross-cut these differences. For example, lay health advisors are defined as "lay people to whom others naturally turn for advice, emotional support, and tangible aid. They provide informal, spontaneous assistance, which is so much a part of everyday life that its value is often not recognized" (Israel, 1985).

The concept of natural neighbors is similar to that of lay health advisors. The term *natural neighbors*, coined by Collins and Pancoast (1976), refers to people who are prompted by empathy or a desire to help others. Many do volunteer work at churches or community organizations.

Some lay health advisors or natural neighbors may not be as "natural" or as skillful as others but are willing to participate in paraprofessional training programs to increase their skills and to identify persons who are in need of support. Examples of such local and state programs are provided by Haber (1989).

Two federally supported model programs that are based on the importance of providing social support are (a) the Senior Companion Program, in which low-income persons, aged 60 and older, receive a small stipend (below minimum wage) to provide companionship to peers in need, and (b) the Foster Grandparent Program, in which low-income persons, aged 60 and older, receive a small stipend to provide companionship and guidance to children with exceptional needs, especially in hospitals, centers for the retarded, correctional facilities, and other institutions that serve children.

Studies of these programs report that, in addition to providing benefits to the young and the old in need, the older volunteers improve their *own* mental and physical health (ACTION, 1984, 1985).

## ONLINE SUPPORT

By 1998 there were already thousands of different self-help groups available online. With appropriate cautions, clinicians may find these services to be a useful adjunct to their care. There is support and information for smokers, alcoholics, people with disabilities, overeaters, diabetics, stroke victims, deaf persons—the list is endless. The American Self-Help Clearinghouse is probably the best online database of national and international support groups. It can be accessed through their Internet address at, www.cmhc.com/selfhelp.

There are several internet support groups used by nurses and other health professionals, particularly in the area of Alzheimer's support. Computerlink, for instance, is a computer network providing information, communication, and decision-support functions for caregivers of persons with Alzheimer's disease. During a 1-year study conducted by several nurses, access to ComputerLink enhanced caregivers' decision-making confidence (Brennan et al., 1995). Another Internet resource for caregivers of an Alzheimer's patient is through the email address: adear@alzheimers.org.

There is a downside to cyberspace support as well. On the Internet, there is rarely a professional available to intervene when bad advice, faulty information, or inappropriate support is being given. Moreover, it is not uncommon to spend excessive amount of time on the Internet to the exclusion of other responsibilities or people who are important to you. Ironically, there is an Internet Addiction Support Group that can be reached through <listserv@net-com.com> Message: subscribe i-a-s-g.

Books on the topic of online health information and support include *Health Online*, Tom Ferguson, MD (Addison-Wesley, 1996); *Dr. Tom Linden's Guide to Online Medicine*, Tom Linden, MD, and Michelle Kienholz (McGraw-Hill, 1995); and *The Internet Health, Fitness & Medicine Yellow Pages*, Matthew Naythons, MD, and Anthony Catsimatides (Osborne/McGraw-Hill, 1996).

## PET SUPPORT

It is estimated that between one third and one half of all households in the English-speaking world contain pets, yet little empirical research has been conducted on animal companionship (Siegel, 1993). Most existing studies have focused on older persons, who are believed to have the greatest need for companionship, but evidence regarding the advantages of pet ownership for these people has been inconsistent (Siegel, 1993).

One study of Medicare enrollees revealed that pet owners demonstrated lower levels of stress and less use of health services for nonserious medical problems than did nonpet owners ("Health and Fitness," 1991). Pet owners with heart disease had a significantly higher 1-year survival rate than did nonpet owners (Friedmann et al., 1980). However, data analysis from the National Senior Citizens Survey of 1968 indicated *no* association between pet ownership and psychological well-being or health (Lawton et al., 1984).

A review of the literature on pets as a therapeutic intervention yields reports of a wide variety of positive consequences (though few conducted through a rigorous scientific design) including reduced medication levels, increased social interaction, lowered blood pressure levels, and reduced mortality rates (Robb & Stegman, 1983). Pet therapy and pet visitation programs with older adults in institutionalized settings appear to have resulted in a variety of mental health benefits, even though the temporary contact restricts the bonding potential between resident and pet (Boldt & Dellmann-Jenkins, 1992).

Unlike most previous pet therapy programs, however, dogs, cats, and other pets live *permanently* with residents in long-term care facilities through the Eden Alternative. The basic premise of the Eden Alternative is that nursing homes should treat residents as people who need attentive care in a homelike setting. To accomplish this goal, nursing homes need to contain plants; children; and, perhaps most important, pets.

The program was initiated by William Thomas, MD, in 1991 when he was medical director at a nursing home in New York. Since then, it has been replicated at least partially by more than 100 nursing homes nationwide. Studies that support the benefits of the program—lower mortality rates, urinary tract infections, respiratory infections, staff turnover, resident depression, and medication costs—are reported in Thomas's book *The Eden Alternative* (1996).

An Eden Alternative Train the Trainer Program was launched in 1996. The 4-day program demonstrates how to create a long-term care environment that supports residents emotionally and spiritually as well as physically.

For information on how successfully the Eden Alternative was replicated in long-term care institutions in the state of Michigan, contact the state ombudsman in Michigan: Hollis Turnham, Michigan State Ombudsman, Citizens for Better Care, 416 North Home Street, #101, Alpha Building, Lansing, MI 48912-4700; 517-336-6753.

Although much less common than nursing home-based programs, hospital nurses have introduced pet therapy programs onto hospital units. One nurse manager evaluated a hospital-based pet therapy program by stating that the staff seemed to be smiling more and laughing more with the patients, and everyone worked as a team while the pets were on the unit (Willis, 1997).

Most of the evaluations of the pet intervention programs, however, have not been rigorous—few have included control groups, and the positive results have not separated out the effects of pet companionship versus novel or intriguing activities and the involvement of children.

Nonetheless, the evidence to date has been consistently positive and indicates that it would be desirable if more "community and volunteer organizations would play a constructive role in facilitating pet ownership among people who wish to own pets" (Siegel, 1993).

Midland Life Insurance in Ohio appears to have been the first insurance company to reduce life insurance premiums for clients who have animal companionship. In 1998, the company lowered premiums as much as 8% for clients with animal companionship. They based this financial policy change on data that showed pet owners live longer and visit the doctor less often than their petless peers.

There are several organizations that promote pet ownership and visitation on a national basis. The Delta Society, for instance, is an international, not-for-profit organization that provides training for volunteers and animals in visiting and therapy programs. The Delta Society also sponsors an annual conference and publishes a quarterly magazine and a scientific journal. Contact: Delta Society, 321 Burnett Avenue South, 3rd Floor, Renton, WA 98055-2569; 425-226-7357.

Jeff's Companion Animal Shelter provides financial support (through a grant from Sandoz Pharmaceuticals Corporation) for organizations and individuals seeking to replicate their pet therapy program, a program that matches elderly people with animals (particularly dogs from animal rescue leagues) or establishes pet therapy programs in nursing homes or hospitals. Contact Jeff's Companion Animal Shelter, 1128 Main Road, Westport, MA 02790. Small grants have been provided to nonprofit organizations working for animals or for older adults.

## RELIGIOUS OR SPIRITUAL SUPPORT

People who attend religious institutions have stronger immune systems, are physically healthier, and are less depressed than those who do not (Koenig et al., 1997; Larson, 1995). The relationship between religious attendance and good health remains even when researchers control for the chronic illnesses and functional abilities of their samples.

Possible explanations for the positive relationship between religion and heath are that many religions encourage healthy lifestyles (e.g., less addiction to smoking and drinking), that congregations are characterized by positive, supportive social relationships, and that positive ideologies and prayer lower harmful stress hormones (Idler, 1994; "Studies Suggest that Religious Activities Can Improve Health," 1996).

Although church attendance decreases with age, a shift to such personal practices like Bible reading and listening to religious radio programs increases. Reduced attendance at religious services is due primarily to decreased mobility and transportation problems rather than declining interest (Lowenthal & Robinson, 1976).

One interesting study that supports the relationship between religious involvement and health status reports that Christians and Jews tended to die less frequently in the month before their own group's religious holidays (Idler & Kasl, 1992). A 14-year longitudinal study, however, reported that being religious had no predictive value in terms of health or psychological well-being (Atchley, 1998).

Health professionals should be sensitive to the religious and spiritual needs of their clients and provide the time to listen to and empathize with their concerns. In addition, health professionals can strengthen the belief systems of their clients, finding out whether they have access to a pastor, rabbi, or religious study group or are receiving the visits of volunteers from their previously attended church or synagogue.

Religion may be especially important as a source of social support for Black elders. Involvement in religious activity correlated with greater self-esteem and personal control in a sample of older Blacks (Krause & Van Tran, 1989), Black caregivers were found to be more likely than White caregivers to use religion as a means of coping (Wykle & Segal, 1991), and the effects of religious consolation or religious comfort are stronger among African-Americans than white church members who are faced with adversity (Ferraro & Koch, 1994).

Health professionals seeking innovative ideas or wanting to identify model programs in the area of spiritual health and the older adult should access *Aging and Spirituality*, published by the American Society on Aging's Forum on Religion, Spirituality, and Aging. To receive a copy, contact the American Society on Aging, 833 Market Street, Suite 512, San Francisco, CA 94103.

Another useful publication is the *Journal of Religious Gerontology*, a quarterly publication of the National Interfaith Coalition on Aging, which is affiliated with the National Council on the Aging, 409 3rd Street SW, Washington, DC 20024.

## INTIMATE SUPPORT

Older adults can share intimate support in many ways, for example, by playing with children, watching a sunset, feeding ducks, walking in the woods, and enjoying sexual intimacy. Playing, watching, feeding, and walking, however, are not problematic for most older adults, but sexual intimacy may present a problem.

According to studies by the Duke University Center for the Study of Aging and Human Development, most older couples remain sexually active between the ages of 65 and 75. Nevertheless, sexuality increasingly focuses on warmth, sharing, touching, and intimate communication. As consumers of research, we might find it useful to pay more attention to studies that report on individual perceptions and experiences than to those that emphasize physiological parameters, performance data, and statistical frequencies (Starr, 1985).

In one study of 800 people between the ages of 60 and 91, 36% reported that sex grew better over time, whereas only 25% said it was worse (Starr & Weiner, 1981). A 1998 study sponsored by the National Council on the Aging and conducted by a national polling firm reported that half the sample aged 60 and over had sex at least once a month, and two-thirds of them said their sex was at least as satisfying as when they were in their 40's.

The sexuality of some aging Americans, however, can get waylaid by psychological factors, such as depression, guilt, monotony, performance anxiety, and anger. Young and old alike can be hampered by negative cohort attitudes that reveal hostility toward the expression of sexuality in late life.

Physical limitations are yet another cause of sexual dysfunction. Arthritic pains, cardiovascular disorders, respiratory conditions, hormonal imbalances, and neurological disorders can interfere with sexual performance. In addition, various medications can lead to sexual dysfunction (Ebersole & Hess, 1990).

But the most significant cause of sexual inactivity, particularly after age 75, is widowhood or lack of opportunity. This problem is exacerbated in older adults who are not accepting of alternative intimacy practices. Family members might try to expand the options of an older adult by arranging to have a respected health professional prescribe the reading of *The Joy of Sex* (Comfort, 1972), in which the physician-author, Dr. Alex Comfort, in addition to presenting a wide variety of sexual ideas, describes alternatives to intercourse, such as fantasizing, masturbating, and touching.

The importance of touching was clearly demonstrated when a yoga class, which had been enthusiastically received by older adults at senior centers and congregate living facilities (Haber, 1983a, 1986), was presented at 10 nursing homes (Haber, 1988). After unsuccessful attempts to engage these nursing home residents were made during the first three classes, we decided to begin each class with massage—mostly instructor-to-resident massage (with help from student assistants), but also resident-to-resident and self-massage (see Figure 9.1).

As a consequence, we witnessed a dramatic increase in—there are no other words that come to mind—*fun and intimacy*. The nursing home residents enthusiastically awaited the remaining classes.

This demonstration of the need for touch and intimacy brought to mind a passage from a book by Ebersole and Hess (1990): "When a group of Boy Scouts completed their performance for (a group of nursing home) residents, (an old woman) beckoned to the scout leader and said, 'Do you suppose I could hug one of those little boys?' "

## CHRONIC ILLNESS AND THE SUPPORT OF INTIMATE OTHERS

Health promotion is applicable even to the chronically ill. Chronic illness may provide an opportunity for older clients or their caregivers to increase intimacy with loved ones. Conversely, from my experience with clients, family members, and myself, I know that chronic diseases, like arthritis, heart disease, cancer, and other conditions associated with aging, can create barriers to intimacy—particularly because of increased frustration and fear.

Frustration and fear are frequent companions of the aging chronically ill—the frustration of immobility; the fear of the unpredictable; the fear of intractable pain; and, perhaps worst of all, the frustration and fear of increasing dependency on caregivers. Being able to trust someone and share feelings with them enables one to deepen and expand emotional ties. This can occur in the context of existing family relationships, through a support group or volunteer companion, or within the client-prac-titioner relationship.

Chronic illness may also offer older persons who are ill, and those who care for them, the motivation and opportunity to reorganize priorities:

# MASSAGE

Massaging your joints and muscles daily helps remove stiffness and aches and pains and helps circulation. It helps to incorporate these massage hints into your exercise routine as well as at various other times of your day—such as while you watch TV. **NOTE: Before massaging any part of your body, rub your hands together briskly until they feel warm with energy. This really helps.**

**SHOULDERS**—Rub the entire shoulder area with a firm, circular motion.

**HEAD**—Start from the temples and rub into the center and back out again. Do between your eyebrows and all the way up into your scalp.

**NECK**—Rub up and down from your throat all the way up and around the back of your neck. Rub firmly with fingers.

**ELBOWS**—Grasp your elbow joint firmly and rotate your hand back and forth around the entire elbow joint.

**LOWER BACK**—Place your hands firmly on your lower back and rub up and down all the way to your tail bone.

SHOULDERS

HEAD

NECK

ELBOWS

LOWER BACK

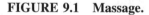

**FIGURE 9.1   Massage.**

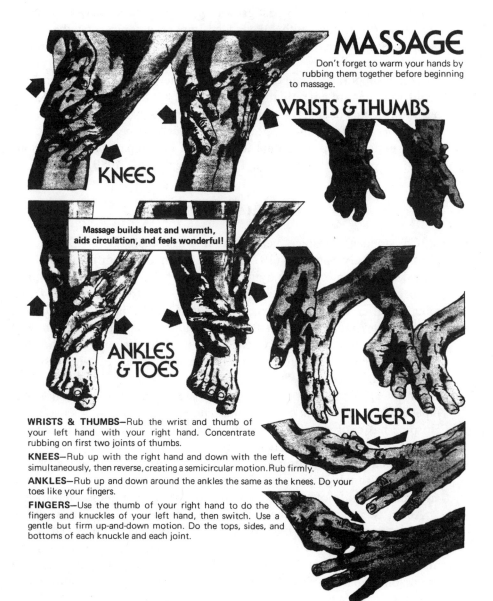

**MASSAGE**

Don't forget to warm your hands by rubbing them together before beginning to massage.

**WRISTS & THUMBS**

**KNEES**

Massage builds heat and warmth, aids circulation, and feels wonderful!

**ANKLES & TOES**

**FINGERS**

**WRISTS & THUMBS**—Rub the wrist and thumb of your left hand with your right hand. Concentrate rubbing on first two joints of thumbs.

**KNEES**—Rub up with the right hand and down with the left simultaneously, then reverse, creating a semicircular motion. Rub firmly.

**ANKLES**—Rub up and down around the ankles the same as the knees. Do your toes like your fingers.

**FINGERS**—Use the thumb of your right hand to do the fingers and knuckles of your left hand, then switch. Use a gentle but firm up-and-down motion. Do the tops, sides, and bottoms of each knuckle and each joint.

**FIGURE 9.1   Massage.** (*continued*)

to ask themselves whether past grievances are still necessary or too petty to pursue, to discuss with loved ones important topics that they have been putting off, and to reach out to old friends and end long-standing mutual neglect.

Social support also appears to play a crucial role in improving the health outcomes of not only the chronically ill but the terminally ill. Long-term follow-ups of several years reveal that not only is survival extended but quality of life is improved among seriously ill persons who receive social support and professional intervention in comparison with persons in control groups (Fawzy et al., 1995; Spiegel et al., 1989).

## HOSPICE SUPPORT

St. Christopher's Hospice, near London, was established in 1967 by the physician Cicely Saunders (1977). It was an independent institution that provided inpatient care for dying patients. The first American hospice, Connecticut Hospice, Inc., in New Haven, was founded in 1974 and modeled after its London prototype. By 1990 the number of hospice programs in America increased to 1,800 and the number of terminally ill persons served to 210,000. Six years later, in 1996, the number of hospice programs increased to almost 5,000, and the number of clients served more than doubled—to 450,000.

Hospice programs have expanded their service sites, providing not only inpatient care but care in private homes, nursing homes, and other settings. Hospice has evolved, therefore, into a type of care, rather than the site of care. Its distinguishing characteristic is the emphasis on psychosocial and spiritual support over medical procedures. By focusing on psychosocial and spiritual support, hospice is able to improve the mental health and quality of life of clients, even as their physical bodies deteriorate.

About two thirds of America's dying, or 1.5 million persons, die in hospitals compared with the 18% who die in hospice settings. There are several barriers to why more persons do not receive hospice care. First, many physicians are still reluctant to refer patients to hospice, seeing it as an admission of defeat. Many family members also see it in the same negative way. Second, most insurance companies including Medicare require that the physician certify that the patient has less than 6 months to live. The problem, however, is that only late-stage cancer tends to be that predictable. Emphysema, aids, congestive heart failure, Parkinson's disease, and other conditions are not.

Finally, a major difficulty facing hospice clients and their supporting families in the future may be the lack of a sufficient number of social support providers, especially for clients who choose to stay at home. Seventy-three percent of hospice clients are over the age of 65, and 83% are living in a private residence (Haupt, 1997). Their spouses and their adult children are often in their 60s and 70s and physically unable to bear the exhausting burden of supporting the terminally ill. Whether we will be able to find sufficient numbers of volunteers to help meet the social and emotional support needs of the terminally ill elderly in the future is problematic (Lupu, 1984–1985).

Medicare covers hospice care by Medicare-approved agencies or facilities for older persons with a terminal illness who elect it in lieu of standard hospital treatment. Most private health insurance plans, and some state Medicaid programs also pay for hospice care. For more information on hospice, contact the National Hospice Organization, 1901 North Moore Street, Suite 901, Arlington, VA 22209; 703-243-5900 or 800-658-8898; or www.nho.org.

## PEER SUPPORT

Growing older presents the challenge, for many people, of coping with chronic conditions—either their own or those of loved ones. A significant number of these people are discovering the rewards of belonging to a peer support group. Such groups unite people with common concerns so that they can share their ideas and feelings, exchange practical information, and benefit from knowing they are not alone. In short, they help members learn to live as fully as possible despite the limitations that accrue with age.

A peer support group can be organized around a health-promoting theme (e.g., weight reduction, exercise, alcohol or smoking cessation), or it can exist to cope with almost any chronic health condition—Alzheimer's, Parkinson's, cancer, arthritis, heart and lung disease, stroke, hearing and visual impairment, and others. Some groups are organized to provide support for spouses or caregivers, whereas others help individuals cope with life-cycle events, like widowhood.

Besides the obvious mental health focus of group activities, group members—whether or not the group is organized around a specific disease—typically exchange ideas on nutrition, exercise, stress management, smoking cessation, and moderating alcohol-drinking patterns.

Peer support groups have certain commonalties; most operate informally, meet regularly, and do not charge fees (although voluntary donations for refreshments may be requested). Most distribute leadership responsibilities among peer members, and many involve health professionals in a significant way.

Peer support groups differ widely in their purpose, structure, and effectiveness. Most Alzheimer's groups, for example, focus primarily on the emotional needs of caregiving members. Other groups may emphasize education, whereas others focus on health advocacy in the legislative arena.

Support groups that meet in an institutional setting with strong professional leadership differ markedly from groups that meet in a home or church and may or may not include professional leadership. Regardless of setting or professional participation, some groups benefit their members greatly (Lieberman & Borman, 1979), whereas others are ineffective (personal experience) or may be psychologically harmful.

By any standard, the self-help group movement is a phenomenon with which to be reckoned. By 1979, 15 million people were participants in 500,000 different groups (Evans, 1979). Today, the 1979 estimates are far too conservative, given the documented growth among groups by self-help group clearinghouses around the nation over the past two decades.

In 1983, according to a probability sample of more than 3,000 households, self-help groups were the number-one source of assistance to persons with mental health problems. More individuals participated in self-help groups (5.8%) than sought help from mental health professionals (5.6%) or consulted with clergy or pastoral sources (5%) (Mellinger & Balter, 1983).

## EMPOWERMENT THROUGH PEER SUPPORT

Several unique characteristics, shared by support groups, *empower* their participants. One is the "helper" principle, described by Frank Riessman (1965): if you help someone else, it is likely you will benefit, at least as much as the person you helped. Research findings support this principle; the benefits accrued by older volunteers helping others through the Senior Companion and Foster Grandparent programs have been documented (ACTION, 1984, 1985).

Modeling behaviors for others and giving encouragement and advice helps us to clarify our ideas and become increasingly conscientious about our own health behaviors. Warning others about how cigarettes, drugs, alcohol, and stress can compromise their cardiovascular, immune, and nervous systems, for instance, may reinforce our own avoidance of these habits.

Members of peer support group empower themselves and others in concrete and practical ways—exchanging information about community resources, assisting with transportation needs, identifying ways to improve home safety, encouraging each other to be assertive with health care professionals and to obtain what is due them in the health care system.

Support group members may be able to empower themselves in psychological and interpersonal ways: validating their experiences by sharing the experiences with others in similar situations; getting feedback from others and developing new behaviors and attitudes based on the collective experience of group members; and obtaining support, when feeling desperate or hopeless, by sharing feelings on the telephone or through a visit.

Peer support group members may be able to empower each other through cognitive restructuring. Members may build new norms for self-esteem, develop new definitions of personal identities, and change their perceptions of the nature of a health problem or their attitudes toward people without their problems. For example, support group members with medical disabilities may view outsiders as "temporarily able-bodied" or potential victims of future disabilities, thereby enhancing their personal capacity for accepting adversity.

Members may empower each other by allowing emotional ventilation in a sympathetic environment. The expression of such difficult emotions as fear, anger, anxiety, sadness, and grief may allow group members to share, accept, and deal with feelings in appropriate ways.

The peer support group may also empower its members by providing them opportunities to participate voluntarily in group activities, to share leadership functions, and to work for causes that are larger than themselves. For example, one support group in New York City, Friends and Relatives of the Institutionalized Aged, blocked the New York State Health Department's attempt to relax standards for nursing home care and pressured the New York State Department of Social Services into revising regulations to allow more residents access to nursing home beds following hospitalization (National Council on the Aging, 1982).

Advocacy can also be personal. A member of the Self-Help Group for the Hard of Hearing in Omaha, Nebraska, expressed frustration with a recalcitrant hearing aid provider who refused to stand behind his promise of "satisfaction guaranteed." The threat of picketing his establishment by a dozen support group peers quickly led to the successful resolution of the hearing aid consumer's problem (personal experience).

## AGE-RELATED PEER SUPPORT GROUPS

Substantial evidence indicates that peer support groups are especially appropriate for aging persons who need chronic care and their caregivers, that the number of such persons in support groups is growing, and that great potential exists for even faster growth rates (Haber, 1989).

The potential for growth of support groups will be fueled, in part, by the same factors that will lead to the declining number of family support persons for future cohorts of older adults. Declining birthrates after the baby-boom generation will mean that fewer children and grandchildren will be available to serve as support persons. Job mobility, retirement relocation, and neighborhood growth and renewal often result in the dispersion of family, friends, and neighbors. At the same time, older adults are afflicted with limited mobility because of health factors or their unwillingness to travel from familiar neighborhoods.

Butler and Lewis (1982) noted that older persons tended to be reluctant to seek help from mental health professionals because of a perceived stigma and a distaste for large, impersonal, and highly bureaucratic organizational structures. Conversely, some mental health professionals perceive mental health problems as irreversible in old age and are reluctant to treat older adults.

In consideration of these societal factors, I have built a peer support group component into almost two dozen grant-funded health promotion, health education, and caregiving training programs for older adults. Members of these peer support groups continue to provide social support and practical assistance to each other for years after a funded project (and the participation of health professionals) is terminated (Haber, 1983b, 1984, 1986, 1989; Haber & Lacy, 1993).

One health education class, for instance, continues to meet several years later as a monthly peer support group. A member of the group sent me the following letter (see Figure 9.2).

Peer support groups may be especially important for the mental health of *widowed* older persons. Studies have reported that widows in support groups adjust to bereavement (Vachon et al., 1980) and undergo reductions in their depression, anxiety, somatic symptoms, and psychotropic medica-

April 1

Dear David,

    You might already know - but the outgrowth of your classes is a continuation of socialization among nearly 20 persons. The "Prime Timers" are going strong - we meet once a month.
    We are never at a loss for agenda! April 24, we will meet at Kountz Memorial Church for Fred Aliano's famous spaghetti, and a relaxation tape to improve our mental health.
    Everyone sends love and we miss you. From your friends....

*Jackie Devaney,*
*secretary for the day*

**FIGURE 9.2   Dear Dr. Haber letter.**

tions (Lieberman & Borman, 1979) more rapidly than widows who do not use support groups. Lieberman and Borman (1979) also noted that support groups for *older* widows may be underused. Although about half the widows in the general population are older than age 60, widows older than age 60 represent only 20% of those who join widowhood support groups nationwide.

Conversely, older adults may prefer the comfort of one-to-one peer support to that of group support. AARP's Widowed Persons Service, for example, has served thousands of persons who were widowed through this type of one-to-one peer support program. Contact the Widowed Persons Service, American Association of Retired Persons, Program Department, 601 E Street NW, Washington, DC 20049; 202-434-6190.

Other one-to-one support programs are the United Ostomy Association, 2001 West Beverly Boulevard, Los Angeles, CA 90057; and the Senior Companion Program; ACTION, 1100 Vermont Avenue NW, Washington, DC 20525.

## HEALTH PROFESSIONAL INVOLVEMENT IN PEER SUPPORT

In its early years, the self-help movement met with resistance from many health professionals. The groups were labeled nonprofessional or antiprofessional and were accused of potentially causing harm by "practicing medicine without a license." Although these attitudes have subsided— indeed, many professionals now initiate or are actively involved in self- help groups—they have not disappeared altogether.

Peer support groups *are* nonprofessional, as are most family members. This is not an indictment against the quality or importance of peer support groups. Although nonprofessional, peer support groups are not antiprofes- sional. The role of the groups is to complement the services of health professionals. A few self-helpers may rail against professionals, but the overwhelming majority do not. Self-help group members are just as likely as those who do not join self-help groups to encourage other members to seek professional assistance (Lieberman & Borman, 1979).

Many factors encourage collaboration between health professionals and support groups. In short, *peer support group members can help health professionals* by (a) meeting existing service gaps or serving persons who are unable or unwilling to access professional assistance, (b) uncovering new knowledge and bringing it to the attention of professionals, (c) provid- ing ongoing social and emotional support that professionals should not be expected to provide to clients, and (d) extending the professional's influence in the community and identifying individuals in need of referral to health professionals.

*Health professionals can aid peer support groups* by (a) improving the effectiveness of some groups by offering training in facilitation skills, providing current knowledge or resource materials, and, perhaps, provid- ing feedback through evaluation studies; and (b) making referrals to ex- isting support groups or starting new groups or peer pairings (Haber, 1989).

A powerful synergy can develop when support groups and health profes- sionals work together. Such collaboration can lead to (a) alerting appro- priate persons to the inadequacies of professional knowledge, agency policies and procedures, insurance coverage, and government legislation, and (b) taking political action in favor of policies that benefit both health professionals and support group members.

Most health science students, with the possible exception of medical students, come into contact with mutual help groups during their educa- tional process. Even students who visit one or two support groups, though, have to be concerned about whether they are adequately informed about such groups in general. Groups differ, for instance, in the unique personali- ties of the members. Some groups are professionally run and others peer led; some are primarily educational, others primarily discussion and emotionally supportive, and yet others advocacy oriented; some are institutional based, and others home or church based; and so forth.

Some older adults may prefer to get their social support in a one-to-one context rather than a group. Health professionals with inexperienced clients ("rookies"), for instance, could match them with their more experienced clients ("veterans") to receive practical tips and support; conversely, more experienced clients who are matched with less experiences clients can receive psychological boosts from helping others and serving as role models.

What can health professionals do to educate themselves about peer support groups?

1. Visit different groups whose members have types of health problems typical of their clientele. Most groups welcome observers who want to educate themselves.
2. Make presentations to some of these groups, allowing plenty of time for questions.
3. Refer clients, and get feedback on the groups' effectiveness.
4. If necessary, start a group, or arrange for peer support between two clients.

The American Self-Help Clearinghouse will provide written materials and verbal advice on all aspects of starting and sustaining mutual help groups. For more information on mutual help groups, contact Ed Madara, Director, American Self-Help Clearinghouse, Northwest Covenant Medical Center, Denville, NJ 07834; www.cmhc.com/selfhelp.

Fitzhugh Mullan, former director of the Bureau of Health Professions and a physician, suggests that "instead of simply going to that white-coated doctor and medical establishment (go) to people who have already 'been there' in some way . . . people who have already had the condition, or who are coping with it" (1992).

## Peer Support Organizations

If you cannot locate the nearest local Area Agency on Aging to identify peer support groups of interest in your community, contact the national organization of area agencies on aging to obtain the address of a local agency: National Association of Area Agencies on Aging, 1112 16th

Street NW, #100, Washington, DC 20036; 202-296-8130. Professional associations are another source of information on local peer support groups. (See the partial listing of national professional associations in chapter 11 on Community Health.)

Oasis is a model program housed at Texas A & M University that trains older volunteers to be mental health paraprofessionals and serve residents of long-term care facilities. A manual and videotape focus on listening skills as well as skills for working with depressed, difficult, or confused clients.

Another program at Texas A & M University is The Minority Peer Educator Project, which trains older minorities to teach nutrition and other health-related topics to their peers at congregate nutrition sites. This program focuses on high blood pressure and diabetes for African-American elderly and obesity and depression for Hispanic elderly.

For more information about these two university-based programs, contact the Texas Agricultural Extension Service, The Texas A & M University, College Station, TX 77843-2112; or call Judy Warren at 409-845-1146.

The Arthritis Club Program is for people with arthritis and their family members who wish to meet with their peers for mutual assistance in satisfying common needs and overcoming common problems. Knowledgeable professionals are readily available to assist lay leaders who have been trained to be positive role models. Generally, clubs meet monthly with sessions that include films, lectures, panel presentations, or group discussions. For individuals who prefer one-to-one support over group support, PALS volunteers from local Arthritis Foundations will call or visit. Contact the Arthritis Foundation, P.O. Box 19000, Atlanta, GA 30326; or call 800-283-7800 or 404-872-7100.

Some older adults may be more willing to talk openly with their peers than with professional counselors. Peer counseling is affordable and can provide positive role models for older adults. Santa Monica's Senior Health and Peer Counseling program, a model training and service program, has been implemented at 41 sites in California. Since its establishment in 1978, a few hundred volunteer counselors, age 55 and older, have been trained to provide counseling service to their peers. For more information, contact Senior Health and Peer Counseling Center, Director of Community Relations, 2125 Arizona Avenue, Santa Monica CA 90404-1398; or call 310-828-1243.

VIEWS (Volunteers Involved for the Emotional Well-being of Seniors), another model peer counseling program, provides 50 hours of training to older peers to prepare them to conduct home visits to elders in need and provide additional counseling by telephone. In addition to one-to-one counseling, there are a half-dozen peer-led groups. For more information, contact VIEWS, Mt. Hood Community Mental Health Center, 400 NE 7th Avenue, Gresham, OR 97030; or call 503-661-5455.

## INTERGENERATIONAL SUPPORT

Older adults and children, though not age peers, are peers in the sense of being outside the full-time employment phase of the life cycle. The Foster Grandparent Program, a national program, trains volunteers age 60 and older to serve 20 hours a week with children in hospitals, shelters, and special care facilities. Low-income volunteers receive a small stipend. Contact the Foster Grandparent Program, ACTION, 1100 Vermont Avenue NW, Washington, DC 20525 (see Figure 9.3).

The Off Our Rockers program is a model program that trains volunteers age 60 and older to visit for 1 hour with kindergarten through third-grade students in the Dallas-area schools. Contact Maria Garza Reynolds, Senior Citizens of Greater Dallas, 2905 Swiss Avenue, Dallas, TX 75204; 214-823-5700 (see Figure 9.4).

For information and ideas on intergenerational programs and projects, order a free copy of the Intergenerational Projects Idea Book from AARP Fulfillment, 601 E Street NW, Washington, DC 20049, and request Stock #D15087.

## SUPPORT OF HEALTH PROFESSIONALS WORKING TOGETHER

Nearly 80% of the American population visit their physician at least once a year (Sullivan, 1990). Because of their unusual degree of access to the general population, and the fact that 85% of adults say a doctor's recommendation would motivate them to get more involved in positive health practices (Harris et al., 1989), physicians are in a unique position to occupy a key role in promoting health.

The physicians' potential for changing client health behavior, however, is not being realized (Haber, 1992b, 1993b; Heath et al., 1993; Lewis, 1988; Maheux et al., 1989; Wechsler et al., 1996; Wheeler et al., 1989). The Council of Scientific Affairs of the American Medical Association

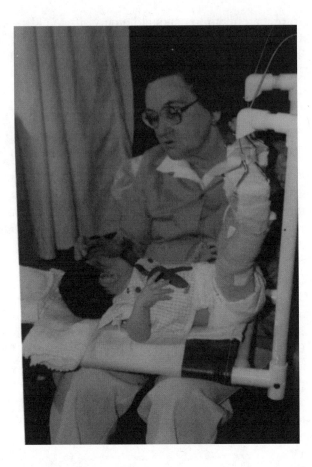

**FIGURE 9.3    Foster Grandparent Program.**

(*JAMA*, 1990) has also concluded that although physicians are well situated to play a leadership role in health promotion, they either do not act on these opportunities or are ineffectual in their daily practice.

The council has suggested, therefore, that physician involvement with patient education should be embedded in a cost-effective framework "by using allied health personnel and providing advice in small-group settings to reduce per capita costs" (United States Preventive Services Task Force, 1996).

Successful applications of the council's strategy have been implemented by the author, using *Physician Wellness Prescriptions* (i.e., prescriptions

**FIGURE 9.4   Off Our Rockers Program.**

or referral forms used by physician to refer to health education programs run by nursing, occupational therapy, and physical therapy students). The programs have consistently led to positive health behavior change on the part of the older participants (Haber, 1991; Haber et al., in press; Haber et al., 1997; Haber & Lacy, 1993).

## QUESTIONS FOR DISCUSSION

1. If you have not already done so, visit at least two peer support groups. Ask five people who have never attended a peer support group whether they have opinions of such groups in general.
2. Think about an older adult you know—a family member, friend, client—who could benefit from a strengthened social support network. What new sources of social support could be relevant to this person? How can you effectively communicate your ideas to this person?

3. What are the advantages and disadvantages of online support versus in-person support?
4. Do you feel health professionals should concern themselves about the religious beliefs and practices of clients?

# 10

# Behavioral and Psychological Management

This life is only a test. If this were an actual life, you would have been given better instructions. (Myrna Neims)

## BEHAVIORAL AND COGNITIVE MANAGEMENT

Operant conditioning, Skinner's (1953) model of behavior control, is based on the premise that behavior is determined by its consequences. Changes in personal behavior or in the behavior of a client or significant other become more or less probable as the rewards or punishments on which they depend change.

Operant conditioning and other methods of behavior modification have been criticized on the basis that it is a type of devious manipulation on the part of the professional (Skinner, 1948). This criticism, however, is easily negated by the fact that clients almost always join behavior modification programs through personal choice, and they control the application of behavior-changing methodologies to their daily life.

Cognitive conditioning, unlike operant conditioning, which focuses on external behaviors, deals with internal changes in thoughts and feelings. Cognitive conditioning advocates assert that behavior and feelings are influenced not by their consequences but by antecedent thoughts.

The first step toward cognitive restructuring, therefore, is the identification of undesirable and unrealistic thoughts. The next step is the substitution and regular repetition of positive thoughts to shape future affect and behavior. Having positively restructured our thoughts, we engage in fewer cognitive distortions, experience less emotional distress, and perform fewer maladaptive behaviors (Burns, 1980).

Because behavior and cognitive conditioning are practiced universally, they do not seem to constitute a formal learning model. All of us use praise and punishment to influence the behavior of others as well as ourselves, and we often substitute positive thoughts for negative ones, leading us to question why these techniques are labeled learning models.

Formal behavior and cognitive management techniques, unlike informal methods for influencing others or ourselves, are applied systematically. This application to behavior management (or, similarly, to cognitive restructuring) consists of the following three components:

1. *Clear definition of the problem.* A need to exercise is vague but to be able to climb steps without having to stop to rest is not.
2. *Implementation of a systematic and measurable response to the problem.* To exercise as often as possible is not systematic nor measurable but to exercise three times a week, for at least 30 minutes at a time, taking one's pulse to determine when one has reached a target heart rate zone is.
3. *Scheduled periodic evaluations.* To feel we are making improvement is vague but to assess the effectiveness of our plan on a weekly basis and alter our plan of action or our goal, as necessary, is not.

## HEALTHY PLEASURES

In contrast to behavior and cognitive management theories based on structure and self-discipline, there is the theory of healthy pleasure (Ornstein & Sobel, 1989). Advocates of this theory propose that healthy behaviors will be sustained when these behaviors are based on joy, intuition, and self-trust. Some advocates go one step further and suggest that a "growing reliance on one's own ability to listen to the body's internal cues for feeling good" can replace behavior-change decisions based on scientific guidelines (Field & Steinhardt, 1992).

My own bias is that this is not an either/or proposition. Joyful, intuitive activities are important in their own right, or they can be converted into healthy routines, or they can be discontinued. Self-disciplined routines can be enjoyable, effective, or they can evolve into stale and counterproductive activity. It is not a question of choosing between activities based on pleasure and spontaneity, or regimens based on self-discipline—both are important.

For ideas on healthy pleasure, clients should read *Healthy Pleasures* (Ornstein & Sobel, 1989). For an understanding of regimens based on self-discipline, it is helpful to examine social learning theory.

## SOCIAL LEARNING THEORY

Several researchers have endorsed a broad learning model, referred to as social learning theory (Bandura, 1977, 1986, 1995; Rodin, 1986; Rotter, 1954), that addresses both the psychosocial dynamics underlying health behavior and the methods of promoting behavior change. This theory actually encompasses a wide range of learning theories that include the operant and cognitive conditioning theories, modeling, guided mastery of tasks on a step-by-step basis, verbal persuasion, social support, and several conceptualizations described later in this chapter, such as personal control, self-efficacy, and health locus of control.

Role modeling, for instance, is an important component of social learning theory. Modeling is most effective when the role model shares many characteristics with the client or student (e.g., physical impairment, age, sex, ethnicity, and socioeconomic status). Professional leaders of health education classes who are not role models in this sense should consider sharing teaching with and deferring problem solving to class members who are.

McAuley and Courneya (1993) suggest that role modeling with older program participants "may be particularly salient. In such cases it is common to look to other people, especially those that bear similar physical characteristics to ourselves, for motivation and information regarding our own prospects of success."

Persuasion is another social learning strategy, one that is probably more popular than effective (Lorig, 1992). Persuasion is most effective when health providers and educators ensure that it is accompanied by realistic goals and includes opportunities for guided mastery of tasks on a step-by-step basis (Bandura, 1995). It is also important that messages are positive and direct ("you can do it," not "try and do it") and are delivered by a source that is respected.

Social learning theory is most effective when it is applied through combined strategies. Studies have demonstrated that the integration of several strategies is more effective than the application of a single technique (Haber & Lacy, 1993; Kottke et al., 1988; United States Preventive Services Task Force, 1996).

Applying multiple behavioral and cognitive strategies to a goal—for example, achieving or maintaining weight loss—might include several of the following techniques.

## HEALTH ASSESSMENT

Make sure that weight control is a high priority for behavior change before establishing it as a goal (see chapter 3 on health assessment). If there appears to be a lack of sufficient motivation, start with another health goal that is easier to achieve. It is important to build a mentality of success before tackling difficult health goals.

## SELF-MONITORING

Self-monitoring is the process of systematically observing one's own patterns of behavior for a limited period. One method of self-monitoring is keeping a written record, or diary, of everything you eat and drink. During a 2-day period (including a weekend day if your weekend eating pattern differs from that of weekdays), carefully record what you eat, how much you eat, the time of day, the location, your companions, and how you feel.

When you carefully observe your eating behaviors, you not only increase your awareness of what triggers unhealthy eating patterns, but you often begin to modify them. You might realize through self-monitoring that you eat automatically in front of the television set or when you socialize in certain settings—even when you are not hungry.

## WRITING A HEALTH CONTRACT

A major task when writing a health contract is identifying a measurable, achievable goal. Dramatic weight losses may be exciting but most likely will not be sustained because realistic eating routines have not been established. Conversely, people who set out to lose a modest amount of weight within a given period—for example, 1 pound every 2 weeks for 8 weeks—are beginning to establish eating habits with which they can live indefinitely. Be pessimistic when setting goals to help choose targets that are realistic; be optimistic when thinking about your ability to achieve them.

A major component in writing a health contract is the establishment of a plan for achieving the goal. The first hurdle is motivation. List the benefits associated with achieving your goal, and post the list in a conspicuous place. Then, identify the barriers to success, and list ways in which to circumvent them. If you are dealing with eating patterns, it is best not to limit your plan just to eating habits but to include a regular exercise routine in your plan of action.

## ESTABLISHING A SUPPORT SYSTEM

Significant others can help motivate, support, and assess your progress. However, a spouse or friend is not necessarily the best source of social support. Another person who is struggling or has grappled with the same eating problem is usually a good source of support. This person can be a relative, a friend, or someone a health professional has identified among his or her other clients.

Health professionals can be good sources of support. Dedicated health professionals will make follow-up telephone calls to clients to check on their progress, record their progress—or lack of it—in the medical record, and consider starting peer support groups. A health professional may be the most influential person to sign off on a health contract, along with your own signature.

It is important to have role models (lay and professional) who are practicing or attempting to practice the behaviors you are striving for. Sharing the commitment to change with a wide variety of people often can instigate support, as well as useful social pressure, from others. It may motivate other individuals as well, who can then join in a collaborative effort, thereby strengthening everyone's resolve.

## EVALUATION

An evaluation schedule can be very useful. The interval between progress checks should be neither too short (e.g., daily weight checks), nor too long. Gradual progress is difficult to detect within short time segments, and anxiety levels are likely to increase. The interval should not be too lengthy, so that steps to correct problems can be taken in a timely fashion. Weekly progress checks may prove practical and effective.

## STIMULUS OR ENVIRONMENTAL CONTROL

Specific stimuli inspire specific behaviors. Controlling stimuli increases the probability of desirable behavior. Stimulus control differs from operant conditioning in that its focus is on the antecedents of behavior rather than on the consequences.

To reduce weight, it is important to control the stimuli provided by foods that are available in your environment. To ensure that your home is well supplied with nutritious foods, rather than junk foods, limit your food shopping to planned events, use shopping lists, and shop on a full stomach. Eliminating spontaneous visits to the store will curtail the purchase of high-calorie foods.

Some people eat large amounts of food unthinkingly, perhaps when watching television or reading a book. To counteract this habitual consumption, create a specific eating environment, designating place (only the dining room, for instance) and time. You might allow some leeway in the number but not in the type of snacks permitted; that is, allow occasional extra snacks of healthy foods, such as fruits or vegetables, but not junk food. It might be useful to banish reading material, the television set, or other objects that trigger semiconscious eating in the dining area.

## RESPONSE SUBSTITUTION

Response substitution and stimulus control interrupt the habitual stimulus/ response relationship. Instead of automatically reaching for food after turning on the television set, clients can be encouraged to occupy their hands with substitute activities, such as knitting. Or they can be encouraged to identify high-calorie foods, such as ice cream, nuts, large portions of high-fat meat, and soda, and plan ahead of time to substitute lower-calorie foods that are somewhat equivalent, for example, ice milk, popcorn, modest portions of fish, and ice water.

Social gatherings constitute a rather common, and dangerous, environment for overeating. A wary individual, so informed, can anticipate the likely response (excess eating) and fill up on low-calorie foods before leaving for an event. In addition, the individual can practice polite ways of declining food (perhaps rehearsing out loud before leaving home, "That looks delicious; sorry I don't have my appetite with me tonight"), substituting this new response for the more typical automatic acquiescence to the offer of food.

## ESTABLISH CUES

Start and end meals with a unique action, a cue, to differentiate between eating and noneating environments. A good beginning action might be saying grace or conducting a brief relaxation ritual. This will help deter spontaneous eating episodes. A good ending ritual is leaving the eating environment and brushing your teeth.

Cues can be expanded to trigger desired responses in other settings. Being given a menu at a restaurant, for instance, can serve as a cue for focusing on the sections describing the salads and vegetables available at the restaurant.

## ASSOCIATIVE LEARNING

Pairing new habits with established habits of daily living may help establish behaviors that quickly become automatic. Examples include jogging before breakfast, thinking about affirmations while brushing teeth, meditating on coming home from work, and diaphragmatic breathing at stoplights. The goal is to replace decision making ("Am I really up for jogging?") with automatic behaviors.

## CONTINGENCY REINFORCEMENT

Praise is a suitable reward from the health professional for a client who accomplishes a goal. A less common reward for accomplishing a health goal might be a small fee rebate from the health professional. The possibilities for rewards from significant others are endless; they might include theater tickets, exemption from a chore, buying a small item of clothing or a book, credit toward a special vacation—anything but food (which should not be viewed as a reward).

Self-generated reinforcers, such as self-praise, over which the client has complete control, should be encouraged. The positive consequences of new behaviors eventually may be reinforcing in themselves.

Reinforcement is most effective when it is received often and in close proximity to desired behaviors, rather than postponed until the achievement of a goal. Negative reinforcement, or punishment, used infrequently in behavior-changing programs, tends to be less effective than positive reinforcement (Kazdin, 1984). One diabolically clever form of punishment, which I personally abhor, is identifying an issue about which a client feels strongly (e.g., euthanasia) and having the client make out several small checks to an organization that promotes a contrary belief. When punishments are to be administered, the checks are mailed by someone other than the client.

## AFFIRMATION AND MOTIVATION

Substitute positive and hopeful thoughts for negative, self-defeating ones. For each negative thought, like "I've never been able to keep weight off before," substitute a positive argument "It may be difficult, but this time, I will persist and accomplish my goal." It is helpful to record affirmations and place them in conspicuous locations.

Other ways to increase motivation are to read books or magazines that inspire you, associate with friends who are supportive of your goal, identify role models who have accomplished what you are striving to achieve, vary your activities so you do not tire of one, and include enjoyable tasks or desirable incentives in your plan of action.

## RATIONAL THOUGHTS

Replace irrational with rational thoughts. A person who fails to adhere to a new eating pattern is not a person "who has no willpower" or "who never succeeds." The more rational thought is, "Most people have setbacks." Failing at one or more attempts neither indicates a permanent absence of willpower nor inability to succeed.

Irrational thoughts can be fostered by inaccurate information and claims. Miracle diets abound but probably require miracles to work. Nothing substitutes for sound education on nutritional principles.

## MODELING

A behavior can be learned through the observation of others. Instructors or health providers who have successfully coped with the same problem as students or clients have the added advantage of being role models. Lay instructors are useful, especially when they have a structured curriculum, adequate training, and professional support or backup. If professional instructors or health providers are not role models, they can identify class members or other clients to serve as role models by encouraging them to share the ways they solved problems or achieved success.

## STRESS MANAGEMENT

Clients who eat when anxious or bored should be advised to substitute a relaxation technique for eating once they have identified the triggering emotion. Diaphragmatic breathing (belly breaths) is adaptable to any setting and quick to implement. If time allows, progressive muscle relaxation (systematically alternating muscle tension and relaxation throughout the body), meditation (repetition of a sound), or some other stress management technique may prevent compulsive eating.

## BIBLIOTHERAPY

A wide array of self-help books and manuals can be found in bookstores or libraries. Professionals can encourage clients to take advantage of their availability. These books typically provide inspiration and step-by-step approaches to mastering various practical techniques. One popular manual, *The Relaxation and Stress Reduction Workbook* (Davis et al., 1995), instructs readers in simple versions of more than a dozen stress management techniques. Write to New Harbinger Publications, Inc., 5674 Shattuck Avenue, Oakland, CA 94609.

## COGNITIVE DISTORTIONS AND MODIFICATIONS

We continuously engage in internal self-talk. This talk often is irrational, based on such words as *should, must, always,* and *never* and consequently leads to anxiety, anger, and depression. Based on a system called rational emotive therapy, Albert Ellis (1975) suggests that irrational self-talk, left unchecked, can lead to diminished mental health.

Examples of irrational self-talk include telling ourselves that we need love and approval from everyone and that we need to be successful in everything we do. This type of search for love and success is described by psychiatrists as *all-or-nothing thinking*—we are either loved or not, successful or not; and *overgeneralization*—a single event can define whether we are loved or successful (Burns, 1980).

A four-step process (substantially modified below) was recommended by Goldfried and Sobocinski (1975) to help clients restructure their irratio- nal cognitions. To help our clients, or ourselves, the authors suggest that we recognize that *statements to ourselves* intervene between events that impact on us and subsequent emotions and behaviors. These statements may occur automatically, and we need to be more conscious of them. Once conscious of them, we can understand that these statements and beliefs are *irrational* and can lead to undesirable emotions and behaviors. *Rehearsing* positive beliefs and statements can support positive emotional states and behaviors.

Positive beliefs and statements can be practiced in the preparatory, confrontational, and reinforcing stages posited by Meichenbaum and Cam- eron (1974):

> *Preparation Stage.* I'm going to be all right. I've succeeded with similar
> challenges before. What exactly do I have to do? It's easier once
> you get started.
> *Confrontation Stage.* Take it step by step. I can do this, I'm doing it
> now. I can do only my best. Any tension I feel is a signal to use
> my coping skills. I can get help if I need it.It's OK to make mistakes.
> *Reinforcement Stage.* Next time I won't worry as much.I did all right.
> I'm in control of my life.

## SELF-EFFICACY, PERSONAL CONTROL, AND HEALTH BELIEFS

As individuals, we strive for confidence and personal control. We want to believe that our decisions and actions will produce desirable outcomes or discourage undesirable ones. Studies show that increased confidence and perceived control is associated with reduced stress, increased motivation, improved health, and enhanced performance (McAuley, 1994; Peterson & Stunkard, 1989).

Perceived control or confidence, however, can have negative effects under specified conditions: when perceived control or confidence exists without sufficient information or skill to support a positive outcome; when excessive demands are made on a person's time, effort, and resources; and when individuals erroneously accept responsibility and blame for health problems, regardless of origin (Rodin, 1986).

## SELF-EFFICACY

Self-efficacy is a belief in one's capabilities to implement a course of action. It is synonymous with confidence within a specific domain and is one dimension of personal control (Bandura, 1986). Self-efficacy theory is often predictive of future health behaviors, especially in regard to sustaining behavior change (McAuley, 1994). One researcher concluded that "self-efficacy affects the amount of effort devoted to a task, and the length of persistence when difficulties are encountered" (O'Leary, 1985).

Self-efficacy can be manipulated experimentally with success. In one study, psychological tests were administered to a group of volunteers in a smoking cessation program. Half the subjects were then randomly assigned to a treatment group and told that in their tests they had demonstrated great potential to quit smoking. The other half were told the truth, that they had been *randomly* assigned to a control group. Fourteen months after treatment, smoking frequency had been reduced by 67% among the efficacy-enhanced group and by 35% among the control group (Blittner et al., 1978).

After reviewing the literature McAuley and Courneya (1993) concluded: "If practitioners and clinicians fail to organize, present, and develop their programs in such a way as to cultivate efficacy beliefs, participants are likely to perceive the activity negatively, become disenchanted, discouraged, and discontinue. On the other hand, adequately organizing (programs) in a manner such that a strong sense of personal efficacy is promoted will result in the individual displaying more positive affect, evaluating their self-worth more positively, embracing more challenging activities, putting forth more effort, and persisting longer. In short, they will be in a position to successfully self-regulate their behavior" (p. 72).

An increasing number of researchers believe that the relationship between beliefs like self-efficacy and behaviors is interactive, not unidirectional (Goldsteen et al., 1991; Lorig et al., 1989; McAuley, 1994). Just as enhancing self-efficacy beliefs may increase the likelihood of sustaining a new health behavior, ongoing adherence to a new health behavior may continue to increase self-efficacy.

Several cautionary notes emerge from research findings. Bandura (1995) reports that behavior change and maintenance are also a function of outcome expectations. Enhancing your belief about your ability to behave in a particular way (self-efficacy) needs to be supplemented by the belief that your performance will lead to a desired outcome (outcome expectancy).

*Extreme* optimism regarding one's self-efficacy may relate inversely to successful performance (Rakowski et al., 1991). Also, self-efficacy is limited to an individual's belief in a specific, not a general, ability. For example, people may perceive themselves to possess the self-efficacy to implement a walking program but not to follow through on a diet. Self-efficacy in one area of behavior does not generalize to another.

The perceived ability to change a health habit or adopt a new health behavior does not guarantee that a person has the necessary skill level, role model, peer or professional support, access, or whatever else might be required. Self-efficacy may be necessary but not sufficient for clients attempting to improve a health behavior.

Self-efficacy is an important part of the Arthritis Self-Help (ASH) course (Lorig et al., 1989) developed at Stanford University in 1978 by Kate Lorig, a nurse and health educator, and Halsted Homan and James Fries, physicians. More than 100,000 persons with arthritis have completed the ASH course, usually in groups of 15 individuals or fewer, and typically led by nonprofessionals who have arthritis. During the 12-hour program, students are taught about arthritis and about how to design an exercise program, manage pain through relaxation techniques, improve nutrition, fight depression and fatigue, and communicate more effectively with physicians.

Participants who complete the program report, in general, about a 15% to 20% reduction in pain; they are more active and visit a physician less frequently. Among those who were depressed when starting the program, fewer depressive symptoms were shown by the end of the program.

The researchers were surprised to find that although changes in behavior, such as exercise and stress management, did occur as a consequence of the program, the factor most closely linked to outcomes (improvements in pain control, depression management, and activity level) was an increase in self-efficacy. In one group of successful patients, self-efficacy was still 17% higher 4 years after they completed the course (Lorig et al., 1989).

## HEALTH LOCUS OF CONTROL

Health locus of control (Wallston & Wallston, 1982) refers to the idea that an individual's health can be controlled through that person's ability to control his or her behavior (i.e., internal locus) or by external forces (i.e., powerful others or luck).

One's health locus of control orientation, similar to perceived self-efficacy, is of limited utility when individuals do not place much value on their health (Lau, 1988; Wallston & Wallston, 1982). Also, medical practices and outcomes, unlike health practices, may not be within one's sphere of influence (Sechrist, 1983). Therefore, it is important that health professionals who encourage their clients to take personal responsibility for their health practices discourage them from overestimating their personal control over medical events.

It may be necessary to help clients differentiate between the realistic goals—increasing their energy, reducing their stress, enhancing their feelings of well-being, and increasing their knowledge and decision-making ability—from the less realistic goal of staving off a deteriorating medical condition.

Research in the future, however, may suggest otherwise. Nursing home residents who were able to exert control over their environment lived twice as long as those who were given assistance without responsibilities (Rodin & Langer, 1977). Spiegel's (1989) 10-year follow-up study of metastasized breast cancer patients reported that patients who participated in supportive therapy groups lived twice as long as those who did not.

As people move from adulthood to old age, their belief in self-efficacy may increase in specific areas (Sarafino, 1990), perhaps because experience has taught them what they can and cannot do. Their belief in health locus of control, conversely, may become more external with age (Lachman, 1986). Older patients are more likely than younger ones, for instance, to prefer that health professionals make health-related decisions for them (Haug, 1979; Woodward & Wallston, 1987).

This increased externality among older adults, however, may be due to *cohort* factors, such as the following:

1. The cultural orientation of specific older cohorts who believe in an authoritarian health professional role, or
2. The lower education levels of the oldest cohorts, which lead to their reluctance to engage in a dialogue with health professionals they might not understand.

Increasing externality with age, on the other hand, may be due to *maturational factors*. For example, the increased physical vulnerability that occurs with age may, over time, discourage an individual's sense of personal control.

Either external or internal health locus of control may correlate with a positive attitude toward the future. A belief in powerful others, like physicians, who can influence the course of an illness, may lead older patients to become more hopeful about the future (Marks et al., 1986).

Conversely, older adults with an internal health locus of control may be more sanguine about the future. Older adults may not believe they can control the outcome of their disease states, but they may feel hopeful that they can affect other aspects of their future, like the ability to control their perception of stress or the ability to acquire the information they need to cope as well as possible with health problems (Wallston & Wallston, 1982).

Information seeking does not necessarily lead to better adjustment. Information about an illness can raise, as well as lower, anxiety. When combined with the adoption of a relaxation technique, however, information seeking may lead to a more desirable outcome (Taylor et al., 1984).

One interesting study matched subjects by their health locus of control profiles. Internals in self-directed programs and externals in peer support groups were more satisfied and lost more weight than nonmatched subjects (Wallston et al., 1976). Unfortunately, another possible, perhaps more powerful, explanation was not examined—that *both* self-direction and peer support may lead to better perceptions and results.

The success of Alcoholics Anonymous (AA) may be attributable to its applicability to both an internal and an external locus of control. On the one hand, AA members must take responsibility for their problem; on the other hand, they are required to acknowledge their inability to control alcoholism without the help of a higher power and the other members of AA (Strecher et al., 1986).

## PERSONAL CONTROL

Two classic studies in personal control reveal that seemingly simple or minor opportunities to control events can affect both physical and mental health. In one study, the residents of two floors of a nursing home were given responsibility for such activities as taking care of a plant, deciding on when to see a movie, and rearranging furniture. The residents of the other two floors were also the beneficiaries of a plant, weekly movie, and furniture, but were given no control over these activities; the staff took care of the plants, decided when the movie would be shown, and rearranged the furniture.

Despite the fact that the residents were similar in physical health, mental health, and prior socioeconomic status, the residents with personal control were physically and mentally healthier, and, 18 months later, only 15% of those with enhanced control had died, versus 30% of those without (Langer & Rodin, 1976; Rodin & Langer, 1977).

Schulz's (1976) experiment with residents of a retirement home revealed that student visits to residents led to more active, happier lives among the residents. Unlike the nursing home experiments of Langer and Rodin (1976), in which personal control opportunities for residents were on a continuing basis, the removal of the students from the retirement home precipitated a drastic decline in health.

## HEALTH BELIEFS

Other factors that help to predict health behaviors are perceived threats, benefits, and barriers. The health belief model, developed during the 1950s to explain why people did not participate in free tuberculosis screenings and other prevention programs (Becker, 1974; Rosenstock, 1990), states that individuals choose to take or not to take preventive action depending on these perceptions.

*Perceived threats* refer to the individual's perception of his or her susceptibility to a particular condition and the degree of severity of that condition that the individual fears. Persons who perceive no threat lack a reason to act.

Perceived susceptibility to and severity of a condition together produce fear. Fear is an effective motivator, yet the optimal level of fear for motivating client behavior is unknown (Sutton & Hallett, 1988). Too little fear may not motivate, but too much can lead to denial and inaction. An important consideration in fear-inducing interventions is the fact that fearful individuals, regardless of their motivation, may lack the necessary skills or confidence to change their health behaviors.

*Perceived benefits* refer to the belief that specific actions on the part of an individual will reduce the threat of negative outcomes or increase the chance of positive outcomes. Perceived benefits must outweigh perceived barriers before a person will initiate an action. *Perceived barriers* may include financial considerations, inconvenience, lack of transportation, lack of knowledge, or potential pain or discomfort.

Evaluations of the health belief model conducted exclusively with older persons have been limited. One such study assessed health beliefs related to osteoporosis—specifically, the likelihood that the older adults in the study would adopt exercise behaviors and increase their calcium intake (Kim et al., 1991). The authors concluded that it is important to focus on perceived barriers, such as the difficulty of changing old habits and the incorporation of new habits into a daily routine.

Each of these belief measures—susceptibility, severity, benefits, and barriers—has a significant, but limited, relationship to subsequent preventive behaviors, such as participation in flu vaccination, breast self-examination, tuberculosis skin tests, and smoking cessation activities (Kirscht, 1988).

The predictability of the model is limited because of the uncertainty surrounding how rational a person will act in a given circumstance (Janis, 1984). In addition, beliefs are not in themselves sufficient conditions for action. "Researchers must seek out that constellation of conditions, including beliefs, which accounts for major variations in behavior" (Rosenstock, 1990). Some of these factors are physiological dependency, economic limitations, environmental influences, skill development, and self-efficacy.

## STRESS AND STRESS MANAGEMENT

### FIGHT OR FLIGHT

The Harvard physiologist Walter Cannon coined two terms, *homeostasis* and *fight or flight*. Homeostasis refers to the body's attempt to preserve the constancy of its internal environment. When cold, for instance, the body shivers to generate heat and, when hot, sweats to reduce it.

When a challenge produces fear, homeostasis is disrupted and the organism prepares for flight or fight. Adrenaline is released, and the heart rate, respiratory rate, blood pressure, coagulability of the blood, and flow of the blood to the brain and large muscles of the extremities increase.

Fight or flight, in response to a physical challenge, prepares the organism to move more quickly, see better, think better, and reduce blood loss. In modern times, however, stress is more likely to be emotional than the reaction to a physical threat. Fighting or running away is often inappropriate. For instance, if we are pressed for time and trapped in big city traffic, there is nothing to fight and no way to flee. The fight or flight response can be harmful, both physically and emotionally.

## GENERAL ADAPTATION SYNDROME

Stress research began with Hans Selye. His general adaptation syndrome consists of three stages: (a) an alarm reaction, which mobilizes the body's resources; (b) a stage of resistance, in which the body tries to adapt to the stressor; and (c) a state of exhaustion. The trapped commuter, who can neither fight nor flee, is vulnerable to being in a prolonged state of resistance. This prolonged stress response, which is harmful to health, may produce pathologic changes, including hypertension, heart disease, arthritis, asthma, and peptic ulcers.

## EXTERNAL, INTERNAL, TRANSACTIONAL

Stress can be viewed from three perspectives. The first perspective is external, focusing on threatening stimuli from the environment. Measuring stress from this perspective may consist of counting stressful events, like divorce and widowhood (Holmes & Rahe, 1967), or calculating hassles, such as being stuck in traffic (Lazarus & Folkman, 1984), that have occurred within the past year.

A second perspective on stress focuses on internal forces, such as our psychological response to stressors. Being stuck in traffic, for instance, can produce anger, anxiety, and frustration. Or we can perceive the traffic delay as an opportunity to converse with our companion or listen to a few additional audiotapes.

The fact that we do not all perceive events in the same way is illustrated in Figure 10.1. Do you see a young or an old woman? Is it difficult to shift your perception between the two?

From the third perspective, stress is viewed as a transactional process, an interaction between forces in the environment and our perception. For example, because we are in a hurry, traffic triggers a stress response. Our anger and frustration then escalate our stress. In this transactional process, however, we can take a pause from our escalating stress level and choose to do a deep-breathing exercise. Thus, we can attempt to neither fight nor flee but to flow.

**FIGURE 10.1   What do you see?**

## PSYCHONEUROIMMUNOLOGY

Over the past two decades, researchers have found several physiological linkages between the nerve cells of the brain and the immune system (Goleman & Gurin, 1993). These nerve cells connect the brain with the spleen and other organs that produce immune system cells. As a consequence, when the brain perceives, for example, a stressful event, immunological changes, such as a decline in the cells that fight tumors and viral infections, result.

Unfortunately for stress researchers, many other factors can also suppress immunity, for example, lifestyle habits (alcohol consumption, smoking, nutritional habits, etc.) and the overall status of the immune system. This latter variable is particularly relevant for older adults because the robustness of the immune system declines with age.

One study, which examined the relationship between lifestyle stress and the immune system of older adults, compared 69 older caregivers of spouses with Alzheimer's disease to a matched sample of older adults living in the community. During this 13-month study, the chronic stress of caring for a family member with dementia led to the reduced function of the immune system of the older caregivers, which, in turn, led to more frequent respiratory tract infections compared with the matched sample in the community (Kiecolt-Glaser et al., 1991).

A more recent study reports that the brain's perception of mental stress may be a better predictor of future heart problems than physical stress recorded through conventional treadmill testing with heart function measured on an electrocardiogram. Persons who responded adversely to mental stress testing (which included reactions to public speaking or solving math problems on a deadline) were two to three times more likely to suffer a heart attack or progressive chest pain in the future (Jiang et al., 1996).

## STRESS AMONG OLDER VERSUS YOUNGER ADULTS

Although many Americans report that stress has had some effect on their health, it is less likely to be reported by older adults (about a third) than younger adults (about half) (USDHHS, 1991). Similarly, in response to the broader question: "How much stress do you feel in your daily life?" older adults are less likely to report considerable stress (about half) than younger adults (almost two thirds) (American Board of Family Practice, 1987).

It is possible that older adults manage their stress better than do younger adults—either through managing their perceptions of stress better, more frequent prayer, or the practice of other informal stress management techniques. It is also possible that they are less willing to report stress. They may find it to be more of a stigma than do younger adults and are reluctant to admit to it. Or they may be less able to recognize it, either because of lack of knowledge about what stress is or because the stress is masked by depression—which older adults are more likely to exhibit symptoms of (George, 1993). This is an empirical question that needs to be tested.

Many adult Americans, regardless of age, report a great deal of stress from time to time, and most of them consciously take steps to control or reduce it. Only a few, however, try formal stress management techniques. The most popular stress management measures are physical exercise (practiced more among younger adults), psychological denial, and avoidance (Taylor & Kagay, 1985).

## MEASUREMENT

Perhaps the most widely known stress study of the second half of the 20th century was the Social Readjustment Rating Scale (SRRS), developed by Thomas Holmes and Richard Rahe at the University of Washington School of Medicine. The SRRS ranks 43 life-change events according to a score derived from more than 5,000 interviews over two decades.

Men and women of different socioeconomic status, age, and marital status were asked to assign numeric values higher or lower than an arbitrary score of 50 for marriage. Ten of the top 15 scores related to the family, with death of a spouse receiving the top score of 100. Surprisingly, the ratings of events was consistent across ethnicities (African Americans and Mexican Americans) and countries (Europe and Japan).

Holmes and Rahe correlated the ratings of life change events over a 12-month period with health risk. Thirty-seven percent of the individuals who scored under 200 underwent an appreciable change of health compared with 79% of those who scored over 300.

An interesting facet of the SRRS scale is its validity despite its mechanistic approach to life events. The instrument does not, for instance, determine whether the individual's perception of a life event is stressful or not. Thus, the death of a cantankerous and burdensome spouse may be met with relief, whereas a codependent spouse may experience hysteria.

Researchers are looking for ways to make stress-measuring instruments more precise and powerful by weighing individual perceptions of stressful events. Lazarus and colleagues have focused on daily hassles (e.g., weight gain, rising prices, losing things), and have found stronger statistical associations with health outcomes than are obtained by merely counting life events (Lazarus & Folkman, 1984).

Over the past decade, it has also become clear that the Holmes and Rahe's Scale is not responsive to the life events of the later years and that many of the items that are included are unlikely to occur in late life. About a dozen age-specific scales have since been developed (Chiriboga, 1992).

## STRESS MANAGEMENT INTERVENTIONS

There are numerous stress management techniques, too many to list in their entirety. Some of the more popular strategies focus on exercise, diet, muscle relaxation, meditation, acupuncture, deep breathing, visualization, desensitization, and biofeedback. Although a service industry has been developing around these techniques, the efficacy of these activities needs further study. In particular, we need to know which technique or, more realistically, combination of techniques works best with which type of person and for what type of problem.

In the meantime, it is best for clients to give a particular technique a trial run of at least 2 weeks before giving up on the technique and moving on to another one. Following is a summary of a few of the more popular techniques.

### DIAPHRAGMATIC BREATHING

One symptom of stress is shallow and rapid breathing. One way to counteract this is through diaphragmatic breathing, also called belly breaths. This technique is easy, convenient, and has face validity for most adherents. In other words, people feel better quickly. From a research perspective, however, the technique's short- or long-term effect on stress management is largely untested.

Imagine your stomach and chest as a pitcher to be filled with air. Place one hand on your stomach and the other on your chest, and inhale for about 6 seconds through the nose (this warms and moistens the air, and screens impurities). First, raise the lower hand as the air fills up the bottom of the pitcher, then the upper hand as the top of the pitcher is filled. Exhale for about 6 to 8 seconds, with the upper hand moving in first as the top of the pitcher is emptied; then draw in the abdomen as the bottom of the pitcher is emptied last and the lower hand moves in.

Because most persons are shallow chest breathers, confusion about the procedure or lightheadedness may occur. To minimize the confusion, the placement of the hands on the stomach and the chest will help to clarify this breathing procedure. To reduce or avoid lightheadedness, decrease the length of the inhalation. After sufficient practice, this exercise can be repeated several times in succession and multiple times over the course of the day (see Figure 10.2).

## PROGRESSIVE MUSCLE RELAXATION/VISUALIZATION

In addition to shallow breathing, another symptom of stress is muscle tension. Edmund Jacobson began his work on reducing muscle tension through progressive muscle relaxation in 1908. The scientific evidence since then has provided a modest amount of support to his claim that relaxation skills can lower tension levels (Pender, 1987). The guiding force behind this technique is twofold: (a) to relax you must first learn to differentiate between tension and relaxation, and (b) tension can manifest itself anywhere throughout the body.

One way to determine the sequence of muscle groups to tense and relax is to start from either the top of your head or from your feet, and continue in the opposite direction.

H3R below refers to "hold for 3 seconds, then relax." When relaxing, exhale slowly and steadily.

1. Tense your forehead by raising your eyebrows, H3R.
2. Wrinkle nose and purse lips together, H3R.
3. Tense your whole face, squeeze in like a prune, H3R.

## BREATHING EXERCISE 1 BELLY BREATH

### HOW TO EXHALE correctly

BREATHE OUT..... BELLY GOES IN.

### HOW TO INHALE correctly

BREATHE IN....... BELLY GOES OUT.

### CORRECT BREATHING

**HOW TO EXHALE.** Sit up straight in your chair **(1)**. Do not lean against the back of the chair. Now put your hands on your belly as in illustration **(2)**. Spread your fingers wide apart so that you cover your belly area. Now press in firmly with your hands and fingers as in **(3)**, and as you press in, breathe out through your nose. **This means that you will be breathing out as you press your belly in (4).**

**HOW TO INHALE.** Now, as you breathe in, release your hands slowly, letting the belly drop down and out **(5)** as though it were being filled with air. **This means that you will be breathing in as your belly goes out.**

In order to see how this will look when it is done correctly, look right at the hands in Figure **(4)**. Now look at the hands in Figure **(5)**. Look back and forth quickly from **(4)** to **(5)** several times and you will see how the belly goes in and out.

**REMEMBER: Don't try to breathe like this all day. Just do 2–5 minutes of breathing exercise every day, morning and evening.**

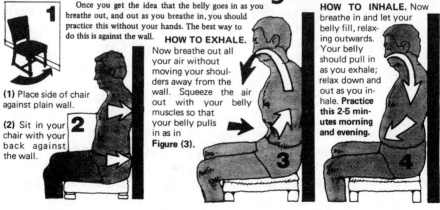

## BREATHING EXERCISE 2 BELLY BREATH against the wall

Once you get the idea that the belly goes in as you breathe out, and out as you breathe in, you should practice this without your hands. The best way to do this is against the wall. **HOW TO EXHALE.** Now breathe out all your air without moving your shoulders away from the wall. Squeeze the air out with your belly muscles so that your belly pulls in as in **Figure (3).**

**(1)** Place side of chair against plain wall.

**(2)** Sit in your chair with your back against the wall.

**HOW TO INHALE.** Now breathe in and let your belly fill, relaxing outwards. Your belly should pull in as you exhale; relax down and out as you inhale. **Practice this 2-5 minutes morning and evening.**

**FIGURE 10.2   Belly breath.**

4. Shrug shoulders, H3R; tense left arm, H3R, then tense right arm, H3R.
5. Tense left fist, H3R, then tense right fist, H3R.
6. Tense shoulders toward the back, slightly arch back, lift head up, H3R.
7. Squeeze abdomen tight, H3R; squeeze buttocks together, H3R.
8. Tense left leg, H3R, then tense right leg, H3R.
9. Bend left toes, cock left ankle, H3R, then bend right toes, cock right ankle, H3R.

Relaxation can be further facilitated by following progressive muscle relaxation with 10 minutes of visualization or imagery. One popular image is to recall the warmth of the sun, the sensation of a gentle breeze, the sound and smell of the ocean, and the sight of a swaying palm tree. Myriad other images can also promote relaxation. For books, tapes, referrals, and a directory of practitioners, contact the Academy for Guided Imagery, P.O. Box 2070, Mill Valley, CA 94942; 800-726-2070.

During progressive muscle relaxation, it is important to become aware of the feelings of tension and relaxation. After some practice at this technique, you will begin to recognize and locate tension in specific parts of your body. You can use a localized version of the procedure to let go of tension lodged in a particular part of the body at any time of the day.

This may not be the ideal relaxation technique for people with painful arthritis or a heart condition. Clients with these conditions need to consult with their physician and may choose to eliminate or just imagine the tension phase of the technique, or to focus exclusively on the visualization phase.

## RELAXATION RESPONSE AND MEDITATION

The relaxation response is based on the technique of meditation without the Eastern spiritual overtones. It operates on the premise that the repetition of a sound or word (like "one" or "peace") is equivalent to the repetition of a mantra (a one- or two-syllable sound) as part of a meditation technique. (For more information on relaxation response techniques and theory, see Benson, 1976, 1984, 1987.)

Researchers at the Maharishi University in Fairfield, Iowa, have reported in research journals that the technique of transcendental meditation—brought into the United States in the 1950s by the Indian guru Maharishi Mahesh Yogi and later popularized by the Beatles—is the best option for lowering high blood pressure. Through 3-month randomized, controlled, single-blinded trials, the researchers report that meditation lowers blood pressure as effectively as hypertension drugs but without the side effects (Alexander et al., 1996; Schneider et al., 1995).

Both the relaxation response and meditation are based on the technique of letting all thoughts drift from one's mind as they arise. This generally is referred to as emptying one's mind but, in actuality, the technique is one in which thoughts are allowed to pass through the mind as they arise, while the participant keeps returning to the chosen repetitive sound.

1. Find a comfortable position. Most people prefer to be seated, though some choose to lie down. (Some people complain that they are likely to nap when they lie down, but it is unclear if, or how much, a short nap is less effective at revitalizing the body and mind than a meditation session.)
2. Sit quietly with eyes closed; then run through a quick version of progressive muscle relaxation.
3. Begin to repeat to yourself, softly, your word or sound (choose one that is pleasing to you and that you are not likely to forget).
4. Continue for 20 minutes, opening an eye to check the time if you like, or set a timer in another room so you hear it as a soft auditory reminder.
5. Practice twice a day, preferably before a meal when digestive processes are not too distracting, and at a consistent time of the day (e.g., before breakfast and dinner) to establish a habit.
6. Most important, do not evaluate each session, even if you believe your thoughts have dominated your attention rather than the repetition of your word or sound. Instead, choose a trial period (perhaps 3 weeks) and determine whether the sessions as a whole are having a favorable impact.

Although repeating a sound or word is the most popular meditative device, some people prefer to focus on a yantra (a geometric form), imagine a peaceful scene (such as the beach or the woods), or pay attention to their inhalation and exhalation pattern.

Stress management techniques are deceptively simple. They are easy to learn but difficult to sustain. To help form a stress management habit, it is important to establish a consistent routine and to have a partner to encourage you and sometimes to remind you of your commitment.

## ACUPUNCTURE

One major source of stress is coping with chronic physical pain. In November 1997, a committee of independent physicians and scientists at the National Institutes of Health (NIH) reviewed a wide range of research findings and reported that acupuncture treatment—the 2,500-year-old Chinese needle therapy that has been on the fringe of American medicine for years—is an effective adjunctive therapy for pain control and has the promise to be beneficial in other areas as well. Only 10% of health plans offer acupuncture benefits, however, and Medicare is not one of them. The NIH committee urged insurers, both public and private, to cover acupuncture services.

The Chinese theory behind acupuncture—that the body is made up of channels of energy flow called Qi and that inserting needles into specific points on the body relieves energy blockages along these channels—has not received support from Western science. Research does support the idea, though, that acupuncture needles inserted into specific nerve junction points on the body and rotated or electrically stimulated, will increase the production of the body's own natural pain-killing chemicals.

Acupuncture is widely used in the treatment of various addictions and has been reported to be successful with rheumatoid arthritis, low-back pain, asthma, relief of postchemotherapy nausea, and improvement of the clinical outcome following cerebrovascular accident (Peterson, 1996). Most of the studies to date, however, have had serious design flaws.

In 1997, 34 states licensed or regulated the practice of acupuncture by nonphysicians and provided training standards for certification. In addition, the FDA regulates the needles as part of its medical device authority. The number of acupuncturists in the United States has grown to 10,000 including almost 3,000 physicians who are members of the American Academy of Medical Acupuncture. To find a licensed or certified specialist, contact the National Commission for the Certification of Acupuncturists (202-232-1404) or the American Academy of Medical Acupuncturists (800-521-2262).

## HYPNOSIS

The committee of independent physicians and scientists at the NIH also reported that hypnosis can be an effective adjunctive therapy for treating cancer-related pain, tension headaches, and other conditions. Hypnosis is a deep state of relaxation, accompanied by inertia, passivity, and a narrowing of consciousness. Guides are available to help clients learn self-hypnosis (Davis et al., 1995), and professional societies that screen hypnotherapists can provide referrals on request. Contact one of the following two organizations: The American Society of Clinical Hypnosis, 2200 East Devon Avenue, Suite 291, Des Plaines, IL 60018; or The Society for Clinical and Experimental Hypnosis, 128-A Kingspark Drive, Liverpool, NY 13090.

## BIOFEEDBACK

The NIH committee also recommended biofeedback for tension headaches. Biofeedback uses a machine to make you aware of bodily processes that you do not ordinarily notice (muscle tension, skin surface temperature, brain wave activity, skin conductivity or moisture, blood pressure, and heart rate), so that you bring them under voluntary control.

A directory of certified biofeedback practitioners in your area is published by the Biofeedback Certification Institute of America, 10200 W. 44th Avenue, Suite 304, Wheatridge, CO 80033.

## MASSAGE

Anyone skeptical of the mental health benefits of massage just needs to receive a good one. To find a qualified massage therapist in your area call the American Massage Therapy Association at 847-864-0123; or connect to: www.amtamassage.org.

## MEDICATIONS

The class of drugs called benzodiazepine, commonly referred to as tranquilizers, have been available since the early 1960s. These drugs are believed to affect the amygdala and hypothalamus regions of the limbic system of the brain within 30 to 40 minutes of ingestion. This quick relief, which requires no effort, is available at an affordable cost to many who are able to participate in the American health care system.

Unfortunately, these drugs have side effects, can be addictive, and do nothing to alter the life events or personality traits that produce stressful situations.

## MENTAL HEALTH AND AGING

### MENTAL HEALTH OF OLDER ADULTS

My personal definition of health greatly emphasizes mental health. It surprised me, therefore, to uncover the comment, "mental wellness . . . is rarely included as a major component in health promotion programs for older adults" (Mettler, 1992, p. 4). Perhaps this is due to the belief that most older adults already experience good mental health.

To some extent, studies bear this out. Researchers consistently report that most (about 85%) older adults are satisfied with their lives, and that older adults are at least as satisfied with their lives as middle-aged and younger adults (George, 1986).

Moreover, neither the average 50% reduction in income at retirement nor a probable increase in loss and caregiving responsibility significantly reduces, in general, the life satisfaction of older adults. As George (1986) notes, "Older adults are apparently masters of the art of lowering aspirations to meet realities" (p. 7).

Conversely, although we must acknowledge the mental health resiliency of older adults in general, we tend to neglect the 15% of older adults who are dissatisfied with their lives. Referrals to psychiatric specialists, for example, are less likely for older than for younger adults because of professional skepticism about its utility and the reluctance of older adults to accept referral (Shapiro, 1986).

### DEPRESSION

Some clinicians and investigators fear that the diagnostic criteria for depressive disorder are not "age fair" (George, 1993). Research findings suggest that older adults are more likely to have depressive symptoms that do not meet the criteria for a diagnosis of depression (the treatment of which could be reimbursed through third-party payers) but do interfere with social role and quality of life.

Barry Lebowitz (1995) of the National Institute of Mental Health estimates that 15% of Americans age 65 and older suffer from serious and persistent symptoms of depression, even though only 3% are reported to be suffering from the clinical diagnosis of major depression as defined by the *Diagnostic and Statistical Manual of Mental Disorders*. Depression in older adults, therefore, may be unrecognized or undertreated in as many as 90% of older adults (Burns & Taub, 1990). This insufficiently treated depression leads to higher risk of subsequent physical decline (Penninx et al., 1998) and, probably, suicide (Klein & Bloom, 1997). The rate of suicide among persons aged 65 and older is twice the national rate, and among white men over age 85, it is six times the national rate.

The most likely *causes* of depression among older adults are chronic illness, medications, genetic predisposition, personalities characterized by low self-esteem, and life events focused on loss. The most likely *signs* of depression are unexplained crying, withdrawal, a focus on despair and helplessness, increased agitation, slow speech, and self-neglect.

A summary of depression assessment scales and how to obtain them, along with practical strategies for reducing depression in older adults can be found in *A Life Worth Living* (Mosher-Ashley & Barrett, 1997). For an assortment of mental health treatment protocols used by nurses in a variety of practice settings see Kurlowicz (1997). Treatment response for depression is effective for up to 80% of older adults (NIH, 1992).

Antidepressant medication and psychotherapy are the standard prescriptions for older persons with depression, but there has been growing interest in treatment through acupuncture, hypnosis, massage, exercise, nutrition, prayer, exposure to bright lights, yoga, deep breathing, guided imagery, and life reviews. The Office of Alternative Medicine at the NIH in Bethesda, Maryland, is beginning to fund small studies in these areas.

## LIFE REVIEW PROCESS

Although not a formal therapy, life reviews are believed to have therapeutic powers. Robert Butler first presented the life review process in 1961 as a way of incorporating reminiscence in the aged as part of a normal aging process. Dr. Butler described the life review as more comprehensive than mere reminiscence, and perhaps more important in old age when there may be a need to put one's life in order and to come to an acceptance of present circumstances (Butler, 1995).

Although life reviews are usually helpful for improving the mental health of most older adults who are seeking meaning, resolution, reconciliation, direction, and atonement, health professionals find it too time-consuming to listen to the reminiscences of older clients in this era of managed care. Health professionals can, however, provide a key role in referring older clients to appropriate forums or helping them obtain relevant materials (see subsection on Mental Health Resources).

There are also helpful reading materials for conducting life reviews. James Birren and colleagues (1996), for instance, review several themes in their book—such as love, money, work, and family—to provide structure to the review process. He encourages small group discussion to help both memory and the acceptance of memories, and notes that in all his years of experience he has not had a group member report having become depressed as a result of a life review (Birren & Deutchman, 1991). He warns, however, that persons who are already depressed or otherwise needing therapy should be under the supervision of a qualified professional.

## MENTAL HEALTH OF THE VERY OLD

The number of centenarians in America doubled between 1980 and 1990, from 18,000 to 36,000 and by the year 2000 the number may reach 100,000 (Bortz, 1996). Although the research on centenarians has been limited by nonrepresentative samples, the existing studies do provide evidence on the importance of mental health and social involvement toward our ability to live long and well.

In 1991 to 1992, psychologist Leonard Poon of the University of Georgia interviewed about 100 centenarians through the Georgia Centenarian Study and tentatively concluded that mental health is more important to survival than the longevity of your parents or what you have eaten over a lifetime. Poon reports that survivors over the age of 100 appear to be optimistic, to be passionately engaged in some activity, and to have the ability to adapt to repeated losses over time.

Alice Day's (1992) interviews of American women in their 70s and 80s uncovered similar qualities among women who were aging successfully; they tended to have a positive attitude, stay involved, and foster social support. These factors can override barriers to physical health and financial well-being.

## COGNITIVE FITNESS

K. Warner Schaie (1997) suggests that "use it or lose it" does not just apply to muscles, it applies to our brains as well. He reports that by 80 years of age, virtually everybody has some decline in mental function, but how much you slip in your 60s and 70s depends in part on mental stimulation.

Dr. Marilyn Albert of Harvard Medical School and her colleagues (1995) conducted interviews with 1,192 people aged 70 to 79 and concluded that mental stimulation like crossword puzzles, reading, and discussion—versus passively viewing television entertainment, idle chit-chat, and doing things from rote—may help stave off dementia and memory loss. They also reported that physical activity, perhaps because it affects the blood flow to the brain, helps sustain mental faculties.

Other researchers also report a connection between physical and mental fitness. Psychologist Robert Dustman (1996) reported that after 4 months, sedentary people over age 55 who increase their aerobic capacity also increase their mental acuity. Hardman and Blair (1995) at a Consensus Conference on the effects of exercise reported that "Exercise has a moderate to large beneficial effect on mild to moderate depression."

## MENTAL HEALTH RESOURCES

Even among the 85% of older adults who are basically satisfied with their lives, there is an inevitable, recurrent need for mental health support, often during times of stress. The American Association of Retired Persons offers a variety of mental health programs and resources to the general public. Two of the programs are

1. The Reminiscence Program, in which trained volunteers help isolated elders in institutions and community settings regain touch with significant past experiences to improve their self-worth.

2. The Widowed Persons Service, a peer support program of trained volunteers, themselves widowed, who assist the newly widowed to recover from their losses and rebuild their lives.

To access these programs, contact the American Association of Retired Persons, Social Outreach and Support, 601 E. Street NW, Washington, DC 20049. A list of other AARP mental health resources, including organizations, publications, and audio programs, is available free of charge, from AARP Fulfillment,Mental Health/Wellness/Older Adults Resource List, 601 E Street NW,Washington, DC 20049.

To borrow a Reminiscence Video Training Kit (Stock Number D13403) at no charge, or to obtain a free 11-page booklet on creative uses of life review in a variety of settings (Stock #D14930), contact AARP Fulfillment, 601 E Street NW, Washington, DC 20049.

Growing Wiser is a community-based mental health program for older adults that has been replicated in many states. Topics covered include memory improvement, mental alertness, coping with loss and life change, maintenance of independence, stress management, and self-image. Contact the Growing Wiser program, Healthwise, Inc., P.O. Box 1989, Boise, ID 83701; 208-345-1161.

The National Institute of Mental Health distributes literature and conducts educational programs to educate the public on the recognition and treatment of depression. One publication especially written for older adults is called *If You're Over 65 and Feeling Depressed . . . Treatment Brings New Hope*. Contact the National Institute of Mental Health, D/ART (Depression Awareness, Recognition, and Treatment Program), 5600 Fishers Lane, Room 15c-05, Rockville, MD 20857; 301-443-4513.

The National Alliance for the Mentally Ill provides information on mental illness and its treatment, including the publication *Mood Disorders, Depression and Manic Depression*. Contact the National Alliance for the Mentally Ill, 2101 Wilson Blvd., Suite 302, Arlington, VA 22201; 800-950-6264.

The National Mental Health Association provides information, referrals, and support for a wide variety of mental health issues. Contact the National Mental Health Association Information Center, 1021 Prince Street, Alexandria, VA 22314-2971; 800-969-6642.

Project Oasis trains older adult volunteers to become mental health paraprofessionals in nursing homes. Benefits accrue not only to nursing home residents, but to the volunteers and the nursing home staff. To find out more about this program, contact Judy Warren, PhD, Texas Agricultural Extension Service, Texas A & M University, College Station, TX 77843; 409-845-1146.

Fostering creativity in older adults can also improve their mental health. "There is some degree of creativity in every person, and the (health practitioner's) function is to assist the aged person to recognize and believe in his or her full potential. Products of creativity are less important than fostering a creative attitude. Curiosity, inquisitiveness, wonderment, puzzlement, and craving for understanding are creative attitudes. [It is possible to help older persons] to break free" (Ebersole & Hess, 1990).

A monograph by McMurray (1990) is a good source of information on sparking creativity in older persons. Ebersole and Hess (1990) refer to several other guides that encourage creative expression in older adults, including art, music, poetry, humor, and self-actualization. Koch's (1977) account describing how he taught poetry to nursing home residents is a particularly enjoyable and useful resource guide.

## QUESTIONS FOR DISCUSSION

1. Choose a health behavior that you would like to improve. Then look at the list of behavior management techniques in this chapter and try one or two for a 2-week period. Write a report on your experience.
2. How would you help older persons increase their self-efficacy so that they can lose weight?
3. Prepare a plan for leading a small group of older persons in a 30-minute stress management routine. Are you confident enough to lead a small group?

# 11
## Community Health

To increase (no baseline data) the proportion of people who had the opportunity to participate during the preceding year in at least one organized health promotion program to 85%.

To increase the percentage of worksites with 50 or more employees that have health promotion programs from 66% in 1985 to 85%. (Public health goals from The U.S. Public Health Service's Healthy People 2000 Initiative) (AARP, 1991)

As of 1992, the proportion of people who had the opportunity to participate during the preceding year in at least one organized health promotion program was 80%; as of 1992, the percentage of worksites with 50 or more employees that have health promotion was 81%. (*Healthy People 2000 Midcourse Review: 1995 Report on Progress*, DHHS, OPHS)

## COMMUNITY HEALTH ORGANIZATIONS

Unless they live in remote rural settings, older persons are likely to have a wide array of health-promoting resources and services available within their communities. Neither frailty nor disability automatically prevents older adults from getting involved in church programs, senior centers, AARP health education or advocacy programs, hospital-based senior health education programs, or other community resources (Haber, 1993b).

A logical place for older clients to begin to locate relevant community resources is the local Area Agency on Aging (AAA). These agencies are responsible for providing information as well as coordinating the more than 20,000 organizations around the country providing services for the aging.

Unfortunately, the 672 AAAs do not have uniform names and can be difficult to locate. The National Association of Area Agencies on Aging (1112 16th Street NW, #100, Washington, DC 20036; 202-296-8130) provides current local information through its *Directory of State and Area Agencies on Aging.*

## SENIOR CENTERS

Older adults are more active at seeking health information than younger adults. A major source of information for 20% to 25% of older adults is the neighborhood senior center (Office of Disease Prevention and Health Promotion, 1990). A national survey revealed that every one of the more than 10,000 senior centers around the country provide some type of health education or screening program (Leanse, 1986). In addition, most centers provide a combination of general health education seminars, exercise and nutrition classes, self-help groups, self-care programs, or referrals to appropriate health services.

Senior centers exist in almost every community, provide a broad spectrum of health education offerings, and have good connections with the medical community. More than 80% are linked to physicians, hospitals, or public health departments (Leanse, 1986).

According to one survey, though, health education and health promotion opportunities are not always linked to senior centers (Campanelli, 1990). Community practitioners who were asked where they would locate information on health education or health promotion for older adults identified a wide array of sites, giving no specific emphasis to senior centers. Identified sites included state and local health departments, institutes of higher education, hospitals, public service agencies, and voluntary organizations.

Nevertheless, many of the senior centers around the country are the best place to go to for a wide range of health promoting activities, including exercise programs, medical screenings, nutrition programs, and health education classes. Summaries describing several innovative senior centers in Texas follow.

The Maurice Barnett Geriatric Wellness Center offers a wide array of wellness programs including health assessments, medical screenings and immunizations, health education, caregiving programs, and support groups. This senior center is unique in two ways. It identifies itself as a wellness center and it involves older adults on the Board of Directors: Maurice Barnett Geriatric Wellness Center, 401 W. 16th Street., P.O. Box 861492, Plano, TX 75086.

Retirees crafted the native stone wall outside of the Comal County Senior Citizens Center and disassembled, hand sanded, and reassembled into squares thousands of inch-long pieces of wood for the parquet tile floor. Retirees continue to make contributions to this senior center including the running of a thrift shop that nets over $2,000 per month: Comal County Senior Citizens Center, 655 Landa Street, New Braunfels, TX 78130.

The Galveston County Multipurpose Senior Center offers a variety of health programs including exercise and country western dance classes. The most innovative aspect of this senior center was an effort to develop older adult leadership through a senior leadership training program (Grasso & Haber, 1995). Galveston County Multipurpose Senior Center, 2201 Avenue L, Galveston, TX 77550; 409-766-2444.

## RELIGIOUS INSTITUTIONS

The church, synagogue, or mosque has the potential to be one of the most important sources of health-promoting programs in this country. Congregational members share values, beliefs, traditions, cultural bonds, and the trust and respect that these engender. Among minority groups, religious institutions may be the only community organizations deemed trustworthy of providing health information and social support (Thomas et al., 1994; Williams, 1996). In addition, religious institutions are able to connect with difficult-to-reach older adults, who may be isolated from other sources of health care.

Religious institutions are often called on to provide a wide array of educational, counseling, and social support services for those persons who are least served by health care institutions—minorities and the poor. It would entail only a small additional step—collaboration with health professionals—for many of these institutions to be able to implement medical screenings and health education programs. Yet the immense potential contribution of religious institutions toward the health promotion of individuals remains largely untapped (Neighbors et al., 1995; Wind, 1990).

More than 80% of Americans past age 65 claim their religious faith is the most important influence in their lives (Moberg, 1983). Of the 5 million persons aged 65 and over who do unpaid volunteer work, for instance, fully 43% perform most of their work at religious organizations. These older volunteers tend to put in more hours per week and more weeks per year than do younger volunteer workers (U.S. Department of Labor, 1989). Many of these older volunteers could be trained to provide health-promoting services to their peers.

Religious institutions have broadened their mission in the mental health arena. A survey of 2,500 self-help groups revealed that 44% of these groups had met in churches or synagogues, more than had met in any other community site (Madara & Peterson, 1986).

## SHEPHERD'S CENTERS OF AMERICA

The Shepherd's Centers of America is a national association of nonprofit organizations, typically housed in local neighborhood congregations, that offer older persons an array of educational courses, services, and resources with a wellness approach. Formed in Kansas City, in 1972, by Dr. Elbert Cole, this organization originally consisted of six men who delivered hot meals to seven homebound women. The organization now reaches more than 200,000 persons, to whom it provides health education, life enrichment classes, bereavement support, transportation services, respite care programs, advocacy, and other activities.

Teams of retired health professionals, trained lay persons, and volunteers develop and implement health programs that may include health education classes, blood pressure screenings, exercise programs, nutrition education, medication seminars, caregiver seminars, and the development of peer support groups.

The empowerment philosophy of the Shepherd Center is embodied in the saying: "No one should do for older persons what they can do for themselves." In 1998, the model was being implemented at 86 centers located in 25 states, with the leadership in the hands of older persons. For more information, contact The Shepherd's Centers of America, 6700 Troost Avenue, Suite 616, Kansas City, MO 64131; contact Dr. Elbert Cole at 816-960-2022.

## OTHER NATIONAL RESOURCES AFFILIATED WITH RELIGIOUS INSTITUTIONS

Two national resources with the goal of maximizing the independence of older adults and which are affiliated with religious institutions, are the

Interfaith Volunteer Caregivers Program (IVCP), 105 Mary's Avenue, P.O. Box 1939, Kingston, NY 12401, contact Virginia Schiaggino at 914-331-1358; and the Forum on Religion and Aging, American Society on Aging, 833 Market Street #512, San Francisco, CA 94103.

IVCP will share a step-by-step approach to linking members of multiple congregations in a specific geographic area into a single organization in order to meet specific caregiving needs, and to enhance the quality of life of older persons who live in the community and want to avoid premature institutionalization.

The Forum on Religion and Aging distributes a newsletter, *Aging and Spirituality*, and assists members of the American Society on Aging who want to address their concerns about spirituality and aging.

## WORKSITE WELLNESS

The Healthy People 2000 goal of 85% of worksites with 50 or more employees having health promotion programs was on the verge of being achieved in 1992 (*Worksite Wellness Works*, 1993). This growth may be attributed to the fact that corporate leaders have become more knowledgeable about the studies that have correlated participation in worksite wellness programs with lower absenteeism and tardiness, fewer medical insurance and disability compensation claims, increased productivity because of higher morale, and lower turnover rates (Kizer, 1987). Among 31 worksite wellness programs evaluated in terms of cost-effectiveness, only one failed to indicate a positive return on investment (Stokols et al., 1995). Another 20 worksite health programs were evaluated, and only one was not associated with reduced costs or increased benefits (Pelletier, 1996).

In 1978, Johnson and Johnson, the nation's largest producer of health care products, began its Live for Life program to improve the health of more than 10,000 employees. Compared with employees at Johnson and Johnson companies who did not have access to the program, participating employees became more active, lost more weight, smoked less, showed greater improvement in applying stress management techniques, and lost less time because of sickness (Nathan, 1984).

A similar program, Control Data Corporation's Staywell Program, was started a year later. As with Live for Life, Staywell begins with a health screening profile, then follows up with professionally run programs and support groups called action teams. Both programs led to corporatewide environmental changes, such as the provision of nutritious foods in the cafeteria and in vending machines, no-smoking areas, and on-site exercise facilities (Naditch, 1984).

With the cost of corporate medical plans rising 25% in 1991 (Meyer, 1991), some companies, like Turner Broadcasting Systems, attempted to lower insurance costs by firing or refusing to hire smokers and overweight people. A more common, and less extreme, response was instituted by companies that raised health care costs for employees who engage in lifestyle risk behaviors. Hershey Foods employees, for instance, pay $1,400 more per year if they become obese (even as a result of eating Hershey bars), or if they smoke, don't exercise, or have high blood pressure, and high cholesterol.

A more positive perspective is taken by Southern California Edison (SCE), which gives premium reductions or reimbursements to employees who undergo screenings or join risk reduction programs. SCE was motivated by the finding that employees with three risk factors averaged insurance claims that were twice as high as those with no risk factors (Meyer, 1991).

One of the major shortcomings of worksite wellness programs is the tendency for those who need them least—the younger and healthier workers—to use them most (International Society of Certified Employee Benefit Specialists, 1985). This is due, in part, to the youth of staff members. "At General Electric, Campbell Soup and Johnson and Johnson, the average age of staff members is less than 30. This is typical for fitness center staff; it is rare to find instructors over the age of 40" (Levin, 1987). Levin (1987) questions whether youth-oriented program staff members understand the special needs and interests of older employees and retirees.

Retirees may be excluded from wellness programs deliberately, for such reasons as space limitations, added staff costs, and possible legal liability. Another reason is failure to extend an invitation. In 1985, only 15% of companies with wellness programs permitted retirees to participate ("Year End Update," 1985).

On the positive side, however, an estimated three fourths of major employers offer preretirement programs (Segal, 1986), and an increasing number are adding a wellness component to their content (Levin, 1987). Even more encouraging, these companies are adopting a life planning theme for their preretirement programs, and including employees in their 40s or younger rather than waiting for the more traditional preretirement eligibility age of 55.

## Worksite Health Promotion Organizations

In 1987, in Omaha, Nebraska, the Wellness Councils of America (WEL-COA) was founded for the purpose of developing community-based wellness councils to encourage health promotion activities at the worksite. The growth of these councils in cities across America peaked in 1993 with 40 such councils, but were reduced to 14 in 1998. WELCOA provides them and other organizations with manuals for starting or strengthening worksite health promoting activities. Contact the Wellness Councils of America, Community Health Plaza, Suite 311, 7101 Newport Avenue, Omaha, NE 68152; 402-572-3590.

The Washington Business Group on Health is another national corporate wellness organization that can provide information on corporate wellness and resources on a wide variety of related topics: Washington Business Group on Health, 777 N. Capitol Street NE, #800, Washington, DC 20002; 202-408-9320.

## Hospitals

Since about half the patients in American hospitals are geriatric patients, it is not surprising that many hospitals in the United States host health education programs for older patients and their families. In addition to fostering good public relations, these programs are considered good marketing strategies.

These rapidly increasing hospital-based senior membership programs for health education and health promotion services typically offer a newsletter, sponsor seminars, implement senior exercise and medical screening programs, provide claims assistance, and offer insurance counseling.

An exemplary program affiliated with the hospitals and outpatient clinics associated with the University of Texas Medical Branch (UTMB) in Galveston, Texas, is called SageSource. This program sponsors luncheons and dinner for adults 55 and older, with faculty and clinicians from the UTMB hospitals and outpatient clinics providing health education; a weekly radio show on senior activities and health issues; Share Your Life Story workshops, which allows older adults to craft memories into words; a quarterly newsletter called *SageSource News*; and the sponsorship of health screenings and health fairs. Contact the UTMB Senior Services

Office, P.O. Box 35081, Galveston, TX 77555-5081; 409-747-2142; www.sagesite.utmb.edu.


## EDUCATIONAL INSTITUTIONS

Elderhostel is an international program that provides low-cost room and board and specially designed classes for adults age 55 and over on college campuses. In 1989, about 90,000 older adults participated in Elderhostel programs at more than 1,600 universities, museums, state and national parks, and other community sites throughout the United States, Canada, and 42 countries overseas.

There are no homework assignments, no examinations, and no grades. Elderhostel's emphasis is on thought-provoking and challenging programs. Typically, noncredit college courses are 1 to 3 weeks long. The elder students often live in dormitories and eat in college dining halls. Classes frequently are taught by college faculty, and cover many different types of subjects, such as music, art, religion, history, health, and astronomy. Free catalogs of programs on a national basis are available. Contact Elderhostel, Inc., 75 Federal Street, Boston, MA 02110; 617-426-7788 (or -8056 for international information).

An interesting Elderhostel program, hosted at Texas A & M University at Galveston, is a sea camp that focuses on the coastal environment and endangered species. During the 5-day residential learning program, the students not only attend classes, they take sailing trips and go netting aboard the *Roamin' Empire*, a 48-foot research vessel. The camps started in January 1992 and have had waiting lists during the "snowbird" months, with participation from throughout the United States and Canada.

In July 1993, an even more unique program began for Elderhostelers who want to share their experience with their grandchildren (ages 9 through 12). The intergenerational participants share firsthand, on-the-water experiences during the day and reside in dormitories on campus at night. For information, contact Elderhostel Program, Texas A & M University, Galveston, TX 77550; 409-740-4726.

Community colleges around the country offer low-cost or sometimes free educational programs for senior adults. The College of the Mainland Senior Adult Program, for example, provides a variety of free educational programs for adults age 55 and older including arts, crafts, exercise classes, computers, area trips, and long-distance travel. For information, contact

College of the Mainland Senior Adult Program, 1200 Amburn Road Texas City, TX 77591; 409-938-1211.

## SHOPPING MALL-BASED PROGRAMS

OASIS (Older Adult Service and Information System) provides shopping mall-based educational programs at 27 May Company Department Stores in 22 cities for 135,000 adults age 55 and older. There is only one paid administrator at each site, with considerable administrative responsibility assumed by older adult volunteers. The courses focus on mental and physical health, intellectual stimulation on a wide scope of subjects, and fun. Contact OASIS, 7710 Carondelet Avenue, Suite 125, St. Louis, MO 63105; contact Marylen Mann, director, 314-862-2933.

The National Organization of Mall Walkers (NOMW), began in 1989, is a clearinghouse with 2,000 members. NOMW president, Tom Cabot, reports nearly 3 million mall walkers nationwide (*AARP Bulletin*, 1991), the overwhelming majority of whom are aged 50 and older. Typically, mall walker programs occur before the opening of the mall to shoppers. A few innovative programs provide incentives (merchandise) to registered walkers who walk and record their mileage on a mileage map. If a mall does not have a walking club, it is not too difficult for a health professional or a lay person to start one. Contact National Organization of Mall Walkers, P.O. Box 191, Hermann, MO 65041; 573-486-3945.

## ACTIVATING YOUR CLIENTS' INTERESTS

For health professionals who want to help their clients to activate or expand their interest in

*Art*, contact the National Center on Arts and the Aging, 409 3rd Street, 2nd Floor SW, Washington, DC 20024; 202-479-1200

*Business*, contact the Service Corps of Retired Executives, 409 3rd Street SW, 4th Floor, Washington, DC 20024; 202-205-6762

*Computers*, contact SeniorNet, One Kearny Street, 3rd Floor, San Francisco, CA 94108; 415-352-1210

*Ecology*, contact Earthwatch, Box 0914, 680 Mount Auburn Street, Watertown, MA 02272; 617-926-8200

*Environmental employment*, contact the Senior Environmental Employment Program, AARP, 601 E. Street NW, Washington, DC 20049

*Games for seniors or competitive sports*, contact the U.S. National Senior Sports Organization, 12520 Live Boulevard, St. Louis, MO 63141; 314-878-4900

*Poetry*, contact the Poetry Society of America, 15 Gramercy Park, New York, NY 10003; 212-254-9628

*Tutoring at-risk youth*, contact the National Association of Service and Conversation Corps, 666 11th Street NW, Room 500, Washington, DC 20001; 202-737-6272

## MODEL HEALTH EDUCATION PROGRAMS

There is no certain method for assuring a high quality health education program. It can be helpful, however, for an interested professional, or older adult, to gain access to a model program to see how it works. Some of these programs have been developed through federal grants and other funding sources and have gone through a program evaluation.

A national directory of selected health programs for older adults, entitled *Health Promotion and Aging*, describes 40 model programs around the country that can be adapted to local conditions, and provides references to more than 200 additional programs. The directory, compiled by the Administration on Aging and the U.S. Public Health Service (DHHS Publication No. [OHDS] 86-20950 [ISBN 1-55672-001-7]), is distributed by the National Council on the Aging, Inc., 409 3rd Street SW, Washington, DC 20024; 202-479-1200.

An additional 24 model programs around the country are described in *Exemplary Contributions to Healthy Aging: Award Winners* (July 1992). These programs were selected by a panel of experts through a cooperative project between AARP and the United States Public Health Service's Office of Disease Prevention and Health Promotion. This document, produced through the Healthy People 2000/Healthy Older Adults' initiative, can be obtained from the: American Association of Retired Persons; Healthy Advocacy Services, Program Coordination and Development Department; 601 E. Street NW; Washington, DC 20049.

The best-known older adult medical self-care program is the Healthwise program in Boise, Idaho. With the assistance of a $2.1 million grant from the Robert Wood Johnson Foundation, Healthwise distributed its medical self-care guide to 125,000 Idaho households, along with toll-free nurse consultation phone service and self-care workshops. The handbook provided information and prevention tips on 180 different health problems along with physician-approved guidelines on when to call a health professional for each health problem covered. Thirty-nine percent reported that the handbook helped them avoid a visit to the doctor (Mettler, 1997). Additional information can be obtained from Healthwise, Inc., P.O. Box 1989; Boise, Idaho 83701; 208-331-6963; www.healthwise.org.

Another model program, Staying Healthy After Fifty, began as a demonstration and research project for the W. K. Kellogg Foundation. This project, completed in 1988, involved 2,500 older adults from more than 70 communities nationwide including Asian, African-American, and Hispanic communities. Although the evaluational component of the project did not address outcomes related to the physical health status of participants or their use of medical care, the older participants reported increased knowledge, improved self-care skills, and positive changes in their health behaviors.

An important outgrowth of the Staying Healthy After Fifty project was the development of a curriculum for community programs that can be taught by trained volunteers. This project was implemented by the American Association of Retired Persons, the Dartmouth Institute for Better Health, and the American Red Cross. For more information, contact: American Association of Retired Persons, Health Advocacy Services, 601 E Street NW, Washington, DC 20049.

Dr. Dean Ornish, a physician at the University of California at San Francisco and founder of the Preventive Medicine Research Institute, has developed a program for reversing heart disease that has been replicated at several sites around the country. Dr. Ornish (1992) recommends a vegetarian diet with fat intake of 10% or less of total calories, exercise at least three times a week, yoga and meditation an hour a day, and group support sessions.

Dr. Ornish and has colleague K. Lance Gould (Gould et al., 1995) have reported that blockages in arteries have decreased in size and blood flow has improved in as many as 82% of their heart patients. However, the applicability of his program to nonheart patients is still of uncertain utility. It may take highly motivated individuals (e.g., severe heart patients) and significant medical and health support (requiring significant resources) for the program to be useful to others.

I observed what may have been the best example of a model health education program—a self-led, tai chi class—while on an early morning jog in China in 1978. Tai chi is a nonstrenuous sequence of physical movements derived from the ancient Chinese martial arts, that increases energy, improves balance, and enhances mental and spiritual health. The participants I observed, over half of whom were older adults, had maximum accessibility to this program—they had only to exit their front doors. There were no fees to be paid, and no professionals to depend on (see Figure 11.1). Tai chi, believed to be beneficial for older adults with balance problems, is now being taught at many senior centers throughout the United States.

## PROFESSIONAL ASSOCIATIONS

Health education programs are sponsored by many disease-specific professional associations. The Arthritis Foundation, for example, offers a wide array of health education programs, among them several self-help and peer support programs, including the Arthritis Self-Help Course, PACE

**FIGURE 11.1  Tai chi in China.**

Exercise, Arthritis Clubs, and Aquatic Programs. All programs are taught by trained volunteer instructors, many of whom cope with arthritis.

It is estimated that everyone over age 60 has some degree of osteoarthritis, and about 30% of older Americans recognize some of its symptoms. Osteoarthritis, the most common form of arthritis, is the gradual wearing away of tissue around the joints of the hands, feet, knees, hips, neck, or back. Arthritic pain may vary from mild to severe, and it may come and go. Arthritis cannot be prevented nor cured, but the function of arthritic joints can be improved and the pain often can be alleviated.

More than 100 local chapters of the Arthritis Foundation offer a 6-week course that provides information on medications, exercise, nutrition, relaxation techniques, coping skills, and the practical concerns of daily living. The practical information can range from places where people who have trouble dressing can purchase Velcro-modified clothing to the location of aquatic exercise programs.

Many of the Arthritis Foundation programs were developed and evaluated at the Stanford Arthritis Center over the past decade. Participants are typically asked to pay a small fee for courses and instructional materials. Besides health education programs, local arthritis chapters distribute free booklets on arthritis as well as information about most arthritis medications.

Many other professional associations offer health education programs and materials as well. If you cannot locate a state or local chapter of a specific professional association, contact one of the following national headquarters for information:

Arthritis Foundation, P.O. Box 19000, Atlanta, GA 30326.

Alzheimer's Association, 919 North Michigan Avenue, Suite 1000, Chicago, IL 60611.

American Cancer Society, 1599 Clifton Road NE, Atlanta, GA, 30329.

American Diabetes Association, P.O. Box 25757, 1660 Duke Street, Alexandria, VA 22313.

American Heart Association, 7320 Greenville Avenue, Dallas, TX 75231.

American Lung Association, 1740 Broadway, New York, NY 10019.

HIP (Help for Incontinent People), P.O. Box 544, Union, SC 29379.

National Osteoporosis Foundation, 2100 M Street NW, Suite 602, Washington, DC 20037.

National Stroke Association, 300 East Hampden Avenue, Suite 240, Englewood, CO 80110.

The Health Promotion Institute, a national membership organization, provides a forum for professional development and legislative advocacy. The institute provides opportunities for health promoters to network and to receive health promotion materials. Contact the National Council on Aging, Health Promotion Institute, Department 5087, Washington, DC 20061-5087; 202-479-6606.

A comparable institute, the National Eldercare Institute on Health Promotion at AARP, was grant funded and terminated in 1997. Past issues of its newsletter and other health information may still be obtained from AARP, 601 E. Street NW, Washington, DC; 202-434-2230.

## TOLL FREE HOTLINES

American Diabetes Association: 800-232-3472
American Dietetic Association: 800-366-1655
Cancer Information Service: 800-422-6237
Diabetes Research Foundation: 800-223-1138
Kidney Fund: 800-638-8299
Liver Foundation: 800-223-0179
National Council on Alcoholism and Drug Dependence, Inc.: 800-622-2255
National Mental Health Association: 800-969-6642
National Stroke Association: 800-787-6537
Office of Minority Health Resource Center: 800-444-6472

## COMMUNITY-ORIENTED PRIMARY CARE

Primary health care traditionally is defined as a first-contact medical practice where care is being sought by individuals on their own initiative, without referral by a physician. Community-Oriented Primary Care (COPC), in contrast, refers to the activities of primary care health care professionals who go out into the community on their own initiative, thereby gaining more understanding of individual clients as well as the community from which they come.

Thus, in addition to the traditional focus on the individual patient, the family and the community are also made the focus of diagnosis, treatment, and ongoing surveillance (Institute of Medicine, 1981; Nutting, 1987). The practitioner of COPC moves from the narrow, biomedical, physician-led, one-to-one form of care, to a new vision of providing health care, one that includes the social environment that shapes an individual's health and behaviors.

## DEFINING COMMUNITY

The two most popular definitions of a community are individuals who share a geographical area, and a group of persons who share values or lifestyles. The concept of community from a COPC perspective, however, is more flexibly defined.

A COPC community typically includes clients of a health professional or a health facility who have a specific type or set of health problems (e.g., diabetes, noncompliance, cancer, alcohol abuse, teenage pregnancy, homelessness). In addition, the COPC community often includes the significant individuals on whom these clients rely (e.g., spouse, minister, *curandero*, pharmacist, peers).

The definition of community can be further expanded to include providers from a variety of community organizations who offer services that are relevant to particular health problems as well as officials of state and federal government agencies who implement the policies that impact on these clients.

A COPC project tends to take a broad view of community, and to systematically examine the status or perceptions of the wide variety of persons who represent the community of interest. The crucial elements of a COPC community, however, are those persons within the community who enlarge our understanding of a health problem, and lead us to find better ways in which to address it.

## COLLECTING DATA

In addition to identifying relevant persons in the community who can shed light on a specific health problem, the COPC practitioner reviews extant data, or collects new data. The County Health Department or other city and county agencies may provide relevant demographic, social, economic, and mortality and morbidity data. Other sources of data include chart reviews of clients, or surveys of clients or residents in the community.

Often, data at the local community level (e.g., widowhood, suicide, teenage pregnancy, size of community, ethnicity, socioeconomic status) are compared with data from similar populations in other parts of the country or with Healthy People 2000 baseline data or projections. Health problems in a local community that are of unusual magnitude tend to stimulate COPC projects.

## JOINING OR FORMING A COMMUNITY COALITION

A community coalition typically ranges from 4 to 20 members. Preferably, it is heterogeneous in composition (age, ethnicity, gender, socioeconomic status) and expertise (different types of professionals, lay leaders, and community residents). Coalition members should be willing and able to inventory community health resources and interact with appropriate persons to address relevant health problems.

Health professionals must be prepared to generate interest in the project. A truly mutual collaboration requires the interest and commitment of community residents or leaders.

## CONDUCTING AND EVALUATING A PROJECT

Developing and implementing a modest, doable plan includes identifying measurable objectives for reducing a health problem or the risk factors that contribute to it; establishing a relatively short time frame in which to accomplish the initial objectives; including a focus on health education, disease prevention, or health promotion; and conducting periodic evaluations of progress.

COPC raises important questions regarding the traditional health care training of most health professionals:

Do clinical experiences that are based heavily on hospital-based learning experiences adequately prepare health care professionals?

Do health care providers trained largely in isolation from each other recognize that a team approach is often essential to an accurate diagnosis and an effective treatment plan?

Are students and practitioners who are trained to work within the health care system able to recognize that providers and consumers have the opportunity, and the responsibility, to be advocates of change, and to make the health care system more responsive to their needs?

Over a 4-year period (1992–1996), I participated in two COPC interdisciplinary teams, one housed in a Public Health Service Section 330 community health clinic for indigent patients and the other in a university-affiliated outpatient clinic (Thompson et al., 1996, 1998). These interdisciplinary teams involved primary care physicians, clinical nurses, community health nurses, a physician's assistant, an epidemiologist, a public health specialist, social workers, a medical sociologist, health educators, and a variety of health science students.

The teams met weekly to conduct and discuss home visits, and to develop, implement, and evaluate community-based health projects that were responsive to the needs expressed by the community residents and the local leaders who met with the teams.

The health professionals on the teams, in collaborating with community residents and leaders on a number of small, achievable projects became more sensitive to the home and community environments of the individual clients. A homeless patient at the clinic, for instance, led to a visit to a homeless shelter, which in turn led to a collaborative effort with community residents to develop a health screening instrument to help shelter staff assess the medical status of their clients, and to provide the staff with referral telephone numbers for dealing with a wide range of health problems.

A visit to another homeless shelter led to the implementation of a health fair at that site. Homeless shelter residents participated in planning and implementing the health fair, and residents in the surrounding community were invited to the fair for the purpose of better integrating the homeless shelter into the community.

Visits from former patients of a recently closed Public Health Service Section 330 community health clinic for the indigent in a neighboring city led team members into the community to interview 80 former patients to determine how they had been receiving medical care since the closing and the barriers to health care generated by the closing. The findings were compiled, and the resulting report distributed to community leaders and government officials as the first step in an attempt to reopen this much-needed medical clinic.

Participation in COPC projects is not without frustration. Sometimes, the health care providers or the students wonder about the relevance of these new community activities to the more traditional form of providing health care. Some projects, conceived within the group of health professionals, lack adequate community collaboration and fizzle out.

Without a mechanism for reimbursement of its activities, the COPC model may have only a modest impact on the average clinical practice in the community. At least two abbreviated elements of the COPC model, however, can supplement traditional clinical practices in a cost-effective way: (a) defining a health problem that affects a significant number of clients and (b) developing small projects in the community that systematically address this problem (Nutting, 1987).

## ALTERNATIVE HEALTH CARE IN THE COMMUNITY

In 1997, 40 percent of American adults used some type of alternative care—herbal medicine, chiropractic, acupuncture, massage therapy, spiritual healing, relaxation techniques, self-help groups, or other nonmedical therapies—in the community (Astin, 1998). This is an increase from 33% of American adults in 1991 (Eisenberg et al., 1993). The 1991 survey reported that the number of visits to providers of alternative healing exceeded, by 37 million, the combined number of visits to all U.S. primary care physicians. Visits to alternative healers resulted in the expenditure of nearly $14 billion a year, with only 25% of the cost covered by health insurance.

Although the study reported that alternative healing is used most often by people between the ages of 25 and 49, it should be noted that these techniques are primarily used for chronic conditions—conditions that increase, both in number and severity, with age.

More than three-quarters of the clients using unconventional therapies neglect to notify their physicians about their treatments. The researchers concluded that communication between the medical and alternative healing communities is poor, and this lack of communication can be dangerous.

The establishment in 1992 of the Office of Alternative Medicine at the NIH represented a small step toward bridging this gap. The mission of this office is to subject as many alternative therapies to scientific scrutiny as possible. This goal could go a long way toward promoting acceptance of legitimate alternative therapies by the allopathic medical community and discredit illegitimate ones.

The Office of Alternative Medicine (OAM) has been limited by its budget of less than $2 million in 1992—increased to $3.5 million in 1994 but still a very small portion of the total NIH budget of more than $10 billion. Between 1993 and 1997, OAM funded 42 pilot studies, but there was concern that most of these studies were *not* randomized, controlled clinical trials that resulted in publication in peer-reviewed journals (Angell & Kassirer, 1998).

Over the past 3 years several peer-reviewed journals devoted to research and trends in alternative medicine have been launched: *Alternative Therapies in Health and Medicine, The Journal of Alternative and Complementary Medicine, Alternative Complementary Therapies*, and *The Scientific Review of Alternative Medicine*. It is too soon to tell what percentage of the articles in these journals will be the product of rigorous testing from the scientific community.

## ALTERNATIVE MEDICINE AT U.S. MEDICAL SCHOOLS

Medical schools have responded to the growing interest in alternative health care practices. Almost two-thirds of traditional U.S. medical schools now offer elective courses in alternative medicine or include such topics as acupuncture, chiropractic, herbal medicine, homeopathy, and mind-body medicine in required courses (Wetzel et al., 1998).

A Harvard-based national survey of 125 medical schools (with 94% responding) in 1997 found that 75 of the 117 responding schools—64%—provided such training. A national survey conducted two years prior reported only 46 medical schools doing so.

The authors of the survey concluded that patients are increasingly seeking to identify physicians who are solidly grounded in conventional medicine and are also knowledgeable about the value and limitations of alternative treatments.

There are also four naturopathic medical colleges in the United States, and 11 states in which licensed naturopaths can legally practice medicine as primary care physicians. The state of Washington leads the country in naturopathic medicine. Seattle is the home to Bastyr University, the largest naturopathic school in the country, and in 1996 the state of Washington became the first state to require insurance companies to cover alternative therapies in their benefit plans. The first publicly funded natural medicine clinic—staffed with naturopaths, other alternative therapists, and conventional health professionals—opened in the Seattle area in October 1996.

Naturopaths complete 4 years in a medical college and take national licensing exams. These physicians receive training that is similar in many ways to traditional physicians, plus they receive excellent training in the areas of nutrition (comparable with registered dietitians) and herbal medicine. These practitioners use herbal medicine, massage, acupuncture; take X-rays, blood and urine tests; and, in some states, perform minor surgery and prescribe antibiotics.

Naturopaths are more inclined than medical doctors, however, to try treatments that have little or no credible scientific backing, such as homeopathy—prescribing infinitesimal doses of herbs and minerals that in larger amounts would produce an ailment's symptoms in order to stimulate the body's curative powers; color therapy—wearing purple to lower blood pressure and yellow to prevent another stroke; and colonic irrigations—a powerful, machine-delivered enema.

## WEIL AND CHOPRA

The two most popular purveyors of alternative medicine are physicians: Andrew Weil and Deepak Chopra. Dr. Weil is on the medical school faculty at the University of Arizona in Tuscon where he has developed a 2-year residency program that integrates traditional medicine with other disciplines, such as meditation, nutrition, herbal medicine, acupuncture, and osteopathic manipulation. Dr. Weil has published best sellers (*Spontaneous Healing* and *Eight Weeks to Optimum Health*) and receives about 50,000 questions a week online (cgi.pathfinder.com/drweil).

Dr. Chopra is an entrepreneur who writes books and a monthly newsletter, recites lyrics and poetry on CDs, delivers lectures and seminars, sells tapes, herbs and aromatic oils, and has plans for breaking into movies, television, and a chain of healing centers. The Chopra Center for Well Being in La Jolla, California, dispenses aromatherapy, massage, and spa food (for almost $3,000 a week, lodging not included), along with conventional medicine.

Charismatic health gurus have been on the rise in the 1980s and 1990s, and include Tony Robbins, John Bradshaw, Robert Bly, Marianne Williamson, James Redfield, and many others. To the extent they advocate critical thinking and do not denounce the medical mainstream, they can serve a very useful purpose of expanding our strategies for improving our health. To the extent that they are interested in idolatry and the bottom line—Chopra enterprises brought in about $15 million in 1997—they may be expanding their wallets more than our health care options.

## HOLISTIC HEALTH ORGANIZATIONS

The American Holistic Medical Association (AHMA) and the American Holistic Nurses Association (AHNA) are educational associations that focus on holistically oriented health care—care that emphasizes the biological, psychological, social, and spiritual dimensions. The associations provide information on alternative healing therapies, as well as referrals in your area. Contact AHMA or AMNA, 6728 Old McLean Village Drive, McLean, VA 22101; 703-556-9728.

The Center for Mind-Body Studies provides information for health professionals and lay persons alike. Its projects include mind-body studies, community programs for the working poor and indigent, and support groups for people with chronic illness. The Center for Mind-Body Studies, 5225 Connecticut Avenue NW, Suite 414, Washington, DC 20015.

Commonweal is a support program for people with cancer who seek physical, mental, emotional, and spiritual healing, and a professional development program for health professionals who care for people with life-threatening illnesses: Commonweal, P.O. Box 316, Bolinas, CA 94924.

The National Wellness Association is an organization for professionals and lay persons who are interested in promoting health and wellness and an advocacy group that redresses national health care policies that focus primarily on the treatment of sickness. The National Wellness Association, South Hall, 1319 Fremont Street, Stevens Point, WI 54481; 715-346-2172.

## QUESTIONS FOR DISCUSSION

1. Have you had experience with any organizations—that are *or* are not included in this chapter—that could be a useful referral resource for an older adult? If so, describe your experiences.
2. Which of the community organizations listed in this chapter that you have not had experience with do you most want to know more about, and why? What plans do you have to learn more about one or more of these organizations or programs?

3. Choose one of the Healthy People 2000 objectives listed at the beginning of a chapter in this book, and then develop a plan (by way of a brief outline) for a Community-Oriented Primary Care project that could move us along toward the accomplishment of the objective.
4. One assumption of mind-body medicine is that clients' feelings, as well as their medical concerns, require attention. In what ways would the health care system differ from our present one if it included this approach? What might the economic impact be?
5. If you suffered from a physical illness that might be helped by an alternative health care technique, how much proof would you require before trying it? What are the risks of such an approach?

# 12
## Health Care Reform

A man dies and finds himself standing before the pearly gates. St. Peter approaches and asks: "What did you do in your lifetime to benefit humanity? The man replies: "I helped develop and implement HMOs." St. Peter responds: "Ah, by all means come in." As the man enters, St. Peter adds a cautionary note: "But remember, you can only stay 3 days."

Health-promoting interventions aimed at changing the behaviors of individuals and groups are insufficient by themselves because, in addition to individual and social factors there is an economic, political, cultural, and environmental milieu to consider. All these macrolevel factors come to a focus in the debate over health care reform. And as we enter the new millennium, one of the most controversial aspects of health care reform is managed care.

### MANAGED CARE: WITH OR WITHOUT CLINTON

In the early 1990s, everyone agreed on the inevitability of health care reform taking place. One of the compelling reasons for reform was to address the needs of the 37 million Americans who had no health insurance, plus an additional 20 million who were underinsured. Another, equally compelling, reason for reform was the exorbitant rise in health care costs, which far exceeded the general rate of inflation, and an inability to demonstrate that the United States was better off than countries that spent far less on health care.

Even among a relatively advantaged sector of the American population—Medicare recipients—there was rising discontent. Out-of-pocket medical costs for older adults had been escalating for some time, and elderly families were spending an ever-increasing percentage of their income on medical care, even more than they spent before Medicare was enacted.

In 1991, elderly families spent an average of $3,305 on out-of-pocket medical costs, in contrast to the $1,589 (in 1991 dollars) spent in 1961. The escalating medical expenses of Medicare recipients over the past three decades were reflected in continual increases in copayments and deductibles, a need to purchase additional medigap insurance, rising prescription and over-the-counter medication prices, and a continuing lack of coverage for nursing home care.

Reinforcing the obvious need for health care reform, presidential candidate Bill Clinton promised in 1991 to deliver comprehensive health care reform legislation within 100 days after his inauguration.

By 1994, however, health care reform appeared to be a dismal failure. President Clinton's health care reform task force, headed by Hillary Rodham Clinton, was conducted in secrecy and its major achievement was dubious at best—1,342 pages of mind-numbing acronyms, elaborate regulations, and complicated systems.

Despite the failed attempt at government leadership, health care reform was occurring anyway, under the banner of "Managed Care." Although there is much promise in managed care in terms of cost control and an emphasis on prevention, the unregulated, business-dominated managed care market that took control of health care in the 1990s produced more anxiety and frustration than promise.

Moreover, the number of uninsured Americans continued to increase, to 43.4 million people in 1997. The percentage of the population that was uninsured, which has been increasing every year since 1987 when it was 14.8%, continued to rise and reached 17.7% of the American population in 1996 ("Growing Uninsured Renews Questions About Health Reform," 1997).

## MANAGED CARE ERA OF THE 1990s

### DEFINITION AND GROWTH

There are three basic types of managed care, HMOs, PPOs, and POSs. Health maintenance organizations (HMOs) combine coverage of health care costs and delivery of health care for a prepaid premium. Members receive services from personnel employed by the HMO and patients are generally required to coordinate care through a primary care physician who refers to specialists and admits to a hospital.

Preferred provider organizations (PPOs) and point-of-service (POSs) options are networks of physicians, hospitals, and other health care providers who contract with an insurance company to provide care at discount rates. Members are given financial incentives to use health care providers within the network, but are allowed to use out-of-network providers at a higher cost.

By 1997, 85% of all U.S. workers were enrolled in some form of managed care, 35% in a PPO, 30% in an HMO, and 20% in a POS plan. Overall, managed care enrollment increased by 35% between 1992 and 1996 ("Managed Care Strives to Recover from '97 Struggles," 1998).

## COSTS

Managed care has been given much of the credit for the decline in health care costs in the 1990s because of its emphasis on cheaper alternatives to hospitalization and limiting doctor fees. Annual health spending inflation had reached a high of 16% in 1981, and then went up and down for the rest of the 1980s. However, as the era of managed care took hold in the 1990s, there was a steady decrease in costs, reaching a low of 4.4% inflation rate in 1996 ("Managed Care Cited for Slowdown in Spending," 1998), the lowest rate since health spending trends were first compiled in 1960.

But experts are less sanguine about future cost containment given that HMOs may have already squeezed much of the fat from the system. In fact, two large managed care organizations that had been making a profit for years—Oxford Health and Kaiser Foundation Health—reported their first ever losses in 1997 ("Managed Care Strives to Recover from '97 Struggles," 1998).They were not alone. Of 506 HMOs examined in 1997, 57% lost money (Jacob, 1998).

And the future is not sanguine. Managed care companies have been attracting a high percentage of healthy customers, which is attractive from a short-term business perspective but is at odds with the demographic trends in this country. Also, consumers and legislators are becoming advocates for better-quality managed care. As state legislative mandates for quality care accumulate because of this advocacy, managed care costs are predicted to increase significantly.

In addition, physicians and hospitals are becoming better negotiators with managed care companies and it is becoming more difficult for managed care plans to achieve low reimbursement rates. Other factors include increasing costs associated with an aging population, rising drug costs, and the need to upgrade computer information systems.

## QUALITY OF MANAGED CARE

The good news regarding the monitoring of the quality of managed care is that the health-plan assessment industry is improving rapidly under the leadership of the National Committee for Quality Assurance (NCQA). NCQA is a nonprofit, independent watchdog of, and accreditation for, managed care organizations. Each year, NCQA issues a report card that is based on HEDIS data (Health Plan Employer Data and Information Set), a collection of measurements on managed care plan performance (for more information contact www.ncqa.org on the Web). Eventually, HEDIS is expected to include comprehensive data on not only which health plans work best, but which treatments work best and which are most cost-effective.

The bad news is that in 1998 most employers were still ignoring the HEDIS data on the quality of competing health care plans and basing their decision on which plan to choose on cost alone (Dentzer, 1998). And costs were being viewed from a short-term perspective. Studies on preventive care at the worksite, for instance, report that employer savings from prevention may not be realized for up to 5 years. Managed care organizations, however, are concerned about spending resources on patients who might not be there in 5 or 6 years ("Must HMOs Cover Diabetes Prevention?" 1998).

It is not surprising, therefore, that 75% of Americans are concerned about the quality of their health care system (*U.S. News & World Report*, 1998). Nor was I surprised about the audience's reaction to Helen Hunt in a movie I saw, *As Good As It Gets*. When Helen Hunt's character denounced her HMO for caring more about money than her son's health, the audience cheered wildly.

## 1998 CONSUMER BILL OF RIGHTS

The Henry J. Kaiser Family Foundation and Harvard University conducted a random sample of more than 1,000 adults and reported, not surprisingly, that an overwhelming percentage of respondents were in favor of: more information about how managed care operates, allowing a woman to see a gynecologist of her choice without first getting approval from a health plan, requiring health plans to provide greater access to medical specialists, allowing patients whose claims had been denied to appeal the decision to an independent reviewer, making health plans pay for emergency room visits, and allowing patients to sue for malpractice (Morin, 1998).

All of these popular proposals were part of President Clinton's "Consumer Bill of Rights," pending before Congress in 1998, and similar to the approximately 200 managed care laws passed by state legislators in 1997. What is unpredictable in 1998 and beyond, however, is the "Harry and Louise" factor—advertisements that complain about the meddling of "Big Government" and its potential to increase health care costs. Harry and Louise ads helped defeat President Clinton's health care reform plan in 1994.

In fact, when the Kaiser Foundation survey probed their respondents a little more they found that most of their respondents were no longer favorable to the popular ideas embodied in the Consumer Bill of Rights—if they had to pay more in insurance premiums, if it meant greater involvement by the federal government in health care, or if it might cause some employers to drop health coverage.

## MEDICARE MANAGED CARE

Since the 1982 Tax Equity and Fiscal Responsibility Act, Medicare enrollees have been allowed to join federally accredited HMOs. Enrollment growth in Medicare managed care was quite slow in the 1980s, and only began to increase rapidly between 1993 and 1996, averaging about a 30% increase per year. Despite this recent growth, the absolute numbers are still small, and only 11% of Medicare beneficiaries were enrolled by 1997 (Angell, 1997).

Medicare HMOs cover all deductibles and coinsurance, plus benefits that are not otherwise covered by Medicare including annual physicals, eyeglasses, dental coverage, low-cost prescription drugs, and some types of preventive care. In addition to financial and service benefits, the Medicare HMOs are practically paperwork-free.

Conversely, Medicare HMO enrollees are limited to the doctors in the HMO network. There is also evidence that less healthy older adults find themselves getting poorer access to care (specifically, expensive tests and procedures) in HMOs than in traditional plans. Dissatisfaction with service in Medicare HMOs is much greater among those reporting poor health (Angell, 1997). Seduced in the beginning by lower copayments and pre-scription drug benefits, healthy enrollees do not report problems until they become seriously sick and have difficulty getting adequate time with health professionals as well as access to expensive, specialized services.

Most managed care plans, Medicare or otherwise, are investor owned, and executives are required to maximize profits within the limits of the law. This fiduciary responsibility creates an incentive for managed care plans to seek healthy enrollees, and to limit services to those with serious disease and functional limitations (Angell, 1997). In conflict with this goal is that Medicare typically means expensive care and, along with more research discoveries and an increasing number of older adults, will become increasingly expensive in the future.

Geriatric care, as described by Cassell (1996), means that widespread osteoarthritis of the hips and knees that used to cause major mobility disorders now can be ameliorated if hip- and knee-replacement surgery is available; that heart disease can now be reduced by medicine, coronary bypass and valve replacement; that geriatric depression can often be alleviated provided there is expert diagnosis; that mild cognitive impair-ment can be treated effectively if the clinician is skilled enough to sift through a variety of potential causes; and that hypertension management can be maintained if there is considerable ongoing medical attention.

In short, older adults require more time and effort from health profes-sionals than younger patients, and health professionals need considerable and ongoing geriatric training as well. This reality challenges our ability to manage costs while maintaining quality.

If older persons have questions about the quality of their Medicare HMO, or about joining one, they can be referred to the brochure "Medicare Health Maintenance Organizations: Your Rights, Risk and Obligations," which can be obtained for $3 from the Medical Rights Center, Box RRO, 1460 Broadway, 8th Floor, New York, NY 10036. Free information can also be obtained from the Kaiser Family Foundation at 800-656-4533, or on the Web site: www.hcfa.gov.

## PREVENTION AND ALTERNATIVE MEDICINE

The great hope of managed care, in addition to controlling costs, is that it can become a vehicle for promoting health and prevention. Members of HMOs have traditionally received a higher level of preventive services than patients of fee-for-service practices (Group Health Association of America, 1988; Manning et al., 1984). In the 1990s, many HMOs have taken a leadership role in prevention programs, including expansion into alternative medicine treatments (Voelker, 1993).

Kaiser Permanente, for instance, set up an Alternative Medicine Clinic at Vallejo, California, and, with a referral from a primary care physician, a patient can receive acupuncture, acupressure (form of massage), herbal medicine, meditation, nutritional counseling, and yoga. Harvard Pilgrim Health Care, a Massachusetts-based HMO, allows patients to refer themselves to a behavioral medicine program whereby they learn how to change feelings and affective states in order to have a positive effect on their bodies and their health. After completing the program, patient visits to both primary care physicians and specialists were down 50% (*Wellness and Prevention Sourcebook*, 1998).

In May 1994, Blue Cross of Washington and Alaska began offering treatments by acupuncturists, homeopaths, and naturopaths to 1,000 of their subscribers on a pilot basis. Benefits include acupuncture and acupressure, biofeedback, dietary counseling and weight management, herbal, homeopathic, and vitamin therapies, hypnotherapy, and stress management.

In 1996, Oxford Health Plans, a Connecticut-based HMO, began offering chiropractic, acupuncture, and naturopathy coverage from a network of prescreened providers for an additional premium cost of 2% to 3%. In addition, members are able to purchase at a discount yoga, massage, nutrition education, herbal remedies, vitamins, and other supplements.

Executives from these managed care organizations report that the tidal wave of aging Baby Boomers has increased the popularity and acceptance of prevention and alternative medicine treatments and will drive the expansion of these services in the decades ahead (*Boomer Report*, 1997).

## REFORM PRIORITY: SERVING CULTURALLY AND GEOGRAPHICALLY DIVERSE POPULATIONS

Culturally and geographically diverse populations are referred to by a variety of terms, among them minority groups, the hard-to-reach, racial groups, the poor, ethnic groups, rural populations, cultural groups, and the disadvantaged. Interest in gathering information on these imprecise and overlapping groups has been considerable in recent years, but has not, as yet, been matched in deed (Dorfman, 1991).

Minority health has, in general, tended to ignore the economic and political contexts in which health-promoting behaviors occur. Community projects and research on the disadvantaged has not focused on health advocacy and health-related policy changes at the state and federal level. Efforts of this type, according to some, will do more to modify individual and group health behaviors among the disadvantaged than a direct health education emphasis (Thomas, 1990).

A survey of 1,599 poor urban residents ("Urban Obstacles to Healthy Living," 1996) revealed that health education is not the primary factor in whether low-income persons practice good health habits. Twice as many low-income adults reported feeling worried about the safety of walking in their neighborhood as in higher-income groups, and they reported less access to safe parks or recreational facilities. Twice as many low-income respondents reported that fresh fruits and vegetables were not readily available where they shopped, and when they were available they cost too much. Another study of low-income versus high-income families reported that low-income families eat more processed foods and less fruits and vegetables, and pay more for what they eat ("Vanishing Inner-City Grocery Stores," 1996).

Most minority elders have grown up without equal rights and protection under the law. Job discrimination over the years has left minorities "with less resources to cope with their old age and a legacy of poverty, poor nutrition, and living in substandard housing that generally translates into poorer health in old age" (Yee, 1990). This history of discrimination also affects the minority older adult's willingness to access the health care system, though the advent of Medicare corrected that problem to a considerable degree.

## AGING MINORITIES AND HEALTH

In 1990, 15% of the population age 65 and over was minority, and this percentage is expected to double by 2050 (Yee, 1990). As the number of minority elders increases, so does their health care needs. During their work years, many minority elders will have had labor intensive jobs, inadequate access to health care, poor diets, and substantial stress (Krause & Wray, 1991). Not surprisingly, therefore, elderly minorities experience greater health problems than elderly Anglos. One consequence is that many minority elders consider "old age" as beginning in the early 50's, or even younger (Lopez & Aguilera, 1991; National Indian Council on Aging, 1984).

Although important for all persons, disease prevention and health promotion practices can have greater impact on minorities. The prevalence of cancer, heart disease, stroke, and diabetes is significantly greater among minorities than among whites. At the same time, minorities are less likely than whites to undergo diagnostic tests for cancer and other health problems, and are more likely to be prone to such health risk factors as smoking, alcohol abuse, high fat diets, and obesity (Report of the Special Committee on Aging, 1996).

When offering disease prevention and health promotion programs to minority or rural-based older adults, the following precautions need to be observed:

1. Communities need to establish their own health priorities, and be involved in program development and implementation.
2. Factors affecting accessibility must be identified and addressed.
3. Language should be familiar, nontechnical, concise, factual, and specific.
4. Nonprint formats, such as videotapes, audiotapes, slide shows, songs, games, and plays, should be encouraged.
5. Printed materials should use large type, be attractive, and make generous use of photographs and drawings.
6. Communications should acknowledge and incorporate cultural beliefs, and visual images should include familiar people, settings, and symbols.
7. Efforts must be sustained and reinforced over time (Dorfman, 1991).

And the following questions should be addressed:

1. Where do individuals go to for health information?
2. Are there ethnic theories that explain specific illness or health problems?
3. What type of traditional medicine or treatment is used, and for which health problems?
4. Do any of a particular ethnic group's religious beliefs or practices conflict with the philosophy of health promotion and disease prevention?

5. What are the group's attitudes toward "Western" medicine, and how is allopathic medicine used?
6. What roles do traditional foods play in health? Are these foods accessible and affordable (Gonzalez et al., 1991)?

Nurses in particular appear to be giving attention to how to incorporate cultural considerations into the care they provide (Giger et al., 1997) and into the patient education materials they create (Wilson, 1996).

## AFRICAN AMERICANS

African Americans have higher overall cancer rates, both for incidence and mortality, and significantly lower survival rates, than any other population group in the United States (Baquet & Gibbs, 1992). At every age, blacks are at higher risk of developing diabetes than whites (Johnson, 1991). Stroke deaths among black males are nearly twice as high as those among white males, and coronary heart disease rates are twice as high in black as in white women. African-American women over age 65 are at greater risk of hypertension than any other group in the United States (Hildreth & Saunders, 1992; Report of the Special Committee on Aging, 1996).

Older blacks are much more likely to rate their health as fair or poor (48%) than older whites (28%), and are almost 50% more burdened by illness or injury that restricts daily activities (44 days per year versus 30 days) (AARP, 1990b). For reasons not clearly understood, however, once blacks reach age 75 a "crossover" phenomenon results and their remaining life expectancy is higher than that of whites (Harper, 1990).

Although it is important to acknowledge and support ethnic food preferences, Black elders are susceptible to eating foods high in fat and sodium like bacon, sausage, pork, pig's feet, foods fried in animal fat, smoked and pickled foods (AARP, 1989). Because African Americans are more likely than others to be salt-sensitive and have high blood pressure, it is important that sodium intake be limited; foods can be seasoned by using herbs, spices and other flavorings, like lemon juice, garlic, pepper, and ginger. Neighborhood grocery stores well stocked with processed foods and short on fruits and vegetables, surrounded by fast-food restaurants, do not offer low-income African Americans very many healthy alternatives to high fat and high salt diets.

## Hispanics

Hispanic Americans comprise the second largest minority group in the United States. They include Mexican Americans, Cuban Americans, Puerto Ricans, and people from Central and South America, and Spain. Although the Hispanic populations share the Spanish language, their dialects, ability to speak English, and length of time in the United States are diverse.

Hispanics in general have high rates of heart disease, diabetes, and cancer, and certain subgroups disproportionately fall prey to poor eating habits, smoking, lack of exercise, and alcohol excess (AARP, 1989).

Hispanics would benefit from eating a higher proportion of traditional foods that are rich in fiber and complex carbohydrates, such as chickpeas, fava, pinto beans, plantains, cassavas, sweet potatoes, taniers, mangoes, guavas, papayas, and corn tortillas (AARP, 1989).

AARP's National Eldercare Institute on Health Promotion (now defunct) conducted a study that examined the barriers to community health promotion programs among primarily Spanish-speaking Hispanic elders. A list of significant barriers follows:

1. Many Hispanic elders are unfamiliar with senior citizens centers, whereas others who visit the centers find the programs to be culturally insensitive to Hispanic elders.
2. Hispanic physicians, followed by Spanish-speaking or bilingual health professionals, are preferred, but are in short supply. The belief in folk medicine and the healing power of God can often result in the postponement of timely doctors' visits.
3. Lack of knowledge of and experience in the American health care system, compounded by financial limitations and lack of transportation, constitute a major barrier to timely health care services.
4. Spanish-language television and radio, followed by the extended family, worksites, churches, community-wide activities, and Hispanic social clubs and organizations are the most credible sources of health information for Hispanic elders.

Health education programs need to involve the extended family, both in program development and implementation. Program presenters need to be sensitized to the spiritual beliefs and folk medicine of Hispanic elders and, when possible, to focus on ideas from both folk and Western medicine. The role of the *curandero*, a traditional healer who provides physical, psychological, social, and spiritual support for the Hispanic family (not just the individual) also needs to be understood and incorporated into health education programs. *Curanderos* believe that morbidity and mortality are associated with strong emotional states, like *biles* (rage) and *susto* (fright) (Maduro, 1983).

## OTHER MINORITY GROUPS

Good places to begin reviewing the literature on populations with small numbers of older Americans, such as American Indians, Alaskan Natives, Asian Americans, Pacific Islanders, and others, are Yee (1990), McCormack and colleagues (1991), and Dorfman (1991).

## MINORITY PROFESSIONAL ASSOCIATIONS

Asian American Health Forum, 116 New Montgomery Street, Suite 531, San Francisco, CA 94105.

National Pacific/Asian Resource Center on Aging, Melbourne Tower, Suite 914, 1511 3rd Avenue, Seattle, WA 98101.

The Association of Asian Pacific Community Health Organizations 310 Eight Street, Suite 310, Oakland, CA 94607.

National Indian Council on Aging, P.O. Box 2088, Albuquerque, NM 87130.

American Indian Health Care Association, 245 E. Sixth Street, Suite 499, St. Paul, MN 55101.

National Hispanic Council on Aging, 2713 Ontario Road NW, Washington, DC 20009.

Asociacion Nacional Pro Personas Mayores, 3325 Wilshire Boulevard, Suite 800, Los Angeles, CA 90010.

National Caucus and Center on Black Aged, Inc., 1424 K Street NW, Suite 500, Washington, DC 20005.

National Council on Black Aging, Box 8522, Durham, NC 27707.

National Black Women's Health Project, 1237 Gordon Street SW, Atlanta, GA 30310.

## RURAL HEALTH CARE

One in every four older adults resides in a rural area. Living in rural areas increases the probability of living in poverty (Coward & Lee, 1986);

income levels for older rural families are about one third lower than those for older urban families (Fry, 1987). Typical consequences and correlates of lower income are: substandard and dilapidated housing, a larger number of health problems, lack of adequate health services, and inadequate transportation.

Such circumstances are more common for minority elders in rural areas. For instance, one third of the older African Americans in urban areas are impoverished, whereas half the Black elderly in rural areas live in poverty (Yee, 1990).

Nurses, social workers, physicians and other health professionals are in short supply in rural settings. Health policies, such as lower reimbursements for providers in rural settings, and a lack of resources in many rural communities—affecting the quality of schools, the availability of cultural opportunities, and the equipment of hospitals—discourage health professionals from locating in rural areas.

The older rural poor are more likely than their urban counterparts to distrust the health care system and the providers who represent it. Because they have been instilled with an attitude of independence and self-reliance, they are less likely to demand needed services. Other factors also inhibit the rural elderly from accessing the health care system. Rural population bases are smaller and more spread out than their urban counterparts, making transportation a major barrier; travel times are long, and public and private means of transportation limited. In addition, a disproportionate number of persons in rural areas lack medical insurance, also affecting the demand for health care services.

## RURAL HEALTH PROMOTION

The rural elderly exhibit more medical problems than the urban elderly, problems that also tend to be more severe (Coward & Lee, 1986). Rural elders are more likely than their urban counterparts to rate their health as poor or fair, to be heavy drinkers, and *not* to be "uniquely advantaged by embeddedness in strong, supportive kin networks" (Lee & Cassidy, 1986, p. 165) despite the stereotypes of rural life.

In addition, rural residents are more likely to be overweight than those in cities ("Wisconsin Study Describes Rural Obesity Problem," 1996) and have higher rates of self-reported depression and chronic conditions that limit activity than their urban counterparts ("Health," 1996).

Whereas health care needs may be greater, in some ways, in rural than in urban areas, the supply of health care services is scarcer, and the prospect of their expansion into rural areas is poor. Inadequate accessibility of health care services makes it especially important that rural residents engage in prevention and health promoting behavior.

The adoption of health promoting practices by older adults in rural areas may be enhanced by encouragement by health care professionals. A survey of family and general practice physicians in rural Mississippi revealed that such encouragement is more likely if a staff person is assigned by the physician to preventive medicine education and if flow charts are used to direct physician attention to needed preventive medicine activities (Bross et al., 1993).

### RURAL RESOURCE MATERIALS

The Center on Rural Elderly at the University of Missouri–Kansas City produced three health-oriented publications: *Health Promotion for the Rural Black Elderly, Leadership Enhancement for the Active Retired*, and the *Directory of Health Programs for Elders*. For order and price information, contact the Center on Rural Elderly, University of Missouri-Kansas City, 5245 Rock Hill Road, Kansas City, MO 64110; 816-235-1747.

## PUBLIC POLICY, PREVENTION, AND HEALTH PROMOTION

Public policy endorsing prevention and health promotion has been traditionally weak in America. As noted in the section on medical screenings in Chapter 3 though, 1998 has been a watershed year when it comes to expanding Medicare's secondary prevention benefits to older adults. Public policy in the areas of tertiary prevention and primary prevention/health promotion, however, continues to lag.

### PUBLIC POLICY AND TERTIARY PREVENTION

For many years Robert Kane, a board-certified physician in preventive medicine, has advocated for Outcome-Based Reimbursement in long term care facilities (Kane & Kane, 1987). The rationale has been that heavy care and time-consuming residents can be a disincentive to administrators and providers within a fixed payment system, or a cost-ineffective incentive within a fee-base system. Neither system, however, is oriented toward providing quality care and good outcomes.

Because there is great variability in health quality and health outcomes, why not reward the ability of administrators and providers to improve resident's function, or to prevent deterioration of function? Especially if this quality care comes at an expenditure comparable to those institutions that are performing largely custodial tasks. Such a reward system, however, needs to be based on comparing observed outcomes with expected outcomes that are based on professionally established norms. Rewards based on improvement only will be confounded by the expected trajectory of the medical condition.

If residents do better than expected, there should be rewards for administrators and providers; if worse, there should be penalties. Such a system encourages institutions that are doing well to expand, and those that are doing poorly to withdraw from the market. This system is probably not only viable in long term care institutions, but in managed health care organizations as well.

## PRIMARY PREVENTION/HEALTH PROMOTION

Public policy in health promotion has been primarily limited to taxes and the bully pulpit. Taxes on cigarettes and liquor, for instance, are designed to not only raise revenue, but are also used as a (partially effective) way to discourage consumption and to pay for consumer education. Consumption taxes can also be applied to junk food as well. For many years policy analysts have brought up the possibility of a "Twinky tax" (i.e., an added tax on junk foods like Twinkies that provide no nutritional value and add to obesity-related diseases and associated costs).

Similar to the cigarette tax, which in many states contributes to smoking cessation education programs and advertisements, the Twinky tax could go to nutrition education programs and advertisements. Additional taxes do tend to lower consumption, but accompanying health education messages lower consumption even more (*American Medical News*, February 8, 1993, p. 31).

For many years, Surgeon General Everett Koop used his bully pulpit very successfully to educate the public on the harmful effects of tobacco.

More recently, the 1996 Surgeon General's Report on Physical Activity and Health has widely promoted the idea that inactivity is a risk factor for heart disease, cancer, diabetes, obesity, and so forth. It remains to be seen if the current Surgeon General's Report on inactivity will be as successful as the one published in 1964 on the health hazards of tobacco.

Another public policy approach to supporting health promotion in America is to increase public funding for health promotion research and training. From time to time, there are isolated federal initiatives supporting health promotion, but usually there is no sustained effort. In 1997, AARP terminated its National Eldercare Institute on Health Promotion because of lack of funding. At the present time the University of Washington in Seattle is the only ongoing federally funded academic center devoted to promoting health in persons aged 65 and over.

## GERIATRIC HEALTH ADVOCACY

Advocacy is the art of influencing the allocation of resources and services. The task of the advocate is to influence legislation as well as organizational and governmental policies.

Inevitably, social systems deny access to some persons in need, offer poor quality services to others, and fail to provide needed services, information, research, or education. To make a social system more responsive to their health needs, health professionals and health consumers must become advocates for change.

It is especially important that health professionals encourage clients who are interested in advocacy because clients have a unique advantage. Lay persons in the advocacy arena can dramatically present firsthand accounts of unmet health care needs to legislators and to the media.

There are many opportunities for health professionals and clients to advocate for a better health care system. If, for example, a client has a spouse with Alzheimer's disease and is disgruntled about the lack of available alternatives in long term care in this country, she or he may be referred to an Alzheimer's Association chapter, to an AARP Vote candidate forum, to a Gray Panther chapter meeting, to the Older Women's League, or elsewhere. Health professionals need to be informed about health advocacy opportunities and, in turn, we need to inform our clients—or better yet, our collaborators.

# ADVOCACY ORGANIZATIONS

## AMERICAN ASSOCIATION OF RETIRED PERSONS (AARP)

### *AARP/VOTE*

AARP/VOTE fields trained volunteers from across the nation to monitor the candidates' stands on issues. In addition, AARP/VOTE produces a voter's guide to inform voters about key issues and each candidate's position. This voter education program focused on health care reform in 1992, with the goal of having the successful presidential candidate making health care reform, including long-term care, a top priority in the next administration. Many of the presidential candidates in 1992, including then-Governor Clinton, did make health care reform a top priority.

### *AARP Citizen Advocate Nursing Home Inspection Program*

Trained volunteers accompany each state's Department of Health survey team on an annual unannounced nursing home inspection.

### *AARP Health Advocacy Services*

Opportunities to meet with and influence state legislators across the country take place at free forums on health care reform, called Building a Better Health Care System. At the state level, volunteers organize health fairs on a variety of health topics, including smoking cessation, walking programs, nutrition, the Staying Healthy After Fifty program, and Medicare/Medicaid assistance. Access your State Volunteer Coordinator by contacting the national AARP office for their address and telephone number. Contact American Association of Retired Persons, 601 E. Street NW, Washington, DC 20049; 202-434-AARP.

## NURSING HOME OMBUDSMAN PROGRAMS

An ombudsman provides information and helps resolve problems. This program trains volunteer ombudsmen, and then assigns them to nursing homes through an Area Agency on Aging staff person, or one of its provider agencies.

There are also independent advocacy groups in most states that are devoted to improving care in nursing homes. These groups attempt to make nursing homes and social service agencies more responsive to consumers. Typically, representatives are not shy about contacting elected officials, like city councilmen, state legislators, or congressmen.

Independent nursing home advocacy groups can be difficult to locate. Oftentimes, the local Area Agency on Aging can help citizens reach them. Another option is to contact the National Citizens' Coalition for Nursing Home Reform, 1424 16th Street NW, #202, Washington, DC 20036-2211; 202-332-2275.

## ALZHEIMER'S ASSOCIATION

The Alzheimer's Association (AA) consists of a 50-state network of 215 official local chapters, a countless number of AA support groups that form in the community or in nursing homes, and 35,000 volunteers. In addition to providing emotional support and practical information, AA members engage in a variety of advocacy activities.

Through its Public Policy Forum, Alzheimer advocates from all 50 states gather together in Washington, D.C., each Spring. Prior to that, town meetings occur nationwide on such topics as Long Term Care Must Be Part of Health Care Reform. For information on the annual Spring trek to Washington, D.C., or the town meetings that precede them, contact the Alzheimer's Association, 70 East Lake Street, Chicago, IL 60601.

## GRAY PANTHERS

Organized in 1970, the Gray Panthers mobilize persons of all ages to work for health care reform and other areas of social change. Among other priorities, Gray Panthers are advocating for a national, comprehensive health care system. The late Maggie Kuhn was the well-known founder and long-time leader of the Gray Panthers. Gray Panthers, P.O. Box 21477, Washington, DC 20009; 202-466-3132.

## SILVER-HAIRED LEGISLATURE

A nonpartisan, elected body of state residents age 60 and over meets before each state legislative session to debate and prioritize issues that affect older adults, which will be addressed by state lawmakers. The first Silver-Haired legislature (SHL) was organized in 1973 in Missouri, and the concept has been adopted by residents in about half the states. Silver-haired legislators have had considerable success with influencing legislation. For information, contact your State Department on Aging.

## OLDER WOMEN'S LEAGUE

The Older Women's League (OWL) focuses on the economic plight of women in the later years (especially social security and pension rights), health insurance, caregiver support services, and the inequities inherent in public policy. OWL maintains a referral resource file and answers letters from women from across the country. For more information, contact the Older Women's League, 666 11th Street NW, Suite 700, Washington, DC 20001; 202-783-6686.

## SENIOR ENVIRONMENT CORPS

The goals of the corps are to address environmental issues affecting older adults, encourage older adults to become involved in conservation and environmental protection, and improve environmental education and awareness among older adults and physicians. For more information, contact Senior Environment Corps, 6410 Rockledge Drive, Suite 203, Bethesda, MD 20817.

## PRESIDENT HABER

The likelihood of my running for President of the United States is extraordinarily small, and the probability that I will be elected if I do decide to run, is slightly less than that. Nonetheless, it does not cost anything to begin to craft my health promotion platform for the country.

It appears to me that politicians are most likely to be successful if they are focused on a few priorities and they do not advocate for "Big Government." Well, one out of two aint bad!

1. The federal government should make sure that *all* Americans are entitled to health care, and that health care does not just mean medical care.
2. Managed care should be required to reimburse physicians and other health care professionals to routinely counsel clients on disease prevention and health promotion, and base that reimbursement on their effectiveness with clients.
3. The Surgeon General in 1996 called physical inactivity a public health challenge for the 21st century. We should provide the Surgeon General's office with a 40 million dollar annual budget (comparable to what the tobacco company spent in a 30-day period in mid-1998) to deliver an important message nationwide—sitting around too much is as taboo as smoking!

## QUESTIONS FOR DISCUSSION

1. Evaluate the role of preventive medicine and health promotion in health care today. Summarize what is, and is not, covered; who does, or does not, provide services; and how services are financed. How would *you* improve the current plan?
2. Choose a Health Priority Area from the beginning of a chapter that interests you and, as a government policy maker, develop a plan to achieve a Healthy People 2000 objective.
3. Add an advocacy component to your plan above, making sure that it includes older adults.
4. Discuss the pros and cons of the idea to tax high-fat and other unhealthy foods, and allocate the proceeds to publicly sponsored nutrition education and exercise programs.

# References

A natural remedy for depression? (1997, October). *The Johns Hopkins Medical Letter, Health After 50: Vol. 9*, pp. 2–3.

A world of information beckons. (1998, February). *AARP Bulletin, 39,* 14.

AARP. (1989). *Health risks and preventive care among older Hispanics. Health risks and preventive care among older blacks* (Health Advocacy Services Program Department, Minority Affairs Initiative). Washington, DC: Author.

AARP. (1990a). Making health promotion work for minority elders. *Perspectives in Health Promotion and Aging, 5,* 1, 5, 6.

AARP. (1990b). *A profile of older Americans: 1990.* Program Resources Department. Washington, DC: Author.

AARP. (1991). *Healthy People 2000: Healthy older adults.* Excerpted from Healthy People 2000 National Health Promotion and Disease Prevention Objectives, U.S. Department of Health and Human Services, Public Health Service, Washington, DC.

AARP. (1992). National Eldercare Institute on Health Promotion, *Perspectives in Health Promotion and Aging,* Washington, DC, *7,* 2.

AARP. (1996). *A profile of older Americans: 1996* (Program Resources Department). Washington, DC: Author.

*AARP Bulletin.* (1990). *31,* 2. Washington, DC: Author.

*AARP Bulletin.* (1991). *32,* 2. Washington, DC: Author.

Accidents don't just happen. (1995). *American Medical News,* March 20, pp. 10–14.

ACTION. (1984). *Descriptive Evaluation of RSVP and FGP Volunteers Working with Headstart.* Washington, DC: Office of Policy and Planning Evaluation Division.

ACTION. (1985). *Senior Companion Program Impact Evaluation.* Alexandria, VA: SRA Technologies.

Adams, W., et al. (1993, September 8). Alcohol-related hospitalizations of elderly people. *JAMA, 270,* 1222–1225.

Adelman, R., et al. (1989). Concordance between physicians and their older and younger patients in the primary care medical encounter. *The Gerontologist, 29,* 808–813.

Agre, J., et al. (1988). Light resistance and stretching exercise in elderly women: Effect upon strength. *Archives of Physical Medicine Rehabilitation, 69,* 273.

Albert, M., et al. (1995, December). Predictors of cognitive change in older persons: MacArthur studies of successful aging. *Psychology and Aging, 10,* 578–586.

Alderman, M., & Cohen, H. (1998). Dietary sodium intake and mortality: The National Health and Nutrition Examination Survey (NHANES I). *The Lancet, 351,* 781–785.

Alexander, C., et al. (1996). Trial of stress reduction for hypertension in older African Americans. *Hypertension, 28,* 228–237.

AMA reports hidden epidemic of elderly alcoholism. (1995, September 25). *American Medical News.*

AMA urges awareness of dehydration in elderly. (1995, November 20). *American Medical News,* p. 15.

American Board of Family Practice. (1987). *Rights and Responsibilities: Part II, The Changing Health Care Consumer and Patient/Doctor Partnership.* A National Survey of Health Care Opinions, Lexington, KY.

American Cancer Society. (1994). *A Survey Concerning Cigarette Smoking.* Princeton, NJ: Gallup Organization.

American Cancer Society. (1990). *Cancer Facts and Figures.* Atlanta, GA: American Cancer Society.

American College of Sports Medicine. (1988). American College of Sports Medicine position stand: The recommended quantity and quality of exercise for developing and maintaining cardiorespiratory and muscular fitness in healthy adults. *Medicine and Science in Sports and Exercise, 22,* 265–274.

*American College of Sports Medicine.* (1995). ACSM's guidelines for exercise testing and prescription (5th ed.). Baltimore: Williams & Wilkins.

American Dietetic Association. (1990, March). ADA-IFIC Gallup Poll. *American Dietetic Association Courier, 29,* 2.

*American Medical News* (1992, May 11).

*American Medical News* (1992, June 16). p. 16.

*American Medical News* (1992, August 10).

*American Medical News* (1993, February 8). p. 31.

Andersen, R., et al. (1998). Can inexpensive signs encourage the use of stairs? Results from a community intervention. *Annals of Internal Medicine, 129*(5), 363–369.

Angell, M. (1997). Fixing Medicare. *The New England Journal of Medicine, 337,* 192–194.

Angell, M., & Kassirer, J. (1998). Alternative medicine—The risks of untested and unregulated remedies. *The New England Journal of Medicine, 339*(12), 839–841.

Applegate, W. (1992). High blood pressure treatment in the elderly. In G. Omenn (Ed.), *Clinics in geriatric medicine* (pp. 103–117). Philadelphia: W. B. Saunders.

Are natural fen-phens safe? (1998, March). *Health,* p. 30.

Are you eating right? (1992, October). *Consumer Reports,* pp. 644-655.

Astin, J. (1998). Why patients use alternative medicine. *JAMA, 279*(19), 1548–1553.

Atchley, R. (1998, March–April). Importance of being religious. *Aging Today, 9,* 12.

Atkins, R. (1997). *Dr. Atkins' new diet revolution.* New York: Avon.

Atkinson, R., et al. (1985). Early versus late onset alcoholism in older persons: Preliminary findings. *Alcoholism, 9,* 513–551.

Atkinson, S. (1998, April). Calcium: Why get more? *Nutrition Action Healthletter,* pp. 3–5.

Bailey, C., & Gates, R. (1996). *Smart eating*. Boston: Houghton-Mifflin.

Bailey, C. (1994). *Smart exercise: Burning fat, getting fat*. London: Aurum Press.

Bailey, C. (1991). *The new fit or fat*. Boston: Houghton Mifflin.

Bandura, A. (1977). *Social learning theory*. Upper Saddle River, NJ: Prentice Hall.

Bandura, A. (1986). *Social foundations of thought and action: A social cognitive theory*. Englewood Cliffs, NJ: Prentice Hall.

Bandura, A. (1995). *Self-efficacy in changing societies*. Cambridge, England: Cambridge University Press.

Baquet, C., & Gibbs, T. (1992). Cancer and black americans (pp. 106–121). In R. Braithwaite & S. Taylor (Eds.), *Health issues in the Black community*. San Francisco: Jossey-Bass.

Becker, M. (1974). The health belief model and personal health behavior. *Health Education Monographs, 2*, 236.

Beisecker, A. (1990, November). *The older patient's companion*. Paper presented at the 43rd Annual Scientific Meeting of the Gerontological Society of America, Boston.

Benson, H. (1976). *The relaxation response*. New York: Avon.

Benson, H. (1984). *Beyond the relaxation response*. New York: Times Books.

Benson, H. (1987). *Your maximum mind*. New York: Times Books.

Berkman, L. (1983). *Health and ways of living: Findings from the Alameda County Study*. New York: Oxford University Press.

Berthold, H., et al. (1998). Effect of a garlic oil preparation on serum lipoproteins and cholesterol metabolism. *JAMA, 279*(23), 1900–1902.

Beta carotene pills. (1997, June). *Mayo Clinic Health Letter: Supplement*, p. 4.

Birch, B. (1995). *Power yoga: The total wellness workout for mind and body*. New York: Fireside.

Birren, J., et al. (1996). *Aging and biography: Explorations in adult development*. New York: Springer.

Birren, J., & Deutchman, D. (1991). *Guiding autobiography groups for older adults*. Baltimore: The Johns Hopkins University Press.

Blair, S., et al. (1992). Physical activity and health: A lifestyle approach. *Medicine, Exercise, Nutrition and Health*. New York: Blackwell Science.

Blair, S., et al. (1989, November 3). Physical fitness and all-cause mortality: A prospective study of healthy men and women. *Journal of the American Medical Association, 262*, 2395–2401.

Blittner, M., et al. (1978). Cognitive self-control factors in the reduction of smoking behavior. *Behavior Therapy, 9*, 53–561.

Blumenthal, J., et al. (1991). Long-term effects of exercise on psychological functioning in older men and women. *Journal of Gerontology, 46*, 352–361.

Blumenthal, R. (1996, September). The many benefits of fiber. *The Johns Hopkins Medical Letter: Health After 50*, p. 4.

Bogden, J., et al. (1995, April). Studies on micronutrient supplements and immunity in older people. *Nutrition Reviews, 3*, pp. S59–S64.

Bogden, J. (1994). Daily micronutrient supplements enhance delayed-hypersensitivity skin test responses in older people. *American Journal of Clinical Nutrition, 60*, 437–447.

Boldt, M., & Dellmann-Jenkins, M. (1992, June). The impact of companion animals in later life and considerations for practice. *The Journal of Applied Gerontology, 11*, 228–239.

*Boomer Report.* (1997, November). Age Wave newsletter, 2000 Powell St., #1555, Emory-ville, CA 94608.

Borkman, T. (1982). Where are older persons in mutual self-help groups? In A. Kolker & P. Ahmed (Eds.), *Aging.* New York: Elsevier.

Bortz, W. (1996). *Dare to Be 100.* New York: Fireside.

Brandsma, J., et al. (1980). *Outpatient treatment of alcoholism: A review and comparative study.* Baltimore: University Park Press.

Brennan, P., et al. (1995, May/June). The effects of a special computer network on caregivers of persons with Alzheimer's disease. *Nursing Research, 44,* 166–171.

Brimer, E., et al. (1991). Why do some women get regular mammographies? *American Journal of Preventive Medicine, 7,* 69–74.

Brody, J. (1998, February 15). Cretan diet rich in fruits, vegetables, grains proves heart-healthy. *Houston Chronicle,* p. 5F.

Brody, J. (1996, February 28). Good habits outweigh genes as key to a healthy old age [Health section]. *The New York Times,* p. 12.

Brookfield, S. (1990). *Understanding and facilitating adult learning.* San Francisco: Jossey-Bass.

Bross, M., et al. (1993, November). Health promotion and disease prevention: A survey of rural family physicians. Presented at Society of Teachers of Family Medicine, Orlando.

Brown, C., & Kessler, L. (1988). Projections of lung cancer mortality in the United States: 1985–2025. *Journal of the National Cancer Institute, 80,* 43–51.

Brownell, K., et al. (1986). Understanding and preventing relapse. *American Psychologist, 41,* 765–782.

Buchner, D., & Wagner, E. (1992). Preventing frail health (pp. 1–18). In G. Omenn (Ed.), *Clinics in geriatric medicine.* Philadelphia: W. B. Saunders.

Buchowski, M., & Sun, M. (1996, March). Energy expenditure, television viewing and obesity. *International Journal of Obesity, 20,* 236–245.

Building immunity. (1997, September). *Nutrition Action Healthletter,* pp. 4–7.

Burack, R., & Liang, J. (1987). The early detection of cancer in the primary care setting: Factors associated with the acceptance and completion of recommended procedures. *Preventive Medicine, 16,* 739–751.

Burack, R., & Liang, J. (1989). Acceptance and completion of mammography by older black women. *American Journal of Public Health, 79,* 721–726.

Burns, D. (1980). *Feeling good: The new mood therapy.* New York: William Mor-row & Company.

*Business and Health.* (1985). Year end update, quality of care. *3,* 35.

Butler, R. (1995). Foreword: The life review (pp. xvii–xxi). In B. Haight & J. Webster (Eds.), *The art and science of reminiscing.* Washington, DC: Taylor & Francis.

Butler, R. (1993, January). Food: You are what you eat (pp. 33–34). *Modern Maturity.*

Butler, R., & Lewis, M. (1982). *Aging and mental health.* St. Louis: C. V. Mosby.

Caggiula, A., et al. (1987). The multiple risk intervention trial (MRFIT): IV. Intervention on blood lipids. *Preventive Medicine, 10,* 443–475.

Calcium and vitamin D. (1996, June). *Mayo Clinic Health Letter* (Medical Essay Suppl.), pp. 4–5.

Campanelli, L. (1990). Promoting healthy aging. *Educational Gerontology, 16,* 517–518.

Campbell, A., et al. (1997). Randomised controlled trial of a general practice programme of home based exercise to prevent falls in elderly women. *British Medical Journal, 315,* 1065–1069.

Cardenas, L., et al. (1987). Adult onset diabetes mellitus: Glycemic control and family function. *American Journal of the Medical Sciences, 293,* 28–33.

Cassel, C. (1996, July–August). Managing chronic illness, disability. *Aging Today,* pp. 9, 11.

Caterson, I. (1990). Management strategies for weight control: Eating, exercise and behavior. *Drugs, 39*(Suppl. 3), 20–32.

Centers for Disease Control. (1992). Cigarette smoking among adults, United States, 1990: Effectiveness of smoking-control strategies—United States. *MMWR, 41,* 354–355, 361–362, 645–647, 653.

Center for Infectious Diseases and Center for Prevention Services. (1990). Centers for Disease Control, Public Health Service, USDHHS, Atlanta, GA.

Chandra, R. (1997, May 7). Graying of the immune system: Can nutrient supplements improve immunity in the elderly? *JAMA, 277,* 1398–1399.

Chandra, R. (1992). Effect of vitamins and trace-element supplementation on immune responses and infection in elderly subjects. *Lancet, 340,* 1124–1127.

Chiriboga, D. (1987). Social supports (pp. 635–636). In G. Maddox et al. (Eds.)., *The encyclopedia of aging.* New York: Springer.

Chiriboga, D. (1992). Paradise lost: Stress in the modern age (pp. 35–71). In M. Wykle et al. (Eds.), *Stress and health among the elderly.* New York: Springer.

Christensen, A., & Rankin, D. (1979). *Easy does it yoga for older people.* San Francisco: Harper & Row.

Cohen, S., et al. (1997, June 25). Social ties and susceptibility to the common cold. *JAMA, 277,* 1940–1944.

Cohen, S., et al. (1989). Encouraging primary care physicians to help smokers quit. *Annals of Internal Medicine, 110,* 648–652.

Cohen, S., et al. (1990). Debunking myths about self-quitting: Evidence from 10 prospective studies of persons who attempt to quit smoking by themselves. *American Psychologist, 44,* 1355–1365.

Colangelo, R., et al. (1997, November/December). The role of exercise in rehabilitation patients with end-stage renal disease. *Rehabilitation Nursing, 22,* 288–292, 302.

Colditz, G. (1998). Relationship between estrogen levels, use of hormone replacement therapy, and breast cancer. *Journal of the National Cancer Institute, 90*(11), 814–823.

Collins, H., & Pancoast, D. (1976). *Natural helping networks: A strategy for prevention.* Washington, DC: National Association of Social Workers.

Comfort, A. (1972). *The joy of sex.* New York: Simon & Schuster.

Connolly, H., et al. (1997). Valvular heart disease associated with fenfluramine-phentermine. *The New England Journal of Medicine, 337,* 581–584.

*Consumer Reports.* (1993, June). Losing weight: What works. What doesn't. pp. 347–357.

*Consumer Reports on Health.* (1997, November). Zinc: The cold facts. p. 123.

Cooper, K. (1994). *Dr. Kenneth H. Cooper's antioxidant revolution.* Nashville: Thomas Nelson.

Cooper, K. (1988–1989, December 1988–January 1989). Coronary combat. *Modern Maturity,* pp. 78–84.

Cooper, K., & Cooper, M. (1988). *The new aerobics for women.* New York: Bantam.

Corbin, D., & Metal-Corbin, J. (1997). *Reach for it!* (3rd ed.). Iowa: Eddie Bowers.

Coward, R., & Lee, G. (1986). *The elderly in rural society.* New York: Springer.

Crowe, R., et al. (1997, September/October). The utility of the brief MAST and the CAGE in identifying alcohol problems. *Archives of Family Medicine, 6,* 447–483.

Curfman, G. (1997). Diet pills redux. *The New England Journal of Medicine, 337,* 629–630.

Curtis, J., et al. (1989). Characteristics, diagnosis and treatment of alcoholism in elderly patients. *Journal of American Geriatrics Society, 37,* 310.

Davis, M., et al. (1985). Living arrangements and dietary patterns of older adults in the U.S. *Journal of Gerontology, 40,* 434–442.

Davis, M., et al. (1995). *The relaxation and stress reduction workbook.* Oakland, CA: New Harbinger.

Davis, R. (1988). Uniting physicians against smoking: The need for a coordinated national strategy. *Journal of the American Medical Association, 259,* 2900–2901.

Dawson, D., et al. (1987). Trends in routine screening examinations. *American Journal of Public Health, 77,* 1004–1005.

Day, A. (1992). *Remarkable survivors: Insights into successful aging among women.* Washington, DC: Urban Institute Press.

De Groen, P., et al. (1996, October 3). Esophagitis associated with the use of Alendronate. *The New England Journal of Medicine, 335,* 1016–1021.

Dean, A., et al. (1990). Effects of social support from various sources on depression in elderly persons. *Journal of Health and Social Behavior, 31,* 148–161.

DeBusk, R., et al. (1990). Training effects of long versus short bouts of exercise in healthy subjects. *American Journal of Cardiology, 65,* 1010–1013.

DeGroen, et al. (1996, October 3). Esophagitis associated with the use of Alendroate. *The New England Journal of Medicine, 335,* 1016–1021.

Delany, S., et al. (1993). *Having our say: The Delany sisters' first 100 years.* New York: Kodansha.

Dentzer, S. (1998, January–February). A guide to managed care. *Modern Maturity,* 35–43.

Department of Agriculture. (1990). *Nutrition and your health: Dietary guidelines for Americans* (p. 25, 3rd ed.). Washington, DC: U.S. Department of Health and Human Services.

Devine, A., et al. (1995). A longitudinal study of the effect of sodium and calcium intakes on regional bone density in postmenopausal women. *American Journal of Clinical Nutrition, 62,* 740–745.

deVries, H., & Hales, D. (1974). *Fitness after 50.* New York: Scribner's.

DHEA. (1998, May). *Nutrition Action Healthletter,* p. 9.

DiGilio, D., & Howze, E. (1984, December). Fitness and full living for older adults. *Parks and Recreation,* pp. 32–37.

Dishman, R., et al. (1985, March–April). The determinants of physical activity and exercise. *Public Health Reports, 100,* 158–171.

Dorfman, S. (1991). *Health promotion for older minority adults.* Washington, DC: AARP National Resource Center on Health Promotion and Aging.

Duffy, M., & MacDonald, E. (1990). Determinants of functional health of older persons. *The Gerontologist, 30,* 503–509.

Dufour, M., et al. (1992). Alcohol and the elderly. In G. Omenn (Ed.), *Clinics in geriatric medicine* (pp. 127–141). Philadelphia: W. B. Saunders.

Dunn, A., et al. (in press). Reduction in cardiovascular disease risk factors. *Preventive Medicine*.

Duncan, J. (1996). Exercise intensity. Unpublished manuscript, Cooper Institute, Dallas.

Dustman, R. (1996, March–April). Think fast. *Health*, pp. 44–46.

Dustman, R., et al. (1984). Aerobic exercise training and improved neuropsychological function of older individuals. *Neurobiology of Aging, 5,* 35–42.

Dychtwald, K. (1986). *Wellness and health promotion for the elderly*. Maryland: Aspen.

Eastman, R. (1997). *Diabetes in America*. Washington, DC: National Institute of Diabetes and Digestive and Kidney Disorders.

Ebersole, P., & Hess, P. (1990). *Toward healthy aging: Human needs and nursing response*. St. Louis: C. V. Mosby.

Elliot, P., et al. (1996, May 18). Intersalt revisited. *British Medical Journal, 312,* 1249–1253.

Ellis, A. (1975). *A new guide to rational living*. North Hollywood, CA: Wilshire Books.

Elmore, J., et al. (1998). Ten-year risk of false positive screening mammograms and clinical breast examinations. *The New England Journal of Medicine, 338*(16), 1089–1096.

Elward, K., & Larson, E. (1992). Benefits of exercise for older adults. In G. Omenn (Ed.), *Clinics in geriatric medicine* (pp. 35–50). Philadelphia: W. B. Saunders.

End of Debate: Fiber's Great. (1996, July–August). *Health*, p. 16.

Eng, E., & Young, R. (1992). Lay health advisors as community change agents. *Family and Community Health, 15,* 24–40.

Ephedrine's Deadly Edge. (1997, July 7). *U.S. News & World Report*, pp. 79–80.

Ettinger, W., et al. (1997, January 1). A randomized trial comparing aerobic exercise and resistance exercise with a health education program in older adults with knee osteoarthritis. *JAMA, 277,* 25–31.

Ettinger, W., et al. (1992). Lipoprotein lipids in older people: Results from the Cardiovascular Heart Study. *Circulation, 86,* 858–869.

Evans, E. (1979). *The family circle guide to self-help*. New York: Ballantine Books.

Evans, L., & Strumpf, N. (1989). Tying down the elderly: A review of the literature on physical restraint. *Journal of American Geriatrics Society, 37,* 65.

Evans, W., et al. (1991). *Biomarkers: The 10 determinants of aging you can control*. New York: Simon & Schuster.

Fawzy, F., et al. (1995, February). Critical review of psychosocial interventions in cancer care. *Archive of General Psychiatry, 52,* 100–113.

Ferraro, K., & Koch, J. (1994). Religion and health among black and white adults: Examining social support and consolation. *Journal for the Scientific Study of Religion, 33,* 362–375.

Ferrini, A., & Ferrini, R. (1989). *Health in the later years*. Dubuque, Iowa: William C. Brown.

Fiatarone, M., et al. (1990, June 13). High-intensity strength training in nonagenarians: Effects on skeletal muscle. *Journal of the American Medical Association, 263,* 3029–3034.

Field, L., & Steinhardt, M. (1992). The relationship of internally-directed behavior to self-reinforcement, self-esteem, and expectancy values for exercise. *American Journal of Health Promotion, 7,* 21–26.

Finn, S. (1988, January). Nutrition: What's your ideal weight? *50 Plus Magazine*, pp. 31–33.

Finucane, T. (1988). Planning with elderly outpatients for contingencies of severe illness: A survey and clinical trial. *Journal of General Internal Medicine, 2,* 322.

Fiore, M., et al. (1990). Methods used to quit smoking in the United States: Do cessation programs help? *Journal of the American Medical Association, 263,* 2760–2765.

Fiore, M. (1992). Trends in cigarette smoking in the United States: The epidemiology of tobacco use. *The Medical Clinics of North America, 76,* 289–303.

Fiore, M., et al. (1992, November 18). Tobacco dependence and the nicotine patch: Clinical guidelines for effective use. *Journal of the American Medical Association, 269,* 2687–2694.

Fishing for Safe Seafood. (1996, November). *Nutrition Action Healthletter*, pp. 3–5.

Fitzgerald, F. (1994, July 21). The tyranny of health. *The New England Journal of Medicine, 331,* 196–198.

Flegal, K., et al. (1995, November 2). The influence of smoking cessation on the prevalence of overweight in the United States. *New England Journal of Medicine, 333,* 1165–1170.

Fletcher, A. (1994). *Thin for life*. Boston: Houghton Mifflin.

Fletcher, G., et al. (1992, July). Statement on exercise: Benefits and recommendations for physical activity programs for all Americans: A statement for health professionals by the Committee on Exercise and Cardiac rehabilitation of the Council on Clinical Cardiology, American Heart Association. *Circulation, 86,* 340–344.

*Food and Nutrition Research Briefs*. (1996, January). Washington, DC: U.S. Department of Agriculture Research Service, pp. 1–2.

Forrest, K., et al. (1997). Driving patterns and medical conditions in older women. *Journal of American Geriatrics Society, 45,* 1214–1218.

Fried, R., et al. (1985). *The clinician's health promotion handbook*. Denver, CO: Mercy Medical Center.

Friedan, B. (1993). *The fountain of age*. New York: Simon & Schuster.

Friedmann, E., et al. (1980). Animal companions and one-year survival of patients after discharge from a coronary care unit. *Public Health Reports, 95,* 307–312.

Fries, J. (1989). *Aging well: A guide for successful seniors*. Reading, MA: Addison-Wesley.

Fries, J., & Crapo, M. (1986). The elimination of premature disease (pp. 19–37). In K. Dychtwald (Ed.), *Wellness and health promotion for the elderly*. Rockville, MD: Aspen.

Fry, C. (1987). Rural elderly (p. 587). In G. Maddox et al. (Eds.), *The encyclopedia of aging*. New York: Springer.

Gallup. (1988). *Research to prevent blindness*. New York.

Gamble, E., et al. (1991). Knowledge, attitudes and behavior of elderly persons regarding living wills. *Archive Internal Medicine, 151,* 277.

Garcia, A., & King, A. (1991). Predicting long-term adherence to aerobic exercise: A comparison of two models. *Journal of Sport & Exercise Physiology, 13,* 394–410.

Gemson, et al. (1988). Differences in physician prevention practice patterns for white and minority patients. *Journal of Community Health, 13,* 53–64.

Genant, H., et al. (1997, December). Low-dose esterified estrogen therapy. *Archives of Internal Medicine, 157,* 2609–2615.

George, L. (1986, spring). Life satisfaction in later life. *Generations*, pp. 5–8.

George, L. (1993, Winter–Spring). Depressive disorders and symptoms in later life. *Generations*, pp. 35–38.

Giger, J., et al. (1997). Health promotion among ethnic minorities: The importance of cultural phenomena. *Rehabilitation Nursing, 22*, 303–308.

Ginzel, K. (1985). The underemphasis on smoking in medical education. *New York State Journal of Medicine, 85*, 299–301.

Glassheim, C. (1992). *Health Partners Program mimeograph*. Albuquerque, New Mexico: The University of New Mexico School of Medicine's Primary Care Curriculum.

Glynn, T. (1990). Methods of smoking cessation: Finally, some answers. *Journal of the American Medical Association, 263*, 2795–2796.

Glynn, T., & Manley, M. (1989). *How to help your patients stop smoking: A National Cancer Institute manual for physicians*. Bethesda, MD: National Cancer Institute, USDHHS.

Goldfried, M., & Sobocinski, D. (1975). The effect of irrational beliefs on emotional arousal. *Journal of Consulting and Clinical Psychology, 43*, 504–510.

Goldsteen, R., et al. (1991, November). Examining the relationship between health locus of control and use of medical services. Paper presented at the Annual Gerontological Society of America meeting, Minneapolis.

Goleman, D., & Gurin, J. (1993). *Mind body medicine: How to use your mind for better health*. Yonkers, New York: Consumer Reports Books.

Gonzalez, V., et al. (1991). *Health promotion in diverse cultural communities*. Palo Alto: Stanford Center for Research in Disease Prevention.

Goodwin, J., et al. (1987). The effect of marital status on stage, treatment, and survival of cancer patients. *Journal of the American Medical Association, 258*, 3125–3130.

Gorman, K., & Posner, J. (1988). Benefits of exercise in old age. *Clinics in Geriatric Medicine, 4*, 181–192.

Gossard, D., et al. (1986). Effects of low- and high-intensity home-based exercise training on functional capacity in healthy middle-aged men. *American Journal of Cardiology, 57*, 466.

Gottlieb, B. (1985). Social networks and social support: An overview of research, practice, and policy implication. *Health Education Quarterly, 12*, 5–22.

Gould, L., et al. (1995). Changes in myocardial perfusion abnormalities by positron emission tomography after long-term, intense risk factor modification. *JAMA, 274*, 894–901.

Grasso, P., & Haber, D. (1995). A leadership training program at a senior center. *Activities, Adaptation and Aging, 20*, 13–24.

Greeley, A. (1990, October). Nutrition and the elderly. *FDA Consumer*, pp. 25–28.

Green, L., et al. (1980). *Health education planning: A diagnostic approach*. Palo Alto, CA: Mayfield.

Green, L., & Kreuter, M. (1991). *Health promotion planning: An educational and environmental approach*. Mountain View, CA: Mayfield.

Green, L., & Lewis, F. (1986). *Measurement and evaluation in health education and health promotion*. Palo Alto, CA: Mayfield.

Greene, M., et al. (1987). Psychosocial concerns in the medical encounter: A comparison of the interactions of doctors with their old and young patients. *The Gerontologist, 27*, 164.

Greene, M., et al. (1989). Concordance between physicians and their older and younger patients in the primary care medical encounter. *The Gerontologist, 29,* 808–813.

Greene, M. (1991, July). *Determinants and outcomes of the physician-elderly patient initial medical encounter* (Final report for the AARP Andrus Foundation). Washington, DC.

Grobbee, D., & Hofman, A. (1986). Does sodium restriction lower blood pressure? *British Medical Journal, 293,* 27–29.

Grodstein, F., et al. (1997). Postmenopausal hormone replacement therapy and mortality. *New England Journal of Medicine, 336*(25), 1769–1775.

Group Health Association of America. (1988). Annual HMO Industry Survey. Washington, DC: Group Health Association.

Growing uninsured renews questions about health reform. (1997, November 17). *American Medical News,* p. 13.

Guralnik, J. (1991, May). Prospects for the compression of morbidity. *Journal of Aging and Health, 3,* 138–154.

Haber, D. (1979, November–December). Old age in China. *Aging,* pp. 7–9.

Haber, D. (1983a). Yoga as a preventive health care program. *The International Journal of Aging and Human Development, 17,* 169–176.

Haber, D. (1983b). Promoting mutual help groups among older persons. *Gerontologist, 23,* 251–253.

Haber, D. (1984). Church-based programs for caregivers of noninstitutionalized elders. *Journal of Gerontological Social Work, 7,* 43–55.

Haber, D. (1986). Health promotion to reduce blood pressure level among older blacks. *The Gerontologist, 26,* 119–121.

Haber, D. (1988). A health promotion program in ten nursing homes. *Activities, Adaptation and Aging, 2,* 73–82.

Haber, D. (1989). *Health Care for an Aging Society: Cost Conscious Community Care and Self-Care Approaches.* New York: Hemisphere/Taylor and Francis Group.

Haber, D. (1991). *Good health contract.* Galveston, TX: University of Texas Medical Branch, School of Allied Health Sciences.

Haber, D. (1992a). Self-help groups and aging (pp. 295–298). In A. Katz et al. (Eds.), *Self-help: Concepts and applications.* Philadelphia: Charles Press.

Haber, D. (1992b). *Geriatric empowerment.* Galveston, TX: University of Texas Medical Branch, School of Allied Health Sciences.

Haber, D. (1992c). An obstacle to physicians recommending medical screenings to older adults (p. 107). *Academic Medicine: Journal of the Association of American Medical Colleges, 67,* 2.

Haber, D. (1993a). Guide to Clinical Preventive Services: A Challenge to Physician Resourcefulness. *Clinical Gerontologist, 12,* 17–29.

Haber, D. (1993b). Chronic illness, aging, and health promotion. *Illness, Crises and Loss, 2,* 2–5.

Haber, D., & George, J. (1981–1982). A preventive health care program with Hispanic elders. *The Journal of Minority Aging, 6,* pp. 1–11.

Haber, D., & Lacy, M. (1993). A socio-behavioral health promotion intervention with older adults. *Behavior, Health, and Aging, 3,* 73–85.

Haber, D. (1996, July). Strategies to promote the health of older persons: An alternative to readiness stages. *Family and Community Health, 19,* 1–10.

Haber, D., et al. (1997). Impact of a geriatric health promotion elective on occupational and physical therapy students. *Gerontology & Geriatrics Education, 18,* 65–76.

Haber, D., et al. (in press). Impact of a geriatric health promotion program on sedentary and overweight older adults. *Family and Community Health.*

Hanna, K. (1989, October). The meaning of health for graduate nursing students. *Journal of Nursing Education, 28,* 372–376.

Hans, C. (1990). Peer Network Nutrition Education report. Ames: Iowa State University Extension.

Hardman, A., & Blair, S. (1995). Physical activity, health and well-being: A summary of the Consensus Conference. World Forum on Physical Activity and Sport. *Quebec City Proceedings,* pp. 86–90.

Harper, M. (1990). *Minority aging: Essential curricula for selected health and allied health professions.* Washington, DC: Department of Health and Human Services, Health Resources and Services Administration.

Harris, L., et al. (1989). *The Prevention Index '89: Summary Report.* Emmaus, PA: Rodale Press.

Haug, M. (1979). Doctor patient relationships and the older patient. *Journal of Gerontology, 34,* 852–860.

Haug, M., & Lavin, B. (1981). Practitioner or patient: Who's in charge? *Journal of Health and Social Behavior, 22,* 212–229.

Haupt, B. (1997, April 25). Characteristics of hospice care discharges: United States, 1993–1994. *Advance Data, 287,* 1–14.

Haynes, R., et al. (1980). *Patient compliance to prescribed antihypertensive medication regimens: A report to the National Heart, Lung and Blood institute* (DHHS Publication No. [PHS]81-2102). Bethesda, MD: USDHHS.

Hayward, R., et al. (1987, April 1). Who gets preventive care? Results from a new national survey. Paper presented at Concurrent Symposium A, SREPCIM Abstracts.

Hazzard, W. (1992). Dyslipoproteinemia in the elderly: Should it be treated? In G. Omenn (Ed.), *Clinics in geriatric medicine* (pp. 89–102). Philadelphia: W. B. Saunders.

Health. (1996, July 1). *American Medical News,* pp. 13–14.

Health and Fitness. (1991, November 19). Special section. *Newsweek.*

Health Care Advisory Board. (1997). *Innovations in Eldercare.* Washington, DC: The Advisory Board Company.

*Healthy people: The surgeon general's report on health promotion and disease prevention.* (1980). USDHHS, Public Health Services. Washington, DC: U.S. Government Printing Office.

*Healthy People 2000 Midcourse Review: 1995 Report on Progress.* (1995). Washington, DC: U.S. Department of Health and Human Services Public Health Service.

Heaney, R. (1993, February 18). Thinking straight about calcium. *The New England Journal of Medicine, 328,* 503–505.

Heath, C., et al. (1993, June). Do family physicians treat obese patients? *Family Medicine, 25,* 401–402.

Heinonen, O., et al. (1998, March 18). Prostate cancer and supplementation with alpha-Tocopherol and beta-Carotene: Incidence and mortality in a controlled trial. *Journal of the National Cancer Institute, 90,* 440–446.

Heinzelmann, F., & Bagley, R. (1970). Response of physical activity programs and their effects on health behavior. *Public Health Reports, 85,* 905–911.

Hesson, J. (1995). *Weight training for life.* Englewood, CO: Morton.

Hildreth, C., & Saunders, E. (1992). Heart disease, stroke and hypertension in blacks (pp. 90–105). In R. Braithwaite & S. Taylor (Eds.), *Health issues in the Black community.* San Francisco: Jossey-Bass.

Hill, D., et al. (1988). Self examination of the breast: Is it beneficial? *British Medical Journal, 297,* 271–275.

Hill, L., & Smith, N. (1985). *Self-care nursing: Promotion of health.* Norwalk, CT: Appleton-Century-Crofts.

Hoeger, W., & Hoeger, S. (1997). *Principles and Labs for Fitness and Wellness* (4th ed.). Englewood, CO: Morton.

Holman, H., & Lorig, K. (1992). Perceived self-efficacy in self-management of chronic disease (pp. 305–323). In R. Schwarzer (Ed.), *Self-efficacy: Thought control of action.* Washington, DC: Hemisphere.

Holmes, T., & Rahe, R. (1967). The social readjustment rating scale. *Journal of Psychosomatic Research, 11,* 213–218.

Horton, J. (1986). Education programs on smoking prevention and smoking cessation for students and house staff in U.S. medical schools. *Cancer Detection and Prevention, 9,* 417–420.

Horwarth, C. (1989). Marriage and diet in elderly Australians: Results from a large random survey. *Journal of Human Nutrition and Dietetics, 2,* 185–193.

Horwath, C. (1991). Nutrition goals for older adults: A review. *The Gerontologist, 31,* 811–821.

House, J., et al. (1988). Social relationships and health. *Science, 241,* 540–545.

Howley, E., & Franks, B. (1997). *Health fitness instructor's handbook* (3rd ed.). IL: Human Kinetics.

Hu, F., et al. (1997). Dietary fat intake and the risk of coronary heart disease in women. *New England Journal of Medicine, 337,* 1491–1499.

Hurley, J. (1992). *Nutrition and health.* Guilford, CT: Dushkin.

Hutchinson, S. (1998, January 12). The new case for patient education. *American Medical News,* p. 13.

Hypertension Detection and Follow-Up Program Cooperative Group. (1988). Persistence of reduction in blood pressure and mortality of participants in the hypertension detection and follow-up program. *Journal of the American Medical Association, 259,* 2113–2122.

Idler, E. (1994). *Cohesiveness and coherence: Religion and the health of the elderly.* New York: Garland.

Idler, E., & Kasl, S. (1992). Religion, disability, depression, and the timing of death. *American Journal of Sociology, 97,* 1052–1079.

Institute of Medicine. (1981). *Report on a meeting of the Community-Oriented Primary Care Planning Committee.* Washington, DC: National Academy of Sciences.

Insull, W., et al. (1990). Results of a randomized feasibility study of a low-fat diet. *Archives of Internal Medicine, 150,* 421–427.

International Society of Certified Employee Benefit Specialists. (1985, November). *Results: Census of certified employee benefit specialists.* Washington, DC.

Israel, B. (1985). Social networks and social support: Implications for natural helper and community level interventions. *Health Education Quarterly, 12,* 65–80.

Israel, B., & Schurman, S. (1990). Social support, control, and the stress process (pp. 196–201). In K. Glanz et al. (Eds.), *Health behavior and health education: Theory, research and practice.* San Francisco: Jossey-Bass.

Jackman, P. (1997, September 15). FTC crackdowns on wellness infomercials. *Houston Chronicle,* Section C, p. 2.

Jacob, J. (1998, September 21). Financial ratings of HMOs slide: Half lost money. *American Medical News.* p. 16.

Jacques, P., et al. (1997). Long-term vitamin C use and prevalence of early age-related lens opacities. *American Journal of Clinical Nutrition, 66,* 911–916.

Jaglal, S., et al. (1993). Past and recent physical activity and the risk of hip fracture. *American Journal of Epidemiology, 138,* 107–118.

Jakicic, J., et al. (1995). Prescription of exercise intensity for the obese patient: The relationship between heart rate, $Vo_2$ and perceived exertion. *International Journal of Obesity, 19,* 382–387.

*JAMA.* (1990). Report of the US Preventive Services Task Force. *Journal of the American Medical Association, 263,* 436–437.

Janis, I. (1984). The patient as decision maker. In W. Gentry (Ed.), *Handbook of behavioral medicine* (pp. 368–376). New York: Guilford.

Janz, N., et al. (1984). Contingency contracting to enhance patient compliance: A review. *Patient Education and Counseling, 5,* 165–178.

Jiang, W., et al. (1996, June 5). Mental stress-induced myocardial ischemia and cardiac events. *JAMA, 275,* 1651–1656.

*The Johns Hopkins Medical Letter.* (1997).

Johnson, C. (1991). The status of health care among Black Americans. *Journal of the National Medical Association, 83,* 125–129.

Jones, L. (1992, November 9). Physicians can do more to promote regular Pap tests. *American Medical News,* p. 6.

Jones, J., & Jones, K. (1997, July). Promoting physical activity in the senior years. *Journal of Gerontological Nursing,* pp. 41–48.

Kane, R., & Kane, R. (1987). *Long-term care: Principles, programs, and policies.* New York: Springer.

Kane-Williams, E., et al. (1986). *Staying healthy after fifty: Instructor's manual.* Washington, DC: AARP.

Kannus, P., et al. (1989). Sports injuries in elderly athletes: A three-year prospective controlled study. *Age and Ageing, 18,* 263.

Kawachi, I., et al. (1997). A prospective study of passive smoking and coronary heart disease. *Circulation, 95,* 2374–2379.

Kazdin, A. (1984). *Behavior modification in applied settings.* Illinois: Dorsey.

Keim, N. (1995, April). Fates of fat. *Research briefs* (p. 2). Washington, DC: U.S. Department of Agricultural Research Service.

Kemper, D., et al. (1985). *Pathways: A success guide for a healthy life.* Boise: Healthwise.

Kemper, D., et al. (1987). *Growing younger handbook.* Boise: Healthwise, Inc.

Kiecolt-Glaser, J., et al. (1991). Spousal caregivers of dementia victims: Longitudinal changes in immunity and health. *Psychosomatic Medicine, 53,* 345–362.

Kiernat, J. (1991). *Occupational therapy and the older adult.* Gaithersburg, MD: Aspen.

Kim, K., et al. (1991). Development and evaluation of the Osteoporosis Health Belief Scale. *Research in Nursing and Health, 14,* 155–163.

King, A., et al. (1997, January 1). Moderate-intensity exercise and self-rated quality of sleep in older adults. *JAMA, 277,* 32–37.

Kinney, J. (1989). *The busy physician's five-minute guide to the management of alcohol problems.* Washington, DC: American Medical Association, Department of Substance Abuse.

Kirscht, J. (1988). The health belief model and predictions of health actions. In D. Gochman (Ed.), *Health behavior: Emerging research perspectives.* New York: Plenum.

Kizer, W. (1987). *The healthy workplace.* New York: John Wiley & Sons.

Klein, W., & Bloom, M. (1997). *Successful aging.* New York: Plenum Publishing.

Klem, M., et al. (1997, August). A descriptive study of individual's successful at long-term maintenance of substantial weight loss. *American Journal of Clinical Nutrition, 66,* 239–246.

Kleyman, P. (1998, January–February). Using the net for good health/media's health role is growing. *Aging Today,* p. 18.

Kligman, E., & Pepin, E. (1992, August). Prescribing physical activity for older patients. *Geriatrics, 47,* 33–47.

Koch, K. (1977). *I never told anybody.* New York: Random House.

Koenig, H., et al. (1997). Attendance at religious services, interleukin-6, and other biological parameters of immune function in older adults. *International Journal of Psychiatry in Medicine, 27,* 233–250.

Kofoed, L., et al. (1987). Treatment compliance of older alcoholics: An elderly-specific approach is superior to "mainstreaming." *Journal of Studies on Alcohol, 48,* 47–51.

Kolata, G. (1996, February 27). New era of robust elderly belies the fears of scientists. *New York Times Science,* p. 1.

Kottke, T., et al. (1988). Attributes of successful smoking cessation interventions in medical practice: A meta-analysis of 42 controlled trials. *JAMA, 259,* 2883–2889.

Krause, N., & Van Tran, T. (1989). Stress and religious involvement among older blacks. *Journal of Gerontology, 44,* 4–13.

Krause, N., & Wray, L. (1991, fall). Psychosocial correlates of health and illness among minority elders. *Generations.*

Kurlowicz, L. (1997). Nursing standard of practice protocol: Depression in elderly patients. *Geriatric Nursing, 18,* 192–199.

Kushi, L., et al. (1997, April 23–30). Physical activity and mortality in postmenopausal women. *JAMA, 277,* 1287–1292.

Kushi, L., et al. (1996). Dietary antioxidant vitamins and death from coronary heart disease in postmenopausal women. *New England Journal of Medicine, 334,* 1156–1162.

Lachman, M. (1986). Personal control in later life: Stability, change and cognitive correlates. In M. Baltes & P. Baltes (Eds.), *The psychology of control and aging* (pp. 25–30). Hillsdale, NJ: Erlbaum.

LaCroix, A., et al. (1996). Does walking decrease the risk of cardiovascular disease hospitalization and death in older adults? *Journal of American Geriatrics Society, 44,* 113–120.

LaCroix, A., & Omenn, G. (1992). Older adults and smoking. In G. Omenn (Ed.), *Clinics in geriatric medicine* (pp. 69–88). Philadelphia: W. B. Saunders.

Lamy, P. (1988, Summer). Actions of alcohol and drugs in older people. *Generations*, pp. 9–13.

Langer, E., & Rodin, J. (1976).The effects of choice and enhanced personal responsibility for the aged: A field experiment in an institutional setting. *Journal of Personality and Social Psychology, 34,* 191–198.

Langlois, J., et al. (1997, March). Characteristics of older pedestrians who have difficulty crossing the street. *American Journal of Public Health, 87,* 393–397.

Larson, D. (1995, May). Faith: The forgotten factor in healthcare. *American Journal of Natural Medicine, 2,* 10–15.

Lau, R. (1988). Beliefs about control and health behavior. In D. Gochman (Ed.), *Health behavior: Emerging research perspectives* (pp. 43–63). New York: Plenum Press.

Laurence, L. (1997, May 14). Experts help consumers untangle web of health information on Net. *Houston Chronicle*, Section D, p. 2.

Lawton, M., et al. (1984). Pet ownership: A research note. *The Gerontologist, 24,* 208–210.

Lazarou, J., et al. (1998). Incidence of adverse drug reactions in hospitalized patients. *JAMA, 279*(15), 1200–1205.

Lazarus, R., & Folkman, S. (1984). *Stress, appraisal, and coping.* New York: Springer.

Leanse, J. (1986). The senior center as a wellness center. In K. Dychtwald (Ed.), *Wellness and health promotion for the elderly* (pp. 105–118). Gaithersburg, MD: Aspen.

LeBars, P., et al. (1997, October 22–29). A placebo-controlled, double-blind, randomized trial of an extract of Ginkgo Biloba for dementia. *JAMA, 278,* 1327–1332.

Lebowitz, B. (1995, spring). Depression in older adults. *Aging and Vision News, 7,* 2.

Lee, G., & Cassidy, M. (1986). Family and kin relations of the rural elderly. In R. Coward & G. Lee (Eds.), *The elderly in rural society* (pp. 151–170). New York: Springer.

Lee, I., et al. (1995). Exercise intensity and longevity in men. *JAMA, 273,* 1179–1184.

Leibel, R., et al. (1995). Changes in energy expenditure resulting from altered body weight. *New England Journal of Medicine, 332,* 621–628.

Leighton, S. (1998). *Sugar busters: Cut sugar to trim fat.* New York: Ballantine.

Leininger, L., et al. (1996, February). An office system for organizing preventive services. *Archives of Family Medicine, 5,* 108–115.

Lentzner, H., et al. (1992, August). Quality of life in the year before death. *American Journal of Public Health, 82,* 1093–1098.

Leslie, M., & Schuster, P. (1991). The effect of contingency contracting on adherence and knowledge of exercise regimen. *Patient Education and Counseling, 18,* 231–241.

Levin, R. (1987). *Wellness Programs for Older Workers and Retirees.* Washington, DC: Washington, Business Group on Health.

Lewis, C. (1988). Disease prevention and health promotion practices of primary care physicians in the United States. *American Journal of Preventive Medicine,* 4(Suppl.), 9–16.

Lewis, C., & Wells, K. (1985). A model for predicting the counseling practices of physicians. *Journal of General Internal Medicine, 1,* 14–19.

Liberman, U., et al. (1995). Effect of oral alendronate on bone mineral density and the incidence of fractures in postmenopausal osteoporosis. *The New England Journal of Medicine, 333,* 1437–1443.

Lieberman, M., & Borman, L. (1979). *Self-help groups for coping with crisis.* San Francisco: Jossey-Bass.

Liebman, B. (1997, July/August). Carbo-Phobia: Zoning out on the new diet books. *Nutrition Action Healthletter,* pp. 3–5.

Liebman, B., & Hurley, J. (1996, November). One size doesn't fit all. *Nutrition Action Healthletter,* pp. 10–12.

Lilly issues warning on use of prozac for weight loss. (1997, October 20). *American Medical News,* Health sub-section, p. 1.

List, N. (1987, August). Perspectives in cancer screening in the elderly. *Clinics in Geriatric Medicine, 3,* 443–445.

Lopez, C., & Aguilera, E. (1991). *On the sidelines: Hispanic elderly and the continuum of care,* Washington, DC: National Council of La Raza.

Lorig, K. (1992). *Patient education: A practical approach.* St. Louis: Mosby–Year Book.

Lorig, K., et al. (1989). Development and evaluation of a scale to measure perceived self-efficacy in people with arthritis. *Arthritis and Rheumatism, 32,* 37–44.

Lorig, K., & Fries, J. (1986). *The arthritis helpbook: A tested self-management program for coping with your arthritis.* Reading, MA: Addison-Wesley.

Loss of appetite. (1997, August). *Mayo Clinic Health Letter,* p. 7.

Lowenthal, M., & Robinson, B. (1976). Social networks and isolation. In R. Binstock & E. Shanas (Eds.), *Handbook on aging and the social sciences.* New York: Van Nostrand.

Lupu, D. (1984–1985). *Hospice services for patients without family caregivers* (AOA and DHHS Grant Project 90-AM-0060). Chevy Chase, MD: Montgomery Hospice Society.

Lynne, J. (1997, July–August). Living wills: Tackle the hard stuff. *Health,* p. 30.

Madara, E., & Peterson, B. (1986). *Hospitals and self-help groups: Practical and promising relationships.* Unpublished manuscript, Denville, NJ.

Maddox, G. (1987). *The encyclopedia of aging.* New York: Springer.

Maddox, G. (1988, summer). Aging, drinking and alcohol abuse. *Generations,* pp. 14–16.

Maduro, R. (1983). Curanderismo and Latino views of disease and caring in cross cultural medicine. *Western Journal of Medicine, 139,* 868–874.

Maheux, B., et al. (1989, July–August). Factors influencing physicians' preventive practices, *American Journal of Preventive Medicine, 5,* 201–206.

Malnutrition, food intake in elderly studied. (1995, November). *American Medical News, 6,* 14.

Managed care cited for slowdown in spending. (1998, February 2). *American Medical News,* pp. 3, 8, 9.

Managed care strives to recover from '97 struggles. (1998, January 12). *American Medical News,* p. 25.

Manton, K., et al. (1993, September). Forecasts of active life expectancy: Policy and fiscal implications. *Journal of Gerontology, 48*(Special Issue), pp. 11–26.

Marcus, M. (1997, August). Health and fitness: Women hit the weight room. *US News & World Report,* pp. 61–62.

Marcus, A., & Crane, L. (1987, March 31). *Current estimates of adult cigarette smoking by race/ethnicity* [Invited Paper]. Washington, DC: Interagency Committee on Smoking and Health.

Mark, E., et al. (1997, August 28). Fatal pulmonary hypertension associated with short-term use of fenfluramine and phentermine. *The New England Journal of Medicine,* 602–605.

Marks, G., et al. (1986). Role of health locus of control beliefs and expectations of treatment efficacy in adjustment to cancer. *Journal of Personality and Social Psychology, 51,* 443–450.

Marmor, T., & Mashaw, J. (1990, fall). Northern light: Canada's lessons for American health care. *The American Prospect,* pp. 18–29.

Marston, W. (1996a, March–April). How much is too much? *Health,* pp. 38, 40.

Marston, W. (1996b, September). High protein diets really do make you lose fat: That's where the problems start. *Health,* pp. 99–102.

*Mayo Clinic Health Letter.* (1997, July). Coffee, p. 7.

McAuley, E. (1994). Physical activity and psychosocial outcomes. In C. Bouchard et al. (Eds.), *Physical activity, fitness, and health* (pp. 561–568). Champaign, IL: Human Kinetics.

McAuley, E. (1993). Self-efficacy and the maintenance of exercise participation in older adults. *Journal of Behavioral Medicine, 16,* 103–113.

McAuley, E., & Courneya, K. (1993). Adherence to exercise and physical activity as health promoting behaviors: Attitudinal and self-efficacy influences. *Applied and Preventive Psychology, 2,* 65–77.

McConnell, J., et al. (1998). The effect of finasteride on the risk of acute urinary retention and the need for surgical treatment among men with benign prostatic hyperplasia. *The New England Journal of Medicine, 338,*(9), 557–563.

McCormack, G., et al. (1991). Culturally diverse elders. In J. Kiernat (Ed.), *Occupational therapy and the older adult* (pp. 11–25). Gaithersburg, MD: Aspen.

McCormick, W., & Inui, T. (1992). Geriatric preventive care: Counseling techniques in practice settings. In G. Omenn (Ed.), *Clinics in geriatric medicine* (pp. 215–218). Philadelphia: W. B. Saunders.

McDowell, I., et al. (1986). Comparison of three methods of recalling patients for influenza vaccination. *Canadian Medical Association Journal, 135,* 991.

McGinnis, J. (1992, summer–fall). Top leading cause of death. *The Interchange, 9,* 5.

McGinnis, J., & Foege, W. (1993, November 10). Actual causes of death in the United States. *JAMA, 270,* 2207–2212.

McGinnis, J., & Lee, P. (1995, April 12). Healthy people 2000 at mid decade. *JAMA, 273,* 1123–1129.

McKinlay, J. (1975). Who is really ignorant: Physician or patient? *Journal of Health and Social Behavior, 16,* 3–11.

McMurray, J. (1990). Creative arts with older people. *Activities, Adaptation and Aging, 14.*

McNeil, J., et al. (1991). The effect of exercise on depressive symptoms in the moderately depressed elderly. *Psychology and Aging, 6,* 487–488.

McTernan, E., & Rice, N. (1986, November). An overview of the role of allied health professionals in the health promotion and disease prevention movement. *Journal of Allied Health, 15,* 289–292.

Measuring alcohol's effect on you. (1996, April). *The Johns Hopkins Medical Letter: Health After 50, 8,* 2–3.

*Medical Tribune.* (1989). Physician's newspaper, 30, 20.

Meichenbaum, D., & Cameron, R. (1974). The clinical potential of modifying what clients say to themselves. In M. Mahoney & C. Thorensen, *Self-control: Power to the person.* New York: Wadsworth.

Meier, K., & Licari, M. (1997). The effect of cigarette taxes on cigarette consumption, 1955 through 1994. *American Journal of Public Health, 87,* 1126–1130.

Mellin, L., et al. (1997). The solution method: 2-year trends in weight, blood pressure, exercise, depression, and functioning of adults trained in development skills. *Journal of the American Dietetic Association, 97,* 1133–1138.

Mellinger, G., & Balter, M. (1983). *Collaborative Project* (GSMIRSB Report). Washington, DC: National Institute of Mental Health.

Mestel, R. (1997, November/December). A safer estrogen. *Health,* pp. 73–75.

Mestel, R. (1997, September). Sleeping lessons from recovered insomniacs. *Health,* pp. 108–115.

Mettler, M. (1992). The number one factor. *Perspectives in Health Promotion and Aging, 7,* 4.

Mettler, M. (1997). Unpublished update on the *Healthwise Handbook* program, Healthwise, Inc., P.O. Box 1989, Boise, ID 83701.

Meydani, S., et al. (1997, May 7). Vitamin E supplementation and in vivo immune response in healthy elderly subjects. *JAMA, 277,* 1380–1386.

Meyer, H. (1991, December 9). Shape up or shell out. *American Medical News,* p. 3.

Midgley, J., et al. (1996). Effect of reduced dietary sodium on blood pressure. *JAMA, 275*(20), 1590–1597.

Miller, J. (1992, November). Washington Perspective. *Worksite Wellness Works, 8.*

Miller, J. (1993, February). Washington Perspective. *Worksite Wellness Works, 9.*

Mishara, B., & Kastenbaus, R. (1980). Alcohol and the elderly: Five thousand years of uncontrolled experimentation. In *Alcohol and old age. Seminars in Psychiatry* (p. 1). New York: Grune & Stratton.

Moberg, D. (1983). The ecological fallacy: Concerns for program planners. *Generations, 8,* 12–14.

Mockenhaupt, R., & Boyle, K. (1992). *Healthy aging.* Santa Barbara, CA: ABC-CLIO.

Montamat, S., & Cusack, B. (1992). Overcoming problems with polypharmacy and drug misuse in the elderly. In G. Omenn (Ed.), *Clinics in geriatric medicine* (pp. 143–158). Philadelphia: W. B. Saunders.

Moore, S., & Nagle, J. (1990). *Physician's guide to outpatient nutrition.* Kansas City, MO: American Academy of Family Physicians.

Morain, C. (1994, July 4). Still a long way to, baby. *American Medical News,* pp. 11–14.

Morales, A., et al. (1994, June). Effects of replacement dose of dehydroepiandrosterone in men and women of advancing age. *Journal of Clinical Endocrinology and Metabolism, 78,* 1360–1367.

Morgan, D. (1993, May 24–31)). The best prescription might be just taking time to care. *American Medical News,* p. 9.

Morin, R. (1998, January 26). Turning the question: Opinions on health care laws shift abruptly when pollsters bring up the issue of cost. *The Washington Post Weekly Edition,* p. 35.

Morreale, P., et al. (1996). Comparison of the antiinflammatory efficacy of chondroitin sulfate and diclofenac sodium in patients with knee osteoarthritis. *Journal of Rheumatology, 23,* 1385–1391.

Morse, R., & Flavin, D. (1992, August). The definition of alcoholism. *The Journal of the American Medical Association, 268,* 1012–1014.

Mosher-Ashley, P., & Barrett, P. (1997). *A life worth living*. Baltimore: Health Professions.

Moyers, B. (1993). *Healing and the mind*. New York: Doubleday.

Mullan, F. (1992). Rewriting the social contract in health. In A. Katz et al. (Eds.), *Self-help: Concepts and applications* (pp. 61–67). Philadelphia: The Charles Press.

Murphy, J., et al. (1982). The long-term effects of spouse involvement upon weight loss and maintenance. *Behavior Therapy, 13,* 681–693.

Must HMOs cover diabetes prevention? (1998, February 9). *American Medical News,* p. 30.

Naditch, M. (1984). The Staywell Program. In J. Matarazzo et al. (Eds.), *Behavioral health: A handbook of health enhancement and disease prevention*. New York: John Wiley & Sons.

Nathan, P. (1984). Johnson and Johnson's Live for Life: A comprehensive positive lifestyle change program. In J. Matarazzo et al. (Eds.), *Behavioral health: A handbook of health enhancement and disease prevention*. New York: John Wiley & Sons.

Nathan, P. (1986). Outcomes of treatment for alcoholism: Current data. *Annals of Behavioral Medicine, 8,* 40–46.

National Center for Health Statistics. (1986). Prevalence of Selected Chronic Conditions: United States, 1979-1981. *Vital and health statistics* (Series 10, No. 155, DHHS Publication No. [PHS]861583-10155). Hyattsville, MD: USDHHS.

National Center for Health Statistics. (1988). *Vital and health statistics* (Series 10, No. 163, DHHS Publication No. [PHS]88-1591). Washington, DC: USDHHS.

National Center for Health Statistics. (1990a). *Health, United States, 1989 and prevention profile* (DHHS Publication No. [PHS]90-1232). Hyattsville, MD: USDHHS.

National Center for Health Statistics. (1990b). *Healthy people 2000: National health promotion and disease prevention objectives* (DHHS Publication No. [PHS]91-50213). Hyattsville, MD: Public Health Service.

National Center for Health Statistics. (1994). Annual summary of births, marriages, divorces, and death: United States, 1993. Monthly vital statistics report, vol. 42, no. 13. Hyattsville, MD: Public Health Service.

National Center Institute. (1989). *Cancer statistics review, 1973–1987* (NIH Publication No. [NIH]88-2789). Bethesda, MD: USDHHS.

National Council on the Aging. (1982, March–April). Public policy agenda, 1986-1987. *Perspective on aging*. Washington, DC: Author.

National Health Interview Survey. (1985, November). *Advance data*. Hyattsville, MD: U.S. Public Health Service.

National Heart, Lung and Blood Institute. (1988). *The 1988 Report of the Joint National Committee on detection, evaluation and treatment of high blood pressure*. Washington, DC: USDHHS.

National Indian Council on Aging. (1984). Indians and Alaskan natives. In E. Palmore (Ed.), *Handbook on the aged in the United States*. Westport, CT: Greenwood Press.

National Institute on Aging. (1994). *NIH Consensus Statement on Optimal Calcium Intake, 12,* 1–31.

Natural relief from arthritis. (1997, October). *The Johns Hopkins Medical Letter, Health After 50, 9,* 1–2.

Neergaard, L. (1998, February 23). Dietary supplement users are advised to use caution. *Houston Chronicle*, p. 3.

Neighbors, H., et al. (1995). Health promotion and African-Americans: From personal empowerment to collective action. *American Journal of Health Promotion, 9,* 281–287.

Nelson, K. (1987). Visual impairment among elderly Americans: Statistics in transition. *Journal of Visual Impairment and Blindness, 81,* 331–334.

Newell, G., et al. (1989). Cancer and age. *Seminars in Oncology, 16,* 3–9.

NIAMSD. (1991). *Osteoporosis research, education and health promotion.* Bethesda, MD: USDHHS, National Institute of Arthritis and Musculoskeletal and Skin Diseases.

Norstrom, J. (1966). *Activity pyramid.* Reprint from Institute for Research and Education Healthy System, Minnesota.

Nutting, P. (1987). Community-oriented primary care: From principle to practice. In P. Nutting (Ed.), *Community-Oriented Primary Care* (pp. xv–xxv). Albuquerque: University of New Mexico Press.

Ockene, J. (1987). Physician-delivered interventions for smoking cessation: Strategies for increasing effectiveness. *Preventive Medicine, 16,* 723–737.

Office of Disease Prevention and Health Promotion. (1990). *Healthy older people: The report of a National Health Promotion Program.* Washington, DC: USDHHS.

Office of Disease Prevention and Health Promotion. (1998). *Clinician's handbook of preventive services* (2nd ed.). Washington, DC: U.S. Department of Health and Human Services.

Office on Smoking and Health. (1989). *Reducing the Health Consequences of Smoking: 25 Years of Progress: A Report of the Surgeon General* (DHHS Publication No. [CDC]89-8411). Washington, DC: USDHHS.

Oldridge, N., et al. (1988). Cardiac rehabilitation after myocardial infarction. *The Journal of the American Medical Association, 260,* 945–950.

O'Leary, A. (1985). Self-efficacy and health. *Behavioral Research and Therapy, 23,* 437–451.

Olestra-Fried Snacks Fat-Free, But Not Free of Concerns. (1996, February). *American Medical News,* American Medical Association.

Ornish, D. (1992). *Dr. Dean Ornish's program for reversing heart disease.* New York: Ballantine.

Ornstein, R., & Sobel, D. (1989). *Healthy pleasures.* Reading, MA: Addison-Wesley.

Paganini-Hill, A., et al. (1991). Exercise and other risk factors in the prevention of hip fracture. *Epidemiology, 2,* 16–25.

Pate, R., et al. (1995). Physical activity and public health. *JAMA, 273,* 402–407.

Pelletier, K. (1996). A review and analysis of the health and cost-effective outcome studies of comprehensive health promotion and disease prevention programs at the worksite: 1993–1995 update. *American Journal of Health Promotion, 10,* 380–388.

Pender, N. (1987). *Health promotion in nursing practice.* Norfolk, CT: Appleton & Lange.

Penninx, B., et al. (1998). Depressive symptoms and physical decline in community-dwelling older persons. *JAMA, 279*(21), 1720–1726.

Persson, I., et al. (1997). Hormone replacement therapy and the risk of breast cancer. *International Journal of Cancer, 72,* 758–761.

Pesticide exposure. (1997, June). *Nutrition Action Healthletter,* pp. 4–6.

Peterson, C., & Stunkard, A. (1989). Personal control and health promotion. *Social Science Medicine, 28,* 819–828.

Peterson, J. (1996, April). Acupuncture in the 1990s. *Archives of Family Medicine, 5,* 237–240.

Peto, R., et al. (1992, May 23). Mortality from tobacco in developed countries: Indirect estimates from national vital statistics. *The Lancet, 339,* 1268–1278.

Pickering, T., et al. (1988). How common is white coat hypertension? *JAMA, 259,* 225.

Pierce, J., et al. (1998). Has the California tobacco control program reduced smoking? *JAMA, 280*(10), 893–899.

Podmore, I., et al. (1998, April 9). Vitamin C exhibits pro-oxidant properties. *Nature, 392.*

Potter, J., & Haigh, R. (1990). Benefits of antihypertensive therapy in the elderly. *British Medical Bulletin, 46,* 77–93.

Prisuta, R. (1984, October). *Evaluation of the AARP Widowed Persons Services.* Washington, DC: AARP, Research and Data Department.

Prochaska, J., et al. (1988). Measuring processes of change: Applications to the cessation of smoking. *Journal of Consulting Clinical Psychology, 56,* 520–528.

Prochaska, J., & Di Clemente, C. (1992). Stages of change in the modification of problem behaviors. In M. Herson et al. (Eds.), *Progress in behavior modification* (pp. 184–218). Newbury Park, CA: Sage.

Protecting yourself against prescription errors. (1996, January). *The Johns Hopkins Medical Letter: Health After 50,* pp. 6–7.

Public Health Service. (1988). *The Surgeon General's Report on Nutrition and Health* (DHHS Publication No. [PHS]88-50210). Washington, DC: USDHHS.

Public Health Service. (1995). *Healthy people 2000 midcourse review and 1995 revisions.* Washington, DC: USDHHS.

Pyke, S., et al. (1997). Change in coronary risk and coronary risk factor levels in couples following lifestyle intervention. *Archives of Family Medicine, 6,* 354–360.

Rakowski, W., et al. (1991). Correlates of expected success at health habit change and its role as a predictor in health behavior research. *American Journal of Preventive Medicine, 7,* 89–94.

Rall, L., et al. (1996). The effect of progressive resistance training in rheumatoid arthritis. *Arthritis & Rheumatism, 39,* 415–426.

Ransdell, L., & Rehling, S. (1996). Church-based health promotion: A review of the current literature. *American Journal of Health Behavior, 20,* 195–207.

Ray, W., et al. (1989). Benzodiazepines for long and short elimination half-life and the risk of hip fracture. *JAMA, 262,* 3303.

Report of the National Cholesterol Education Program. (1988). Evaluation, and treatment of high blood cholesterol in adults. *Archives of Internal Medicine, 148,* 1993–1997.

Report of the Special Committee on Aging. (1996). (1991). (1985). *Developments in Aging, Vol. 1.* U.S. Senate. Washington, DC: US Government Printing Office.

Report on Medical Guidelines and Outcomes Research. (1991). Health and Sciences Communication, 1909 Vermont Avenue NW, Suite 700, Washington, DC 20005.

Retchin, S., & Anapolle, J. (1993, May). An overview of the older driver. *Clinics in Geriatric Medicine, 9,* 279–296.

Revicki, D., & Mitchell, J. (1990). Strain, social support, and mental health in rural elderly individuals. *Journal of Gerontology, 45,* 267–274.

Rexrode, K., et al. (1997). A prospective study of body mass index, weight change, and risk of stroke in women. *JAMA, 277,* 1539–1545.

Riessman, F. (1965). The helper therapy principle. *Social Work, 10,* 27–32.

Rimer, B. (1988). Health promotion and aging: Smoking among older adults. In F. Abdellah & S. Moore (Eds.), *Surgeon general's workshop: Health promotion and aging background papers* (pp. I.l–I.20). Washington, DC: DHHS.

Rimer, G., et al. (1983). Planning a cancer control program for older citizens. *The Gerontologist, 23,* 384–389.

Rimm, E., et al. (1996, February 14). Vegetable, fruit, and cereal fiber intake and risk of coronary heart disease among men. *JAMA, 14,* 447–451.

Rivara, F., et al. (1997). Injury prevention. *The New England Journal of Medicine, 337,* 613–614.

Robb, S., & Stegman, C. (1983). Companion animals and elderly people: A challenge for evaluators of social support. *The Gerontologist, 23,* 277–282.

Roberts, S., et al. (1996). Effects of age on energy expenditure and susbtrate oxidation during experimental overfeeding and underfeeding in healthy men. *Journal of Gerontology, 51A,* B148–B166.

Roberts, S., et al. (1994, November 23–30). Control of food intake in older men. *JAMA, 272,* 1601–1606.

Robertson, N. (1988, February 21). The changing world of Alcoholics Anonymous. *New York Times Magazine,* 40–47, 57, 92.

Rodin, J. (1986). Aging and health: Effects of the sense of control. *Science, 233,* 1271–1275.

Rodin, J., & Langer, E. (1977). Long-term effects of a control-relevant intervention with the institutionalized aged. *Journal of Personality and Social Psychology, 35,* 897–902.

Rosen, M., et al. (1984). Prevention and health promotion in primary care: Baseline results on physicians from the INSURE project on life cycle preventive health services. *Preventive Medicine, 13,* 535–548.

Rosendahl, E., & Kirschenbaum, P. (1992, November). Weight loss and mood among older adults. Paper presentation at the 45th Gerontological Society of America Annual Meeting, Washington, DC.

Rosenstock, I. (1990). The health belief model: Explaining health behavior through expectancies. In K. Glanz et al. (Eds.), *Health behavior and health education: Theory, research, and practice* (pp. 39–61). San Francisco: Jossey-Bass.

Rost, K. (1990, October 1). *Introduction of the elderly patient's agenda in the medical visit* (Final report for AARP Andrus Foundation). Washington, DC.

Rotter, J. (1954). *Social learning and clinical psychology.* Upper Saddle River, NJ: Prentice Hall.

Rowe, J., & Kahn, R. (1987, July 10). Human aging: Usual and successful. *Science, 137,* 143–149.

Sainsbury, R., & Hanger, H. (1991). Preventive medicine in the elderly population. *Drugs and Aging, 1,* 345–352.

Salon, I. (1997). Weight control and nutrition: Knowing when to intervene. *Geriatrics, 52,* 33–41.

Sano, M., et al. (1997). A controlled trial of Selegilene, Alpha-Tocopherol, or both as treatment for Alzheimer's disease. *New England Journal of Medicine, 336,* 1216–1222.

Sarafino, E. (1990). *Health psychology: Biopsychosocial interactions.* New York: John Wiley & Sons.

Sarason, I., et al. (1983). Assessing social support: The Social Support Questionnaire. *Journal of Personality and Social Psychology, 44,* 127–139.

Saunders, C. (1977). Dying they live: St Christopher's Hospice. In H. Feifel (Ed.), *New meanings of death.* New York: McGraw-Hill.

Schaie, K. (1997, May). Exercising the mind. *Nutrition Action Healthletter,* p. 7.

Schneider, D., et al. (1997, February 19). Timing of postmenopausal estrogen for optimal bone mineral density. *JAMA, 277,* 543–547.

Schneider, R., et al. (1995). A randomized controlled trial of stress reduction for hypertension in older African Americans. *Hypertension, 26,* 820–827.

Schonfeld, L. (1993, January–February,). Research findings on a hidden population. *The Counselor,* pp. 20–26.

Schonfeld, L., et al. (1992). Age-related differences in antecedents to substance abuse. Paper presented at the centennial meeting of the American Psychological Association, Washington, DC.

Schulz, R. (1976). Effects of control and predictability on the physical and psychological well-being of the institutionalized aged. *Journal of Personality and Social Psychology, 33,* 563–573.

Schwartz, J. (1997, May 26). Health information on Internet is plentiful, but can you trust it? *Houston Chronicle,* p. 34.

Sears, B. (1997). *Mastering the zone.* New York: HarperCollins.

Sears, B. (1995). *Entering the zone.* New York: HarperCollins.

Sechrist, W. (1983, March–April). Causal attribution and personal responsibility for health and disease. *Health Education, 14,* 51–54.

Segal, S. (1986, February). Retirement programs in the '80s. *Personnel Administration.*

Selzer, M. (1971, February). The Michigan Alcohol Screening Test: The quest for a new diagnostic instrument. *American Journal of Psychiatry, 127,* 1653.

Senate Special Committee on Aging. (1985). *Developments in Aging: Vol. 1.* Washington, DC: U.S. Government Printing Office.

Sennott-Miller, L., & Kligman, E. (1992, December). Healthier lifestyles: How to motivate older patients to change. *Geriatrics, 47,* 52–59.

Shamblin, G. (1997). *The Weigh Down Diet.* New York: Doubleday.

Shapiro, S. (1986, spring). Are elders underserved? *Generations,* pp. 14–17.

Shapiro, S., et al. (1985). Selection, followup and analysis in the Health Insurance Plan Study: A randomized trail with breast cancer screening. *National Cancer Institute Monographs, 67,* 65–74.

Sharp, D. (1997, November–December). The calcium problem. *Health,* pp. 103–107.

Shmerling, R., et al. (1988). Discussing cardiopulmonary resuscitation: A study of elderly outpatients. *Journal of General Internal Medicine, 3,* 317.

Sidney, K., & Shephard, R. (1977). Activity patterns of elderly men and women. *Journal of Gerontology, 32,* 25.

Siegel, J. (1993). Companion animals: In sickness and in health. *Journal of Social Issues, 49,* 157–167.

Skinner, B. (1948). *Walden two.* New York: Macmillan.

Skinner, B. (1953). *Science and human behavior.* New York: MacMillan.

Sloan, R. (1986). *Practical geriatric therapeutics.* New Jersey: Medical Economics Books.

Smith, H., et al. (1986). The value of permixon in benign prostatic hypertrophy. *British Journal of Urology, 58,* 36–40.

Sox, H. (1997, October). Expert questions call to expand prostate cancer screenings. *Aging Research & Training News,* p. 119.

Speechley, M., & Tinetti, M. (1991). Falls and injuries in frail and vigorous community elderly persons. *Journal of American Geriatrics Society, 39,* 46.

Spiegel, D., et al. (1989, October 14). Effect of psychosocial treatment on survival of patients with metastatic breast cancer. *The Lancet,* pp. 888–891.

Spiegel, D., & Bloom, J. (1983). Group therapy and hypnosis reduce metastatic breast cancer pain. *Psychosomatic Medicine, 45,* 333.

Spirduso, W. (1995). *Physical dimensions of aging.* Champaign, IL: Human Kinetics.

Stamler, J., et al. (1986). Is relationship between serum cholesterol and risk of premature death from coronary heart disease continuous and graded? Findings in 356,222 primary screenees of the Multiple Risk Factor Intervention Trial (MRFIT). *Journal of the American Medical Association, 256,* 2823–2828.

Stapleton, S. (1997, May 5). Wrong focus for mammogram debate? *American Medical News,* pp. 3, 34–35.

Starr, B. (1985). Sexuality and aging. In M. Lawton & G. Maddox (Eds.), *Annual review of gerontology and geriatrics* (5th ed.). New York: Springer.

Starr, B., & Weiner, M. (1981). *Sex and sexuality in the mature years.* New York: McGraw-Hill.

Starting to exercise? Do you need a stress test? (1998). *UC Berkeley Wellness Letter, 14,* 11, p. 6.

Stephens, N., et al. (1996). Randomised controlled trial of vitamin E in patients with coronary disease: Cambridge Heart Antioxidant Study (CHAOS). *Lancet, 347,* 781–786.

Stokols, D., et al. (1995). Integration of medical care and worksite health promotion. *JAMA, 273,* 1136–1142.

Strecher, V., et al. (1986, spring). The role of self-efficacy in achieving health behavior change. *Health Education Quarterly, 13,* 73–91.

Stuart, R., & Davis, B. (1972). *Slim chance in a fat world.* Chicago: Research Press.

Studies suggest religious activities can improve health. (1996, March 4). *American Medical News.*

Stunkard, A. (1987). Conservative treatments for obesity. *American Journal of Clinical Nutrition, 45,* 1142–1154.

Sullivan, L. (1990). *Healthy people 2000: Healthy older Adults. A report of the surgeon general.* Washington, DC: USDHHS.

Survival guide. (1988, June). A survival guide to the greasy kid stuff. *Consumer Reports,* p. 355.

Sutton, S., & Hallett, R. (1988). Understanding the effects of fear-arousing communications: The role of cognitive factors and the amount of fear aroused. *Journal of Behavioral Medicine, 11,* 353–360.

Switkes, B. (1982). *Senior-cize: Exercises and dances in a chair.* Washington, DC: Senior-cize.

Take vitamin B-12, new study advises. (1998). *AARP Bulletin, 39,* 3.

Tayback, M., et al. (1990, May). Body weight as a risk factor in the elderly. *Archives of Internal Medicine, 150,* 1065–1072.

Taylor, H., & Kagay, M. (1985). *Prevention in America III: Steps people take—or fail to take—for better health.* New York: Louis Harris and Associates.

Taylor, R., et al. (1982). *Health promotion: Principles and clinical applications.* Norfolk, CT: Appleton-Century-Crofts.

Taylor, S., et al. (1984). Attributions, beliefs about control, and adjustment to breast cancer. *Journal of Personality and Social Psychology, 46,* 489–502.

The many benefits of fiber. (1996, September). *The Johns Hopkins Medical Letter: Health After 50,* p. 4.

Theodosakis, J. (1997). *The arthritis cure.* New York: St. Martin's Press.

Thomas, S. (1990, spring). Community health advocacy for racial and ethnic minorities in the United States: Issues and challenges for health education. *Health Education Quarterly, 17,* 13–19.

Thomas, W. (1996). *The Eden alternative.* Acton, MA: VanderWyk & Burnham.

Thompson, R., et al. (1998, January 30). Orientation to community in a family medicine residency program. *Family Medicine, 1,* 22–26.

Thompson, R., et al. (1996, May). COPC in a family medicine residency program. *Family Medicine, 28,* 326–330.

Thun, M., et al. (1997). Alcohol consumption and mortality among middle-aged and elderly U.S. adults. *The New England Journal of Medicine, 337,* 1705–1714.

Tinetti, M., et al. (1993). FICSIT: Risk factor abatement strategy for fall prevention. *Journal of American Geriatric Society, 41,* 315–320.

Trans: The phantom fat. (1996, September). *Nutrition Action Healthletter,* pp. 10–11.

Turkoski, B., et al. (1997, May–June). Clinical nursing judgment related to reducing the incidence of falls by elderly patients. *Rehabilitation Nursing, 22,* 124–130.

Tyler, V. (1993). *The honest herbal* (3rd ed.). Pharmaceutical Products Press.

United States Department of Agriculture. (1997, July). *Briefs.* Agricultural Research Service.

USDHHS. (1979). *Health People: The Surgeon General's Report on Health Promotion and Disease Prevention.* Washington, DC: U.S. Government Printing Office.

United States Department of Health and Human Services. (1985, June). *A Resource Guide for Injury Control Programs for Older Persons.* Washington, DC: USGPO.

USDHHS. (1989). *Surgeon General's Report on Smoking and Health.* Washington, DC: U.S. Government Printing Office.

United States Department of Health and Human Services. (1990). *Healthy People 2000: National Health Promotion and Disease Prevention Objectives.* Washington, DC: USGPO.

United States Department of Labor. (1989, March 29). *Thirty-eight million persons do volunteer work.* Bureau of Labor Statistics' press release USDL 90-154.

United States Preventive Services Task Force. (1989). *Guide to clinical preventive services: An assessment of the effectiveness of 169 interventions.* Baltimore: Williams & Wilkins.

United States Preventive Services Task Force. (1996). *Guide to clinical preventive services.* Baltimore: Williams & Wilkins.

United States Public Health Service Reports. (1980). DHHS, Publication No. (PHS) 83-1572. Series 10, no. 144.

University of California at Berkeley Wellness Newsletter. (1995). *The new wellness encyclopedia*. Boston: Houghton Mifflin.

Urban Obstacles to Healthy Living. (1996, March–April). *Health*, p. 35.

Uriri, J., & Thatcher-Winger, R. (1995). Health risk appraisal and the older adult. *Journal of Gerontological Nursing, 21,* 25–31.

US News & World Report. (1998, March 9). Who is worried about health care and why? p. 48.

Vachon, M., et al. (1980). A controlled study of self-help intervention for widows. *American Journal of Psychiatry, 137,* 1179–1184.

Vanishing inner-city grocery stores. (1996, February 12). *American Medical News*, p. 23.

Van Itallie, T., & Lew, E. (1990). Health implications of overweight in the elderly. *Progress in Clinical and Biological Research, 326,* 89–108.

Vita, A., et al. (1998). Aging, health risks, and cumulative disability. *New England Journal of Medicine, 338*(15), 1035–1041.

Vitamin and nutritional supplements. (1997, June). *Mayo Clinic Health Letter*, pp. 1–8.

Vitamin B-12. (1998, May). *Nutrition Action Healthletter*, p. 5.

Vitamin E. (1996, April). *Nutrition Action Healthletter*, p. 5.

Vitamin report. (1994). *University of California at Berkeley Wellness Letter*, October. Palm Coast, Florida.

Vitiello, M. (1997). Sleep disorders and aging: Understanding the causes. *Journal of Gerontology: Medical Sciences, 52A,* M189–M191.

Voelker, R. (1993, February 15). HMOs taking prevention to expansive new heights. *American Medical News*, pp. 1, 35.

Wagner, E., et al. (1991). Factors associated with participation in a senior health promotion program. *The Gerontologist, 31,* 598–602.

Wallechinsky, D., & Wallace, A. (1993). *The people's almanac presents the book of lists: The '90s edition*. Boston: Little, Brown.

Wallston, K., & Wallston, B. (1982). Who is responsible for your health? The construct of health locus of control. In G. Saunders & J. Suls (Eds.), *Social psychology of health and illness*. New Jersey: Erlbaum.

Wallston, B., et al. (1976). Development and validation of the health locus of control scale. *Journal of Consulting and Clinical Psychology, 44,* 58–585.

Walsh, B., et al. (1998). Effects of Raloxifene on serum lipids and coagulation factors in healthy postmenopausal women. *JAMA, 279*(18), 1445–1451.

Wechsler, H., et al. (1983). The physician's role in health promotion: A survey of primary care practitioners. *The New England Journal of Medicine, 308,* 97–100.

Wechsler, H., et al. (1996, April 11). The physician's role in promotion revisited: A survey of primary care practitioners. *The New England Journal of Medicine, 334,* 996–998.

Weight control: What works and why. (1994). *Mayo Clinic Health Letter Supplement*, pp. 1–8.

Weinberg, A., & Minaker, K. (1995). Dehydration: Evaluation and management in older adults. *JAMA, 274,* 1552–1556.

Weininger, B., & Menkin, J. (1978). *Aging is a lifelong affair*. Los Angeles, CA: The Guild of Tutors Press.

WELCOA (Wellness Councils of America). (1994, August). Health risk assessment use up. *Worksite Wellness Works, 10,* 3.

WELCOA. (1997, April). Health risk appraisals. *Worksite Wellness Works, 13*, 2.

*Wellness and Prevention Sourcebook.* (1998). New York: Faulkner & Gray.

Wetzel, M., et al. (1998). Courses involving complementary and alternative medicine at U.S. medical schools. *JAMA, 280*(9), 784–787.

Wheeler, F., et al. (1989, February). Health Promotion beliefs and attitudes of physicians: A survey of two communities in South Carolina. *The Journal of South Carolina Medical Association, 1*, 121–134.

Whelton, P., et al. (1998). Sodium reduction and weight loss in the treatment of hypertension in older persons. *JAMA, 279*(11), 839–846.

Whitehead, M. (1997). Editorial: How useful is the 'stages of change' model? *Health Education Journal, 56*, 111–112.

Williams, M. (1996). Increasing participation in health promotion among older African-Americans. *American Journal of Health Behaviors, 20*, 389–399.

Williams, P. (1997a, September). *Health*, pp. 27–29.

Williams, P. (1997b, January 27). Relationship of distance run per week to coronary heart disease risk factors in 8283 male runners. *Archives of Internal Medicine, 157*, 191–198.

Williams, R., et al. (1992). Prognostic importance of social and economic resources among medically treated patients with angiographically documented coronary artery disease. *Journal of the American Medical Association, 267*, 520–524.

Willis, C. (1986, November). The future of allied health in the health promotion/disease prevention movement. *Journal of Allied Health, 15*, 349–355.

Willis, D. (1997, March–April). Animal therapy. *Rehabilitation Nursing, 22*, 78–81.

Wilson, F. (1996). Patient education materials nurses use in community health. *Western Journal of Nursing Research, 18*, 195–205.

Wind, J. (1990, March). Striving for the fullness of life: The church's challenge in health. *Second Opinion, 13*, 8–73.

Wisconsin study describes rural obesity problem. (1996, April 1). *American Medical News*, p. 25.

Wold, J., & Williams, A. (1996). Student/faculty practice and research in occupational health: Health promotion and outcome evaluation. *Journal of Nursing Education, 35*, 252–257.

Wolf, S., et al. (1996). Reducing frailty and falls in older persons: An investigation of Tai Chi and computerized balance training. *Journal of the American Geriatrics Society, 44*, 489–497.

Wolfson, L., et al. (1996). Balance and strength training in older adults: Intervention gains and Tai Chi maintenance. *Journal of Geriatrics Society, 44*, 498–506.

Wolk, A., et al. (1998). A prospective study of association of monounsaturated fat and other types of fat with risk of breast cancer. *Archives of Internal Medicine, 158*, 41–45.

Wood, P., et al. (1988). Changes in plasma lipids and lipoproteins in overweight men during weight loss through dieting as compared with exercise. *New England Journal of Medicine, 2319*, 1173–1179.

Woodward, N., & Wallston, B. (1987). Age and health care beliefs: Self-efficacy as a mediator of low desire for control. *Psychology and Aging, 2*, 3–8.

*Worksite Wellness Works.* (1993, May). Quarterly newsletter of the Wellness Councils of America, *9*, 8.

Wykle, M., & Musil, C. (1993, winter–spring). Mental health of older persons: Social and cultural factors. *Generations*, pp. 7–12.

Wykle, M., & Segal, M. (1991). A comparison of black and white family caregivers' experience with dementia. *Journal of the Black Nurses Association, 5*, 29–41.

Year end update: Quality of care. (1985). *Business and Health, 3*, 35.

Yee, B. (1990). *Variations in Aging: Older Minorities*. Galveston, Texas: The University of Texas Medical Branch.

Young, R., & Kahana, E. (1989, February). Age, medical advice about cardiac risk reduction, and patient compliance. *Journal of Aging and Health, 1*, 121–134.

Young, T., & Gelskey, D. (1995). Is noncentral obesity metabolically benign? *JAMA, 274*, 1939–1941.

Your elderly patients may be hungry or malnourished. (1993, December 6). *American Medical News*, p. 11.

Zajac, B. (1992, fall). Put a patch on your smoking habit. *Discover Health*, pp. 2–4.

Zeni, A., et al. (1996). Energy expenditure with indoor exercise machines. *JAMA, 275*, 1424–1427.

Zimmerman, R., & Connor, C. (1989). Health promotion in context: The effects of significant others on health behavior change. *Health Education Quarterly, 16*, 57–75.

# Index

('i' indicates an illustration, 't' indicates a table)